A HISTORY OF
THE WORK OF
REDEMPTION

A HISTORY OF
THE WORK OF
REDEMPTION

JONATHAN EDWARDS

THE BANNER OF TRUTH TRUST

THE BANNER OF TRUTH TRUST
3 Murrayfield Road, Edinburgh EH12 6EL, UK
P.O. Box 621, Carlisle, PA 17013, USA

*

First published by W. Gray, Edinburgh, 1774
First Banner of Truth edition, 2003

ISBN 0 85151 844 3

*

Typeset in 12 /14 pt Goudy Old Style at
the Banner of Truth Trust, Edinburgh
Printed and bound in Great Britain
at the University Press,
Cambridge

CONTENTS

PREFACE

It has long been desired by the friends of Mr Edwards, that a number of his manuscripts should be published; but the disadvantage under which all posthumous publications must necessarily appear, and the difficulty of getting any considerable work printed in this infant country hitherto, have proved sufficient obstacles to the execution of such a proposal. The first of these obstacles made me doubt, for a considerable time after these manuscripts came into my hands, whether I could, consistently with that regard which I owe to the honour of so worthy a parent, suffer any of them to appear in the world. However, being diffident of my own sentiments, and doubtful whether I were not over jealous in this matter, I determined to submit to the opinion of gentlemen, who are friends both to the character of Mr Edwards and to the cause of truth. The consequence was, that they gave their advice for publishing them.

The other obstacle was removed by a gentleman[1] in the church of Scotland, who was formerly a correspondent of Mr Edwards. He engaged a bookseller to undertake the work, and also signified his desire that these following discourses in particular might be made public.

Mr Edwards had planned a body of divinity, in a new method, and in the form of a history; in which he was first to show how the most remarkable events in all ages from the Fall to the present times, recorded in sacred and profane history, were adapted to promote the work of redemption; and then to trace, by the light of Scripture prophecy, how the same work should be yet further carried on even to the end of the world. His heart was so much set on executing this plan, that he was considerably averse to accept the presidentship of Princeton College, lest the duties of that office should put it out of his power.

[1] The Rev. John Erskine of Edinburgh (1721–1803).

The outlines of that work are now offered to the public, as contained in a series of sermons preached at Northampton in 1739,[2] without any view to publication. On that account, the reader cannot reasonably expect all that from them which he might justly have expected, had they been written with such a view, and prepared by the Author's own hand for the press.

As to elegance of composition, which is now esteemed so essential to all publications, it is well known, that the Author did not make that his chief study. However, his other writings, though destitute of the ornaments of fine language, have, it seems, that solid merit, which has procured both to themselves and to him a considerable reputation in the world, and with many an high esteem. It is hoped that the reader will find in these discourses many traces of plain good sense, sound reasoning, and thorough knowledge of the sacred oracles, and real unfeigned piety: and that, as the plan is new, and many of the sentiments uncommon,[3] they may afford entertainment and improvement to the ingenious, the inquisitive, and the pious reader; may confirm their faith in God's government of the world, in our holy Christian religion in general, and in many of its peculiar doctrines; may assist in studying with greater pleasure and advantage the historical and prophetical books of Scripture; and may excite to a conversation becoming the gospel.

That this volume may produce these happy effects in all who shall peruse it, is the hearty desire and prayer of the reader's most humble servant,

JONATHAN EDWARDS [Jr.]
New Haven, 25 February 1773[4]

[2] See Iain H. Murray, *Jonathan Edwards: A New Biography* (Edinburgh: Banner of Truth, 1987), pp. 150, 156, 451, 455.

[3] The work was originally published with the subtitle 'Containing the Outlines of a Body of Divinity, including a View of Church History, in a Method Entirely New'.

[4] It seems appropriate that, two hundred and seventy years after these words were written, and three hundred after the birth of Jonathan Edwards (5 October 1703), this work should again be published, like the first edition, in Edinburgh.

INTRODUCTION

'For the moth shall eat them up like a garment, and the worm shall eat them like wool: but my righteousness shall be for ever, and my salvation from generation to generation'

(Isa. 51:8).

The design of this chapter of Isaiah is to comfort the church under her sufferings, and the persecutions of her enemies; and the argument of consolation insisted on is the constancy and perpetuity of God's mercy and faithfulness towards her, which shall be manifest in continuing to work salvation for her, protecting her against all assaults of her enemies, and carrying her safely through all the changes of the world, and finally owning her with victory and deliverance.

In the text, this happiness of the church of God is set forth by comparing it with the contrary fate of her enemies that oppress her. And therein we may observe:

1. HOW SHORT LIVED THE POWER AND PROSPERITY OF THE CHURCH'S ENEMIES IS: 'The moth shall eat them up like a garment, and the worm shall eat them like wool'; that is, however great their prosperity is, and however great their present glory, they shall by degrees consume and vanish away by a secret curse of God, until they come to nothing; and all their power and glory, and so their persecutions, eternally cease, and they be finally and irrecoverably ruined, as the finest and most

glorious apparel will in time wear away, and be consumed by moths and rottenness. We learn who those are that shall thus consume away, by the foregoing verse, namely, those that are the enemies of God's people: 'Hearken unto me, ye that know righteousness, the people in whose heart is my law; fear ye not the reproach of men, neither be ye afraid of their revilings.'

2. THE CONTRARY HAPPY LOT AND PORTION OF GOD'S CHURCH, expressed in these words, 'My righteousness shall be for ever, and my salvation from generation to generation.' Who are meant as those that shall have the benefit of this, we also learn by the preceding verse, namely, they 'that know righteousness', and 'the people in whose heart is God's law'; or, in one word, the church of God. And concerning this happiness of theirs here spoken of, we may observe two things: i. *Wherein it consists;* ii. *Its continuance.*

i. *Wherein it consists,* namely, in God's righteousness and salvation towards them. By God's righteousness here, is meant his faithfulness in fulfilling his covenant promises to his church, or his faithfulness towards his church and people in bestowing the benefits of the covenant of grace upon them; which benefits, though they are bestowed of free and sovereign grace, as being altogether undeserved; yet as God has been pleased, by the promises of the covenant of grace, to bind himself to bestow them, so they are bestowed in the exercise of God's righteousness or justice. And therefore the Apostle says, 'God is not unrighteous to forget your work and labour of love' (*Heb.* 6:10). And so, 'If we confess our sins, he is faithful and just to forgive us our sins, and to cleanse us from all unrighteousness' (*1 John* 1:9). So the word *righteousness,* is very often used in Scripture for God's covenant faithfulness; so it is used in Nehemiah 9:8. 'Thou hast performed thy words, for thou art righteous.' So we are often to understand righteousness and covenant mercy for the same thing; as, 'He shall receive the blessing from the LORD, and righteousness from the God of his salvation' (*Psa.* 24:5).'Continue thy loving kindness to them that know thee, and thy righteousness to the upright in heart' (*Psa.* 36:10). And, 'Deliver me from blood guiltiness, O God, thou God of my salvation: and my tongue shall sing aloud of thy righteousness' (*Psa.* 51:14). 'O Lord, according to thy righteousness, I beseech thee, let thine anger and thy fury be turned away' (*Dan.* 9:16). And so in innumerable other places.

The other word here used is *salvation.* Of these two, God's righteousness and his salvation, the one is the cause, of which the other is the effect. God's righteousness, or covenant mercy, is the root of which his salvation is the fruit. Both of them relate to the covenant of grace. The one is God's covenant mercy and faithfulness, the other intends that work of God by which this covenant mercy is accomplished in the fruits of it. For salvation is the sum of all those works of God by which the benefits that are by the covenant of grace are procured and bestowed.

ii. We may observe *its continuance,* signified here by two expressions; *for ever,* and *from generation to generation.* The latter seems to be explanatory of the former. The phrase *for ever,* is variously used in Scripture. Sometimes it means as long as a man lives. So it is said, the servant that has his ear bored through with an awl to the door of his master, should be his *for ever.* Sometimes thereby is meant during the continuance of the Jewish state. So of many of the ceremonial and Levitical laws it is said that they should be statutes *for ever.* Sometimes it means as long as the world shall stand, or to the end of the generations of men. So it is said, 'One generation passeth away, and another cometh; but the earth abideth *for ever*' (*Eccles.* 1:4). Sometimes thereby is meant to all eternity.

So it is said, God is 'blessed *for ever*' (*Rom.* 1:25). And so it is said, 'If any man eat of this bread, he shall live *for ever*' (*John* 6:51).

And which of these senses is here to be understood, the next words determine, that is, to the end of the world, or to the end of the generations of men. It is said in the next words, 'and my salvation, *from generation to generation*'. Indeed the fruits of God's salvation shall remain after the end of the world, as appears by the end of verse 6: 'Lift up your eyes to the heavens, and look upon the earth beneath: For the heavens shall vanish away like smoke, and the earth shall wax old like a garment, and they that dwell therein shall die in like manner, but my salvation shall be for ever, and my righteousness shall not be abolished.'

But the work of salvation itself towards the church shall continue to be wrought: until the end of the world God will go to accomplish deliverance and salvation for the church, from all her enemies; for that is what the prophet is here speaking of; until the end of the world, until her enemies cease to be, as to any power to molest the church. And this expression, *'from generation to generation'*, may determine us as to the time which God continues to carry on the work of salvation for his church, both with respect to the beginning and end. It is *from generation to generation*, that is, throughout all generations; beginning with the generations of men on the earth, and not ending until these generations end, at the end of the world. And therefore we deduce from these words this DOCTRINE:

THE WORK OF REDEMPTION IS A WORK THAT GOD CARRIES ON FROM THE FALL OF MAN TO THE END OF THE WORLD.

The generations of mankind on the earth did not begin until after the Fall. The beginning of the posterity of our first parents was after the Fall; for all their posterity, by ordinary generation, are partakers of the Fall, and of the corruption of nature that followed from it; and these generations, by which the human race is propagated, shall continue to the end of the world. So these two are the limits of the generations of men on the earth; the Fall of man, the beginning; and the end of the world, or the day of judgment, the end. The same are the limits of the work of redemption, as to those progressive works of God by which that redemption is brought about and accomplished, though not as to the fruits of it; for they, as was said before, shall be to all eternity.

The work of redemption and the work of salvation are the same thing. What is sometimes in Scripture called God's saving his people is in other places called his redeeming them. So Christ is called both the Saviour and the Redeemer of his people.

Before entering on the proposed *History of the Work of Redemption*, I would

1. Explain the terms made use of in the doctrine; and,

2. Show what those things are that are designed to be accomplished by this great work of God.

First, I would show in what sense the terms of the doctrine are used. And, i. I would show how I would be understood when I use the word *redemption;* and, ii. How I would be understood when I say, this work is a work of God carried on from the Fall of man to the end of the world.

i. I would show how I would be understood when I use the word *redemption.* And here it may be observed that the work of redemption is sometimes understood in a more limited sense for the purchase of salvation; for so the word strictly signifies, a purchase of deliverance; and if we take the word in this restrained sense, the work of redemption was not so long in doing. But it was begun and finished with Christ's humiliation. It was all wrought while Christ was upon earth. It was begun with Christ's incarnation, and carried on through Christ's life, and finished with his death, or the time of his remaining under the power of death, which ended in his resurrection. And so we say, that the day of Christ's resurrection is the day when Christ finished the work of redemption, that is, then the purchase was finished, and the work itself, and all that appertained to it, was *virtually* done and finished, but not *actually*.

But then sometimes the work of redemption is taken more largely, including all that God works or accomplishes tending to this end; not only the purchasing of redemption, but also all God's works that were properly preparatory to the purchase, or as applying the purchase and accomplishing the success of it. So that the whole dispensation, as it includes the preparation and the purchase, and the application and success of Christ's redemption, is here called the work of *redemption*.

All that Christ does in this great affair as mediator, in any of his offices, either of prophet, priest, or king; either when he was in this world, in his human nature, or before, or since; and not only what Christ the mediator has done, but also what the Father, or the Holy Ghost, has done, as united or confederated in this design of redeeming sinful men; or, in one word, all that is wrought in the execution of the eternal covenant of redemption; this is what I call the work of redemption in the doctrine; for it is all but one work, one design. The various dispensations or works that belong to it, are but the several parts of one scheme. It is but one design that is formed, to which all the persons of the Trinity do conspire, and all the various dispensations that belong to it are united; and the several wheels are one machine, to answer one end, and produce one effect.

ii. When I say, this work is carried on from the Fall of man to the end of the world; in order to the full understanding of my meaning in it, I would desire two or three things to be observed.

a. That it is not meant, that nothing was done in order to it before the Fall of man. There were many things done in order to this work of redemption before that. Some things were done before the world was created, yea, from all eternity. The persons of the Trinity were as it were confederated in a design and a covenant of redemption; in which covenant the Father had appointed the Son, and the Son had undertaken the work; and all things to be accomplished in the work were stipulated and agreed. And besides these, there were things done at the creation of the world, in order to that work, before man fell; for the world itself seems to have been created in order to it. The work of creation was in order to God's works of providence. So that if it be inquired, Which of these kinds of works are the greatest, the works of creation or the works of providence? I answer, the works of providence; because God's works of providence are the end of his works of creation, as the building a house, or the forming an engine or machine, is for its use. But God's main work of providence is this great work of God that the doctrine speaks of, as may more fully appear hereafter.

The creation of heaven was in order to the work of redemption: it was to be a habitation for the redeemed: 'Then shall the King say unto them on his right hand, Come, ye blessed of my Father, inherit the kingdom prepared for you from the foundation of the world' (*Matt.* 25:34). Even the angels were created to be employed in this work. And therefore the apostle calls them 'ministering spirits, sent forth to minister for them who shall be heirs of salvation' (*Heb.* 1:14). As to this lower world, it was doubtless created to be a stage upon which this great and wonderful work of redemption should be transacted: and therefore, as might be shown, in many respects this lower world is wisely fitted, in its formation, for such a state of man as he is in since the Fall, under a possibility of redemption; so that when it is said, that the work of redemption is carried on from the Fall of man to the end of the world, it is not meant, that all that ever was done in order to redemption has been done since the Fall.

b. Nor is it meant that there will be no remaining fruits of this work after the end of the world. The greatest fruits of all will be after that. That glory and blessedness that will be the sum of all the fruits will remain to all the saints after that. The work of redemption is not an eternal work, that is, it is not a work always a-doing and never accomplished. But the fruits of this work are eternal fruits. The work has an issue. But in the issue the end will be obtained; which end will never have an end. As those things that were in order to this work before the beginning of the world, as God's electing love, and the covenant of redemption, never had a beginning; so the fruits of this work, that shall be after the end of the world, never will have an end. And therefore,

c. When it is said in the DOCTRINE that this is a work that God is carrying on from the Fall of man to the end of the world, what I mean is, that those things that belong to this work itself, and are parts of this scheme, are all this while accomplishing. There are things that are in order to it that are before the beginning of it, and fruits of it that are after it is finished. But the work itself is so long a-doing, even from the Fall of man to the end of the world; it is all this while a-carrying on. It was begun immediately upon the Fall, and will continue to the end of the world, and then will be finished. The various dispensations of God that are in this space, do belong to the same work, and to the same design, and have all one issue; and therefore are all to be reckoned but as several parts of one work, as it were several successive motions of one machine, to bring about in the conclusion one great event.

And here also we must distinguish between the parts of redemption itself, and the parts of the work by which that redemption is wrought out. There is a difference between the parts of the benefits procured and bestowed, and the parts of the work of God by which those benefits were procured and bestowed. As, for example, there is a difference between the parts of the benefit that the children of Israel received, consisting in their redemption out of Egypt, and the parts of that work of God by which this was wrought. The redemption of the children of Israel out of Egypt, considered as the benefit which they enjoyed, consisted of two parts, namely, their deliverance from their former Egyptian bondage and misery, and their being brought into a more happy state, as the servants of God, and heirs of Canaan. But there are many more things which are parts of that work of God which is called his work of redemption of Israel out of Egypt. To this belongs his calling of Moses, his sending him to Pharaoh, and all the signs and wonders he wrought in Egypt, and his bringing such terrible judgments on the Egyptians, and many other things.

It is this work by which God effects redemption that we are speaking of. This work is carried on from the Fall of man to the end of the world; and it is so in two respects.

i. *With respect to the effect wrought on the souls of the redeemed;* which is common to all ages from the Fall of man to the end of the world. This effect that I here speak of, is the application of redemption with respect to the souls of particular persons, in converting, justifying, sanctifying and glorifying them. By these things the souls of particular persons are actually redeemed, and do receive the benefit of the work of redemption in its effect in their souls. And in this sense the work of redemption is carried on in all ages of the world, from the Fall of man to the end of the world. The work of God in converting souls, opening blind eyes, unstopping deaf ears, raising dead souls to life, and rescuing the miserable capti- vated souls out of the hands of Satan, was begun soon after the Fall of man, has been carried on in the world ever since to this day, and will be to the end of the world. God has always, ever since the first erecting of the church of the redeemed after the Fall, had such a church in the world. Though oftentimes it has been reduced to a very narrow compass and to low circumstances, yet it has never wholly failed.

And as God carries on the work of converting the souls of fallen men through all these ages, so he goes on to justify them, to blot out all their sins, and to accept them as right- eous in his sight, through the righteousness of Christ, and adopt and receive them from being the children of Satan, to be his own children; so also he goes on to sanctify them, or to carry on the work of his grace, which he has begun in them, and to comfort them with the consolations of his Spirit, and to glorify them, to bestow upon them, when their bodies die, that eternal glory which is the fruit of the purchase of Christ. What is said, Romans 8:30, 'Whom he did predestinate, them he also called; and whom he called, them he also justified; and whom he justified, them he also glorified': I say this is appli- cable to all ages, from the Fall, to the end of the world.

The way that the work of redemption, with respect to these effects of it on the souls of the redeemed, is carried on from the Fall to the end of the world, is by repeating and continu- ally working the same work over again, though in different persons, from age to age. But,

ii. *The work of redemption with respect to the grand design in general*, as it respects the universal subject and end, is carried on from the Fall of man to the end of the world in a different manner, not merely by repeating or renewing the same effect in the different subjects of it, but by many successive works and dispensations of God, all tending to one great end and effect, all united as the several parts of a scheme, and all together making up one great work. Like a house or temple that is building; first, the workmen are sent forth, then the materials are gathered, then the ground fitted, then the foundation is laid, then the superstructure is erected, one part after another, until at length the top stone is laid, and all is finished.

Now the work of redemption, in that large sense that has been explained, may be compared to such a building, that is carrying on from the Fall of man to the end of the world. God went about it immediately after the Fall of man. Some things were done towards it immediately, as may be shown hereafter; and so God has proceeded, as it were, getting materials and building, ever since; and so will proceed to the end of the world; and then the time will come when the top stone shall be brought forth, and all will appear complete and consummate. The glorious structure will then stand forth in its proper perfection.

This work is carried on in the former respect that has been mentioned, namely, as to the effect on the souls of particular persons that are redeemed, by its being an effect that is common to all ages. The work is carried on in this latter respect, namely, as it respects the church of God, and the grand design in general, not only by that which is common to all ages, but by successive works wrought in different ages, all parts of one whole, or one great scheme, whereby one work is brought about by various steps, one step in one age, and another in another. It is this carrying on of the work of redemption that I shall chiefly insist upon, though not excluding the former; for one necessarily supposes the other.

Having thus explained what I mean by the *terms* of the doctrine; that you may the more clearly see how the great design and work of redemption is carried on from the Fall of man to the end of the world,

2. I now proceed, in the second place, to show what is *the design of this great work*, or what things are designed to be done by it. In order to see how a design is carried on, we must first know what the design is. To know how a workman proceeds, and to understand the various steps he takes in order to accomplish a piece of work, we need to be informed what he is about, or what the thing is that he intends to accomplish; otherwise we may stand by, and see him do one thing after another, and be quite puzzled and in the dark, seeing nothing of his scheme, and understanding nothing of what he means by it. If an architect, with a great number of hands, were building some great palace, and one that was a stranger to such things should stand by, and see some men digging in the earth, others bringing timber, others hewing stones, and the like, he might see that there was a great deal done; but if he knew not the design it would all appear to him confusion.

And therefore, that the great works and dispensations of God that belong to this great affair of redemption may not appear like confusion to you, I would set before you briefly the main things designed to be accomplished in this great work, to accomplish which God began to work presently after the Fall of man, and will continue working to the end of the world, when the whole work will appear completely finished. And the main things designed to be done by it are these that follow.

i. *It is to put all God's enemies under his feet, and that the goodness of God should finally appear, triumphing over all evil.* Soon after the world was created, evil entered into the world in the Fall of the angels and man. Presently after God had made rational creatures, there were enemies who rose up against him from among them; and in the Fall of man evil entered into this lower world, and God's enemies rose up against him here. Satan rose up against God, endeavouring to frustrate his design in the creation of this lower world, to destroy his workmanship here, and to wrest the government of this lower world out of his hands, and usurp the throne himself, and set up himself as god of this world instead of the God that made it. And to these ends he introduced sin into the world; and having made man God's enemy, he brought guilt on man, and brought death and the most extreme and dreadful misery into the world.

Now one great design of God in the affair of redemption was, to reduce and subdue those enemies of God, until they should all be put under God's feet, 'He must reign until he hath put all enemies under his feet' (*1 Cor.* 15:25). Things were originally so planned and designed that he might disappoint and confound, and triumph over Satan, and that he might be bruised under Christ's feet (*Gen.* 3:15). The promise was given, that the seed of the woman should bruise the serpent's head.

It was a part of God's original design in this work to destroy the works of the devil, and confound him in all his purposes: 'For this purpose was the Son of God manifested, that he might destroy the works of the devil' (*1 John* 3:8). It was a part of his design, to triumph over sin, and over the corruptions of men, and to root them out of the hearts of his people, by conforming them to himself. He designed also that his grace should triumph over man's guilt and that infinite demerit that there is in sin. Again, it was a part of his design, to triumph over death; and, however this is the last enemy that shall be destroyed, yet that shall finally be vanquished and destroyed.

God thus appears gloriously above all evil; and triumphing over all his enemies was one great thing that God intended by the work of redemption; and the work by which this was to be done, God immediately went about as soon as man fell; and so goes on until he fully accomplishes it in the end of the world.

ii. *In doing this, God's design was perfectly to restore all the ruins of the Fall, so far as concerns the elect part of the world, by his Son;* and therefore we read of the 'restitution of all things' (*Acts* 3:21), 'Whom the heaven must receive, until the times of the restitution of all things', and of the 'times of refreshing' from the presence of the Lord Jesus: 'Repent ye, therefore, and be converted, that your sins may be blotted out, when the times of refreshing shall come from the presence of the Lord' (*Acts* 3:19).

Man's soul was ruined by the Fall; the image of God was ruined; man's nature was corrupted and destroyed, and man became dead in sin. The design of God was to restore the soul of man; to restore life to it, and the image of God, in conversion, and to carry on the restoration in sanctification, and to perfect it in glory.

Man's body was ruined; by the Fall it became subject to death. The design of God was to restore it from this ruin, and not only to deliver it from death in the resurrection, but to deliver it from mortality itself, in making it like unto Christ's glorious body. The world was ruined as to man, as effectually as if it had been reduced to chaos again; all heaven and earth were overthrown. But the design of God was to restore all, and as it were to create a new heaven and a new earth: 'Behold, I create new heavens, and a new earth; and the former shall not be remembered, nor come into mind' (*Isa.* 65:17). 'Nevertheless we, according to his promise, look for new heavens, and a new earth, wherein dwelleth righteousness' (2 *Pet.* 3: 13).

The work by which this was to be done was begun immediately after the Fall, and so is carried on until all is finished at the end, when the whole world, heaven and earth, shall be restored; and there shall be, as it were, new heavens, and a new earth, in a spiritual sense, at the end of the world. Thus it is represented, 'And I saw a new heaven, and a new earth; for the first heaven and the first earth were passed away' (*Rev.* 21:1).

iii. *Another great design of God in the work of redemption was to gather together in one all things in Christ, in heaven and in earth, that is, all elect creatures;* to bring all elect creatures, in heaven and in earth, to a union one to another in one body, under one head, and to unite all together in one body to God the Father. This was begun soon after the Fall, and is carried on through all ages of the world, and finished at the end of the world.

iv. *God designed by this work to perfect and complete the glory of all the elect by Christ.* It was a design of God to advance the elect to an exceeding pitch of glory, such as 'eye hath not seen, nor ear heard, nor has ever entered into the heart of man'. He intended to bring them to perfect excellency and beauty in his image, and in holiness, which is the proper beauty of spiritual beings; and to advance them to a glorious degree of honour, and also to an ineffable pitch of pleasure and joy; and thus to glorify the whole church of elect men in soul and body, and with them to bring the glory of the elect angels to its highest pitch under one head. The work which tends to this, God began immediately after the Fall, and carries on through all ages, and will have perfected at the end of the world.

v. *In all this God designed to accomplish the glory of the blessed Trinity in an exceeding degree.* God had a design of glorifying himself from eternity; to glorify each person in the Godhead. The end must be considered as first in the order of nature, and then the means; and therefore we must conceive that God, having professed this end, had then as it were the means to choose; and the principal mean that he pitched upon was this great work of redemption that we are speaking of. It was his design in this work to glorify his only begotten Son, Jesus Christ; and it was his design, by the Son to glorify the Father: 'Now is the Son of man glorified, and God is glorified in him. If God be glorified in him, God also shall glorify him in himself, and shall straightway glorify him' (*John* 13:31-32). It was his design that the Son should thus be glorified, and should glorify the Father by what should be accomplished by the Spirit to the glory of the Spirit, that the whole Trinity, conjointly, and each person singly, might be exceedingly glorified. The work that was the appointed means of this was begun immediately after the Fall and is carried on until, and finished at, the end of the world, when all this intended glory shall be fully accomplished in all things.

Having thus explained the terms made use of in the DOCTRINE, and shown what the things are which are to be accomplished by this great work of God, I proceed now to the proposed *History*; that is, to show how what was designed by the work of redemption has been accomplished, in the various steps of this work, from the Fall of man to the end of the world.

In order to do this, I would divide this whole space of time into three periods:

THE FIRST, reaching from the Fall of man to the incarnation of Christ;

THE SECOND, from Christ's incarnation until his resurrection; or the whole time of Christ's humiliation;

THE THIRD, from thence to the end of the world.

It may be some may be ready to think this a very unequal division; and it is so indeed in some respects. It is so, because the second period is so much the greatest. For although it be so much shorter than either of the other, being but between thirty and forty years, whereas both the other contain thousands; yet in this affair that we are now upon, it is more than both the others.

I would therefore proceed to show distinctly how the work of redemption is carried on from the Fall of man to the end of the world, through each of these periods in their order; which I would do under three propositions, one concerning each period.

1. That from the Fall of man until the incarnation of Christ, God was doing those things that were preparatory to Christ's coming and working out redemption, and were forerunners and earnests of it.

2. That the time from Christ's incarnation until his resurrection was spent in procuring and purchasing redemption.

3. That the space of time from the resurrection of Christ to the end of the world is all taken up in bringing about or accomplishing the great effect or success of that purchase.

In a particular consideration of these three propositions the great truth taught in the DOCTRINE may perhaps appear in a clear light, and we may see how the work of redemption is carried on from the Fall of man to the end of the world.

PERIOD I

FROM THE FALL OF MAN TO THE INCARNATION OF CHRIST

M y first task is to show how the work of redemption is carried on from the Fall of man to the incarnation of Christ, under the first proposition, namely,

THAT THE SPACE OF TIME FROM THE FALL OF MAN TO THE INCARNATION OF CHRIST WAS TAKEN UP IN DOING THOSE THINGS THAT WERE FORERUNNERS AND EARNESTS OF CHRIST'S COMING AND WORKING OUT REDEMPTION, AND WERE PREPARATORY TO IT.

The great works of God in the world during this whole space of time were all preparatory to this. There were many great changes and revolutions in the world, and they were all only the turning of the wheels of providence in order to this, to make way for the coming of Christ, and what he was to do in the world. They all pointed hither, and all issued here. Hither tended especially all God's great works towards his church. The church was under various dispensations of providence, and in very various circumstances, before Christ came. But all these dispensations were to prepare the way for his coming. God wrought salvation for the souls of men through all that space of time, though the number was very small to what it was afterwards; and all this salvation was, as it were, by way of anticipation. All the souls that were saved before Christ came were only, as it were, the earnests of the future harvest.

God wrought many lesser salvations and deliverances for his church and people before Christ came. These salvations were all but so many images and forerunners of the great salvation Christ was to work out when he should come. God revealed himself of old, from time to time, from the Fall of man to the coming of Christ. The church during that space of time enjoyed the light of divine revelation, or God's Word. They had in a degree the light of the gospel. But all these revelations were only so many forerunners and earnests of the great light that he should bring who came to be the light of the world. That whole space of time was as it were the time of night, wherein the church of God was not indeed wholly without light; but it was like the light of the moon and stars that we have in the night; a dim light in comparison with the light of the sun, and mixed with a great deal of darkness. It had no glory, by reason of the glory that excelleth (*2 Cor.* 3:10). The church had indeed the light of the sun, but it was only as reflected from the moon and stars. The church all that while was a minor. This the apostle evidently teaches in Galatians 4: 1-3. 'Now I say, that the heir as long as he is a child, differeth nothing from a servant, though he be lord of all; but is under tutors and governors, until the time appointed of the father. Even so we, when we were children, were in bondage under the elements of the world.'

But here, for the greater clearness and distinctness, I would subdivide this period, from the Fall of man to the coming of Christ into six lesser periods, or parts.

   i. from the Fall to the flood;
  ii. from thence to the calling of Abraham;
 iii. from thence to Moses;
 iv. from thence to David;
  v. from David to the captivity in Babylon;
 vi. from thence to the incarnation of Christ.

PART 1

◈

FROM THE FALL TO THE FLOOD

This was a period farthest of all distant from Christ's incarnation; yet then this great work was begun to be carried on, then was this glorious building begun that will not be finished until the end of the world, as I would now show you. And to this purpose I would observe,

1. As soon as ever man fell, Christ entered on his Mediatorial work. Then it was that Christ first took on him the work and office of a Mediator. He had undertaken it before the world was made. He stood engaged with the Father to appear as man's Mediator, and to take on him that office when there should be occasion, from all eternity. But now the time was come. When man fell, then the occasion came; and then Christ immediately, without further delay, entered on his work, and took on him that office that he had stood engaged to take on him from eternity. As soon as ever man fell, Christ the eternal Son of God clothed himself with the Mediatorial character, and therein presented himself before the Father. He immediately stepped in between a holy, infinite, offended Majesty, and offending mankind; and was accepted in his interposition; and so wrath was prevented from going forth in the full execution of that amazing curse that man had brought on himself.

It is manifest that Christ began to exercise the office of Mediator between God and man as soon as ever man fell because mercy began to be exercised towards man immediately. There was mercy in the forbearance of God, that he did not destroy him, as he did the angels when they fell. But there is no mercy exercised toward fallen man but through a Mediator. If God had not in mercy restrained Satan, he would immediately have seized on his prey. Christ began to do the part of an intercessor for man as soon as he fell. There is no mercy exercised towards man but what is obtained through Christ's intercession; so that now Christ was entered on his work that he was to continue in throughout all ages of the world.

From that day forward Christ took on him the care of the church of the elect: He took on him the care of fallen man in the exercise of all his offices; he undertook thenceforward to teach mankind in the exercise of his prophetical office; and also to intercede for fallen man in his priestly office; and he took on him, as it were, the care and burden of the government of the church, and of the world of mankind, from this day forward. He from that time took upon him the care of the defence of his elect church from all their enemies. When Satan, the grand enemy, had conquered and overthrown man, the business of resisting and conquering him was committed to Christ. He thenceforward undertook to manage that subtle powerful adversary. He was then appointed the Captain of the Lord's hosts, and the Captain of their salvation, and always acted as such thenceforward: and so he appeared from time to time, and he will continue to act as such to the end of the world. Henceforward this lower world, with all its concerns, was, as it were, devolved upon the Son of God; for when man had sinned, God the Father would have no more to do with man immediately; he would no more have any immediate concern with this world of mankind, that had apostatized from and rebelled against him. He would henceforward have no concern with man, but only through a Mediator, either in teaching men, or in governing or bestowing any benefits on them.

And therefore, when we read in sacred history what God did from time to time towards his church and people, and what he said to them, and how he revealed himself to them, we are to understand it especially of the second Person of the Trinity. When we read of God's appearing after the Fall, from time to time, in some visible form or outward symbol of his presence, we are ordinarily, if not universally, to understand it of the second Person of the Trinity: which may be argued from John 1:18, 'No man hath seen God at any time; the only begotten Son, which is in the bosom of the Father, he hath declared him.' He is therefore called, 'the image of the invisible God' (*Col.* 1:15), intimating, that though God the Father be invisible, yet Christ is his image or representation, by which he is seen, or by which the church of God hath often had a representation of him that is not invisible, and in particular that Christ has after appeared in a human form.

Yea, not only was this lower world devolved on Christ, that he might have the care and government of it, and order it agreeably to his design of redemption, but also in some respect the whole universe. The angels from that time were committed to him, to be subject to him in his Mediatorial office, to be ministering spirits to him in this affair; and accordingly were so from this time forward, as is manifest by the Scripture history, wherein we have accounts from time to time of their acting as ministering spirits in the affairs of the church of Christ.

And therefore we may suppose that, immediately on the Fall of man, it was made known in heaven among the angels that God had a design of redemption with respect to fallen man, and that Christ had now taken upon him the office and work of a Mediator between God and man, that they might know their business henceforward, which was to be subservient to Christ in this office. And as Christ, in this office, has since that, as God-man and Mediator, been solemnly exalted and installed the King of heaven, and is thenceforward as God-man, Mediator, the light, and as it were, the Sun of heaven, agreeable to Revelation 21: 23: 'And the city had no need of the sun, neither of the moon, to shine in it; for the glory of God did lighten it, and the Lamb is the light thereof'; so this revelation that was made in heaven among the angels, of Christ's now having taken on him the office of a Mediator between God and man, was as it were the first dawning of this light in heaven. When Christ ascended into heaven after his passion, and was solemnly installed on the throne as King of heaven, then this sun rose in heaven, even the Lamb that is the light of the new Jerusalem. But the light began to dawn immediately after the Fall.

2. Presently upon this the gospel was first revealed on earth, in these words (*Gen.*3:15), 'And I will put enmity between thee and the woman, and between thy seed and her seed. It shall bruise thy head, and thou shalt bruise his heel.' We must suppose that God's intention of redeeming fallen man was first signified in heaven, before it was signified on earth, because the business of the angels as ministering spirits of the Mediator required it; for as soon as ever Christ had taken on him the work of a Mediator, it was requisite that the angels should be ready immediately to be subservient to him in that office: so that the light first dawned in heaven; but very soon after the same was signified on earth. In those words of God there was an intimation of another surety to be appointed for man, after the first surety had failed. This was the first revelation of the covenant of grace; this was the first dawning of the light of the gospel on earth.

This lower world before the Fall enjoyed noonday light; the light of the knowledge of God, the light of his glory, the light of his favour. But when man fell, all this light was at once extinguished, and the world reduced back again to total darkness; a worse darkness than that which was in the beginning of the world, that we read of (*Gen.* 1:2); 'And the earth was without form, and void; and darkness was upon the face of the deep.' This was a darkness a thousand times more remediless than that. Neither men nor angels could find out any way whereby this darkness might be scattered.

This darkness appeared in its blackness when Adam and his wife saw that they were naked and sewed fig leaves, and when they heard the voice of the LORD God walking in the garden, and hid themselves among the trees of the garden; and when God first called them to an account, and said to Adam, 'What is this that thou hast done? Hast thou eaten of the tree, whereof I commanded thee, that thou shouldest not eat?' Then we may suppose that their hearts were filled with shame and terror. But these words of God (*Gen.* 3:15), were the first dawning of the light of the gospel after this darkness. Now first appeared some glimmering of light after this dismal darkness, which before this was without one glimpse of light, any beam of comfort, or any the least hope. It was an obscure revelation of the gospel; and was not made to Adam or Eve directly, but it was in what God said to the serpent. But yet it was very comprehensive, as might be easily shown, were it not that it would take up too much time.

Here was a certain intimation of a merciful design by the 'seed of the woman', which was like the first glimmerings of the light of the sun in the east when the day first dawns. This intimation of mercy was given them even before sentence was pronounced on either Adam or Eve, from tenderness to them, to whom God designed mercy, lest they should be overborne with a sentence of condemnation, without having any thing held forth whence they could gather any hope.

One of those great things that were intended to be done by the work of redemption is more plainly intimated here than the rest, namely God's subduing his enemies under the feet of his Son. This was threatened now, and God's design of this was now first declared, which was the work Christ had now undertaken, and which he soon began, and carried on thenceforward, and will perfectly accomplish at the end of the world. Satan probably had triumphed greatly in the Fall of man, as though he had defeated the designs of God in the creation of man and the world in general. But in these words God gives him a plain intimation that he should not finally triumph, but that a complete victory and triumph should be obtained over him by the seed of the woman.

This revelation of the gospel in this verse was the first thing that Christ did in his prophetical office. You may remember that it was said in the first of those three propositions that have been mentioned that from the Fall of man to the incarnation of Christ, God was doing those things that were preparatory to Christ's coming and working out redemption, and were forerunners and earnests of it. And one of those things which God did in this time to prepare the way for Christ's coming into the world, was to foretell and promise it, as he did from time to time, from age to age, until Christ came. This was the first promise that ever was given of it, the first prediction that ever was made of it on earth.

3. Soon after this, the custom of sacrificing was appointed, to be a steady type of the sacrifice of Christ until he should come and offer up himself a sacrifice to God. Sacrificing was not a custom first established by the Levitical law of Moses; for it had been a part of God's instituted worship long before, even from the beginning of God's visible church on earth. We read of the patriarchs, Abraham, Isaac, and Jacob, offering sacrifice, and before them Noah, and before him Abel. And this was by divine appointment; for it was a part of God's worship in his church, that was offered up in faith, and that he accepted: which proves that it was by his institution; for sacri-

ficing is no part of natural worship. The light of nature does not teach men to offer up beasts in sacrifice to God; and seeing it was not enjoined by the law of nature, if it was acceptable to God, it must be by some positive command or institution; for God has declared his abhorrence of such worship as is taught by the precept of men without his institution (*Isa.* 29:13), 'Wherefore the LORD said, Forasmuch as this people draw near me with their mouth, and with their lips do honour me, but have removed their heart far from me, and their fear towards me is taught by the precept of men; therefore behold, I will proceed to do a marvellous work', etc.

And such worship as hath not a warrant from divine institution, cannot be offered up in faith, because faith has no foundation where there is no divine appointment. It cannot be offered up in faith of God's acceptance; for men have no warrant to hope for God's acceptance in that which is not of his appointment, and in that to which he hath not promised his acceptance; and therefore it follows that the custom of offering sacrifices to God was instituted soon after the Fall; for the Scripture teaches us, that Abel offered 'the firstlings of his flock, and of the fat thereof' (*Gen.* 4:4) and that he was accepted of God in this offering, Hebrews 11:4. And there is nothing in the story that looks as though the institution was first given then when Abel offered up that sacrifice to God; but it appears as though Abel only therein complied with a custom already established.

And it is very probable that it was instituted immediately after God had revealed the covenant of grace, in Genesis 3:15, which covenant and promise was the foundation on which the custom of sacrificing was built. That promise was the first stone that was laid towards this glorious building, the work of redemption, which will be finished at the end of the world. And the next stone which was laid upon that, was the institution of sacrifices, to be a type of the great Sacrifice.

The next thing that we have an account of after God had pronounced sentence on the serpent, on the woman, and on the man, was that God made them coats of skins, and clothed them; which by the generality of divines are thought to be the skins of beasts slain in sacrifice; for we have no account of anything else that should be the occasion of man's slaying beasts, but only to offer them in sacrifice, until after the flood. Men were not wont to eat the flesh of beasts as their common food until after the flood. The first food of man in paradise before the Fall was the fruit of the trees of paradise; and when he was turned out of paradise after the Fall, then his food was the herb of the field (*Gen.* 3:18). The first grant that he had to eat flesh as his common food was after the flood (*Gen.* 9:3): 'Every moving thing that liveth shall be meat for you; even as the green herb have I given you all things.' So that it is likely that these skins that Adam and Eve were clothed with were the skins of their sacrifices. God's clothing them with these was a lively figure of their being clothed with the righteousness of Christ. This clothing was no clothing of their own obtaining; but it was God that gave it them. It is said, 'God made them coats of skins, and clothed them', as the righteousness our naked souls are clothed with is not our righteousness but the righteousness which is of God. It is he only that clothes the naked soul.

Our first parents, who were naked, were clothed at the expense of life. Beasts were slain, and resigned up their lives a sacrifice to God, to afford clothing to them to cover their nakedness. So doth Christ, to afford clothing to our naked souls. The skin signifies the life: So, 'Skin for skin, yea all that a man hath will he give for his life' (*Job* 2:4); that is, life for life. Thus our first parents were covered with skins of sacrifices, as the tabernacle in the wilderness, which signified the church, was, when it was covered with rams skins dyed red, as though they were dipped in blood, to signify that Christ's righteousness was wrought out through the pains of death, under which he shed his precious blood.

We observed before that the light that the church enjoyed from the Fall of man until Christ came was like the light which we enjoy in the night; not the light of the sun directly, but as reflected from the moon and stars; which light did foreshow Christ the Sun of righteousness that was afterwards to arise. This light of the Sun of righteousness to come they had chiefly two ways. One was by predictions of Christ to come, whereby his coming was foretold and promised; the other was by types and shadows, whereby his coming and redemption were prefigured. The first thing that was done to prepare the way for Christ in the former of these ways was in that promise that was just taken notice of in the foregoing particular; and the first thing of the latter kind, namely, of types, to foreshow Christ's coming, was that institution of sacrifices that we are now upon. As that promise in Genesis 3:15 was the first dawn of gospel light after the Fall in prophecy; so the institution of sacrifices was the first hint of it in types. The giving of that promise was the first thing that was done after the Fall, in this work, in Christ's prophetical office; the institution of sacrifices was the first thing that we read of after the Fall, by which especially Christ exhibited himself in his priestly office.

The institution of sacrifices was a great thing done towards preparing the way for Christ's coming, and the sacrifices of the Old Testament were the principal Old Testament types of Christ and his redemption. They tended to establish in the minds of God's visible church the necessity of a propitiatory sacrifice in order to the Deity's being satisfied for sin; and so prepared the way for the reception of the glorious gospel that reveals the great sacrifice in the visible church, and not only so, but through the world of mankind. For from this institution of sacrifices that was after the Fall all nations derived the custom of sacrificing. For this custom of offering up sacrifices to the gods, to atone for their sins, was common to all nations. No nation, however barbarous, was found without it anywhere. This is a great evidence of the truth of the Christian religion; for no nation, but only the Jews, could tell how they came by this custom, or to what purpose it was to offer sacrifices to their deities. The light of nature did not teach them any such thing. That did not teach them that the gods were hungry, and fed upon the flesh which they burnt in sacrifice; and yet they all had this custom; of which no other account can be given but that they derived it from Noah, who had it from his ancestors, on whom God had enjoined it as a type of the great sacrifice of Christ. However, by this means all nations of the world had their minds possessed with this notion, that an atonement or sacrifice for sin was necessary; and a way was made for their more readily receiving the great doctrine of the gospel of Christ, which teaches us the atonement and sacrifice of Christ.

4. God did soon after the Fall begin actually to save the souls of men through Christ's redemption. In this Christ, who had lately taken upon him the work of Mediator between God and man, did first begin that work, wherein he appeared in the exercise of his kingly office, as in the sacrifices he was represented in his priestly office, and in the first prediction of redemption by Christ he had appeared in the exercise of his prophetical office. In that prediction the light of Christ's redemption first began to dawn in the prophecies of it; in the institution of sacrifices it first began to dawn in the types of it; in this, namely, his beginning actually to save men, it first began to dawn in the fruit of it.

It is probable, therefore, that Adam and Eve were the first fruits of Christ's redemption; it is probable by God's manner of treating them, by his comforting them as he did, after their awakenings and terrors. They were awakened, and ashamed with a sense of their guilt, after their Fall, when their eyes were opened, and they saw that they were naked, and sewed fig leaves to cover their nakedness; as the sinner, under the first awakenings, is wont to endeavour to hide the nakedness of his soul, by patching up a righteousness of his own. Then they were further terrified and awakened by hearing the voice of God, as he was coming to condemn them. Their coverings of fig leaves do not answer the purpose; but notwithstanding these, they ran to hide themselves among the trees of the garden, because they were naked, not daring to trust to their fig leaves to hide their nakedness from God.

Then they were further awakened by God's calling of them to a strict account. But while their terrors were raised to such a height, and they stood, as we may suppose, trembling and astonished before their judge, without any thing to catch hold of whence they could gather any hope, then God took care to hold forth some encouragement to them, to keep them from the dreadful effects of despair under their awakenings, by giving a hint of a design of mercy by a Saviour, even before he pronounced sentence against them. And when after this he proceeded to pronounce sentence, whereby we may suppose their terrors were further raised, God soon after took care to encourage them, and to let them see that he had not wholly cast them off, by taking a fatherly care of them in their fallen, naked, and miserable state, by making them coats of skins and clothing them. Which also manifested an acceptance of those sacrifices that they offered to God for sin, that those were the skins of, which were types of what God had promised, when he said, 'The seed of the woman shall bruise the serpent's head'; which promise, there is reason to think, they believed and embraced. Eve seems plainly to express her hope in and dependence on that promise, in what she says at the birth of Cain (*Gen.* 4:1), 'I have gotten a man from the LORD'; that is, as God has promised, that my seed should bruise the serpent's head, so now has God given me this pledge and token of it, that I have a seed born. She plainly owns that this, her child, was from God, and hoped that her promised seed was to be of this her eldest son; though she was mistaken, as Abraham was with respect to Ishmael, as Jacob was with respect to Esau, and as Samuel was with respect to the first-born of Jesse. And what she said at the birth of Seth especially expresses her hope and dependence on the promise of God. See verse 25, 'For God hath appointed me another seed instead of Abel, whom Cain slew.'

Thus it is exceeding probable, if not evident, that as Christ took on him the work of Mediator as soon as man fell, so he now immediately began his work of redemption in its effect, and that he immediately encountered his great enemy the devil, whom he had undertaken to conquer, and rescued those two first captives out of his hands; therein baffling him, soon after his triumph on account of the victory he had obtained over them, whereby he had made them his captives. And though he was, as it were, sure of them and all their posterity, Christ the Redeemer soon showed him that he was mistaken, and that he, Christ, was able to subdue him, and deliver fallen man. He let him see it in delivering those first captives of his; and so soon gave him an instance of the fulfilment of that threatening, 'The seed of the woman shall bruise the serpent's head'; and in this instance a presage of the fulfilment of one great thing he had undertaken, namely, his subduing all his enemies under his feet.

After this we have another instance of redemption in one of their children, namely, in righteous Abel, as the Scripture calls him, whose soul perhaps was the first that went to heaven through Christ's redemption. In him we have at least the first instance of the death of a redeemed person that is recorded in Scripture. If he was the first, then as the redemption of Christ began to dawn before in the souls of men in their conversion and justification, in him it first began to dawn in glorification; and in him the angels began first to do the part of ministering spirits to Christ, in going forth to conduct the souls of the redeemed to glory. And in him the elect angels in heaven had the first opportunity to see so wonderful a thing as the soul of one of the fallen race of mankind, that had been sunk by the Fall into such an abyss of sin and misery, brought to heaven and in the enjoyment of heavenly glory, which was a much greater thing than if they had seen him returned to the earthly paradise. Thus they, by this, saw the glorious effect of Christ's redemption in the great honour and happiness that was procured for sinful, miserable creatures by it.

5. The next remarkable thing that God did in the further carrying on of this great affair of redemption that I shall take notice of was the first remarkable pouring out of the Spirit through Christ that ever was, which was in the days of Enos. This seems to have been the next remarkable thing that was done toward erecting this glorious building that God had begun and laid the foundation of in Christ the Mediator. We read (*Gen.* 4:26), 'Then began men to call upon the name of the LORD.' The meaning of these words has been considerably controverted among divines. We cannot suppose the meaning is that that was the first time that man ever performed the duty of prayer. Prayer is a duty of natural religion, and a duty to which a spirit of piety does most naturally lead men. Prayer is, as it were, the very breath of a spirit of piety; and we cannot suppose, therefore, that those holy men that had been before for above two hundred years had lived all that while without any prayer. Therefore some divines think that the meaning is that then men first began to perform public worship, or to call upon the name of the Lord in public assemblies. Whether it be so to be understood or not, yet so much

must necessarily be understood by it, namely, that there was something new in the visible church of God with respect to the duty of prayer, or calling upon the name of the Lord; that there was a great addition to the performance of this duty; and that in some respect or other it was carried far beyond what it ever had been before, which must be the consequence of a remarkable pouring out of the Spirit of God.

If it was now first that men were stirred up to get together in assemblies to help and assist one another in seeking God, so as they never had done before, it argues something extraordinary as the cause; and could be from nothing but uncommon influences of God's Spirit. We see by experience, that a remarkable pouring out of God's Spirit is always attended with such an effect, namely, a great increase of the performance of the duty of prayer. When the Spirit of God begins a work on men's hearts he immediately sets them to calling on the name of the Lord. As it was with Paul: after the Spirit of God had laid hold of him, the next news is, 'Behold, he prayeth!' So it has been in all remarkable pourings out of the Spirit of God in the latter days. It is foretold that the Spirit will be poured out as a Spirit of grace and supplications, Zechariah 12:10. See also Zephaniah 3:9, 'For then will I turn to the people a pure language, that they may all call upon the name of the LORD, to serve him with one consent.'

And when it is said, 'Then began men to call upon the name of the LORD', no more can be intended by it, than that this was the first remarkable season of this nature that ever was. It was the beginning, or the first, of such a kind of work of God, such a pouring out of the Spirit of God. Similar expressions are commonly used in Scripture: So (1 Sam. 14:35), 'And Saul built an altar unto the LORD; the same was the first altar that he built unto the LORD.' In the Hebrew it is, as you may see in the margin, 'That altar he began to build unto the Lord.' 'How shall we escape, if we neglect so great salvation; which at the first began to be spoken by the Lord?' (*Heb.* 2:3).

It may here be observed that, from the Fall of man to this day wherein we live, the work of redemption in its effect has mainly been carried on by remarkable pourings out of the Spirit of God. Though there is a more constant influence of God's Spirit always in some degree attending his ordinances, yet the way in which the greatest things have been done towards carrying on this work always has been by remarkable pourings out of the Spirit at special seasons of mercy, as may fully appear hereafter in our further prosecution of the subject we are upon. And this pouring out of the Spirit in the days of Enos was the first remarkable pouring out of the Spirit of God that ever was. There had been a saving work of God on the hearts of some before; but now God was pleased to grant a more large effusion of his Spirit, for the bringing in of a harvest of souls to Christ; so that in this we see that great building that is the subject of our present discourse, of which God laid the foundation immediately after the Fall of man, carried on further, and built higher, than ever it had been before.

6. The next thing I shall take notice of, is the eminently holy life of Enoch, who we have reason to think was a saint of greater eminence than any ever had been before him; so that in this respect the work of redemption was carried on to a greater height than ever it had been before. With respect to its effect in the visible church in general, we observed just now how it was carried higher in the days of Enos than ever it had been before. Probably Enoch was one of the saints of that harvest; for he lived all the days that he did live on earth in the days of Enos. And with respect to the degree to which this work was carried out in the soul of a particular person, it was raised to a greater height in Enoch than ever before. His soul, as it was built on Christ, was built up in holiness to a greater

height than there had been any instance of before. He was a wonderful instance of Christ's redemption, and the efficacy of his grace.

7. In Enoch's time, God did more expressly reveal the coming of Christ than he had done before, in the prophecy of Enoch that we have an account of in Jude 14–15, 'And Enoch also, the seventh from Adam, prophesied of these, saying, Behold, the Lord cometh with ten thousand of his saints, to execute judgment upon all, and to convince all that are ungodly among them, of their ungodly deeds which they have ungodly committed, and of all their hard speeches which ungodly sinners have spoken against him.'

Here Enoch prophesies of the coming of Christ. It does not seem to be confined to any particular coming of Christ; but it has respect in general to Christ's coming in his kingdom, and is fulfilled to a degree in both the first and second comings of Christ, and indeed in every remarkable manifestation Christ has made of himself in the world, for the saving of his people, and the destroying of his enemies. It is very parallel in this respect with many other prophecies of the coming of Christ that were given under the Old Testament; and, in particular, it seems to be parallel with that great prophecy of Christ's coming in his kingdom that we have in the 7th chapter of Daniel, whence the Jews principally took their notion of the kingdom of heaven. See verse 10: 'A fiery stream issued and came forth from before him: thousand thousands ministered unto him, and ten thousand times ten thousand stood before him: the judgment was set, and the books were opened.' And verses. 13, 14: 'I saw in the night visions, and behold, one like the Son of Man came with the clouds of heaven, and came to the Ancient of Days, and they brought him near before him. And there was given him dominion, and glory, and a kingdom, that all people, nations, and languages, should serve him. His dominion is an everlasting dominion, which shall not pass away, and his kingdom that which shall not be destroyed.' And though it is not unlikely that Enoch might have a more immediate respect in this prophecy to the approaching destruction of the old world by the flood, which was a remarkable resemblance of Christ's destruction of all his enemies at his second coming, yet it doubtless looked beyond the type to the antitype.

And as this prophecy of Christ's coming is more express than any had been before, so it is an instance of the increase of that gospel light that began to dawn presently after the Fall of man; and is an instance of that building that is the subject of our present discourse being yet further carried on, and built up higher than ever it had been before.

And here, by the way, I would observe, that the increase of gospel light, and the carrying on of the work of redemption, as it respects the elect church in general, from the first erecting of the church to the end of the world, is very much after the same manner as the carrying on of the same work and the same light in a particular soul, from the time of its conversion, until it is perfected and crowned in glory. The work in a particular soul has its ups and downs; sometimes the light shines brighter, and sometimes it is a dark time; sometimes grace seems to prevail, at other times it seems to languish for a great while together, and corruption prevails, and then grace revives again. But in general, grace is growing. From its first infusion, until it is perfected in glory, the kingdom of Christ is building up in the soul. So it is with respect to the great affair in general, as it relates to the universal subject of it, as it is carried on from the first beginning of it, after the Fall, until it is perfected at the end of the world, as will more fully appear by a particular view of this affair from beginning to end in the prosecution of this subject, if God give opportunity to carry it through as I propose.

8. The next remarkable thing towards carrying on this work that we have an account of in Scripture is the translation of Enoch into heaven. The account we have of it is in Genesis 5:24: 'And Enoch walked with God, and he was not; for God took him.' Here Moses, in giving an account of the genealogy of those that were of the line of Noah, does not say concerning Enoch, 'He lived so long, and he died', as he does of the rest; but, 'He was not, for God took him'; that is, he translated him; in body and soul carried him to heaven without dying, as it is explained in Hebrews 11:5, 'By faith Enoch was translated that he should not see death.' By this wonderful work of God, the work of redemption was carried to a greater height in several respects, than it had been before.

You may remember that, when I was showing what were the great things that God aimed at in the work of redemption, or what the main things were that he intended to bring to pass, I mentioned among other things the perfect restoring of the ruins of the Fall with respect to the elect, and restoring man from that destruction that he had brought on himself, in both soul and body. Now this translation of Enoch was the first instance that ever was of restoring the ruins of the Fall with respect to the body.

There had been many instances of restoring the soul of man by Christ's redemption, but none of redeeming and actually saving the body until now. All the bodies of the elect are to be saved as well as their souls. At the end of the world, all the bodies of the saints shall actually be redeemed; those that then shall have been dead by a resurrection; and others, that then shall be living, by causing them to pass through a glorious change. A number of the bodies of the saints were raised and glorified at the resurrection and ascension of Christ; and, before that, there was an instance of a body glorified in Elijah. But the first instance of all was this of Enoch that we are now speaking of.

And the work of redemption by this was carried on further than ever it had been before, as, by this wonderful work of God, there was a great increase of gospel light to the church of God, in this respect: that hereby the church had a clearer manifestation of a future state, and of the glorious reward of the saints in heaven. We are told (2 *Tim.* 1:10) that life and immortality are 'brought to light through the gospel'. And the more of this that is brought to light, the more clearly does the light shine in that respect. What was said in the Old Testament of a future state is very obscure, in comparison with the more full, plain, and abundant revelation given of it in the New. But yet, even in those early days, the church of God, in this instance, was favoured with an instance of it set before their eyes, in that one of their brethren was actually taken up to heaven without dying; which we have all reason to think the church of God knew then, as they afterwards knew of Elijah's translation. And as this was a clearer manifestation of a future state than the church had had before, so it was a pledge or earnest of that future glorification of all the saints which God intended through the redemption of Jesus Christ.

9. The next thing that I shall observe, was the upholding of the church of God in the family of which Christ was to proceed, in the time of that great and general defection of the world of mankind that was before the flood. The church of God, in all probability, was small in comparison with the rest of the world from the beginning of the time that mankind first began to multiply on the face of the earth, or from the time of Cain's defection and departing from among the people of God; the time we read of in Genesis 4:16, when 'Cain went out from the presence of the LORD, and dwelt in the land of Nod'; which, being interpreted, is the land of banishment: I say, from this time of Cain's departure and separation from the church of God, it is probable that the

church of God was small in comparison with the rest of the world.

The church seems to have been kept up chiefly in the posterity of Seth; for this was the seed that God appointed instead of Abel, whom Cain slew. But we cannot reasonably suppose that Seth's posterity were one fiftieth part of the world: 'For Adam was one hundred and thirty years old when Seth was born.' But Cain, who seems to have been the ringleader of those that were not of the church, was Adam's eldest child, and probably was born soon after the Fall, which doubtless was soon after Adam's creation; so that there was time for Cain to have many sons before Seth was born, and besides many other children that probably Adam and Eve had before this time, agreeably to God's blessing that he gave them, when he said, 'Be fruitful, and multiply, and replenish the earth'; and many of these children might have children. The story of Cain before Seth was born seems to imply that there were great numbers of men on the earth (*Gen.* 4:14–15): 'Behold, thou hast driven me out this day from the face of the earth; and from thy face shall I be hid; and I shall be a fugitive and a vagabond in the earth; and it shall come to pass, that every one that findeth me shall slay me. And the LORD said unto him, Therefore whosoever slayeth Cain, vengeance shall be taken on him seven-fold. And the LORD set a mark upon Cain, lest any finding him should kill him.' And all those that were then in being when Seth was born, must be supposed then to stand in equal capacity of multiplying their posterity with him; and therefore, as I said before, Seth's posterity were but a small part of the inhabitants of the world.

But after the days of Enos and Enoch, (for Enoch was translated before Enos died); I say, after their days, the church of God greatly diminished, in proportion as multitudes that were of the line of Seth, and had been born in the church of God, fell away, and joined with the wicked world, principally by means of intermarriages with them, as in Genesis 6:1, 2, 4: 'And it came to pass, when men began to multiply on the face of the earth, and daughters were born unto them, that the sons of God saw the daughters of men, that they were fair; and they took them wives of all which they chose . . . There were giants in the earth in those days; and also after that, when the sons of God came in unto the daughters of men, and they bare children to them, the same became mighty men, which were of old, men of renown.'

By the sons of God here are doubtless meant the children of the church. It is a denomination often given them in Scripture. They intermarried with the wicked world, and so had their hearts led away from God; and there was a great and continual defection from the church. And the church of God, that used to be a restraint on the wicked world, diminished exceedingly, and so wickedness went on without restraint. And Satan, that old serpent, the devil, that tempted our first parents, and set himself up as god of this world, raged exceedingly; and every imagination of the thoughts of man's heart was only evil continually, and the earth was filled with violence. It seemed to be deluged with wickedness now; it was with water afterwards: and mankind in general were drowned in this deluge; almost all were swallowed up in it. And now Satan made a most violent and potent attempt to swallow up the church of God; and had almost done it. But yet God restored it in the midst of all this flood of wickedness and violence.

He kept it up in that line of which Christ was to proceed. He would not suffer it to be destroyed, for a blessing was in it. The Lord the Redeemer was in this branch of mankind, and was afterwards to proceed from it. There was a particular family that was a root in which the great Redeemer of the world was, and whence the branch of righteousness was afterwards to shoot forth. And therefore, however the branches were lopped off, and the tree seemed to be destroyed, yet God, in the midst of all this, kept alive this root, by his wonderful redeeming power and grace, so that the gates of hell could not prevail against it.

Thus I have shown how God carried on the great affair of redemption; how the building went on that God began after the Fall, during this first period of the times of the Old Testament, namely, from the Fall of man until God brought the flood on the earth. And I would take notice upon it that, though the history which Moses gives of the great works of God during that space is very short, yet it is exceeding comprehensive and instructive. And it may also be profitable for us here to observe the efficacy of that purchase of redemption that had such great effects even in the old world so many ages before Christ appeared himself to purchase redemption; that his blood should have such great efficacy so long before it was shed.

PART 2

❦

FROM THE FLOOD TO THE CALLING OF ABRAHAM

I proceed now to show how the same work was carried on through the second period of the Old Testament, that from the beginning of the Flood until the calling of Abraham. For though that mighty, overflowing, universal deluge of waters overthrew the world, yet it did not overthrow this building of God, the work of redemption. But this went on yet; and instead of being overthrown, continued to be built up, and was carried on to a farther preparation for the great Saviour's coming into the world and working out of redemption for his people. And here I would observe:

1. The Flood itself was a work of God that belonged to this great affair and tended to promote it. All the great and mighty works of God from the Fall of man to the end of the world are reducible to this work, and, if seen in a right view of them, will appear as parts of it, and so many steps that God has taken in order to it, or as carrying it on; and doubtless so great a work, so remarkable and universal a catastrophe as the deluge was, cannot be excepted. It was a work that God wrought for redemption, since thereby God removed out of the way the enemies and obstacles of it, that were ready to overthrow it.

Satan seems to have been in a dreadful rage just before the flood, and his rage then doubtless was, as it always has been, chiefly against the church of God to overthrow it; and he had filled the earth with violence and rage against it. He had drawn over almost all the world to be on his side, and they enlisted under his banner against Christ and his church. We read that the earth 'was filled with violence'; and doubtless that violence was chiefly against the church, in fulfilment of what was foretold, 'I will put enmity between thy seed and her seed'. And their enmity and violence was so great, and the enemies of the church so numerous, the whole world being against the church, that it was come to the last extremity. Noah's reproofs, and his preaching of righteousness, were utterly disregarded. God's Spirit had striven with them a hundred and twenty years, and all in vain; and the church was almost swallowed up. It seems to have been reduced to so narrow limits as to be confined to one family. And there was no prospect of any thing else but of their totally swallowing up the church, and that in a very little time, and so wholly destroying that small root that had the blessing in it, whence the Redeemer was to proceed.

And therefore, God's destroying those enemies of the church by the flood belongs to this affair of redemption: for it was one thing that was done in fulfilment of the covenant of grace, as it was revealed to Adam: 'I will put enmity between thee and the woman, and between thy seed and her seed; it shall bruise thy head.' This destruction was only a destruction of the seed of the serpent in the midst of their most violent rage against the seed of the woman, and so delivering the seed of the woman from them, when in utmost peril by them.

We read of scarce any great destruction of nations any where in Scripture but that one main reason given for it is their enmity and injuries against God's church; and doubtless this was one main reason of the destruction of all nations by the flood. The giants that were in those days, in all likelihood, got themselves their renown by their great exploits against

Heaven, and against Christ and his church, the remaining sons of God that had not corrupted themselves.

We read that, just before the world shall be destroyed by fire, the nations that are in the four quarters of the earth, shall gather together against the church as the sand of the sea, and shall go up on the breadth of the earth, and compass the camp of the saints about, and the beloved city; and then fire shall come down from God out of heaven, and devour them (*Rev.* 20:8-9). And it seems as though there was that which was very parallel to it, just before the world was destroyed by water. And therefore their destruction was a work of God that did as much belong to the work of redemption as the destruction of the Egyptians belonged to the redemption of the children of Israel out of Egypt, or as the destruction of Sennacherib's mighty army that had compassed about Jerusalem to destroy it belonged to God's redemption of that city from them.

By means of this flood, all the enemies of God's church, against whom that little handful had no strength, were swept off at once. God took their part, and appeared for them against their enemies, and drowned those of whom they had been afraid in the flood of water, as he drowned the enemies of Israel that pursued them in the Red Sea.

Indeed God could have taken other methods to deliver his church. He could have converted all the world instead of drowning it; and so he could have taken another method than drowning the Egyptians in the Red Sea. But that is no argument that the method that he did take was not a method to show his redeeming mercy to them.

By the wicked world's being drowned, the wicked, the enemies of God's people, were dispossessed of the earth, and the whole earth given to Noah and his family to possess in quiet; as God made room for the Israelites in Canaan, by casting out their enemies from before them. And God's thus taking the possession of the enemies of the church and giving it all to his church, was agreeable to that promise of the covenant of grace: 'For evildoers shall be cut off: but those that wait upon the LORD, they shall inherit the earth. For yet a little while, and the wicked shall not be: yea, thou shalt diligently consider his place, and it shall not be. But the meek shall inherit the earth; and shall delight themselves in the abundance of peace' (*Psa.* 37:9-11).

2. Another thing here belonging to the same work, was God's so wonderfully preserving that family of which the Redeemer was to proceed when all the rest of the world was drowned. God's drowning the world, and saving Noah and his family, both were works reducible to this great work. Saving Noah and his family belonged to it in two ways.

As that family was the family of which the Redeemer was to proceed, and as that family was the church that he had redeemed, it was the mystical body of Christ that was there saved. The manner of God's saving those persons, when all the world besides was so overthrown, was very wonderful and remarkable. It was a wonderful and remarkable type of the redemption of Christ, of that redemption that is sealed by the baptism of water, and is so spoken of in the New Testament: 'Which sometime were disobedient, when once the long-suffering of God waited in the days of Noah, while the ark was a preparing, wherein few, that is, eight souls were saved by water. The like figure, whereunto, even baptism, doth also now save us, (not the putting away of the filth of the flesh, but the answer of a good conscience towards God,) by the resurrection of Jesus Christ' (1 *Pet.* 3:20-21). That water that washed away the filth of the world, that cleared the world of wicked men, was a type of the blood of Christ, that takes away the sin of the world. That water that delivered Noah and his sons from their enemies is a type of the blood that delivers God's church from their sins, their worst enemies. That water that was so plentiful and abundant that it filled the world, and reached above the tops of the highest mountains, was a type of that blood, the sufficiency of which is so abundant that it is sufficient for the whole world; sufficient to bury the highest mountains of sin. The ark, that was the refuge and hiding place of the church in this time of storm and flood, was a type of Christ, the true hiding place of the church from the storms and floods of God's wrath.

3. The next thing I would observe is the new grant of the earth that God made to Noah and his family immediately after the flood, as founded on the covenant of grace. The sacrifice of Christ was represented by Noah's building an altar to the Lord, and offering a sacrifice of every clean beast, and every clean fowl. And we have an account of God's accepting this sacrifice: and thereupon he blessed Noah, and established his covenant with him, and with his seed, promising to destroy the earth in like manner no more; signifying that it is by the sacrifice of Christ that God's favour is obtained, and his people are in safety from God's destroying judgments, and do obtain the blessing of the Lord. And God now, on the occasion of this sacrifice that Noah offered to God, gives him and his posterity a new grant of the earth; a new power of dominion over the creatures, as founded on that sacrifice, and so founded on the covenant of grace. And so it is to be looked upon as a diverse grant from that which was made to Adam, that we have in Genesis 1: 28: 'And God blessed them, and God said unto them, Be fruitful, and multiply and replenish the earth, and subdue it; and have dominion over the fish of the sea, and over the fowl of the air, and over every living thing that moveth upon the earth.' This grant was not founded on the covenant of grace, for it was given to Adam while he was under the covenant of works, and therefore was made obsolete when that covenant ceased. The first grant of

the earth to Adam was founded on the first covenant; and therefore, when that first covenant was broken, the right conveyed to him by that first covenant was forfeited and lost.

And hence it came to pass, that the earth was taken away from mankind by the flood: for the first grant was forfeited; and God had never made another after that, until after the flood. If the first covenant had not been broken, God never would have drowned the world, and so have taken it away from mankind. For then the first grant made to mankind would have stood good. But that was broken; and so God, after a while destroyed the earth, when the wickedness of man was great.

But after the flood, on Noah's offering a sacrifice that represented the sacrifice of Christ, God in smelling a sweet savour, or accepting that sacrifice, as it was a representation of the true sacrifice of Christ, which is a sweet savour indeed to God, gives Noah a new grant of the earth, founded on that sacrifice of Christ, or that covenant of grace which is by that sacrifice of Christ, with a promise annexed, that now the earth should no more be destroyed, until the consummation of all things; as you may see in Genesis 8:20-22; 9:1-3, 7. The reason why such a promise, that God would no more destroy the earth, was added to this grant made to Noah, and not to that made to Adam, was because this was founded on the covenant of grace, of which Christ was the Surety, and therefore could not be broken. And therefore it comes to pass now that, though the wickedness of man has dreadfully raged, and the earth has been filled with violence and wickedness thousands of times, and one age after another, and much more dreadful and aggravated wickedness than the world was full of before the flood, being against so much greater light and mercy, especially in these days of the gospel, yet God's patience holds out; God does not destroy the earth; his mercy and forbearance abide according to his promise; and his grant established with Noah and his sons abides firm and good, being founded on the covenant of grace.

4. At this point God renews with Noah and his sons the covenant of grace: 'And I, behold, I establish my covenant with you, and with your seed after you; and with every living creature that is with you . . . (*Gen.* 9:9–10), which was the covenant of grace; which even the brute creation have this benefit of, that it shall never be destroyed again until the consummation of all things. When we have this expression in Scripture, 'My covenant', it commonly is to be understood of the covenant of grace. The manner of expression, 'I will establish my covenant with you, and with your seed after you', shows plainly that it was a covenant already in being, that had been made already, and that Noah would understand what covenant it was by that denomination, namely, the covenant of grace.

5. The work of God in disappointing the design of building the city and tower of Babel belongs to the great work of redemption. For that building was undertaken in opposition to this great building of God that we are speaking of. Men's going about to build such a city and tower was an effect of the corruption that mankind were now soon fallen into. This city and tower was set up in opposition to the city of God, as the god that they built it to was their pride. Being sunk into a disposition to forsake the true God, the first idol they set up in his room was themselves, their own glory and fame. And as this city and tower had their foundation laid in the pride and vanity of men and the haughtiness of their minds, so it was built on a foundation exceedingly contrary to the nature of the foundation of the kingdom of Christ, and his redeemed city, which has its foundation laid in humility.

Therefore God saw that it tended to frustrate the design of that great building that was founded not in the haughtiness of men but in Christ's blood: and therefore the thing that they did displeased the Lord, and he baffled and confounded the design, and did not suffer them to bring it to perfection; as God will frustrate and confound all other buildings, that are set up in opposition to the great building of the work of redemption.

In the second chapter of Isaiah, where the prophet is fore-telling God's setting up the kingdom of Christ in the world, he foretells how God will, in order to it, bring down the haughtiness of men, and how the day of the LORD shall be on every high tower, and upon every fenced wall, etc. Christ's kingdom is established, by bringing down every high thing to make way for it (2 *Cor.* 10:4-5), 'For the weapons of our warfare are not carnal, but mighty through God to the pulling down of strong holds; casting down imaginations and every high thing that exalteth itself against the knowledge of God.' What is done in a particular soul to make way for the setting up of Christ's kingdom is to destroy Babel in that soul.

They intended to have built Babel up to heaven. That building that is the subject we are upon is a building that is intended to be built so high that its top shall reach to heaven indeed, as it will to the highest heavens at the end of the world when it shall be finished; and therefore God would not suffer the building of his enemies, that they designed to build up to heaven in opposition to it, to prosper. If they had gone on and prospered in building that city and tower, it might have kept the world of wicked men, the enemies of the church, together, as that was their design. They might have remained united in one vast, powerful city; and so they might have been too powerful for the city of God, and quite swallowed it up.

This city of Babel is the same with the city of Babylon; for Babylon in the original is Babel. But Babylon was a city that is always spoken of in Scripture as chiefly opposite to the city of God. Babylon and Jerusalem, or Zion, are opposed to each other often both in the Old Testament and the New. This city was a powerful and terrible enemy to the city of God afterwards, notwithstanding this great check put to the building of it in the beginning. But it might have been, and probably would have been, vastly more powerful, and able to vex and destroy the church of God, if it had not been thus checked.

Thus it was in kindness to his church in the world, and in prosecution of the great design of redemption, that God put a stop to the building of the city and tower of Babel.

6. The dispersing of the nations and dividing the earth among its inhabitants, immediately after God had caused the building of Babel to cease, are the next events I would notice. This was done so as most to suit that great design of redemption. And particularly God therein had an eye to the future propagation of the gospel among the nations. They were so placed, the bounds of their habitation so limited round about the land of Canaan, the place laid out for the habitation of God's people, as most suited the design of propagating the gospel among them: 'When the Most High divided to the nations their inheritance, when he separated the sons of Adam, he set the bounds of the people according to the number of the children of Israel' (*Deut.* 32:8). God 'hath made of one blood all nations of men, for to dwell on all the face of the earth, and hath determined the times before appointed, and the bounds of their habitation; that they should seek the Lord, if haply they might feel after him, and find him' (*Acts* 17:26-27).

The land of Canaan was the most conveniently situated of any place in the world for the purpose of spreading the light of the gospel thence among the nations in general. The inhabited world was chiefly in the Roman Empire in the times immediately after Christ, which was in the countries round about Jerusalem, and properly situated for the purpose of diffusing the light of the gospel among them from that place. The devil, seeing the advantage of this situation of the nations for promoting the great work of redemption, and the disadvantage of it with respect to the interests of his kingdom, afterwards led away many nations into the remotest parts of the world to that end: to get them out of the way of the gospel. Thus he led some into America; and others to northern cold regions that are almost inaccessible.

7. Another thing I would mention in this period was God's preserving the true religion in the line of which Christ was to proceed when the world in general apostatized to idolatry and the church was in imminent danger of being swallowed up in the general corruption.

Although God had lately wrought so wonderfully for the deliverance of his church and had shown so great mercy towards it as, for its sake, even to destroy all the rest of the world; and although he had lately renewed and established his covenant of grace with Noah and his sons; yet so prone is the corrupt heart of man to depart from God, and to sink into the depths of wickedness, and so prone to darkness, delusion, and idolatry, that the world soon after the flood fell into gross idolatry; so that before Abraham the distemper was become almost universal. The earth was become very corrupt at the time of the building of Babel; and even God's people themselves, even that line of which Christ was to come, were corrupted in a measure with idolatry: 'Your fathers dwelt on the other side of the flood in old time, even Terah the father of Abraham, and the father of Nahor; and they served other gods' (*Josh.* 24:2). The 'other side of the flood' means beyond the river Euphrates, where the ancestors of Abraham lived.

We are not to understand, that they were wholly drawn off to idolatry, to forsake the true God. For God is said to be the God of Nahor: 'The God of Abraham, and the God of Nahor, the God of their father, judge betwixt us' (*Gen.* 31:53). But they only partook in some measure of the general and almost universal corruption of the times; as Solomon was in a measure infected with idolatrous corruption; and as the children of Israel in Egypt are said to serve other gods, though yet there was the true church of God among them; and as there were images kept for a considerable time in the family of Jacob, the corruption being brought from Padan-aram, whence he fetched his wives.

This was the second time that the church was almost brought to nothing by the corruption and general defection of the world from true religion. But still the true religion was kept up in the family from which Christ was to proceed. This is another instance of God's remarkably preserving his church in a time of a general deluge of wickedness; and wherein, although the god of this world raged, and had almost swallowed up God's church, yet God did not suffer the gates of hell to prevail against it.

PART 3

❧❀❧

FROM THE CALLING OF
ABRAHAM TO MOSES

I proceed now to show how the work of redemption was carried on through the third period of the times of the Old Testament, beginning with the calling of Abraham, and extending to Moses. And here:

1. It pleased God now to separate that person of whom Christ was to come from the rest of the world, that his church might be upheld in his family and posterity until Christ should come; as he did in calling Abraham out of his own country and from his kindred to go into a distant country that God should show him, and bringing him first out of Ur of the Chaldees to Charran, and then to the land of Canaan.

It was before observed, that the corruption of the world with idolatry was now become general; mankind were almost wholly overrun with idolatry. God therefore saw it necessary, in order to uphold true religion in the world, that there should be a family separated from the rest of the world. It proved to be high time to take this course, lest the church of Christ should wholly be carried away with the apostasy. For the church of God itself, that had been upheld in the line of Abraham's ancestors, was already considerably corrupted. Abraham's own country and kindred had most of them fallen off; and without some extraordinary interposition of providence, in all likelihood, in a generation or two more, the true religion in this line would have been extinct. And therefore God saw it to be time to call Abraham, the person in whose family he intended to uphold the true religion, out of his own country and from his kindred to a far distant country, that his posterity might there remain a people separate from all the rest of the world; that so the true religion might be upheld there, while all mankind besides were swallowed up in heathenism.

The land of the Chaldees that Abraham was called to go out of was the country about Babel; Babel, or Babylon, was the chief city of the land of Chaldea. Learned men suppose, by what they gather from some of the most ancient accounts of things, that it was in this land that idolatry first began; that Babel and Chaldea were the original and chief seat of the worship of idols, whence it spread into other nations. And therefore the land of the Chaldeans, or the country of Babylon, is in Scripture called the land of graven images; as you may see: 'As word is upon the Chaldeans, saith the LORD, and upon the inhabitants of Babylon, and upon her princes, and upon her wise men . . . A drought is upon her waters, and they shall be dried up: for it is the land of graven images, and they are mad upon their idols' (*Jer.* 50:35,38). God calls Abraham out of this idolatrous country, to a great distance from it. And when he came there, he gave him no inheritance in it, no, not so much as to set his foot on; but he remained a stranger and a sojourner, that he and his family might be kept separate from all the world.

This was a new thing: God had never taken such a method before. His church had not in this manner been separated from the rest of the world until now. They were wont to dwell with them, without any bar or fence to keep them separate; the mischievous consequences of which had been found once and again. The effect before the flood of God's people living intermingled with the wicked world, without any remarkable wall of separation, was that the sons of the church joined in marriage with others, and thereby almost all soon became infected, and the church was almost brought to nothing. The method that God took then to fence the church was to drown the wicked world and save the church in the ark. And now the world, before Abraham was called, was become corrupt again. But now God took another method. He did not destroy the wicked world and save Abraham and his wife, and Lot, in an ark; but he calls these persons to go and live separate from the rest of the world.

This was a new thing, and a great thing, that God did toward the work of redemption. This thing was done now about the middle of the space of time between the Fall of man and the coming of Christ; and there were about two thousand years yet to come before Christ the great Redeemer was to come. But by this calling of Abraham, the ancestor of Christ, a foundation was laid for the upholding of the church of Christ in the world, until Christ should come. For, the world having become idolatrous, there was a necessity that the seed of the woman should be thus separated from the idolatrous world for that purpose.

And then it was needful that there should be a particular nation separated from the rest of the world to receive the types and prophecies that were needful to be given of Christ to prepare the way for his coming; that to them might be committed the oracles of God; and that by them the history of God's great works of creation and providence might be upheld; and that so Christ might be born of this nation; and that from thence the light of the gospel might shine forth to the rest of the world. These ends could not be well obtained if God's people, through all these two thousand years, had lived intermixed with the heathen world. So that this calling of Abraham may be looked upon as a kind of a new foundation laid for the visible church of God, in a more distinct and regular state, to be upheld and built up from henceforward until Christ should actually come, and then through him to be propagated to all nations. So that Abraham, being the person in whom this foundation is laid, is represented in Scripture as though he were the father of all the church, the father of all them that believe; as it were a root whence the visible church thenceforward through Christ, Abraham's root and offspring, rose as a tree, distinct from all other plants; of which tree Christ was the branch of righteousness; and from which tree, after Christ came, the natural branches were broken off, and the Gentiles were grafted into the same tree.

So that Abraham still remains the father of the church, or root of the tree, through Christ, his seed. It is the same tree that flourishes from that small beginning that was in Abraham's time, and has in these days of the gospel spread its branches over a great part of the earth, and will fill the whole earth in due time, and at the end of the world shall be transplanted from an earthly soil into the paradise of God.

2. There accompanied this a more particular and full revelation and confirmation of the covenant of grace than ever had been before. There had before this been, as it were, two particular and solemn editions or confirmations of this covenant: one at the beginning of the first period, which was that whereby the covenant of grace was revealed to our first parents, soon after the Fall, the other at the beginning of the second period, whereby God solemnly renewed the covenant of grace with Noah and his family soon after the flood. And now there is a third, at the beginning of the third period, at and after the calling of Abraham. And it now being much nearer the time of the coming of Christ than when the covenant of grace was first revealed, it being, as was said before, about halfway between the Fall and the coming of

Christ, the revelation of the covenant now was much more full than any that had been before. The covenant was now more particularly revealed. It was now revealed, not only that Christ should be, but it was revealed to Abraham, that Christ should be his seed; and it was now promised, that all the families of the earth should be blessed in him. And God was much in the promises of this to Abraham.

The first promise was when he first called him: 'And I will make of thee a great nation, and I will bless thee, and make thy name great; and thou shalt be a blessing' (*Gen.* 12:2). And again the same promise was renewed after he came into the land of Canaan, chapter 13:14-17. And the covenant was again renewed after Abraham had returned from the slaughter of the kings, chapter 15:5-6. And again, after his offering up Isaac, chapter 22:16-18.

In this renewal of the covenant of grace with Abraham, several particulars concerning that covenant were revealed more fully than they had ever been before; not only that Christ was to be of Abraham's seed, but also the calling of the Gentiles and the bringing of all nations into the church, that all the families of the earth were to be blessed, was now made known. And then the great condition of the covenant of grace, which is faith, was now more fully made known. 'And he said unto him, So shall thy seed be. And he believed in the LORD; and he counted it to him for righteousness' (*Gen.* 15:5-6). This is much taken notice of in the New Testament as that whence Abraham was called the father of them that believe.

And as there was now a further revelation of the covenant of grace, so there was a further confirmation of it by seals and pledges, than ever had been before; as, particularly, God did now institute a certain sacrament to be a steady seal of this covenant in the visible church, until Christ should come, namely, circumcision. Circumcision was a seal of this covenant of grace, as appears by the first institution, as we have an account of it in Genesis 17. It there appears to be a seal of that covenant by which God promised to make Abraham a father of many nations, as appears by the 5th verse, compared with the 9th and 10th verses. And we are expressly taught, that it was a seal of the righteousness of faith, Romans 4:11. Speaking of Abraham, the apostle says, 'He received the sign of circumcision, a seal of the righteousness of faith.'

As I observed before, God called Abraham so that his family and posterity might be kept separate from the rest of the world, until Christ should come, which God saw to be necessary on the forementioned accounts. And this sacrament was the principal wall of separation; it chiefly distinguished Abraham's seed from the world, and kept up a distinction and separation more than any other particular observance whatsoever.

And besides this, there were other occasional seals, pledges, and confirmations, that Abraham had of this covenant; as, particularly, God gave Abraham a remarkable pledge of the fulfilment of the promise he had made him in his victory over Chedorlaomer and the kings that were with him. He seems to have been a great emperor that reigned over a great part of the world at that day; and though he had his seat at Elam, which was not much if any thing short of a thousand miles distant from the land of Canaan, yet he extended his empire so as to reign over many parts of the land of Canaan, as appears by Genesis 14:4-7.

It is supposed by learned men that he was a king of the Assyrian empire at that day, which had been before begun by Nimrod at Babel. And as it was the honour of kings in those days to build new cities to be made the seat of their empire, as appears by Genesis 10:10-12, so it is conjectured, that he had gone forth and built him a city in Elam and made that his seat; and that those other kings who came with him were his deputies in the several cities and countries where they reigned.

But yet, as mighty an empire as he had, and as great an army as he now came with into the land where Abraham was, yet Abraham, with only his trained servants that were born in his own house, conquered, subdued and baffled this mighty emperor and the kings that came with him and all their army. This he received of God as a pledge of what he had promised, namely, the victory that Christ, his seed, should obtain over the nations of the earth, whereby he should possess the gates of his enemies. It is plainly spoken of as such in Isaiah 41. In that chapter is foretold the future glorious victory the church shall obtain over the nations of the world; as you may see in verses 1, 10, 15 and so on. But here this victory of Abraham over such a great emperor and his mighty forces is spoken of as a pledge and earnest of this victory of the church, as you may see in Isaiah 41:2-3: 'Who raised up the righteous man from the east, called him to his foot, gave the nations before him, and made him rule over kings? he gave them as the dust to his sword, and as driven stubble to his bow. He pursued them, and passed safely; even by the way that he had not gone with his feet.'

Another remarkable confirmation Abraham received of the covenant of grace was when he returned from the slaughter of the kings, when Melchisedec the king of Salem, the priest of the most high God, that great type of Christ, met him and blessed him and brought forth bread and wine. The bread and wine signified the same blessings of the covenant of grace, that the bread and wine do in the sacrament of the Lord's supper. So that, as Abraham had a seal of the covenant in circumcision that was equivalent to baptism, so now he had a seal of it equivalent to the Lord's supper. And Melchisedec's coming to meet him with such a seal of the covenant of grace, on the occasion of this victory of his over the kings of the north, confirms that that victory was a pledge of God's fulfilment of the same covenant; for that is the mercy that Melchisedec with his bread and wine takes notice of; as you may see by what he says in Genesis 14:19-20.

Another confirmation that God gave to Abraham of the covenant of grace was the vision that he had, in the deep sleep that fell upon him, of the smoking furnace and burning lamp that passed between the parts of the sacrifice, as in the latter part of Genesis 15. The sacrifice, as all sacrifices do, signified the sacrifice of Christ. The smoking furnace that passed through the midst of that sacrifice first signified the sufferings of Christ. But the burning lamp that followed, which shone with a clear bright light, signified the glory that followed Christ's sufferings and was procured by them.

Another remarkable pledge that God gave Abraham of the fulfilment of the covenant of grace was his giving of the child of whom Christ was to come, in his old age. This is spoken of as such in Scripture, in Hebrews 11:11-12, and also in Romans 4:18-22.

Again, another remarkable pledge that God gave Abraham of the fulfilment of the covenant of grace was his delivering Isaac after he was laid upon the wood of the sacrifice to be slain. This was a confirmation of Abraham's faith in the promise that God had made of Christ, that he should be of Isaac's posterity; and was a representation of the resurrection of Christ; as you may see, Hebrews 11:17-19. And because this was given as a confirmation of the covenant of grace, therefore God renewed that covenant with Abraham on this occasion, as you may see, Genesis 22:15-18.

Thus you see how much more fully the covenant of grace was revealed and confirmed in Abraham's time than ever it had been before, by means of which Abraham seems to have had a more clear understanding and sight of Christ the great Redeemer, and the future things that were to be accomplished by him, than any of the saints that had gone before. And therefore Christ takes notice of it, that Abraham rejoiced to see his day, and he saw it, and was glad (*John* 8:56). So great an advance did it please God now to make in this building, which he had been carrying on from the beginning of the world.

3. The next thing that I would take notice of here is God's preserving the patriarchs for so long a time in the midst of the wicked inhabitants of Canaan, and all other enemies. The patriarchs Abraham, Isaac and Jacob were those of whom Christ was to proceed; and they were now separated from the world, so that in them his church might be upheld. Therefore, in preserving them, the great design of redemption was upheld and carried on. He preserved them, and kept the inhabitants of the land where they sojourned from destroying them, which was a remarkable dispensation of providence. For the inhabitants of the land were at that day exceedingly wicked, though they grew more wicked afterwards. This appears by Genesis 15:16: 'In the fourth generation they shall come hither again; for the iniquity of the Amorites is not yet full'; as much as to say, Though it be very great, yet it is not yet full. And their great wickedness also appears by Abraham and Isaac's aversion to their children marrying any of the daughters of the land. Abraham, when he was old, could not be content until he had made his servant swear that he would not take a wife for his son of the daughters of the land. And Isaac and Rebecca were content to send away Jacob to so great a distance as Padan-aram, to take him a wife from thence. And when Esau married some of the daughters of the land, we are told that they were a grief of mind to Isaac and Rebecca.

Another argument of their great wickedness, was the instances we have in Sodom and Gomorrah, Admah and Zeboim, which were some of the cities of Canaan, though they were probably distinguished for their wickedness. And they being thus wicked, were likely to have the most bitter enmity against these holy men; agreeable to what was declared at first, 'I will put enmity between thee and the woman, and between thy seed and her seed.' Their holy lives were a continual condemnation of their wickedness. And besides, it could not be otherwise but that they must be much in reproving their wickedness, as we find Lot was in Sodom; who, we are told, vexed his righteous soul with their unlawful deeds, and was a preacher of righteousness to them.

And they were the more exposed to them, being strangers and sojourners in the land, and having no inheritance there as yet. Men are more apt to find fault with strangers, and to be irritated by any thing in them that offends them, as they were with Lot in Sodom. He very gently reproved their wickedness; and they say upon it, 'This fellow came in to sojourn, and he will needs be a ruler and a judge'; and threatened what they would do to him.

But God wonderfully preserved Abraham and Lot, and Isaac and Jacob and their families, amongst them, though they were few in number, and they might quickly have destroyed them; which is taken notice of as a wonderful instance of God's preserving mercy toward his church: 'When they were but a few men in number; yea, very few, and strangers in it; when they went from one nation to another, from one kingdom to another people; he suffered no man to do them wrong: yea, he reproved kings for their sakes, saying, Touch not mine anointed, and do my prophets no harm' (*Psa.* 105:12-15).

This preservation was, in some instances especially, very remarkable, as in those instances that we have an account of wherein the people of the land were greatly irritated and provoked, as they were by Simeon and Levi's treatment of the Shechemites, as you may see in Genesis 34:30. God then

strangely preserved Jacob and his family, restraining the provoked people by an unusual terror on their minds, as you may
see in Genesis 35:5: 'And the terror of God was upon the
cities that were round about them, and they did not pursue
after the sons of Jacob.'

And God's preserving them, not only from the Canaanites,
but from all others that intended mischief to them, is here to
be taken notice of, as his preserving Jacob and his company
when pursued by Laban, full of rage, and a disposition to over-
take him as an enemy. God met him and rebuked him and
said to him, 'Take heed that thou speak not to Jacob either
good or bad.' How wonderfully did he also preserve him from
Esau his brother when he came forth with an army, with a full
design to cut him off! How did God, in answer to his prayer,
when he wrestled with Christ at Peniel, wonderfully turn
Esau's heart and make him, instead of as an enemy with
slaughter and destruction, to meet him as a friend and brother,
doing him no harm! And thus were this handful, this little
root that had the blessing of the Redeemer in it, preserved in
the midst of enemies and dangers; which was not unlike the
preserving of the ark in the midst of the tempestuous deluge.

4. The next thing I would mention is the awful destruction
of Sodom and Gomorrah and the neighbouring cities. This
tended to promote the great design and work that is the
subject of my present undertaking in two ways. It did so as it
tended powerfully to restrain the inhabitants of the land from
injuring those holy strangers that God had brought to sojourn
amongst them. Lot was one of those strangers; he came into
the land with Abraham and Sodom was destroyed for their
abusive disregard of Lot, the preacher of righteousness, that
God had sent among them. And their destruction came just
after their committing a most injurious and abominable insult
on Lot and the strangers that were come into his house, even
those angels whom they probably took to be some of Lot's

former acquaintance come from the country that he came from to visit him. They in a most outrageous manner beset Lot's house, intending a monstrous abuse and act of violence on those strangers that were come thither, and threatening to serve Lot worse than them.

But in the midst of this, God smote them with blindness; and the next morning the city and the country about it was overthrown in a most terrible storm of fire and brimstone; which dreadful destruction, as it was in the sight of the rest of the inhabitants of the land, and therefore greatly tended to restrain them from hurting holy strangers any more, doubtless struck a dread and terror on their minds, and made them afraid to hurt them, and probably was one principal means to restrain them and preserve the patriarchs.

And when reason is given why the inhabitants of the land did not pursue after Jacob, when they were so provoked by the destruction of the Shechemites, namely, that 'the terror of the Lord was upon them', it is very probable, that his was the terror that was set home upon them. They remembered the amazing destruction of Sodom and the cities of the plain that came upon them on account of their abusive treatment of Lot, and so they durst not hurt Jacob and his family, though they were so much provoked to it.

Another way that this awful destruction tended to promote this great affair of redemption was that hereby God did remarkably exhibit the terrors of his law, to make men sensible of their need of redeeming mercy. The work of redemption never was carried on without this. The law, from the beginning, is made use of as a schoolmaster to bring men to Christ. But under the Old Testament there was much more need of some extraordinary, visible and sensible manifestation of God's wrath against sin than in the days of the gospel, since a future state, and the eternal misery of hell, are more clearly revealed, and since the awful justice of God against the sins of men has been so wonderfully displayed in the sufferings of Christ.

And therefore the revelation that God gave of himself in those days used to be accompanied with much more terror than it is in these days of the gospel. So when God appeared at Mount Sinai to give the law, it was with thunders and lightnings, and a thick cloud, and the voice of the trumpet exceeding loud. But some external awful manifestations of God's wrath against sin were on some accounts especially necessary before the giving of the law: and therefore, before the flood, the terrors of the law handed down by tradition from Adam served.

Adam lived nine hundred and thirty years himself to tell the church of God's awful threatenings denounced in the covenant made with him, and how dreadful the consequences of the Fall were, as he was an eye witness and subject; and others that conversed with Adam lived until the flood. And the destruction of the world by the flood served to exhibit the terrors of the law and manifest the wrath of God against sin, and so to make men sensible of the absolute necessity of redeeming mercy. And some that saw the flood were alive in Abraham's time.

But this was now in a great measure forgotten. Now therefore God was pleased again, in a most amazing manner, to show his wrath against sin, in the destruction of these cities. This was after such a manner as to be the liveliest image of hell of any thing that ever had been; and therefore the apostle Jude says, 'They suffer the vengeance of eternal fire' (*Jude* 7). God rained storms of fire and brimstone upon them. The way that they were destroyed probably was by thick flashes of lightning. The streams of brimstone were so thick as to burn up all these cities, so that they perished in the flames of divine wrath. By this might be seen the dreadful wrath of God against the ungodliness and unrighteousness of men; which tended to show men the necessity of redemption, and so to promote that great work.

5. God again renewed and confirmed the covenant of grace to Isaac and to Jacob. He did so to Isaac, as you may see: 'And I will perform the oath which I sware unto Abraham thy father; and I will make thy seed to multiply as the stars in heaven, and will give unto thy seed all these countries; and in thy seed shall all the nations of the earth be blessed' (*Gen.* 26:3-4). And afterwards it was renewed and confirmed to Jacob: first in Isaac's blessing him, wherein he acted and spoke by extraordinary divine direction.

In that blessing, the blessings of the covenant of grace were established with Jacob and his seed: 'Let people serve thee, and nations bow down to thee; be lord over thy brethren, and let thy mother's sons bow down to thee: cursed be every one that curseth thee, and blessed be he that blesseth thee' (*Gen.* 27:29). And therefore Esau, in missing this blessing, missed being blessed as an heir of the benefits of the covenant of grace.

This covenant was again renewed and confirmed to Jacob at Bethel, in his vision of the ladder that reached to heaven; which ladder was a symbol of the way of salvation by Christ. For the stone that Jacob rested on was a type of Christ, the stone of Israel, which the spiritual Israel or Jacob rests upon. This is evident because this stone was on this occasion anointed and made use of as an altar. But we know that Christ is the anointed of God, and is the only true altar of God. While Jacob was resting on this stone and saw this ladder, God appeared to him as his covenant God and renewed the covenant of grace with him: 'And thy seed shall be as the dust of the earth; and thou shalt spread abroad to the west, and to the east, and to the north, and to the south; and in thee and in thy seed shall all the families of the earth be blessed' (*Gen.* 26:3-4).

And Jacob had another remarkable confirmation of this covenant at Peniel, where he wrestled with God and prevailed; where Christ appeared to him in a human form, in the form of that nature which he was afterwards to receive into a personal union with his divine nature.

And God renewed his covenant with him again, after he was come out of Padan-aram, and was come up to Bethel, to the stone that he had rested on, and where he had the vision of the ladder; as you may see in Genesis 35:10.

Thus the covenant of grace was now often renewed, much oftener than it had been before. The light of the gospel now began to shine much brighter, as the time drew nearer that Christ should come.

6. The next thing I would observe, is God's remarkably preserving the family of which Christ was to proceed from perishing by famine by the instrumentality of Joseph. When there was a seven years' famine approaching, God was pleased, by a wonderful providence, to send Joseph into Egypt, there to provide for and feed Jacob and his family, and to keep the holy seed alive, which otherwise would have perished. Joseph was sent into Egypt for that end, as he observes (*Gen.* 50:20): 'But as for you, ye thought evil against me; but God meant it unto good, to save much people alive.' How often had this holy root that had the future branch of righteousness, the glorious Redeemer, in it been in danger of being destroyed! But God wonderfully preserved it.

This salvation of the house of Israel by the hand of Joseph, was upon some accounts very much a resemblance of the salvation of Christ. The children of Israel were saved by Joseph their kinsman and brother, from perishing by famine; as he that saves the souls of the spiritual Israel from spiritual famine is their near kinsman, and one that is not ashamed to call them brethren. Joseph was a brother that they had hated, and sold and as it were killed; for they had designed to kill him. So Christ is one that we naturally hate and, by our wicked lives, have sold for the vain things of the world, and by our sins have slain. Joseph was first in a state of humiliation. He was a servant, as Christ appeared in the form of a servant. Then he was cast into a dungeon, as Christ descended into the grave; and then when he rose out of the dungeon he was in a state of great exaltation, at the king's right hand as his deputy, to reign over all his kingdom, to provide food, to pre-serve life. And being in this state of exaltation, he dispenses food to his brethren, and so gives them life; as Christ was exalted at God's right hand to be a Prince and a Saviour to his brethren, and received gifts for men, even for the rebellious, and for them that hated and had sold him.

7. After this there was a prophecy given forth of Christ, on some accounts more particular than ever any had been before, even that which was in Jacob's blessing of his son Judah. This was more particular in that it showed of whose posterity he was to be. When God called Abraham, it was revealed that he was to be of Abraham's posterity. Before, we have no account of any revelation concerning Christ's pedigree, confined to narrower limits than the posterity of Noah. After this it was confined to still narrower limits; for though Abraham had many sons, yet it was revealed that Christ was to be of Isaac's posterity. And then it was limited more still, for when Isaac had two sons it was revealed that Christ was to be of Israel's posterity. And now, though Israel had twelve sons, yet it is revealed that Christ should be of Judah's posterity; Christ is the lion of the tribe of Judah. Respect is chiefly had to his great acts when it is said here, 'Judah, thou art he whom thy brethren shall praise; thy hand shall be in the neck of thine enemies: thy father's children shall bow down before thee. Judah is a lion's whelp; from the prey, my son, thou art gone

up: he stooped down, he couched as a lion, and as an old lion. Who shall rouse him up?' (*Gen.* 49:8). And then this prediction is more particular concerning the time of Christ's coming than any had been before (verse. 10): 'The sceptre shall not depart from Judah, nor a lawgiver from between his feet, until Shiloh come; and unto him shall the gathering of the people be.' The prophecy here, of the calling of the Gentiles consequent on Christ's coming seems to be more plain than any had been before in the expression, 'To him shall the gathering of the people be'.

Thus you see how that gospel light which dawned immediately after the Fall of man gradually increases.

8. The work of redemption was carried on in this period in God's wonderfully preserving the children of Israel in Egypt, when the power of Egypt was engaged utterly to destroy them. They seemed to be wholly in the hands of the Egyptians; they were their servants, and were subject to the power of Pharaoh; and Pharaoh set himself to weaken them with hard bondage. And when he saw that that did not do, he set himself to extirpate the race of them by commanding that every male child should be drowned. But after all that Pharaoh could do God wonderfully preserved them; and not only so but increased them exceedingly; so that, instead of being extirpated, they greatly multiplied.

9. Here is to be observed, not only the preservation of the nation, but God's wonderfully preserving and upholding his invisible church in that nation, when in danger of being overwhelmed in the idolatry of Egypt. The children of Israel, being long among the Egyptians, and being servants under them, and so not under advantages to keep God's ordinances among themselves and maintain any public worship or public instruction whereby the true religion might be up-

held, and there being now no written Word of God, they, by degrees, in a great measure lost the true religion and borrowed the idolatry of Egypt; and the greater part of the people fell away to the worship of their gods. This we learn by Ezekiel 20:6-8; 23:8.

This was now the third time that God's church was almost swallowed up and carried away with the wickedness of the world; once before the flood; the other time, before the calling of Abraham; and now, the third time, in Egypt. But yet God did not suffer his church to be quite overwhelmed; he still saved it, like the ark in the flood, and as he saved Moses in the midst of the waters, in an ark of bulrushes, where he was in the utmost danger of being swallowed up. The true religion was still kept up with some; and God had still a people among them, even in this miserable, corrupt, and dark time. The parents of Moses were true servants of God, as we may learn from Hebrews 11:23: 'By faith Moses, when he was born, was hid three months of his parents, because they saw that he was a proper child; and they were not afraid of the king's commandment.'

I have now gone through the third period of the Old Testament time; and have shown how the work of redemption was carried on from the calling of Abraham to Moses; in which we have seen many great things done towards this work, and a great advancement of this building, beyond what had been before.

PART 4

❧❀❧

FROM MOSES TO DAVID

I proceed to the fourth period, which reaches from Moses to David. I would show how the work of redemption was carried on through this also.

1. The first thing that offers itself to be considered is the redemption of the church of God out of Egypt; the most remarkable of all the Old Testament redemptions of the church of God and that which was the greatest pledge and forerunner of the future redemption of Christ, of any. It is much more insisted on in Scripture than any other of those redemptions. And indeed it was the greatest type of Christ's redemption of any providential event whatsoever.

This redemption was by Jesus Christ, as is evident from this, that it was wrought by him that appeared to Moses in the bush; for that was the person that sent Moses to redeem that people. But that was Christ, as is evident, because he is called 'the angel of the LORD' (*Exod.* 3:2). The bush represented the human nature of Christ, who is called the Branch. The bush grew on Mount Sinai or Horeb, which is a word that signifies a dry place, as the human nature of Christ was a root out of a dry ground. The bush burning with fire represented the sufferings of Christ in the fire of God's wrath. It burned and was not consumed; so Christ, though he suffered extremely, yet perished not, but overcame at last, and rose from his sufferings. Because this great mystery of the incarnation and sufferings of Christ was here represented, therefore Moses said, 'I will now turn aside, and see this great sight.' A great sight he might well call it, when there was represented God manifest in the flesh, and suffering a dreadful death, and rising from the dead.

This glorious Redeemer was he that redeemed the church out of Egypt, from under the hand of Pharaoh; as Christ, by his death and sufferings, redeemed his people from Satan, the spiritual Pharaoh. He redeemed them from hard service and cruel drudgery, as Christ redeems his people from the cruel slavery of sin and Satan. He redeemed them, as it is said, from the iron furnace, as Christ redeems his church from a furnace of fire and everlasting burnings. He redeemed them with a strong hand and outstretched arm, and great and terrible judgments on their enemies, as Christ with mighty power triumphs over principalities and powers, and executes terrible judgments on his church's enemies, bruising the serpent's head. He saved them, when others were destroyed, by the sprinkling of the blood of the paschal lamb, as God's church is saved from death by the sprinkling of the blood of Christ, when the rest of the world is destroyed. God brought forth the people sorely against the will of the Egyptians, when they could not bear to let them go; so Christ rescues his people out of the hands of the devil, sorely against his will, when his proud heart cannot bear to be overcome.

In that redemption, Christ did not only redeem the people from the Egyptians, but he redeemed them from the devils, the gods of Egypt; for before, they had been in a state of servitude to the gods of Egypt, as well as to the men. And Christ, the seed of the woman, did now, in a very remarkable manner, fulfil the curse on the serpent in bruising his head: 'For I will pass through the land of Egypt this night, and will smite all the first born in the land of Egypt, both man and beast, and against all the gods of Egypt will I execute judgment' (*Exod.* 12: 12). Hell was as much and more engaged in that affair, than Egypt was. The pride and cruelty of Satan, that old serpent, were more concerned in it than Pharaoh's. He did his utmost against the people, and to his utmost opposed their redemption. But it is said that when God redeemed his people out of Egypt, he broke the heads of the dragons in the waters, and broke the head of leviathan in pieces, and gave him to be meat for the people inhabiting the wilderness (*Psa.* 74:12-14). God forced their enemies to let them go, that they might serve him; as also Zacharias observes with respect to the church under the gospel (*Luke* 1:74-75).

The people of Israel went out with a high hand, and Christ went before them in a pillar of cloud and fire. There was a glorious triumph over earth and hell in that deliverance. And when Pharaoh and his hosts, and Satan by them, pursued the people, Christ overthrew them in the Red Sea; the Lord triumphed gloriously; the horse and his rider he cast into the sea, and there they slept their last sleep, and never followed the children of Israel any more; as all Christ's enemies are overthrown in his blood, which by its abundant sufficiency, and the greatness of the sufferings with which it was shed, may well be represented by a sea. The Red Sea did represent Christ's blood, as is evident, because the apostle compares the children of Israel's passage through the Red Sea to baptism (*1 Cor.* 10: 1-2). But we all know that the water of baptism represents Christ's blood.

Thus Christ, the angel of God's presence, in his love and his pity, redeemed his people, and carried them in the days of old as on eagles' wings, so that none of their proud and spiteful enemies, neither Egyptians nor devils, could touch them.

This was quite a new thing that God did towards this great work of redemption. God never had done any thing like it before (*Deut.* 4:32-34). It was a great advancement of the work of redemption, that had been begun and carried on from the Fall of man; a great step taken in divine providence towards a preparation for Christ's coming into the world, and working out his great and eternal redemption: for this was the people of whom Christ was to come. And now we may see how that plant flourished that God had planted in Abraham. Though the family of which Christ was to come, had been in a degree separated from the rest of the world before, in the calling of Abraham; yet that separation that was then made, appeared not to be sufficient, without further separation. For though, by that separation, they were kept as strangers and sojourners, kept from being united with other people in the same political societies, yet they remained mixed among them, by which means, as it had proved, they had been in danger of wholly losing the true religion, and of being overrun with the idolatry of their neighbours.

God now, therefore, by this redemption, separated them as a nation from all other nations, to subsist by themselves in their own political and ecclesiastical state, without having any concern with the heathen nations, that they might so be kept separate until Christ should come; and so that the church of Christ might be upheld, and might keep the oracles of God, until that time; that in them might be kept up those types and prophecies of Christ, and those histories, and other previous divine instructions, that were necessary to prepare the way for Christ's coming.

2. As this people were separated to be God's peculiar people, so all other people upon the face of the whole earth were wholly rejected and given over to heathenism. This, so far as the providence of God was concerned in it, belongs to the great affair of redemption that we are upon, and was one thing that God ordered in his providence to prepare the way for Christ's coming, and the great salvation he was to accom-

plish in the world; for it was only to prepare the way for the more glorious and signal victory and triumph of Christ's power and grace over the wicked and miserable world, and that Christ's salvation of the world of mankind might become the more sensible.

This is the account the Scripture itself gives us of the matter in Romans 11:30-32. The apostle there, speaking to the Gentiles that had formerly been heathens, says, 'As ye in times past have not believed God, yet have now obtained mercy through their unbelief; even so have these also now not believed, that through your mercy they also may obtain mercy. For God hath concluded them all in unbelief, that he might have mercy upon all.'

That is, it was the will of God that the whole world, Jews and Gentiles, should be concluded in visible and professed unbelief, that so God's mercy and Christ's salvation towards them all might be visible and sensible. For the apostle is not speaking only of that unbelief that is natural to all God's professing people as well as others, but that which appears, and is visible; such as the Jews fell into, when they openly rejected Christ, and ceased to be a professing people. The apostle observes how that first the Gentiles, even the Gentile nations, were included in a professed unbelief and open opposition to the true religion before Christ came, to prepare the way for the calling of the Gentiles, which was soon after Christ came, that God's mercy might be the more visible to them; and that the Jews were rejected, and apostatized from the visible church, to prepare the way for the calling of the Jews which shall be in the latter days: so that it may be seen of all nations, Jews and Gentiles, that they are visibly redeemed by Christ, from being visibly aliens from the commonwealth of Israel, without hope, and without God in the world.

We cannot certainly determine precisely at what time the apostasy of the Gentile nations from the true God, or their being concluded in visible unbelief, became universal. Their falling away was a gradual thing, as we observed before. It was general in Abraham's time, but not universal: for then we find Melchisedec, one of the kings of Canaan, was priest of the most high God. And after this the true religion was kept up for a while among some of the rest of Abraham's posterity, besides the family of Jacob; and also in some of the posterity of Nahor, as we have instances of, in Job, and his three friends, and Elihu. The land of Uz, where Job lived, was a land possessed by the posterity of Uz, or Huz, the son of Nahor, Abraham's brother, of whom we read in Genesis 22:21. Bildad the Shuhite was of the offspring of Shuah, Abraham's son by Keturah (*Gen.* 25:1-2), and Elihu the Buzite was of Buz, the son of Nahor, the brother of Abraham. So the true religion lasted among some other people, besides the Israelites, a while after Abraham.

But it did not last long: and it is probable that the time of their total rejection, and giving up to idolatry, was about the time when God separated the children of Israel from Egypt to serve him; for they are often put in mind on that occasion that God had now separated them to be his peculiar people, or to be distinguished from all other people upon earth to be his people alone; to be his portion, when others were rejected. This seems to hold forth thus much to us, that God now chose them in such a manner, that this visible choice of them was accompanied with a visible rejection of all other nations in the world; that God visibly came, and took up his residence with them, as forsaking all other nations.

And so, as the first calling of the Gentiles after Christ came was accompanied with a rejection of the Jews, so the first calling of the Jews to be God's people, when they were called out of Egypt, was accompanied with a rejection of the Gentiles.

Thus all the Gentile nations throughout the whole world, all nations, except the Israelites, and those that embodied themselves with them, were left and given up to idolatry; and so continued a great many ages, even from this time until Christ came, which was about fifteen hundred years. They were concluded so long a time in unbelief that there might be a thorough proof of the necessity of a Saviour; that it might appear by so long a trial, past all contradiction, that mankind were utterly insufficient to deliver themselves from that gross darkness and misery, and subjection to the devil, that they had fallen under; that it might appear that all the wisdom of the philosophers, and the wisest men that the heathen had among them, could not deliver them from their darkness, for the greater glory to Jesus Christ, who, when he came, enlightened and delivered them by his glorious gospel. Herein the wonderful wisdom of God appeared, in thus preparing the way for Christ's redemption. This the Scripture teaches us, 'For after that, in the wisdom of God, the world by wisdom knew not God, it pleased God by the foolishness of preaching to save them that believe' (*1 Cor. 1. 21*).

Here I might consider as another work of God, whereby the general work of redemption was carried on, that wonderful deliverance which he wrought for the children of Israel at the Red Sea, when they were pursued by the hosts of the Egyptians, and were just ready to be swallowed up by them, there being, to human appearance no possibility of an escape. But as this may be referred to their redemption out of Egypt, and considered as a part of that more general work, I shall not further enlarge upon it.

3. The next thing that I shall take notice of here, that was done towards the work of redemption is God's giving the moral law in so awful a manner at Mount Sinai. This was another new thing that God did, a new step taken in this great affair. 'Did ever a people hear the voice of God speaking out of the midst of the fire, as thou hast heard, and live?' (*Deut.*

4: 33). And it was a great thing that God did towards this work, whether we consider it as delivered as a new exhibition of the covenant of works, or given as a rule of life. The covenant of works was here exhibited to be as a schoolmaster to lead to Christ, not only for the use of that nation in the ages of the Old Testament, but for the use of God's church throughout all ages of the world; as an instrument that the great Redeemer makes use of to convince men of their sin and misery, and helpless state, and of God's awful and tremendous majesty and justice as a lawgiver, and so to make men sensible of the necessity of Christ as a Saviour. The work of redemption, in its saving effect on men's souls, in all the progress of it to the end of it, is not carried on without the use of this law that was now delivered at Sinai.

It was given in an awful manner, with a terrible voice, exceedingly loud and awful, so that all the people that were in the camp trembled; and Moses himself, though so intimate a friend of God, yet said, I exceedingly fear and quake; the voice being accompanied with thunders and lightnings, the mountain burning with fire to the midst of heaven, and the earth itself shaking and trembling; to make all sensible how great that authority, power, and justice was, that stood engaged to exact the fulfilment of this law, and to see it fully executed; and how strictly God would require the fulfilment; and how terrible his wrath would be against every breaker of it; that men, being sensible of these things, might have a thorough trial of themselves, and might prove their own hearts, and know how impossible it is for them to have salvation by the works of the law, and might see the absolute necessity they stood in of a mediator.

If we regard this law now given at Mount Sinai not as the covenant of works but as a rule of life, so it is made use of by the Redeemer, from that time to the end of the world, as a directory to his people, to show them the way in which they must walk as they would go to heaven; for a way of sincere and universal obedience to this law is the narrow way that leads to life.

4. The next thing that is observable in this period was God's giving the typical law, in which I suppose to be included most or all those precepts that were given by Moses that did not properly belong to the moral law; not only those laws that are commonly called ceremonial, in distinction from judicial laws, which are the laws prescribing the ceremonies and circumstances of the Jewish worship, and their ecclesiastical state, but also many if not all those divine laws that were political, and for regulating the Jewish commonwealth, commonly called judicial laws; these were at best many of them typical. The giving this typical law was another great thing that God did in this period, tending to build up this glorious structure of redemption that God had been carrying on from the beginning of the world.

There had been many typical events of providence before that represented Christ and his redemption, and some typical ordinances, as particularly those two of sacrifices and circumcision; but now, instead of representing the great Redeemer in a few institutions, God gives forth a law full of nothing else but various and innumerable typical representations of good things to come, by which that nation were directed how, every year, month, and day, in their religious actions, and in their conduct of themselves, in all that appertained to their ecclesiastical and civil state, to show forth something of Christ; one observance showing one thing, exhibiting one doctrine, or one benefit; another, another: so that the whole nation by this law was, as it were, constituted a typical state. Thus the gospel was abundantly held forth to that nation; so that there is scarce any doctrine of it, but is particularly taught and exhibited by some observance of this law, though it was in shadows, and under a veil, as Moses put a veil on his face when it shone.

To this typical law belong all the precepts that relate to

building the tabernacle that was set up in the wilderness, and all the form, circumstances, and utensils of it.

5. About this time was given to God's church the first written Word of God that ever was enjoyed by God's people. This was another great thing done towards the affair of redemption, a new and glorious advancement of the building. Not far from this time, was the beginning of the great written rule, which God has given for the regulation of the faith, worship, and practice of his church in all ages henceforward to the end of the world; which rule grew, and was added to from that time, for many ages, until it was finished, and the canon of Scripture completed by the apostle John. It is not very material whether the first written word that ever was, was the ten commandments written on the tables of stone with the finger of God, or the book of Job; and whether the book of Job was written by Moses, as some suppose, or by Elihu, as others. If it was written by Elihu, it was written before this period that we are now upon; but yet could not be far from it, as appears by considering whose posterity the persons were that are spoken of in it, together with Job's great age, that was past before this was written.

The written Word of God is the main instrument Christ has made use of to carry on his work of redemption in all ages since it was given. There was a necessity now of the Word of God being committed to writing, for a steady rule to God's church. Before this, the church had the Word of God by tradition, either by immediate tradition from eminent men that were inspired, that were then living (for it was a common thing in those days, before there was a written Word, for God to reveal himself immediately to eminent persons, as appears by the book of Job, and many other things that might be mentioned, in the book of Genesis), or else they had it by tradition from former generations, which might be had with tolerable certainty in ages preceding this, by reason of the long lives of men. Noah might converse with Adam, and receive traditions from him; and Noah lived until about Abraham's time; and the sons of Jacob lived a considerable time to deliver the revelations made to Abraham, Isaac, and Jacob, to their posterity in Egypt. But the distance from the beginning of things was become so great, and the lives of men become so short, being brought down to the present standard about Moses' time, and God having now separated a nation to be a peculiar people, partly for that end, to be the keepers of the oracles of God, God saw it to be a needful and convenient time now to commit his Word to writing, to remain henceforward for a steady rule throughout all ages. And therefore, besides the book of Job, Christ wrote the ten commandments on tables of stone, with his own finger; and after this the whole law, as containing the substance of the five books of Moses, was by God's special command committed to writing, which was called the book of the law, and was laid up in the tabernacle, to be kept there for the use of the church; as you may see in Deuteronomy 31:24-26.

6. God was pleased now wonderfully to represent the progress of his redeemed church through the world to their eternal inheritance by the journey of the children of Israel through the wilderness, from Egypt to Canaan. Here all the various steps of the redemption of the church by Christ were represented, from the beginning to its consummation in glory. The state they are redeemed from is represented by Egypt, and their bondage there, which they left. The purchase of their redemption was represented by the sacrifice of the paschal lamb, which was offered up that night that God slew all the first born of Egypt. The beginning of the application of the redemption of Christ's church in their conversion was represented by Israel's going out of Egypt, and passing through the Red Sea in so extraordinary and miraculous a manner. The

travel of the church through this evil world, and the various changes through which the church passes, in the different stages of it, were represented by the journey of the Israelites through the wilderness. The manner of their being conducted by Christ, was represented by the Israelites being led by the pillar of cloud by day, and the pillar of fire by night. The manner of the church's being supported in their progress, and supplied from the beginning to the end of it, with spiritual food, and continual daily communications from God, was represented by God's supplying the children of Israel with bread, or manna, from heaven, and water out of the rock. The dangers that the saints must meet with in their course through the world, were represented by the fiery flying serpents which the children of Israel met with in the wilderness. The conflicts the church has with her enemies, were represented by their battle with the Amalekites, and others they met with there.

And so innumerable other things might be mentioned, wherein the things they met with were lively images of things which the church and saints meet with in all ages of the world. That these things are typical of things that pertain to the Christian church, is manifest from 1 Corinthians 10:11: 'Now all these things happened unto them for ensamples, and they are written for our admonition, upon whom the ends of the world are come.' Here the apostle is speaking of those very things which we have now mentioned, and he says expressly that they happened unto them for types; so it is in the original.

7. Another thing here must not be omitted, which was a great and remarkable dispensation of providence respecting the whole world of mankind finished in this period; and that was the shortening of the days of man's life, whereby it was brought down from being between nine hundred and a thousand years to be but about seventy or eighty. The life of man

began to be shortened immediately after the flood. It was brought down in the first generation to six hundred years, and in the next to between four and five hundred years; and so the life of man gradually grew shorter and shorter, until about the time of the great mortality that was in the congregation of Israel, after they had murmured at the report of the spies, and their carcasses fell in the wilderness, whereby all the men of war died. Then the life of man was reduced to its present standard, as Moses observes in the psalm that he wrote on the occasion of that mortality: 'The days of our years are three-score years and ten; and if by reason of strength they be fourscore years, yet is their strength labour and sorrow: for it is soon cut off, and we fly away' (*Psa.* 90: 10).

This great dispensation of God tended to promote the grand design of the redemption of Christ. Man's life being cut so very short in this world, tended to prepare the way for poor, mortal, short-lived men, the more joyfully to entertain the glad tidings of everlasting life in another world, that are brought to light by the gospel; and more readily to embrace a Saviour that purchases and offers such a blessing. If men's lives were still commonly about nine hundred years, how much less would they have to move them to regard the proffers of a future life; how much greater temptation would they have to rest in the things of this world, they being of such long continuance, and to neglect any other life but this? This probably contributed greatly to the wickedness of the antediluvians. But now, how much greater motives have men to seek redemption and a better life than this, by the great Redeemer, since the life of man is not one twelfth part of what it used to be and men now universally die at the age when men formerly used to be but, as it were, setting out in the world!

8. The same work was carried on in preserving that people, of whom Christ was to come, from totally perishing in the

wilderness, by a constant miracle of forty years continuance. I observed before many times, how God preserved those of whom the Redeemer was to proceed in a very wonderful manner, as he preserved Noah and his family from the flood; and as he preserved Abraham, Isaac, and Jacob, with their families, from the wicked inhabitants of Canaan; and as he preserved Jacob and his family from perishing by the famine, by Joseph in Egypt.

But this preservation of the children of Israel for so long a time in the wilderness, was on some accounts more remarkable than any of them; for it was by a continual miracle of so long duration. There was, as may be fairly computed, at first two millions of souls in that congregation, that could not subsist any better without meat and drink than other men. But if this had been withheld, they must all have perished, every man, woman, and child, in less than one month's time, so that there would not have been one of them left. But yet this vast multitude subsisted for forty years together, in a dry barren wilderness, without sowing or reaping, or tilling any land, having their bread daily rained down to them out of heaven, and being furnished with water to satisfy them all, out of a rock; and the same clothes with which they came out of Egypt, lasting, without wearing out all that time. Never was any instance like this, of a nation being so upheld for so long a time together. Thus God upheld his church by a continual miracle, and kept alive that people in whom was the blessing, the promised seed, and great Redeemer of the world.

9. God was pleased, in this time of the children of Israel's being in the wilderness, to give a further revelation of Christ the Redeemer in the predictions of him than had been before. Here are three prophecies given at this time that I would take notice of. The first is that of Balaam, 'I shall see him, but not now; I shall behold him, but not nigh: there shall come a Star

out of Jacob, and a Sceptre shall rise out of Israel, and shall smite the corners of Moab, and destroy all the children of Sheth. And Edom shall be a possession, Seir also shall be a possession for his enemies, and Israel shall do valiantly. Out of Jacob shall come he that shall have dominion, and shall destroy him that remaineth of the city' (*Num.* 24:17-19). This is a plainer prophecy of Christ, especially with regard to his kingly office, than any that had been before.

But we have another, which God gave by Moses, that is plainer still, especially with regard to his prophetical office: 'I will raise up a prophet from among their brethren, like unto thee, and will put my words in his mouth, and he shall speak unto them all that I command him' (*Deut.* 18:18). This is a plainer prophecy of Christ than any that had been before in this respect, that all the prophecies that had been before of Christ, were in figurative mystical language. The first prophecy was so, that the seed of the woman should bruise the serpent's head. The promises made to Abraham, Isaac, and Jacob, that in their seed all the families of the earth should be blessed, were also mystical and not so particular, because the expression, 'Thy seed', is general, and not plainly limited to any particular person. The prophecy of Jacob in blessing Judah in Genesis 49:8 is in mystical language; and so is that of Balaam, which speaks of Christ under the figurative expression of a star. But this is a plain prophecy, not veiled in any mystical language at all.

There are several things contained in this prophecy of Christ. Here is his mediatorial office in general, verse 16. Here it is revealed how he should be a person to stand between them and God, who was so terrible a Being, a Being of such awful majesty, holiness, and justice, that they could not have come to him, and have intercourse with him immediately, without a mediator to stand between them. If they came to such a dreadful sin-revenging God immediately, they should die; God would prove a consuming fire to them. And then also, here is a particular revelation of Christ with respect to his prophetical office: 'I will raise them up a prophet from among their brethren, like unto thee.' And further, it is revealed what kind of a prophet he should be, a prophet like Moses, who was the head and leader of all the people, and who, under God, had been their redeemer, to bring them out of the house of bondage. He was, as it were, their shepherd, by whom God led them through the Red Sea and wilderness, and was an intercessor for them with God, and was both a prophet and a king in the congregation; for Moses had the power of a king among them. It is said of him in Deuteronomy 33:5, 'He was king in Jeshurun', and he was the prophet by whom God, as it were, built up his church, and delivered his instructions of worship. Thus Christ was to be a prophet like unto Moses; so that this is both the plainest and fullest prophecy of Christ that ever had been from the beginning of the world to this time.

The next prophecy that I shall take notice of, respects only the calling of the Gentiles, which should be after Christ's coming, of which God gave a very plain prophecy by Moses in the wilderness in Deuteronomy 32:21. Here is a very plain prophecy of the rejection of the Jews and the calling the Gentiles. They moved God to jealousy by that which was not a god, by casting him off, and taking other gods that were no gods, in his room. So God declares that he will move them to jealousy in the like manner, by casting them off, and taking other people, that had not been his people, in their room. The Apostle Paul takes notice of this prophecy as foretelling the calling of the Gentiles, 'But I say, Did not Israel know? First, Moses saith, I will provoke you to jealousy by them that are no people, and by a foolish nation I will anger you. But Esaias is very bold, and saith, I was found of them that sought me not; I was made manifest to them that asked not after me' (*Rom.* 10:19–20).

Thus you see how the light of the gospel, which first began to dawn and glimmer immediately after the Fall, gradually increases the nearer we come to Christ's time.

10. Another thing by which God carried on this work in this time, was a remarkable pouring out of his Spirit on the young generation in the wilderness. The generation that was grown up when they came out of Egypt, from twenty years old and upward, was a very froward and perverse generation. They were tainted with the idolatry and wickedness of Egypt, and were not weaned from it, as the prophet Ezekiel takes notice, Ezekiel 20:6-8. Hence they made the golden calf in imitation of the idolatry of Egypt, that was wont to worship a bull or an ox; and therefore cattle are called the abomination of the Egyptians, that is, their idol (*Exod.* 8:26). This generation God was exceeding angry with, and swore in his wrath that they should not enter into his rest.

But the younger generation were not so; the generation that were under twenty years old when they came out of Egypt, and those that were born in the wilderness, the generation spoken of, 'But your little ones, who ye said should be a prey, them will I bring in; and they shall know the land that ye have despised' (*Num.* 14:31). This was the generation with whom the covenant was renewed, as we have an account in Deuteronomy, and that entered into the land of Canaan. This generation God was pleased to make a generation to his praise, and they were eminent for piety; as appears by many things said in Scripture about them; as, particularly, 'I remember thee, the kindness of thy youth, the love of thine espousals, when thou wentest after me in the wilderness, in a land that was not sown. Israel was holiness to the LORD, and the first fruits of his increase' (*Jer.* 2:2-3). Here the generation that went after God in the wilderness is spoken of with very high commendations, as eminent for holiness: 'Israel was holiness to the LORD, and the first fruits of his increase.' And their love to God is spoken of as distinguished like the love of a bride at her espousals. The going after God in the wilderness that is here spoken of is not the going of the children of Israel out of Egypt into the wilderness of Sinai, but their following God through that dreadful wilderness, that the congregation long wandered in, after they went back from Kadesh-barnea, which is spoken of, 'Who led thee through the great and terrible wilderness, wherein were fiery serpents and scorpions, and drought, where there was no water' (*Deut.* 8:15).

Though this generation had a much greater trial than the generation of their fathers had before they came to Kadesh-barnea, yet they never murmured against God in any wise, as their fathers had done: but their trials had a contrary effect upon them, to awaken them, convince, and humble them, and fit them for great mercy. They were awakened by those awful judgments of God that he inflicted on their fathers, whereby their carcases fell in the wilderness. And God poured out his Spirit with those awakening providences toward their fathers, and their own travel in the wilderness, and the word preached to them by Moses; whereby they were greatly awakened, and made to see the badness of their own hearts, and were humbled, and at length multitudes of them savingly converted: 'And thou shalt remember the way which the LORD thy God led thee these forty years in the wilderness, to humble thee, and to prove thee, to know what was in thine heart whether thou wouldest keep his commandments, or no. And he humbled thee' (*Deut.* 8:2–3). And, verse 15: 'Who led thee through that great and terrible wilderness, that he might humble thee, and that he might prove thee, to do thee good at thy latter end.'

And therefore it is said, 'I did know thee in the wilderness, in the land of great drought' (*Hos.* 13:5). God allured them, and brought them into that wilderness and spake comfortably to them, as it was foretold that he would do afterwards (*Hos.* 2:14).

Those terrible judgments that were executed in the congregation after their turning back from Kadesh-barnea, in the matter of Korah, and the matter of Peor, were chiefly on the old generation, whom God consumed in the wilderness. Those rebellions were chiefly among the elders of the congregation, who were of the older generation that God had given up to their hearts' lust; and they walked in their own counsels, and God was grieved with their manners forty years in the wilderness. But that this younger congregation were eminent for piety, appears by all their history. The former generation were wicked, and were followed with curses; but this was holy, and wonderful blessings followed them. God did great things for them; he fought for them, and gave them the possession of Canaan. And it is God's manner, when he hath very great mercies to bestow on a visible people, first, to fit them for them, and then to bestow them on them. So it was here: they believed in God, and by faith overcame Sihon and Og, and the giants of Canaan; and are commended for cleaving to the Lord: Joshua says to them, 'Cleave unto the LORD your God, as ye have done unto this day' (*Josh.* 23:8).

And so Israel did all the while that generation lived. But when Joshua and all that generation were dead, there arose another generation that knew not the Lord. This pious generation showed a laudable and fervent zeal for God on several occasions; on occasion of Achan's sin; but especially when they suspected the two tribes and a half had set up an altar in opposition to the altar of burnt offering There never was any generation of Israel that so much good and so little evil is mentioned of, as this generation. It is further observable, that in the time of this generation was the second general circumcision, whereby the reproach of Israel was fully rolled away, and they became pure; and when afterwards they were polluted by Achan, they purged themselves again.

The men of the former generation being dead, and God having sanctified this younger generation to himself, he solemnly renewed his covenant with them, which we have a particular account of in the 29th chapter of Deuteronomy. We find that such solemn renovations of the covenant commonly accompanied any remarkable pouring out of the Spirit, causing a general reformation. So we find it was in Hezekiah's and Josiah's times. It is questionable whether there ever was a time of so great a flourishing of religion in the Israelitish church, as in that generation; and as, in the Christian church, religion was in its most flourishing circumstances in the day of its espousals, or first setting up of that church, in the days of the apostles, so it seems to have been with the Jewish church in the days of its first establishment in Moses's and Joshua's times.

Thus God at this time did gloriously advance the work of redemption, both by his Word and Spirit. By this pouring out of the Spirit of God, the work of redemption was promoted, not only as it was in itself a glorious instance of the carrying on of that redemption in the application of it, but as this was what God made use of as a means of the good and orderly establishment of the church of Israel at its first beginning, when it was first settled in the regular observance of God's ordinances in Canaan. Even so, the pouring out of the Spirit, in the beginning of the Christian church, was a great means God made use of for the well establishing of the Christian church in the world in all succeeding ages.

11. The next thing I would observe was God's bringing the people of Israel under the hand of Joshua, and settling them in that land where Christ was to be born, and which was the great type of the heavenly Canaan, which Christ has

purchased. This was done by Joshua, who was of Joseph's posterity, and was an eminent type of Christ, and is therefore called the shepherd, the stone of Israel, in Jacob's blessing of Joseph, Genesis 49:24. Being such a type of Christ, he bore the name of Christ. Joshua and Jesus are the same name, only the one is Hebrew, the other is Greek: and therefore, in the New Testament, which was originally written in Greek, Joshua is called Jesus, 'Which also our fathers brought in with Jesus', i.e. Joshua (*Acts* 7:45). 'If Jesus had given them rest, he would not have spoken of another day' (*Heb.* 4:8), i.e., if Joshua had given them rest.

God wonderfully possessed his people of this land, conquering the former inhabitants of it, and the mighty giants, as Christ conquered the devil; first conquering the great king of that part of the land that was on the eastern side of Jordan, Sihon, king of the Amorites, and Og, king of Bashan; and then dividing the river Jordan, as before he had done the Red Sea; causing the walls of Jericho to fall down at the sound of the trumpets of the priests; that sound typifying the sound of the gospel by the preaching of the gospel ministers, the walls of the accursed city Jericho signifying the walls of Satan's kingdom; and after this wonderfully destroying the mighty host of the Amorites under the five kings; causing the sun and moon to stand still, to help the people against their enemies, at the prayer of the typical Jesus; plainly holding this forth, that God would make the whole course of nature to be subservient to the affair of redemption; so that every thing should yield to the purposes of that work, and give place to the welfare of God's redeemed people.

Thus did Christ show his great love to his elect, that he would make the course of nature, in the frame of the world that he had made, and that he governed, to give place to their happiness and prosperity; and showed that the sun and moon, and all things, visible and invisible, were theirs by his purchase. At the same time, Christ fought as the captain of their host, and cast down great hailstones upon their enemies, by which more were slain than by the sword of the children of Israel. And after this Christ gave the people a mighty victory over a yet greater army in the northern part of the land, that were gathered together at the waters of Merom, as the sand of the sea shore, as it is said (*Josh.* 11:4).

Thus God gave the people whence Christ was to proceed the land where he was to be born, and live, and preach, and work miracles, and die, and rise again, and whence he was to ascend into heaven, as the land which was a great type of heaven; which is another thing whereby a great advance was made in the affair of redemption.

12. Another thing that God did towards carrying on this affair was his actually setting up his stated worship among the people, as it had been before instituted in the wilderness. This worship was appointed at Mount Sinai, wholly in subserviency to this great affair of redemption. It was to make way for the coming of Christ; and the innumerable ceremonial observances of it were typical of him and his redemption. This worship was chiefly instituted at Mount Sinai; but it was gradually set up in practice. It was partly set up in the wilderness, where the tabernacle and its vessels were made; but there were many parts of their instituted worship that could not be observed in the wilderness, by reason of their unsettled, itinerant state there; and then there were many precepts that respect the land of Canaan, and their cities and places of habitation there; which therefore could not be put in practice until they came into that land. But now, when this was brought to pass, God set up his tabernacle in the midst of his people, as he had before promised them (*Lev.* 26:11), 'I will set up my tabernacle amongst you.' The tabernacle was set up at Shiloh (*Josh.* 18:1). And the priests and Levites had their

offices appointed them, and the cities of refuge were appointed. And now the people were in a condition to observe their feasts of the first fruits, and their feasts of ingathering, and to bring all their tithes and appointed offerings to the Lord; and most parts of God's worship were set up, though there were some things that were not observed until afterwards.

13. The next thing I would take notice of, was God's wonderfully preserving that people, from this time forward, when all the males went up, three times in the year, to the place where God's ark was. The people of Israel were generally surrounded with enemies that sought all opportunities to destroy them, and dispossess them of their land; and until David's time there were great numbers in the land of the remains of the Canaanites, and the other former inhabitants of the land, that were bitter enemies to the people of Israel: and these had from year to year, three times in the year, a fair opportunity of overrunning their country, and getting possession of their cities, when all the males were gone, and only the women, and those who were not able to go up, were left behind.

And yet they were remarkably preserved throughout all generations at such seasons, agreeable to the promise that God had made (*Exod.* 34:24), 'Neither shall any man desire thy land, when thou shalt go up to appear before the LORD thy God thrice in the year.' So wonderfully did God order affairs, and influence the hearts of their enemies, that though they were so full of enmity against Israel, and desired to dispossess them of their land, and had so fair an opportunity so often in their hands, that the whole country was left naked and empty of all that could resist them, and it would have been only for them to have gone and taken possession, and they could have had it without opposition, and they were so eager to take other opportunities against them; yet we never read, in all their history, of any of their enemies taking these opportunities against them; which could be no less than a continual miracle, that God, for the preservation of his church, kept up for so many generations, even throughout the ages of the Old Testament. It was surely a wonderful dispensation of divine providence to maintain and promote God's great design of redemption.

14. God preserved his church and the true religion from becoming wholly extinct in the frequent apostasies of the Israelites in the time of the Judges. How prone was that people to forsake the true God, that had done such wonderful things for them, and to fall into idolatry! And how did the land, from time to time, seem to be almost overrun with idolatry! But yet God never suffered his true worship to be totally rooted out. His tabernacle stood, the ark was preserved, the book of the law was kept from being destroyed, God's priesthood was upheld, and God still had a church among the people. And time after time, when religion seemed to be almost gone, and it was come to the last extremity, then God granted a revival, and sent some angel or prophet, or raised up some eminent person, to be an instrument of their reformation.

15. God preserved that nation from being destroyed, and delivering them from time to time, although they were so often subdued and brought under the dominion of their enemies. It is a wonder, not only that the true religion was not wholly rooted out, and so the church destroyed that way; but also that the very nation in which that church was, was not utterly destroyed, who were so often brought under the power of their enemies. One while they were subdued by Chushanrishathaim king of Mesopotamia, another while they were brought under the Moabites; and then they were sold into the

hand of Jabin, king of Canaan; and then they were under the dominion of the Midianites; and then were sorely distressed by the children of Ammon; and then by the Philistines. But yet God, in all these dangers, preserved them, and kept them from being wholly overthrown. And from time to time, when it was come to extremity, and God saw that they were upon the very brink of ruin, then God raised up a deliverer (agreeable to Deuteronomy 32: 36), 'For the LORD shall judge his people, and repent himself for his servants; when he seeth their power is gone, and there is none shut up or left.' Those remarkable dispensations of providence are very lively and elegantly set forth by the Psalmist, Psalm 106:34-46.

These deliverers that God raised up from time to time were all types of Christ, the great Redeemer and Deliverer of his church; and some of them very remarkably so; as, particularly, Barak, Jephthah, Gideon, and Samson, in very many particulars; and above all in the acts of Samson, as might be shown, were it not that this would take up too much time.

16. It is observable that when Christ appeared to manage the affairs of his church in this period, he often appeared in the form of that nature that he took upon him in his incarnation. So he seems to have appeared to Moses from time to time, and particularly at that time when God spake to him face to face, as a man speaketh to his friend, and he beheld the similitude of the LORD (*Num.* 12:8), after he had besought him to show him his glory; which was the most remarkable vision that ever he had of Christ. There was a twofold discovery that Moses had of Christ. One was spiritual, made to his mind, by the word that was proclaimed, when he proclaimed his name, saying, 'The LORD, The LORD God, merciful and gracious, long suffering, and abundant in goodness and truth, keeping mercy for thousands, forgiving iniquity and transgression and sin, and that will by no means clear the guilty;

visiting the iniquity of the fathers upon the children, and upon the children's children, unto the third and to the fourth generation' (*Exod.* 34:6-7). Another was external, which was that which Moses saw, when Christ passed by, and put him in a cleft of the rock, and covered him with his hand, so that Moses saw his back parts. What he saw was doubtless the back parts of a glorious human form, in which Christ appeared to him, and in all likelihood the form of his glorified human nature, in which he should afterwards appear. He saw not his face; for it is not to be supposed that any man could subsist under a sight of the glory of Christ's human nature as it now appears.

So it was a human form in which Christ appeared to the seventy elders, of which we have an account (*Exod.* 24:9-11), 'Then went up Moses and Aaron, Nadab and Abihu, and seventy of the elders of Israel: and they saw the God of Israel: and there was under his feet, as it were a paved work of a sapphire stone, and as it were the body of heaven in his clearness. And upon the nobles of the children of Israel he laid not his hand: also they saw God, and did eat and drink.' So Christ appeared afterwards to Joshua in the form of the human nature (*Josh.* 5:13-14): 'And it came to pass when Joshua was by Jericho, he lift up his eyes, and looked, and behold, there stood a man over against him, with his sword drawn in his hand: and Joshua went unto him, and said unto him, Art thou for us, or for our adversaries? And he said, Nay, but as captain of the host of the LORD am I now come.' And so he appeared to Gideon, Judges 6:11-24; and so also to Manoah, Judges 13:17-21. Here Christ appeared to Manoah in a representation both of his incarnation and death; of his incarnation, in that he appeared in a human form; and of his death and sufferings, represented by the sacrifice of a kid, and by his ascending up in the flame of the sacrifice; intimating that it was he that was the great sacrifice, that must be offered up to

God for a sweet savour, in the fire of his wrath, as that kid was burned and ascended up in the flame. Christ thus appeared, time after time, in the form of that nature he was afterwards to take upon him; because he now appeared on the same design, and to carry on the same work, that he was to appear in that nature to work out and carry on.

17. Another thing I would mention, done in this period towards the work of redemption, is the beginning of a succession of prophets, and erecting a school of the prophets, in Samuel's time. There was something of this spirit of prophecy in Israel after Moses, before Samuel. Joshua and many of the judges had a degree of it. Deborah was a prophetess; and some of the high priests were inspired with this spirit; particularly Eli. And that space of time was not wholly without instances of those that were set apart of God especially to this office, and so were called prophets. Such a one we read of (*Judg.* 6:8), 'The LORD sent a prophet unto the children of Israel, which said unto them,' etc. Such a one he seems to have been that we read of (*1 Sam.* 2:27) 'And there came a man of God to Eli,' etc.

But there was no such order of men upheld in Israel for any constancy, before Samuel; the want of it is taken notice of (in *1 Sam.* 3:1) 'And the word of the LORD was precious in those days; there was no open vision.' But in Samuel there was begun a succession of prophets, that was maintained continually from that time, at least with very little interruption, until the spirit of prophecy ceased, about Malachi's time: and therefore Samuel is spoken of in the New Testament as the beginning of this succession of prophets (*Acts* 3:24) 'And all the prophets from Samuel, and those that follow after, as many as have spoken, have foretold of these days.' After Samuel was Nathan, and Gad, and Iddo, and Heman, and Asaph, and others. And afterwards, in the latter end of

Solomon's reign, we read of Ahijah; and in Jeroboam and Rehoboam's time we read of prophets; and so continually one prophet succeeded another, until the captivity. We read in the writings of those prophets that are inserted into the canon of the Scriptures, of prophets as being a constant order of men upheld in the land in those days: and in the time of the captivity there were prophets still, as Ezekiel and Daniel; and after the captivity there were prophets, as Zechariah, Haggai, and Malachi.

And because God intended a constant succession of prophets from Samuel's time, therefore in his time was begun a school of the prophets; that is, a school of young men, that were trained up under some great prophet, who was their master and teacher in the study of divine things, and the practice of holiness, to fit them for this office as God should call them to it. Those young men that belonged to these schools, were called the sons of the prophets; and oftentimes they are called prophets.

These at first were under the tuition of Samuel. Thus we read of Samuel's being appointed over them (*1 Sam.* 19:20), 'And when they saw the company of prophets prophesying, and Samuel standing as appointed over them.' The company of prophets that we read of, 1 Samuel 10:5, were the same. Afterwards we read of their being under Elijah. Elisha was one of his sons; but he desired to have a double portion of his spirit, as his successor, as his first born, as the eldest son was wont to have a double portion of the estate of his father; and therefore the sons of the prophets, when they perceived that the spirit of Elijah rested on Elisha, submitted themselves to him, and owned him for their master, as they had done Elijah before him; as you may see (*2 Kings* 2:15), 'And when the sons of the prophets which were to view at Jericho, saw him, they said, The spirit of Elijah doth rest on Elisha. And they bowed themselves to the ground before him.'

And so after this Elisha was their master or teacher; he had the care and instruction of them; as you may see (*2 Kings* 4: 38), 'And Elisha came again to Gilgal, and there was a dearth in the land, and the sons of the prophets were sitting before him: and he said unto his servant, Set on the great pot, and seethe pottage for the sons of the prophets.' In Elijah's and Elisha's time, there were several places where there resided companies of these sons of the prophets; as there was one at Bethel, and another at Jericho, and another at Gilgal, unless that at Gilgal and Jericho were the same. And possibly that which is called the college, where the prophetess Huldah resided, was another at Jerusalem; see 2 Kings 22:14. It is there said of Huldah the prophetess, that 'she dwelt in Jerusalem in the college'. They had houses built where they used to dwell together; and therefore those at Jericho being multiplied, and finding their house too little for them, desired leave of their master and teacher Elisha, that they might go and hew timber to build a bigger; as you may see, 2 Kings 6:1–2.

At some times there were numbers of these sons of the prophets in Israel; for when Jezebel cut off the prophets of the Lord, it is said, that Obadiah took an hundred of them, and hid them by fifty in a cave, 1 Kings 18:4.

These schools of the prophets being set up by Samuel, and afterwards kept up by such great prophets as Elijah and Elisha, must be of divine appointment; and accordingly we find, that those sons of the prophets were often favoured with a degree of inspiration, while they continued under tuition in the schools of the prophets; and God commonly, when he called any prophet to the constant exercise of the prophetical office, and to some extraordinary service, took them out of these schools; though not universally. Hence the prophet Amos, speaking of his being called to the prophetical office, says, that he was one that had not been educated in the schools of the prophets, and was not one of the sons of the prophets (*Amos*

7:14-15). But Amos's taking notice of it as remarkable, that he should be called to be a prophet that had not been educated at the schools of the prophets, shows that it was God's ordinary manner to take his prophets out of these schools; for therein he did but bless his own institution.

Now this remarkable dispensation of providence that we are upon, namely, God's beginning a constant succession of prophets in Samuel's time, that was to last for many ages; and to that end, establishing a school of the prophets under Samuel, thenceforward to be continued in Israel, was a step that God took in that great affair of redemption that we are upon. For the main business of this succession of prophets was, to foreshow Christ, and the glorious redemption that he was to accomplish, and so to prepare the way for his coming; as appears by that forementioned place, Acts 3:24, and by Acts 10:43: 'To him give all the prophets witness'; and by Acts 3:18: 'But those things which God before had shewed by the mouth of all his prophets, that Christ should suffer, he hath so fulfilled.'

As I observed before, the Old Testament time was like a time of night, wherein the church was not wholly without light. She had not the light of the sun directly, but as reflected from the stars. Now these prophets were the stars that reflected the light of the sun; and accordingly they spoke abundantly of Jesus Christ, as appears by what we have of their prophecies in writing. And they made it very much their business, when they studied in their schools or colleges, and elsewhere, to search out the work of redemption; agreeable to what the apostle Peter says of them (*1 Pet.* 1:10-11), 'Of which salvation the prophets have inquired, and searched diligently, who prophesied of the grace that should come unto you; searching what, or what manner of time the spirit of Christ that was in them did signify, when it testified beforehand the sufferings of Christ, and the glory that should follow.' We are told, that the church of the Redeemer is built on the foundation of the prophets and apostles, the Redeemer himself being the chief corner stone (*Eph.* 2:20).

This was the first thing of this nature that ever was done in the world; and it was a great thing that God did towards further advancing this great building of redemption. There had been before occasional prophecies of Christ, as was shown; but now, the time drawing nearer when the Redeemer should come, it pleased God to appoint a certain order of men, in constant succession, whose main business it should be to foreshow Christ and his redemption, and, as his forerunners, to prepare the way for his coming. And God established schools wherein multitudes were instructed and trained up to that end: 'I am thy fellow servant, and of thy brethren that have the testimony of Jesus; for the testimony of Jesus is the spirit of prophecy' (*Rev.* 19:10).

PART 5

⊷⊷⊷

FROM DAVID TO THE
BABYLONISH CAPTIVITY

I come now to the fifth period of the times of the Old Testament, beginning with David, and extending to the Babylonish captivity, and would now proceed to show how the work of redemption was carried on through this period also. And here,

1. The first thing to be taken notice of is God's anointing that person that was to be the ancestor of Christ, to be king over his people. The dispensations of providence that have been taken notice of through the last period, from Moses to this time, respect the people whence Christ was to proceed. But now the Scripture history leads us to consider God's providence towards that particular person whence Christ was to proceed, namely, David. It pleased God at this time remarkably to select out that person of whom Christ was to come, from all the thousands of Israel, and to put a most honourable mark of distinction upon him by anointing him to be king over his people. It was only God that could find him out. His father's house is spoken of as being little in Israel, and he was the youngest of all the sons of his father, and was least expected to be the man that God had chosen by Samuel. God had before, in the former ages of the world, remarkably distinguished the persons from whom Christ was to come; as he did

Seth, and Noah, and Abraham, and Isaac, and Jacob. But the last that we have any account of God's marking out in any notable manner, the very person of whom Christ was to come, was in Jacob's blessing his son Judah; unless we reckon Nahshon's advancement in the wilderness to be the head of the tribe of Judah. But this distinction of the person of whom Christ was to come, in David, was very honourable; for it was God's anointing him to be king over his people. And there was something further denoted by David's anointing than was in the anointing of Saul. God anointed Saul to be king personally; but God intended something further by sending Samuel to anoint David, viz. to establish the crown of Israel in him and in his family, as long as Israel continued to be a kingdom; and not only so, but what was infinitely more still, establishing the crown of his universal church, his spiritual Israel, in his seed, to the end of the world, and throughout all eternity.

This was a great dispensation of God, and a great step taken towards a further advancing of the work of redemption, according as the time drew near wherein Christ was to come. David, as he was the ancestor of Christ, so he was the greatest personal type of Christ of all under the Old Testament. The types of Christ were of three sorts: types of institution, or instituted types; providential types; and personal types. The ordinance of sacrificing was the greatest of the instituted types; the redemption out of Egypt was the greatest of the providential types; and David was the greatest of the personal types.

Hence Christ is often called David in the prophecies of Scripture, as Ezekiel 34:23-24, 'And I will set up one shepherd over them, and he shall feed them, even my servant David . . . my servant David a prince among them.' And so in many other places. And he is very often spoken of as the seed of David and the son of David.

David being the ancestor and great type of Christ, his being solemnly anointed by God to be king over his people, that the kingdom of his church might be continued in his family for ever, may in some respects be looked on as an anointing of Christ himself. Christ was as it were anointed in him; and therefore Christ's anointing and David's anointing are spoken of as one in Scripture, as Psalm 89:20, 'I have found David my servant; with my holy oil have I anointed him.' And David's throne and Christ's are spoken of as one: 'And the Lord shall give him the throne of his father David' (*Luke* 1:32). David knew 'that God had sworn with an oath to him, that of the fruit of his loins, according to the flesh, he would raise up Christ to sit on his throne' (*Acts* 2:30).

Thus God's beginning of the kingdom of his church in the house of David, was, as it were, a new establishing, of the kingdom of Christ; the beginning of it in a state of such visibility as it thenceforward continued in. It was, as it were, God's planting the root whence that branch of righteousness was afterwards to spring up that was to be the everlasting king of his church; and therefore this everlasting king is called the branch from the stem of Jesse. 'And there shall come forth a rod out of the stem of Jesse, and a branch shall grow out of his roots' (*Isa.* 11:1). 'Behold, the days come, saith the LORD, that I will raise up unto David a righteous branch, and a king shall reign and prosper' (*Jer.* 23:5). So chapter 33:15, 'In those days, and at that time, I will cause the branch of righteousness to grow up unto David, and he shall execute judgment and righteousness in the land.' So Christ, in the New Testament, is called the root and offspring of David (*Rev.* 22:16).

It is observable that God anointed David after Saul to reign in his room. He took away the crown from him and his family who was higher in stature than any of his people, and was in their eyes fittest to bear rule, to give it to David, who was low of stature, and in comparison, of despicable appearance:

so God was pleased to show how Christ who appeared despicable, without form or comeliness, and was despised and rejected of men, should take the kingdom from the great ones of the earth. And also it is observable that David was the youngest of Jesse's sons, as Jacob the younger brother supplanted Esau, and got the birthright and blessing from him; and as Pharez, another of Christ's ancestors, supplanted Zarah in the birth; and as Isaac, another of the ancestors of Christ, cast out his elder brother Ishmael. Thus was that frequent saying of Christ fulfilled, 'The last shall be first, and the first last.'

2. The next thing I would observe is God's so preserving David's life, by a series of wonderful providences, until Saul's death. I before took notice of the wonderful preservation of other particular persons that were the ancestors of Christ, as Noah, Abraham, Isaac, and Jacob; and have observed how, in that Christ the great Redeemer was to proceed, from them, in their preservation, the work of redemption itself may be looked upon as preserved from being defeated, and the whole church, which is redeemed through him, from being overthrown. But the preservation of David was no less remarkable than that of any others that have been already taken notice of. How often was it so, that there was but a step between him and death. The first instance of it we have in his encountering a lion and a bear, when they had caught a lamb out of his flock, which, without miraculous assistance, could at once have rent this young stripling in pieces, as they could the lamb that he delivered from them. So afterwards the root and offspring of David was preserved from the roaring lion that goes about seeking whom he may devour, and conquered him and rescued the poor souls of men, that were as lambs in the mouth of this lion.

Another remarkable instance was, in preserving him from that mighty giant Goliath, who was strong enough to have taken him, and picked him to pieces with his fingers, and given his flesh to the beasts of the field, and to the fowls of the air, as he threatened him. But God preserved him from him, and gave him the victory over him, so that he cut off his head with his own sword, and God made him therein the deliverer of his people, as Christ slew the spiritual Goliath with his own weapon, the cross, and so delivered his people.

And how remarkably did God preserve him from being slain by Saul, when he first sought his life, by giving him his daughter to be a snare to him, that the hand of the Philistines might be upon him, requiring him to pay for her by an hundred foreskins of the Philistines, that so his life might be exposed to them; and in preserving him afterwards, when Saul spake to Jonathan, and to all his servants, to kill David; and in inclining Jonathan, instead of killing him, as his father bade him, to love him as his own soul, and to be a great instrument of his preservation, even so as to expose his own life to preserve David, though one would have thought that none would have been more willing to have David killed than Jonathan, seeing that he was competitor with him for his father's crown.

And again God saved him, when Saul threw a javelin at him to smite him even to the wall; and again preserved him, when he sent messengers to his house, to watch him, and to kill him, when Michal, Saul's daughter, let him down through a window; and when he afterwards sent messengers, once and again, to Naioth in Ramah, to take him, and they were remarkably prevented time after time, by being seized with miraculous impressions of the Spirit of God; and afterwards, when Saul, being resolute in the affair, went himself, he also was among the prophets. And after this, how wonderfully was David's life preserved at Gath, among the Philistines, when he went to Achish, the king of Gath, and was there in the hands of the Philistines, who, one would have thought, would have dispatched him at once, he having so much provoked them by his exploits against them, and he was again wonderfully preserved at Keilah, when he had entered into a fenced town, where Saul thought he was sure of him. And how wonderfully was he preserved from Saul when he pursued and hunted him in the mountains!

How remarkably did God deliver him in the wilderness of Maon, when Saul and his army were compassing David about! How was he delivered in the cave of Engedi when, instead of Saul's killing David, God delivered Saul into his hands in the cave, and he cut off his skirt, and might as easily have cut off his head; and afterwards delivering him in like manner in the wilderness of Ziph; and afterwards again preserving him in the land of the Philistines, though David had fought against the Philistines, and conquered them at Keilah, since he was last among them; which one would think, would have been suffi-cient warning to them not to trust him, or let him escape a second time, if ever they had him in their hands again; but yet now, when they had a second opportunity, God wonderfully turned their hearts to him to befriend and protect him, instead of destroying him!

Thus was the precious seed that virtually contained the Redeemer, and all the blessings of his redemption, wonder-fully preserved, when hell and earth were conspired against it to destroy it. How often does David himself take notice of this, with praise and admiration, in the book of Psalms!

3. About this time, the written Word of God, or the canon of Scripture, was added to by Samuel. I have before observed, how that the canon of Scripture was begun, and the first writ-ten Word of God, the first written rule of faith and manners that ever was, was given to the church about Moses' time and many, and I know not but most divines, think it was added to by Joshua, and that he wrote the last chapter of Deuteronomy, and most of the book of Joshua. Others think that Joshua,

Judges, Ruth, and part of the first book of Samuel, were written by Samuel. However that was, we have good evidence of this, that Samuel made an addition to the canon of Scripture; for Samuel is manifestly mentioned in the New Testament, as one of the prophets whose writings we have in the Scriptures, as already mentioned, 'Yea, and all the prophets from Samuel, and those that follow after, as many as have spoken, have likewise foretold of these days' (*Acts* 3:24). By that expression, 'as many as have spoken', cannot be meant, 'as many as have spoken by word of mouth', for there never was any prophet but did that; but the meaning must be, 'as many as have spoken by writing, so that what they have spoken has come down to us, that we may see what it is'.

And the way that Samuel spoke of these times of Christ and the gospel was by giving the history of those things that typified them, and pointed to them, particularly the things concerning David that he wrote. The Spirit of God moved him to commit those things to writing chiefly for that reason, because they pointed to Christ, and the times of the gospel; and, as was said before, this was the main business of all that succession of prophets that began in Samuel, to foreshow these times.

That Samuel added to the canon of the Scriptures, seems further to appear from 1 Chronicles 29:29, 'Now the acts of David the king, first and last, behold, they are written in the book of Samuel the seer.'

Whether the book of Joshua was written by Samuel or not, yet it is the general opinion of divines, that the books of Judges, and Ruth, and part of the first book of Samuel, were penned by him. The book of Ruth was penned for the reason that, though it seemed to treat of private affairs, yet the persons chiefly spoken of in that book were of the family whence David and Christ proceeded, and so it pointed to what the apostle Peter observed of Samuel and the other prophets, in the third chapter of Acts. This adding to the canon of the Scriptures, the great and main instrument of the application of redemption, is to be looked upon as a further carrying on of that work, and an addition made to that great building.

4. Another thing God did towards this work, at that time, was his inspiring David to show forth Christ and his redemption, in divine songs, which should be for the use of the church, in public worship, throughout all ages. David was himself endued with the spirit of prophecy. He is called a prophet in Acts 2:29-30, 'Let me freely speak to you of the patriarch David, that he is both dead and buried, and his sepulchre is with us unto this day. Therefore being a prophet, and knowing that God had sworn with an oath,' etc. So that herein he was a type of Christ, that he was both a prophet and a king. We have no certain account of the time when David was first endued with the spirit of prophecy; but it is manifest, that it either was at the time that Samuel anointed him, or very soon after; for he appears soon after actuated by this spirit, in the affair of Goliath: and then great part of the Psalms were penned in the time of his troubles, before he came to the crown; as might be made manifest by an induction of particulars.

The oil that was used in anointing David was a type of the Spirit of God; and the type and the antitype were given both together, as we are told in 1 Samuel 16:13: 'Then Samuel took the horn of oil, and anointed him in the midst of his brethren; and the Spirit of the LORD came upon David from that day forward.' And it is probable that he now came upon him in his prophetical influences.

The way that this Spirit influenced him was to inspire him to show forth Christ, and the glorious things of his redemption, in divine songs, sweetly expressing the breathings of a pious soul, full of admiration of the glorious things of the

Redeemer, inflamed with divine love, and lifted up with praise; and therefore he is called the sweet psalmist of Israel. 'David the son of Jesse said, and the man who was raised up on high, the anointed of the God of Jacob, and the sweet psalmist of Israel' (2 *Sam.* 23:1). The main subjects of these sweet songs were the glorious things of the gospel; as is evident by the interpretation that is often put upon them, and the use that is made of them, in the New Testament; for there is no one book of the Old Testament that is so often quoted in the New, as the book of Psalms.

Joyfully did this holy man sing of those great things of Christ's redemption that had been the hope and expectation of God's church and people from the beginning of the church of God on earth; and joyfully did others follow him in it, as Asaph, Heman, Ethan, and others; for the book of Psalms was not all penned by David, though the greater part of it was. Hereby the canon of Scripture was further added to; and an excellent portion of divine writ it was that was added.

This was a great advancement that God made in this building. And the light of the gospel, which had been gradually growing from the Fall, was exceedingly increased by it: for whereas before there was but here and there a prophecy given of Christ in a great many ages, now here Christ is spoken of by his ancestor David abundantly, in multitudes of songs, speaking of his incarnation, life, death, resurrection, ascension into heaven, his satisfaction, intercession; his prophetical, kingly, and priestly office; his glorious benefits in this life and that which is to come; his union with the church, and the blessedness of the church in him; the calling of the Gentiles, the future glory of the church near the end of the world, and Christ's coming to the final judgment. All these things, and many more, concerning Christ and his redemption, are abundantly spoken of in the book of Psalms.

This was also a glorious advancement of the affair of redemption, as God hereby gave his church a book of divine songs for their use in that part of their public worship, namely, singing his praises, throughout all ages to the end of the world. It is manifest the book of Psalms was given of God for this end. It was used in the church of Israel by God's appointment. This is manifest by the title of many of the Psalms, in which they are inscribed to the chief musician, that is, to the man that was appointed to be the leader of divine songs in the temple, in the public worship of Israel.

So David is called the sweet psalmist of Israel, because he penned psalms for the use of the church of Israel; and accordingly we have an account that they were actually made use of in the church of Israel for that end, even ages after David was dead, as in 2 Chronicles 29:30: 'Moreover, Hezekiah the king, and the princes, commanded the Levites to sing praises unto the LORD, with the words of David, and of Asaph the seer.' And we find that the same are appointed in the New Testament to be made use of in the Christian church, in their worship: 'Speaking to yourselves in psalms and hymns and spiritual songs' (*Eph.* 5:19); 'Admonishing one another in psalms and hymns and spiritual songs' (*Col.* 3:16). And so they have been, and will to the end of the world be, made use of in the church to celebrate the praises of God. The people of God were wont sometimes to worship God by singing songs to his praise before; as they did at the Red Sea; and they had Moses's prophetical song in the 32nd chapter of Deuteronomy committed to them for that end; and Deborah and Barak, and Hannah, sang praises to God; but now first did God commit to his church a book of divine songs for their constant use.

5. The next thing I would take notice of is God's actually exalting David to the throne of Israel, notwithstanding all the

opposition made to it. God was determined to do it, and he made every thing give place that stood in the way of it. He removed Saul and his sons out of the way and first set David over the tribe of Judah; and then, having removed Ishbosheth, set him over all Israel. Thus did God fulfil his Word to David. He took him from the sheepcote, and made him king over his people Israel (*Psa.* 178:70-71). And now the throne of Israel was established in that family in which it was to continue for ever, even for ever and ever.

6. Now first it was that God proceeded to choose a particular city out of all the tribes of Israel to place his name there. Several times mention is made in the law of Moses of the children of Israel's bringing their oblations to the place which God should choose, as Deuteronomy 12:5-7, and so in many other places; but God had never proceeded to do it until now. The tabernacle and ark were never fixed, but sometimes in one place, and sometimes in another; but now God proceeded to choose Jerusalem. The city of Jerusalem was never thoroughly conquered, or taken out of the hands of the Jebusites, until David's time. It is said in Joshua 15:63, 'As for the Jebusites, the inhabitants of Jerusalem, the children of Judah could not drive them out: but the Jebusites dwell with the children of Judah at Jerusalem unto this day.' But now David wholly subdued it, as described in 2 Samuel 5. And now God proceeded to choose that city to place his Name there, as appears by David's bringing up the ark thither soon after; and therefore this is mentioned afterwards as the first time God proceeded to choose a city to place his name there, 2 Chronicles 6:5-6; 12:13. Afterwards God proceeded to show David the very place where he would have his temple built, viz. in the threshing floor of Araunah the Jebusite.

This city of Jerusalem is therefore called the holy city; and it was the greatest type of the church of Christ in all the Old

Testament. It was redeemed by David, the captain of the hosts of Israel, out of the hands of the Jebusites to be God's city, the holy place of his rest for ever, where he would dwell, as Christ, the captain of his people's salvation, redeems his church out of the hands of devils, to be his holy and beloved city. And therefore, how often does the Scripture, when speaking of Christ's redemption of his church, call it by the names of Zion and Jerusalem.

This was the city that God had appointed to be the place of the first gathering and erecting of the Christian church after Christ's resurrection, the place of the pouring out of the Spirit of God on the apostles and primitive Christians, and the place whence the gospel was to sound forth into all the world. The first Christian church there was to be, as it were, the mother of all other churches throughout the world, agreeable to that prophecy, 'Out of Zion shall go forth the law, and the word of the LORD from Jerusalem: and he shall judge among the nations, and shall rebuke many people' (*Isa.* 2:3-4).

Thus God chose Mount Zion, whence the gospel was to be sounded forth, as the law had been from Mount Sinai.

7. The next thing to be observed here is God's solemnly renewing the covenant of grace with David, and promising that the Messiah should be of his seed. We have an account of it in the seventh chapter of the second book of Samuel. It was done on occasion of the thoughts David entertained of building God a house. On this occasion God sends Nathan the prophet to him, with the glorious promises of the covenant of grace. It is especially contained in these words in verse sixteen: 'And thine house and thy kingdom shall be established for ever before thee: thy throne shall be established for ever.' This promise has respect to Christ, the seed of David, and is fulfilled in him only, for the kingdom of David has long since ceased, in any other sense than as it is upheld in Christ. The

temporal kingdom of the house of David has now ceased for a great many ages, much longer than ever it stood.

That this covenant that God now established with David by Nathan the prophet was the covenant of grace is evident by the plain testimony of Scripture in Isaiah 55:1-3. There we have Christ inviting sinners to come to the waters, etc., and in the third verse he says, 'Incline your ear, and come unto me; hear, and your soul shall live; and I will make an everlasting covenant with you, even the sure mercies of David.' Here Christ offers to poor sinners, if they will come to him, an interest in the same everlasting covenant that he had made with David, conveying to them the same sure mercies. But what is that covenant that sinners obtain an interest in, when they come to Christ, but the covenant of grace?

This was the fifth solemn establishment of the covenant of grace with the church after the Fall. The covenant of grace was revealed and established all along. But there had been particular seasons, wherein God had, in a very solemn manner, renewed this covenant with his church, giving forth a new edition and establishment of it, revealing it in a new manner. The first was with Adam, the second with Noah, the third with the patriarchs, Abraham, Isaac, and Jacob, the fourth in the wilderness by Moses, and now the fifth is this made to David.

This establishment of the covenant of grace with David, David always esteemed the greatest smile of God upon him, the greatest honour of all that God had put upon him. He prized it and rejoiced in it above all the other blessings of his reign. You may see how joyfully and thankfully he received it, when Nathan came to him with the glorious message, in 2 Samuel 7:18-29. And so David, in his last words, declares this to be all his salvation, and all his desire, as you may see: 'He hath made with me an everlasting covenant, ordered in all things and sure: for this is all my salvation, and all my desire' (*2 Sam.* 23:5).

8. It was by David that God first gave his people Israel the possession of the whole promised land. I have before shown how God's giving the possession of the promised land belonged to the covenant of grace. This was done in a great measure by Joshua, but not fully. Joshua did not wholly subdue that part of the promised land that was strictly called the land of Canaan, and that was divided by lot to the several tribes; but there were great numbers of the old inhabitants left unsubdued, as we read in the books of Joshua and Judges; and there were many left to prove Israel, and to be thorns in their sides, and pricks in their eyes. There were the Jebusites in Jerusalem, and many of the Canaanites, and the whole nation of the Philistines, who all dwelt in that part of the land that was divided by lot, and chiefly in that part of the land that belonged to the tribes of Judah and Ephraim.

And thus these remains of the old inhabitants of Canaan continued unsubdued until David's time; but he wholly subdued them all. This is agreeable to what Stephen observes, 'Which also our fathers . . . brought in with Jesus (that is, Joshua) into the possession of the Gentiles, whom God drave out before the face of our fathers, unto the days of David' (*Acts* 7:45). They were until the days of David in driving them out, before they had wholly subdued them. But David entirely brought them under. He subdued the Jebusites, and he subdued the whole nation of the Philistines, and all the rest of the remains of the seven nations of Canaan: 'Now after this it came to pass, that David smote the Philistines, and subdued them, and took Gath and her towns out of the hands of the Philistines' (*1 Chron.* 18:1).

After this all the remains of the former inhabitants of Canaan were made bond servants to the Israelites. The posterity of the Gibeonites became servants before, hewers of wood and drawers of water, for the house of God. But Solomon, David's son and successor, put all the other remains of the seven nations of Canaan to bond service; at least he made them pay a tribute of bond service, as you may see in 1 Kings 9:20-22. And hence we read of the children of Solomon's servants, after the return from the Babylonish captivity, Ezra 2:55 and Nehemiah 11:3. They were the children or posterity of the seven nations of Canaan that Solomon had subjected to bond service.

Thus David subdued the whole land of Canaan, strictly so called. But then that was not one half, nor quarter, of the land God had promised to their fathers. The land that God had often promised to their fathers included all the countries from the river of Egypt to the river Euphrates.

These were the bounds of the land promised to Abraham: 'In the same day the LORD made a covenant with Abram, saying, Unto thy seed have I given this land, from the river of Egypt, unto the great river, the river Euphrates' (*Gen.* 15:18). So again God promised at Mount Sinai (*Exod.* 23: 31), 'And I will set thy bounds from the Red Sea even unto the sea of the Philistines, and from the desert unto the river: for I will deliver the inhabitants of the land into your hand and thou shalt drive them out before thee.' So again in Deuteronomy 11:24: 'Every place whereon the soles of your feet shall tread, shall be yours: from the wilderness, and Lebanon, from the river, the river Euphrates, even unto the uttermost sea, shall your coast be.' Again, the same promise is made to Joshua: 'Every place that the sole of your feet shall tread upon, that have I given unto you, as I said unto Moses. From the wilderness and this Lebanon even unto the great river, the river Euphrates, all the land of the Hittites, and unto the great sea, towards the going down of the sun, shall be your coast' (*Josh.* 1:3-4). But the land that Joshua gave the people the possession of, was but a little part of this land. And the people never had had the possession of it, until now when God gave it them by David.

This large country did not only include that Canaan that was divided by lot to those who came in with Joshua but the land of the Moabites and Ammonites, the land of the Amalekites, and the rest of the Edomites, and the country of Zobah. All these nations were subdued and brought under the children of Israel by David. And he put garrisons in the several countries, and they became David's servants, as we have a particular account of in the eighth chapter of 2 Samuel. And David extended their border to the river Euphrates, as was promised; see verse 3: 'And David smote also Hadadezer the son of Rehob, king of Zobah, as he went to recover his border at the river Euphrates.' And accordingly we read, that Solomon his son reigned over all the regions on this side the river, 'For he had dominion over all the region on this side the river, from Tiphsah even unto Azzah, over all the kings on this side the river' (*1 Kings* 4:24). This Artaxerxes king of Persia takes notice of long after: 'There have been mighty kings also over Jerusalem, which have ruled over all countries beyond the river; and toll, tribute, and custom was paid unto them' (*Ezra* 4:20).

So that Joshua, that type of Christ, did but begin the work of giving Israel the possession of the promised land; but left it to be finished by that much greater type and ancestor of Christ, even David, who subdued far more of that land than ever Joshua had done. And in this extent of his and Solomon's dominion was some resemblance of the great extent of Christ's kingdom; and therefore the extent of Christ's kingdom is set forth by this very thing, of its being over all lands, from the Red Sea to the sea of the Philistines, and over all lands from thence to the river Euphrates: 'He shall have dominion also from sea to sea, and from the river unto the ends of the earth' (*Psa.* 72:8). See also 1 Kings 8:56.

9. God by David perfected the Jewish worship, and added to it several new institutions. The law was given by Moses, but

yet all the institutions of the Jewish worship were not given by Moses; some were added by divine direction. So this greatest of all personal types of Christ did not only perfect Joshua's work, in giving Israel the possession of the promised land, but he also finished Moses's work, in perfecting the instituted worship of Israel. Thus there had to be a number of typical prophets, priests, and princes to complete one figure or shadow of Christ the antitype, he being the substance of all the types and shadows. Of so much more glory was Christ accounted worthy than Moses, Joshua, David, and Solomon, and all the great prophets, priests, princes, judges, and saviours of the Old Testament put together.

The ordinances of David are mentioned as of parallel validity with those of Moses: 'Also Jehoiada appointed the offices of the house of the LORD by the hand of the priests the Levites, whom David had distributed in the house of the LORD, to offer the burnt offerings of the LORD, as it is written in the law of Moses, with rejoicing and with singing, as it was ordained by David' (2 *Chron.* 23:18).

The worship of Israel was perfected by David by the addition that he made to the ceremonial law, which we have an account of in 1 Chronicles 23–26, consisting in the several orders and courses into which David divided the Levites and the work and business to which he appointed them, differing from what Moses had appointed them to; and also in the divisions of the priests, the sons of Aaron, into twenty-four courses, assigning to every course their business in the house of the LORD, and their particular stated times of attendance there. He also appointed some of the Levites to a new office that had not been appointed before, the office of singers, and particularly ordered and regulated them in that office, as you may see in 1 Chronicles 25, and he appointed others of the Levites by law to the several services of porters, treasurers, officers, and judges. These ordinances of David were kept up henceforth in the church of Israel as long as the Jewish church lasted. Thus we find the several orders of priests, and the Levites, porters, and singers after the captivity. So we find the courses of the priests appointed by David still continuing in the New Testament. Zacharias the father of John the Baptist was a priest of the course of Abia, which is the same as the course of Abijah appointed by David (*1 Chron.* 24:10).

Thus David, as well as Moses, was made like to Christ the son of David in this respect, that by him God gave a new ecclesiastical establishment and new institutions of worship. David did not only add to the institutions of Moses but, by those additions, he abolished some of the old institutions of Moses that had been in force until that time; particularly those laws of Moses that appointed the business of the Levites, which we have in the third and fourth chapters of Numbers. These very much consisted in their charge of the several parts and utensils of the tabernacle there assigned to them, and in carrying those several parts of the tabernacle. But those laws were now abolished by David: they were no more to carry those things, as they had been used to do until David's time. But David appointed them to other work instead of it: 'And also unto the Levites; they shall no more carry the tabernacle, nor any vessels of it for the service thereof' (*1 Chron.* 23:26), a sure evidence that the ceremonial law given by Moses is not perpetual, as the Jews suppose, but might be wholly abolished by Christ. For if David, a type of the Messiah, might abolish the law of Moses in part, much more might the Messiah himself abolish the whole.

David, by God's appointment, abolished all use of the tabernacle that was built by Moses, of which he had the pattern from God, for God now revealed it to David to be his will that a temple should be built instead of the tabernacle: a great presage of what Christ, the son of David, would do, when he should come, namely, abolish the whole Jewish ecclesiastical constitution, which was but as a movable tabernacle, to set up the spiritual gospel temple, which was to be far more glorious and of greater extent, and was to last for ever.

David had the pattern of all things pertaining to the temple shown him, even as Moses had the pattern of the tabernacle, and Solomon built the temple according to the pattern which he had from his father David, which he received from God. 'Then David gave to Solomon his son the pattern of the porch, and of the houses thereof, and of the treasuries thereof, and of the upper chambers thereof, and of the inner parlours thereof, and of the place of the mercy seat, and the pattern of all that he had by the spirit, of the courts of the house of the LORD, and of all the chambers round about, of the treasuries of the house of God, and of the treasuries of the dedicated things' (*1 Chron.* 28:11-12). And in verse 19: 'All this, said David, the LORD made me understand in writing by his hand upon me, even all the works of this pattern.'

10. The canon of Scripture seems at or after the close of David's reign to be added to by the prophets Nathan and Gad. It appears probable by the Scriptures that they carried on the history of the two books of Samuel from the place where Samuel left it and finished it. These two books of Samuel seem to be the book that in the Scripture is called the book of Samuel the seer, and Nathan the prophet, and Gad the seer, as in 1 Chronicles 29:29: 'Now the acts of David the king, first and last, behold, they are written in the book of Samuel the seer, and in the book of Nathan the prophet, and in the book of Gad the seer.'

11. The next thing I would take notice of is God's wonderfully continuing the kingdom of his visible people in the line of Christ's legal ancestors, as long as they remained an independent kingdom. Thus it was without any interruption

worth taking notice of. Indeed, the kingdom of all the tribes of Israel was not kept in that line, but the dominion of that part of Israel in which the true worship of God was upheld, and so of those who were God's visible people, was always kept in the family of David, as long as there was any such thing as an independent king of Israel, according to God's promise to David. And not only in the family of David, but always in that part of David's posterity that was the line whence Christ was legally to descend; so that the very person that was Christ's legal ancestor was always in the throne, excepting Jehoahaz, who reigned three months, and Zedekiah, as you may see in Matthew's genealogy of Christ.

Christ was legally descended from the kings of Judah, though he was not naturally descended from them. He was both legally and naturally descended from David. He was naturally descended from Nathan the son of David, for Mary his mother was one of the posterity of David by Nathan, as you may see in Luke's genealogy. But Joseph, the reputed and legal father of Christ, was naturally descended from Solomon and his successors, as we see in Matthew's genealogy. Jesus Christ, though he was not the natural son of Joseph, yet, by the law and constitution of the Jews, he was Joseph's heir, because he was the lawful son of Joseph's lawful wife, conceived while she was his legally espoused wife. The Holy Ghost raised up seed to him. A person, by the law of Moses, might be the legal son and heir of another whose natural son he was not; as sometimes a man raised up seed to his brother. A brother, in some cases, was to build up a brother's house; so the Holy Ghost built up Joseph's house.

Joseph, being in the direct line of the kings of Judah, of the house of David, was the legal heir of the crown of David; and Christ, being legally his firstborn son, was his heir. And so Christ, by the law, was the proper heir of the crown of David, and is therefore said to sit upon the throne of his father David.

The crown of God's people was wonderfully kept in the line of Christ's legal ancestors. When David was old, and not able any longer to manage the affairs of the kingdom, Adonijah, one of his sons, set up to be king, and seemed to have obtained his purpose; all things for a while seemed fair on his side, and he thought himself strong. The thing he aimed at seemed to be accomplished. However, Adonijah was not the son of David who was the ancestor of Joseph, the legal father of Christ; and therefore how wonderfully did providence work here! What a strange and sudden revolution! All Adonijah's kingdom and glory vanished away as soon as it was begun; and Solomon, the legal ancestor of Christ, was established in the throne.

And after Solomon's death, when Jeroboam had conspired against the family, and Rehoboam carried himself so that it was a wonder all Israel was not provoked to forsake him, and ten tribes did actually forsake him, and set up Jeroboam in opposition to him; and though he was a wicked man, and deserved to have been rejected altogether from being king; yet, he being the legal ancestor of Christ, God kept the kingdom of the two tribes, in which the true religion was upheld, in his possession. And though he had been wicked, and his son Abijam was another wicked prince, yet they, being legal ancestors of Christ, God still continued the crown in the family, and gave it to Abijam's son, Asa.

And afterwards, though many of the kings of Judah were very wicked men, and horridly provoked God, as particularly Jehoram, Ahaziah, Ahaz, Manasseh and Amon, yet God did not take away the crown from their family, but gave it to their sons, because they were the ancestors of Christ. God's remembering his covenant that he had established with David is given as the reason why he did thus, notwithstanding their wicked lives, as in 1 Kings 15:4, where, speaking of Abijam's wickedness, it is said, 'Nevertheless, for David's sake did the

LORD his God give him a lamp in Jerusalem, to set up his son after him, and to establish Jerusalem.' So in 2 Chronicles 21:7, speaking of Jehoram's great wickedness, it is said, 'Howbeit the LORD would not destroy the house of David, because of the covenant that he had made with David, and as he promised to give a light unto him, and to his sons for ever.'

The crown of the ten tribes was changed from one family to another continually. First, Jeroboam took it, but the crown remained in his family for only one generation after his death. It only descended to his son Nadab, and then Baasha, who was of another family, took it. And it remained in his posterity but one generation after his death. Then Zimri, who was his servant, and not of his posterity, took it. Then, without it descending at all to his posterity, Omri, from another family, took it. The crown continued in his family for three successions, and then Jehu, who was of another family, took it, and the crown continued in his family for three or four successors. Then Shallum, of another family, took it, and the crown did not descend at all to his posterity, but Menahem, that was of another family, took it; and it remained in his family only one generation after him. Then Pekah, of another family, took it: and after him Hoshea, that was of still another family, took it.

So great a difference was there between the crown of Israel and the crown of Judah. The one was continued evermore in the same family, and with very little interruption, in one right line; the other was continually tossed about from one family to another, as if it were the sport of fortune. The reason was not that the kings of Judah, many of them, were better than the kings of Israel; but that these kings had the blessing in them: they were the ancestors of Christ, whose right it was to sit on the throne of Israel. With the kings of Israel it was not so, and therefore divine providence exercised a continual care, through all the changes that happened through so many generations, and such a long space of time, to keep the crown of Judah in one direct line, in fulfilment of the everlasting covenant he had made with David, the mercies of which covenant were sure mercies. But in the other case there was no such covenant, and so no such care of providence.

And here it must not be omitted that there was once a very strong conspiracy of the kings of Syria and Israel, in the time of that wicked king of Judah, Ahaz, to dispossess Ahaz and his family of the throne of Judah, and to set one of another family, even the son of Tabeal, on it, as you may see in Isaiah 7:6: 'Let us go up against Judah, and vex it, and let us make a breach therein for us, and set a king in the midst of it, even the son of Tabeal.' And they seemed very likely to accomplish their purpose. There seemed to be so great a likelihood of it that the hearts of the people sank within them; they gave up the cause. It is said, 'The heart of Ahaz and his people was moved as the trees of the wood are moved with the wind.' And on this occasion God sent the prophet Isaiah to encourage the people, and tell them that it should not come to pass. And because it looked so much like a lost cause, and Ahaz and the people would hardly believe that it would not be, therefore God directs the prophet to give them this sign of it, viz. that Christ should be born of the legal seed of Ahaz: 'Therefore the Lord himself shall give you a sign; behold, a virgin shall conceive, and bear a son, and shall call his name Immanuel' (*Isa.* 7:14). This was a good sign, and a great confirmation of the truth of what God promised by Isaiah, namely, that the kings of Syria and Israel should never accomplish their purpose of dispossessing the family of Ahaz of the crown of Judah and setting up the son of Tabeal; for Christ the Immanuel was to be of them.

I have mentioned this dispensation of providence in this place because, though it was continued for so long a time, yet it began in Solomon's succession to the throne of David.

12. The next thing I would take notice of is the building of the temple, a great type of three things: of Christ, especially his human nature; of the church of Christ; and of heaven. The tabernacle seemed rather to represent the church in its movable, changeable state, here in this world. But that beautiful, glorious, costly structure of the temple, which succeeded the tabernacle and was a fixed and not a movable thing, seems especially to represent the church in its glorified state in heaven. This temple was built according to the pattern shown by the Holy Ghost to David, and by divine direction given to David, in the place where the threshing floor of Ornan the Jebusite was, in Mount Moriah (*2 Chron.* 3:1). This was in the same mountain, and doubtless in the very same place, where Abraham offered up his son Isaac; for that is said to be a mountain in the land of Moriah (*Gen.* 22:2), which mountain was called the mountain of the Lord, as this mountain of the temple was: 'And Abraham called the name of that place Jehovah-jireh; as it is said to this day, In the mount of the LORD it shall be seen' (*Gen.* 22:14).

This was the house where Christ dwelt until he came to dwell in the temple of his body, or human nature, which was the antitype of this temple; as appears in that Christ, on the occasion of his being shown the temple of Jerusalem, says, 'Destroy this temple, and in three days I will raise it up', speaking of the temple of his body (*John* 2:19–20).

This house, or a house built in this place, continued to be the house of God, the place of the worship of his church, until Christ came. Here was the place that God chose, where all their sacrifices were offered up until the great sacrifice came, and made the sacrifice and oblation to cease. Into his temple in this place the Lord came, even the messenger of the covenant. Here he often delivered his heavenly doctrine, and wrought miracles; here his church was gathered by the pouring out of the Spirit, after his ascension. In Luke 24:53, speaking of the disciples after Christ's ascension, it is said, 'And they were continually in the temple, praising and blessing God.' And in Acts 2:46, speaking of the multitudes that were converted by that great outpouring of the Spirit on the day of Pentecost, it is said, 'And they continued daily with one accord in the temple.' And in Acts 5: 42, speaking of the apostles, it is said, 'And daily in the temple, and in every house, they ceased not to teach and preach Jesus Christ.' And hence the sound of the gospel went forth, and the church spread into all the world.

13. It is here worthy to be observed that at this time, in Solomon's reign, after the temple was finished, the Jewish church had risen to its highest external glory. The Jewish church, or the ordinances and constitution of it, is compared to the moon in Revelation 12:1: 'And there appeared a great wonder in heaven, a woman clothed with the sun, and the moon under her feet, and upon her head a crown of twelve stars.' As this church was like the moon in many other respects, so it was in this, that it waxed and waned like the moon. From the first foundation of it, laid in the covenant made with Abraham, when this moon was now beginning to appear, it had to this time been gradually increasing in its glory. The time wherein the temple was finished and dedicated was about mid-way between the calling of Abraham and the coming of Christ, and now it was full moon. After this the glory of the Jewish church gradually decreased until Christ came, as I shall have occasion more particularly to observe afterwards.

Now the church of Israel was in its highest external glory. Now Israel was multiplied exceedingly, so that they seemed to have become like the sand on the seashore (*1 Kings* 4:20). Now the kingdom of Israel was firmly established in the right family, the family of which Christ was to come. Now God had chosen the city where he would place his name. Now God had fully given his people the possession of the promised land. And they now possessed the dominion of it all in quietness and peace, even from the river of Egypt to the great river Euphrates. All those nations that had formerly been their enemies quietly submitted to them. None pretended to rebel against them. Now the Jewish worship in all its ordinances was fully settled. Now, instead of a movable tent and tabernacle, they had a glorious temple; the most magnificent, beautiful, and costly structure that there was then, ever had been, or ever has been since. Now the people enjoyed peace and plenty, and sat every man under his vine and fig tree, eating and drinking, and making merry, as in 1 Kings 4:20. Now they were in the highest pitch of earthly prosperity, silver being as plenty as stones, and the land full of gold and precious stones and other precious foreign commodities, brought by Solomon's ships from Ophir, and which came from other parts of the world. Now they had a king reigning over them that was the wisest of men, and probably the greatest earthly prince that ever was. Now their fame went abroad into all the earth, so that they came from the utmost parts of the earth to see their glory and their happiness.

Thus God was pleased, in one of the ancestors of Christ, remarkably to shadow forth the kingdom of Christ, reigning in his glory. David, who was a man of war, a man who had shed much blood, and whose life was full of troubles and conflicts, was more of a representation of Christ in his state of humiliation, his militant state, wherein he was in conflict with his enemies. But Solomon, who was a man of peace, was a representation more especially of Christ exalted, triumphing, and reigning in his kingdom of peace. And the happy, glorious state of the Jewish church at that time, did remarkably represent two things: 1. That glorious state of the church on earth that shall be in the latter ages of the world; those days of peace, when nation shall not lift sword against nation, nor learn war any more. 2. The future glorified state of the church in heaven. The earthly Canaan never was so lively a type of the heavenly Canaan as it was then, when the happy people of Israel did indeed enjoy it as a land flowing with milk and honey.

14. After this the glory of the Jewish church gradually declined more and more until Christ came; yet not so but that the work of redemption still went on. Whatever failed or declined, God still carried on this work from age to age; this building was still advancing higher and higher. Things still went on, during the decline of the Jewish church, towards a further preparation of things for the coming of Christ, as well as during its increase. For so wonderfully were things ordered by the infinitely wise Governor of the world that whatever happened was ordered for good to this general design, and made a means of promoting it.

When the people of the Jews flourished, and were in prosperity, he made that to contribute to the promoting of this design; and when they were in adversity, God made that also to contribute to the carrying on of the same design. While the Jewish church was in its increasing state, the work of redemption was carried on by their increase; and when they came to their declining state, which they were in from Solomon's time until Christ, God carried on the work of redemption by that. That decline itself was one thing that God made use of as a further preparation for Christ's coming.

As the moon, from the time of her full, is approaching nearer and nearer to her conjunction with the sun, so her light is still more and more decreasing, until at length, when the conjunction comes, it is wholly swallowed up in the light of the sun. So it was with the Jewish church from the time of its highest glory in Solomon's time. In the latter end of

Solomon's reign, the state of things began to darken, as Solomon corrupted himself with idolatry, which much obscured the glory of this mighty and wise prince. And withal troubles began to arise in his kingdom; and after his death the kingdom was divided, and ten tribes revolted, and withdrew their subjection from the house of David, withal falling away from the true worship of God in the temple at Jerusalem and setting up the golden calves of Bethel and Dan. And presently after this the number of the ten tribes was greatly diminished in the battle of Jeroboam with Abijah, wherein there fell down slain of Israel five hundred thousand chosen men. This loss the kingdom of Israel probably never recovered in any measure.

The ten tribes finally apostatized from the true God under Jeroboam, and the kingdom of Judah was greatly corrupted. From that time forward they were more generally in a corrupt state than otherwise. In Ahab's time the kingdom of Israel did not only worship the calves of Bethel and Dan but the worship of Baal was introduced. Before, they pretended to worship the true God by these images, the calves of Jeroboam; but now Ahab introduced gross idolatry, and the direct worship of false gods in the room of the true God. And soon after the worship of Baal was introduced into the kingdom of Judah, namely, in Jehoram's reign, by his marrying Athaliah, the daughter of Ahab. After this God began to cut Israel short, by finally destroying and sending into captivity that part of the land that was beyond Jordan, as you may see in 2 Kings 10:32. And then after this Tiglath-pileser subdued and captivated all the northern parts of the land (*2 Kings* 15:29). Then at last all the land of the ten tribes was subdued by Shalmaneser, and they were finally carried captive out of their own land. After this also the kingdom of Judah was carried captive into Babylon, and a great part of the nation never returned. Those that returned were but a small number, compared with what had been carried captive; and for the most part after this they were dependent on the power of other states, being subject at one time to the kings of Persia, then to the monarchy of the Grecians, and then to the Romans. And before Christ's time, the church of the Jews had become exceedingly corrupt, over-run with superstition and self-righteousness. And how small a flock was the church of Christ in the days of his incarnation!

God, by this gradual decline of the Jewish state and church from Solomon's time, prepared the way for the coming of Christ in several ways.

i. The decline of the glory of this legal dispensation made way for the introduction of the more glorious dispensation of the gospel. The evangelical dispensation was so much more glorious that the legal dispensation had no glory in compari-son with it. The glory of the ancient dispensation, such as it was in Solomon's time, consisting, so much in external glory, was but a childish glory compared with the spiritual glory of the dispensation introduced by Christ. The church, under the Old Testament, was a child under tutors and governors, and God dealt with it as a child. Those pompous externals are called by the apostle, 'weak and beggarly elements'.

It was fit that those things should be diminished as Christ approached, just as John the Baptist, the forerunner of Christ, speaking of Christ, says, 'He must increase, but I must decrease' (*John* 3:30). It is fit that the twinkling stars should gradually withdraw their glory when the sun is ap-proaching towards his rising. The glory of the Jewish dispensation must be gradually diminished to prepare the way for the more joyful reception of the spiritual glory of the gospel. If the Jewish church, when Christ came, had been in the same external glory that it was in, in the reign of Solo-mon, men would have had their eyes so dazzled with it that they would not have been likely joyfully to exchange such great external glory for only the spiritual glory of the poor despised Jesus. Again,

ii. This gradual decline of the glory of the Jewish state tended to prepare the way for Christ's coming in another way, namely, as it tended to make the glory of God's power, in the great effects of Christ's redemption, the more conspicuous. God's people being so diminished and weakened by one step after another, until Christ came, was very much like the diminishing of Gideon's army. God told Gideon that the people that was with him was too many for him to deliver the Midianites into their hands, lest Israel should vaunt themselves against him, saying, 'My own hand hath saved me.' And therefore all that were fearful were commanded to return; and there returned twenty and two thousand, and there remained ten thousand. But still they were too many; and so, by trying the people at the water, they were reduced to three hundred men. So the people in Solomon's time were too many, and mighty, and glorious for Christ; therefore he diminished them; first, by sending off the ten tribes; and then by diminishing them again by the captivity into Babylon; and then they were further diminished by the great and general corruption that there was when Christ came. So that Christ found very few godly persons among them, yet with a small handful of disciples Christ conquered the world. Thus high things were brought down, that Christ might be exalted.

iii. This prepared the way for Christ's coming as it made the salvation of those Jews that were saved by Christ to be more sensible and visible. Though the greater part of the nation of the Jews was rejected, and the Gentiles called in their place, yet there were a great many thousands of the Jews that were saved by Christ after his resurrection (*Acts* 21:20). They being taken from so low a state under temporal calamity in their bondage to the Romans, and from the state of great superstition and wickedness that the Jewish nation was then fallen into, made their redemption the more sensibly and visibly glorious.

I have taken notice of this dispensation of providence in the gradual decline of the Jewish church in this place because it began in the reign of Solomon.

15. I would here take notice of the additions that were made to the canon of Scripture in or soon after the reign of Solomon. Considerable additions were made by Solomon himself. He wrote the books of Proverbs and Ecclesiastes, probably near the close of his reign. His writing of the Song of Songs, as it is called, is what is especially here to be taken notice of, which is wholly on the subject that we are upon, viz. Christ and his redemption, representing the high and glorious relation, and union, and love, that is between Christ and his redeemed church. And the history of the Scripture seems, in Solomon's reign and some of the next succeeding reigns, to have been added to by the prophets Nathan and Ahijah, and Shemaiah and Iddo. It is probable that that part of the history which we have in the First Book of Kings was written by them, by what is said in 2 Chronicles 9:29, and in 12:15 and 13:22.

16. God wonderfully upheld his church and the true religion through this period. It was very wonderful, considering the many and great apostasies of that people to idolatry. When the ten tribes had generally and finally forsaken the true worship of God, God kept up the true religion in the kingdom of Judah; and when they corrupted themselves, as they very often did exceedingly, and idolatry was ready totally to swallow all up, yet God kept the lamp alive, and was often pleased, when things seemed to be come to an extremity, and religion at its last gasp, to grant blessed revivals by remarkable

outpourings of his Spirit, particularly in the time of Hezekiah and Josiah.

17. God remarkably kept the book of the law from being lost in times of general and long-continued neglect of and enmity against it. The most remarkable instance of this kind that we have was the preservation of the book of the law in the time of the great apostasy during the greater part of the long reign of Manasseh, which lasted fifty-five years, and then, after that, the reign of Amon, his son. During this time the book of the law was so much neglected, and such a careless and profane management of the affairs of the temple prevailed, that the book of the law, which used to be laid up by the side of the ark in the Holy of Holies, was lost for a long time. Nobody knew where it was. But yet God preserved it from being finally lost. In Josiah's time, when they came to repair the temple, it was found buried in rubbish, after it had been lost so long that Josiah himself seems to have been much a stranger to it until now. See 2 Kings 22:8 and the following verses.

18. God remarkably preserved the tribe from which Christ was to proceed from being ruined through the many and great dangers of this period. The visible church of Christ from Solomon's reign was mainly in the tribe of Judah. The tribe of Benjamin, which was annexed to them, was but a very small tribe, and the tribe of Judah exceeding large. And, as Judah took Benjamin under his covert when he went into Egypt to bring corn, so the tribe of Benjamin seemed to be under the covert of Judah ever after. And though, on occasion of Jeroboam's setting up the calves at Bethel and Dan, the Levites resorted to Judah out of all the tribes of Israel (*2 Chron.* 11:13), yet they were also small, and not reckoned among the tribes. And though many of the ten tribes did also on that

occasion, for the sake of the worship of God in the temple, leave their inheritances in their several tribes, and remove and settle in Judah, and so were incorporated with them, as we read in the chapter just quoted at the 16th verse, yet the tribe of Judah was so much the prevailing part, that they were called by one name, Judah. Therefore God said to Solomon, 'I will not rend away all the kingdom; but will give one tribe to thy son, for David my servant's sake, and for Jerusalem's sake, which I have chosen' (*1 Kings* 11:13; see also verses 32 and 36). So when the ten tribes were carried captive it is said that there was none left but the tribe of Judah only: 'Therefore the LORD was very wroth with Israel, and removed them out of his sight: there was none left but the tribe of Judah only' (*2 Kings* 17:18). Whence they were all called 'Jews', which is a word derived from 'Judah'.

This was the tribe of which Christ was to come, and in this chiefly did God's visible church consist from Solomon's time. And this was the people over whom the kings that were legal ancestors of Christ, and were of the house of David, reigned. This people was wonderfully preserved from destruction during this period; when they often seemed to be upon the brink of ruin, and just ready to be swallowed up. So it was in Rehoboam's time, when Shishak, king of Egypt, came against Judah with such a vast force; yet then God manifestly preserved them from being destroyed. Of this we read in the beginning of the 12th chapter of 2 Chronicles. So it was again in Abijah's time, when Jeroboam set the battle in array against him with eight hundred thousand chosen men; a mighty army indeed. We read of it in 2 Chronicles 13:3. Then God wrought deliverance for Judah, out of regard to the covenant of grace established with David, as is evident by verses 4 and 5, and the victory they obtained was because the Lord was on their side, as you may see, verse 12. So it was again in Asa's time, when Zerah the Ethiopian came against him with a yet larger army of a thousand thousand, and three hundred chariots (*2 Chron.* 14:9). On this occasion Asa cried to the Lord, and trusted in him, being sensible that it was nothing with him to help those that had no power: 'And Asa cried unto the LORD his God, and said, LORD, it is nothing with thee to help, whether with many, or with those that have no power' (verse 11). And accordingly God gave them a glorious victory over this mighty host.

So again it was in Jehoshaphat's time, when the children of Moab, and the children of Ammon, and the inhabitants of Mount Seir, combined together against Judah with a mighty army, a force vastly superior to any that Jehoshaphat could raise; and Jehoshaphat and his people were greatly afraid. Yet they set themselves to seek God on this occasion, and trusted in him; and God told them by one of his prophets, that they need not fear them, nor should they have any occasion to fight in this battle, they should only stand still and see the salvation of the Lord. And, according to his direction, they only stood still, and sang praises to God, and God made their enemies do the work themselves, and set them to killing one another; and the children of Judah had nothing to do but to gather the spoil, which was more than they could carry away. We have the story in 2 Chronicles 20.

So it was again in Ahaz's time when Rezin the king of Syria and Pekah the son of Remaliah, the king of Israel, conspired against Judah, and seemed to be sure of their purpose; of which we have spoken already. So it was again in Hezekiah's time, when Sennacherib, that great king of Assyria, and head of the greatest monarchy that was then in the world, came up against all the fenced cities of Judah, after he had conquered most of the neighbouring countries, and sent Rabshakeh, the captain of his host, against Jerusalem. He came and in a very proud and scornful manner insulted Hezekiah and his people, as being sure of victory; and the people were trembling for fear, like lambs before a lion. Then God sent Isaiah the prophet to comfort them, and assure them that the enemy should not prevail, as a token of which he gave them this sign, viz. that the earth, for two years successively should bring forth food of itself, from the roots of the old stalks, without their ploughing or sowing; and then the third year they should sow and reap, and plant vineyards, and eat the fruit of them, and live on the fruits of their labour, as they were wont to do before (*2 Kings* 19:29). This is mentioned as a type of what is promised (in verses 30-31), 'And the remnant that is escaped of the house of Judah, shall yet again take root downward, and bear fruit upward. For out of Jerusalem shall go forth a remnant, and they that escape out of Mount Zion: the zeal of the LORD of hosts shall do this.' The corn's springing again after it had been cut off with the sickle, and bringing forth another crop from the roots, that seemed to be dead, and so once and again, represents the church's reviving again, as it were out of its own ashes, and flourishing like a plant after it had seemingly been cut down past recovery.

When the enemies of the church have done their utmost, and seem to have gained their point, and to have overthrown the church, so that the being of it is scarcely visible, but like a living root hid under ground, yet there is a secret life in it that will cause it to flourish again, and to take root downward, and bear fruit upward. This was fulfilled now at this time, for the king of Assyria had already taken and carried captive the ten tribes, and Sennacherib had also taken all the fenced cities of Judah, and ranged the country round about, and Jerusalem only remained. And Rabshakeh had in his own imagination already swallowed that up, as he had also in the fearful apprehensions of the Jews themselves. But yet God wrought a wonderful deliverance. He sent an angel that, in one night, smote one hundred fourscore and five thousand in the enemy's camp.

19. In the reign of Uzziah, and the following reigns, God was pleased to raise up a set of eminent prophets who should commit their prophecies to writing, and leave them for the use of his church in all ages. We before observed how that God began a constant succession of prophets in Israel in Samuel's time, and many of these prophets wrote by divine inspiration and so added to the canon of Scripture before Uzziah's time. But none of them are supposed to have written books of prophecies until now.

Several of them wrote histories of the wonderful dispensations of God towards his church. This we have observed already of Samuel, who is supposed to have written Judges and Ruth, and part of the first of Samuel, if not the book of Joshua. And Nathan and Gad seem to have written the rest of the two books of Samuel; and Nathan, with Ahijah and Iddo, wrote the history of Solomon, which is probably that which we have in the first book of Kings. The history of Israel seems to have been further carried on by Iddo and Shemaiah: 'Now the acts of Rehoboam, first and last, are they not written in the book of Shemaiah the prophet, and Iddo the seer, concerning genealogies?' (2 *Chron.* 12:15). And after that the history seems to have been further carried on by the prophet Jehu, the son of Hanani: 'Now the rest of the acts of Jehoshaphat, first and last, behold, they are written in the book of Jehu, the son of Hanani, who is mentioned in the book of the kings of Israel' (2 *Chron.* 20:34), as we find him to be (*1 Kings* 16:1, 7). And then it was further continued by the Prophet Isaiah: 'Now the rest of the acts of Uzziah, first and last, did Isaiah the prophet the son of Amoz write' (2 *Chron.* 26:22). He probably did so in the second book of Kings, as well as in the book of his prophecy. And the history was carried on and finished by other prophets after him.

Thus the prophets, even from Samuel's time, had from time to time been adding to the canon of Scripture by their historical writings. But now, in the days of Uzziah, did God first raise up a set of great prophets, not only to write histories, but to write books of their prophecies. The first of these is thought to be Hosea the son of Beeri, and therefore his prophecy, or the word of the LORD by him, is called 'The beginning of the word of the LORD by Hosea' (*Hos.* 1:2); that is, the beginning, or the first part, of the written Word of that kind, viz. that which is written in books of prophecy. He prophesied in the days of Uzziah, Jotham, Ahaz, and Hezekiah, kings of Judah, and in the days of Jeroboam, the son of Joash, king of Israel. There were many other witnesses for God raised up about the same time, to commit their prophecies to writing: Isaiah, and Amos, and Jonah, and Micah, and Nahum, and probably some others; and so from that time forward God seemed to continue a succession of writing prophets.

This was a great dispensation of providence, and a great advance made in the affair of redemption, which appears, if we consider what was said before, that the main business of the prophets was to foreshow Christ and his redemption. They were all forerunners of the great prophet. The main end why the spirit of prophecy was given them was that they might give testimony to Jesus Christ, the great Redeemer, that was to come; and therefore the testimony of Jesus, and the spirit of prophecy, are spoken of as the same thing: 'And I fell at his feet to worship him: and he said unto me, See thou do it not: I am thy fellow servant, and of thy brethren that have the testimony of Jesus: worship God: for the testimony of Jesus is the spirit of prophecy' (*Rev.* 19:10). And therefore we find that the great and main thing that most of the prophets in their written prophecies insist upon is Christ and his redemption, and the glorious times of the gospel, which should be in the latter days, according to their manner of expression.

And though many other things were spoken of in their prophecies, yet it seems to be only as introductory to their prophecy of these great things. Whatever they prophesy of, here their prophecies commonly terminate, as you may see by a careful perusal of their writings.

These prophets were set to writing their prophecies by the Spirit of Christ that was in them, chiefly for that end: to foreshow and prepare the way for the coming of Christ, and the glory that should follow. And in what an exalted strain do they all speak of those things! Many other things they speak of in men's usual language. But when they come upon this subject, what a joyful heavenly sublimity is there in the language they use about it! Some of them are very particular and full in their predictions of these things, and above all the Prophet Isaiah, who is therefore deservedly called the evangelical prophet. He seems to teach the glorious doctrines of the gospel almost as plainly as the apostles did, who preached after Christ was actually come. The Apostle Paul therefore takes notice, that the Prophet Esaias is very bold, Romans 10: 20. That is, as the meaning of the word as used in the New Testament is, very plain. He speaks out very plainly and fully; so being 'very bold' is used in 2 Corinthians 3:12: we use 'great plainness of speech', or 'boldness', as it is in the margin.

How plainly and fully does the Prophet Isaiah describe the manner and circumstances, the nature and end, of the sufferings and sacrifice of Christ, in the 53rd chapter of his prophecy. There is scarce a chapter in the New Testament itself which is more full on it! And how much, and in what a glorious strain, does the same prophet speak from time to time of the glorious benefits of Christ, the unspeakable blessings which shall redound to his church through his redemption! Jesus Christ, the Person that this prophet spoke so much of, once appeared to Isaiah in the form of human nature, the nature that he should afterwards take upon him. We have an account of it in the 6th chapter of his prophecy at the beginning: 'I saw also the LORD sitting on a throne, high and lifted up, and his train filled the temple,' etc. This was Christ that Isaiah now saw, as we are expressly told in the New Testament. See John 12:39-41.

And if we consider the abundant prophecies of this and the other prophets, what a great increase is there of the light of the gospel, which had been growing from the Fall of man to this day! How plentiful are the revelations and prophecies of Christ now, to what they were in the first period of the Old Testament, from Adam to Noah! Or to what they were in the second, from Noah to Abraham! Or to what they were before Moses, or in the time of Moses, Joshua, and the Judges! This dispensation that we are now speaking of was also a glorious advance of the work of redemption by the great additions that were made to the canon of Scripture. A great part of the Old Testament was written now, from the days of Uzziah to the captivity in Babylon. And how excellent are those portions of it! What a precious treasure have those prophets committed to the church of God, tending greatly to confirm the gospel of Christ, and which has been of great comfort and benefit to God's church in all ages since, and doubtless will be to the end of the world.

PART 6

❧❧❧

FROM THE BABYLONISH CAPTIVITY
TO THE COMING OF CHRIST

I come now to the last period of the Old Testament, viz. that which begins with the Babylonish captivity and extends to the coming of Christ, being the greatest part of six hundred years, to show how the work of redemption was carried on through this period.

But before I enter upon particulars, I would observe in three things wherein this period is distinguished from the preceding periods of the times of the Old Testament.

1. Though we have no account of a great part of this period in the Scripture history, yet the events of this period are more the subject of Scripture prophecy than any of the preceding periods. There are two ways wherein the Scriptures give account of the events by which the work of redemption is carried on; one is by history, and another is by prophecy: and in one or the other of these ways we have contained in the Scripture an account how the work of redemption is carried on from the beginning to the end. Although the Scriptures do not contain a proper history of the whole, yet there is contained the whole chain of great events by which this affair hath been carried on from the foundation soon after the Fall of man to the finishing of it at the end of the world, either in history or prophecy. And it is to be observed, that where the

Scripture is wanting in one of these ways, it is made up in the other. Where Scripture history fails, there prophecy takes its place; so that the account is still carried on, and the chain is not broken until we come to the very last link of it in the consummation of all things.

And accordingly it is observable of this period or space of time that we are upon that, though it is so much less the subject of Scripture history than most of the preceding periods, so that there is above four hundred years of it that the Scriptures give us no history of, yet the events of this period are more the subject of Scripture prophecy than the events of all the preceding periods put together. Most of those remarkable prophecies of the book of Daniel do refer to events that were accomplished in this period. So also most of those prophecies in Isaiah, Jeremiah and Ezekiel, against Babylon, Tyrus, Egypt, and many other nations, were fulfilled in this period.

So that the reason why the Scriptures give us no history of so great a part of this period is not because the events of this period were not so important as the events of the foregoing periods; for I shall hereafter show how great and distinguishedly remarkable the events of this period were. But there are several other reasons which may be given of it.

One is that it was the will of God that the spirit of prophecy should cease in this period (for reasons that may be given hereafter); so that there were no prophets to write the history of these times; and therefore God, designing this, took care that the great events of this period should not be without mention in his Word; and so ordered it that the prophecies of Scripture should be more full here than in the preceding periods. It is observable that that set of writing prophets that God raised up in Israel were raised up at the latter end of the foregoing period, and at the beginning of this; which it is likely was partly for that reason, that the time was now approaching of which, the spirit of prophecy having ceased, there was to be no Scripture history, and therefore no other Scripture account but what was given in prophecy.

And another reason that may be given why there was so great a part of this period left without an historical account in Scripture is that God in his providence took care that there should be authentic and full accounts of the events of this period preserved in profane history. It is remarkable, and very worthy to be taken notice of, that with respect to the events of the five preceding periods, of which the Scriptures give the history, profane history gives us no account, or at least of but very few of them. There are many fabulous and uncertain accounts of things that happened before; but the beginning of the times of authentic profane history is judged to be but a little before Nebuchadnezzar's time, about an hundred years before. The learned men among the Greeks and Romans used to call the ages before that the fabulous age; but the times after that they called the historical age. And from about that time to the coming of Christ, we have undoubted accounts in profane history of the principal events; accounts that wonderfully agree with the many prophecies that we have in Scripture of those times.

Thus did the great God, that disposes all things, order it. He took care to give an historical account of things from the beginning of the world through all those former ages which profane history does not reach, and ceased not until he came to those later ages in which profane history related things with some certainty. And concerning those times he gives us abundant account in prophecy, that by comparing profane history with those prophecies, we might see the agreement.

2. This period being the last period of the Old Testament, and the next to the coming of Christ, seems to have been remarkably distinguished from all others in the great revolutions that were among the nations of the earth, to make way

for the kingdom of Christ. The time now drawing nigh wherein Christ, the great King and Saviour of the world, was to come, great and mighty were the changes that were brought to pass in order to it. The way had been preparing for the coming of Christ from the Fall of man, through all the foregoing periods. But now, the time drawing nigh, things began to ripen apace for Christ's coming; and therefore divine providence wrought wonderfully now.

The greatest revolutions that any history whatsoever gives an account of, that ever had been from the Flood, fell out in this period. Almost all the then known world, that is, all the nations that were round about the land of Canaan, far and near, that were within the reach of their knowledge, were overturned again and again. All lands were in their turns subdued, captivated, and as it were emptied, and turned upside down, and that, most of them, repeatedly, in this period; agreeable to that prophecy, 'Behold, the LORD maketh the earth empty, and maketh it waste, and turneth it upside down, and scattereth abroad the inhabitants thereof' (*Isa.* 24:1).

This emptying and turning upside down began with God's visible church, in their captivity by the king of Babylon. And then the cup, from them, went round to other nations, agreeable to what God revealed to the prophet Jeremiah (25:15-27). Here special respect seems to be had to the great revolutions that there were in the face of the earth in the times of the Babylonish empire. But after that there were three general overturnings of the world before Christ came in the succession of the three great monarchies of the world that were after the Babylonish empire. The king of Babylon is represented in Scripture as overturning the world; but after that the Babylonish empire was overthrown by Cyrus, who founded the Persian empire in the room of it; which was of much greater extent than the Babylonish empire in its greatest glory. Thus the world was overturned the second time. And then, after that the Persian empire was overthrown by Alexander, and the Grecian empire was set up upon the ruins of it; which was still of much greater extent than the Persian empire. And thus there was a general overturning of the world a third time. And then, after that, the Grecian empire was overthrown by the Romans, and the Roman empire was established, which vastly exceeded all foregoing empires in power and extent of dominion. And so the world was overturned the fourth time.

These several monarchies, and the great revolutions of the world under them, are abundantly spoken of in the prophecies of Daniel. They are represented in Nebuchadnezzar's image of gold, silver, brass, and iron, and Daniel's interpretation of it in Daniel 2; and then in Daniel's vision of the four beasts, and the angel's interpretation of it in Daniel 7. And the succession of the Persian and Grecian monarchies is more particularly represented in chapter 8 in Daniel's vision of the ram and the he-goat, and again in Daniel 11.

And besides these four general overturnings of the world, the world was kept in a constant tumult between whiles. And indeed the world was, as it were, in a continual convulsion through this whole period until Christ came. Before this period, the face of the earth was comparatively in quietness. Though there were many great wars among the nations, yet we read of no such mighty and universal convulsions and overturnings as there were in this period.

The nations of the world, most of them, had long remained on their lees, as it were, without being emptied from vessel to vessel, as is said of Moab (*Jer.* 48:11). Now these great overturnings were because the time of the great Messiah drew nigh. That they were to prepare the way for Christ's coming is evident by Scripture, particularly by Ezekiel 21:27: 'I will overturn, overturn, overturn it, and it shall be no more, until he come whose right it is, and I will give it him.' The prophet, by repeating the word overturn three times, has respect to three overturnings, as, in Revelation 8:13, the repetition of the word 'woe' three times signifies three distinct woes, as appears by what follows, 'One woe is past' (*Rev.* 9: 12), and 'The second woe is past; and, behold, the third woe cometh quickly' (*Rev.* 11:14).

It must be noted that the Prophet Ezekiel prophesied in the time of the Babylonish captivity, and therefore there were three great and general overturnings of the world to come after this prophecy, before Christ came: the first by the Persians, the second by the Grecians, the third by the Romans. And then after that Christ, whose right it was to take the diadem and reign, should come. Here these great overturnings are evidently spoken of as preparatory to the coming and kingdom of Christ. But, to understand the words aright, we must note the particular expression, 'I will overturn, overturn, overturn it', that is, the diadem and crown of Israel, or the supreme temporal dominion over God's visible people. This, God said, should be no more, that is, the crown should be taken off, and the diadem removed, as it is said in the fore-going verse. The supreme power over Israel should be no more in the royal line of David, to which it properly belonged, but should be removed away, and given to others, and over-turned from one to another: first the supreme power over Israel should be in the hands of the Persians; and then it should be overturned again; and then it should be in the hands of the Grecians; and then it should be overturned again, and come into the hands of the Romans, and should be no more in the line of David, until that very Person should come that was the son of David, whose proper right it was, and then God would give it to him.

That those great shakings and revolutions of the nations of the world were all to prepare the way for Christ's coming and the setting up of his kingdom in the world is further manifest by Haggai 2:6-7: 'For thus saith the LORD of hosts; Yet once, it is a little while, and I will shake the heavens, and the earth, and the sea, and the dry land; and I will shake all nations, and the desire of all nations shall come: and I will fill this house with glory, saith the LORD of hosts.' See also verses 21–23. It is evident by this that these great revolutions and shakings of the nations, whereby the thrones of kingdoms and armies were overthrown, and every one came down by the sword of his brother, were to prepare the way for the coming of him who is the desire of all nations.

The great changes and troubles that have sometimes been in the visible church of Christ are in Revelation 12:2 compared to the church's being in travail to bring forth Christ; so these great troubles and mighty revolutions that were in the world before Christ was born were, as it were, the world's being in travail to bring forth the Son of God. The apostle, in Romans 8, represents the whole creation as groaning and travailing in pain together until now, to bring forth the liberty and manifestation of the children of God. So the world as it were travailed in pain, and was in continual convulsions, for several hundred years together, to bring forth the first-born child, and the only begotten Son of God. And those mighty revolutions were as so many pangs and throes in order to it. The world being so long a time kept in a state of war and bloodshed prepared the way for the coming of the Prince of Peace, as it showed the great need the world stood in of such a prince, to deliver the world from its miseries.

It pleased God to order it in his providence that earthly power and dominion should be raised to its greatest height, and appear in its utmost glory, in those four great monarchies that succeeded one another, and that every one should be greater and more glorious than the preceding, before he set up the kingdom of his Son. By this it appeared how much more glorious his spiritual kingdom was than the most glorious temporal kingdom. The strength and glory of Satan's kingdom in these four mighty monarchies, appeared in its greatest height, for those monarchies were the monarchies of the heathen world, and so the strength of them was the strength of Satan's kingdom. God suffered Satan's kingdom to rise to so great a height of power and magnificence before his Son came to overthrow it, to prepare the way for the more glorious triumph of his Son.

Goliath must have on all his splendid armour when the stripling David comes against him with a sling and a stone, for the greater glory of David's victory. God suffered one of those great monarchies to subdue another, and erect itself on the other's ruins, appearing still in greater strength, and the last to be the strongest and mightiest of all; that so Christ, in overthrowing that, might as it were overthrow them all at once, as the stone cut out of the mountain without hands, is represented as destroying the whole image, the gold, the silver, the brass, the iron, and the clay; so that all became as the chaff of the summer threshing floor (*Dan.*2:35).

These mighty empires were suffered thus to overthrow the world, and destroy one another. And though their power was so great, yet they could not uphold themselves, but fell one after another, and came to nothing, even the last of them, that was the strongest, and had swallowed up the earth. It pleased God thus to show in them the instability and vanity of all earthly power and greatness; which served as a foil to set forth the glory of the kingdom of his Son, which never shall be destroyed, as appears by Daniel 2:44, 'In the days of these kings shall the God of heaven set up a kingdom, which shall never be destroyed: and the kingdom shall not be left to other people, but it shall break in pieces, and consume all these kingdoms, and it shall stand for ever.' So greatly does this kingdom differ from all those kingdoms: they vanish away, and are left to other people; but this shall not be left to other people, but shall stand forever. God suffered the devil to do his utmost, and to establish his interest, by setting up the greatest, strongest, and most glorious kingdoms in the world that he could, before the despised Jesus overthrew him and his empire. Christ came into the world to bring down the high things of Satan's kingdom, that the hand of the Lord might be on every one that is proud and lofty, and every high tower, and every lofty mountain, as the prophet Isaiah says (*Isa.* 2:12-17). And therefore these things were suffered to rise very high, that Christ might appear so much the more glorious in being above them.

Thus wonderfully did the great and wise Governor of the world prepare the way for the erecting of the glorious kingdom of his beloved Son Jesus.

3. Another thing for which this last period or space of time before Christ was particularly remarkable was the wonderful preservation of the church through all those overturnings. The preservation of the church was on some accounts more remarkable through this period than through any of the foregoing. It was very wonderful that the church, which in this period was so weak, and in so low a state, and mostly subject to the dominion of heathen monarchies, should be preserved for five or six hundred years together, while the world was so often overturned, and the earth was rent in pieces, and made so often empty and waste, and the inhabitants of it came down so often every one by the sword of his brother.

I say, it was wonderful that the church in its weak and low state, being but a little handful of men, should be preserved in all these great convulsions, especially considering that the land of Judea, the chief place of the church's residence, lay in the midst of them, as it were in the middle between the contending parties. It was very much the seat of war amongst them, and was often overrun and subdued, and sometimes in the hands of one people, and sometimes another, and very much the object of the envy and hatred of all heathen nations, and often almost ruined by them. Often great multitudes of its inhabitants were slain, and the land in a great measure depopulated; and those who had them in their power, often intended the utter destruction of the whole nation. Yet they were upheld; they were preserved in their captivity in Babylon, and they were upheld again under all the dangers they passed through under the kings of Persia, and the much greater dangers they were liable to under the empire of the Greeks, and afterwards when the world was trodden down by the Romans.

And their preservation through this period was also distinguishingly remarkable in that we never read of the church's suffering persecution in any former period in any measure to such a degree as they did in this, under Antiochus Epiphanes, of which more afterwards. This wonderful preservation of the church through all these overturnings of the world gives light and confirmation to what we read in the beginning of the Psalm 46: 'God is our refuge and strength, a very present help in trouble. Therefore will not we fear, though the earth be removed, and though the mountains be carried into the midst of the sea; though the waters thereof roar, and be troubled; though the mountains shake with the swelling thereof.'

Thus I have taken notice of some general things wherein this last period of the Old Testament times was distinguished. I come now to consider how the work of redemption was carried on in particulars.

1. The first thing that here presents itself is the captivity of the Jews into Babylon. This was a great dispensation of providence, and such as never was before. The children of Israel in the time of the Judges had often been brought under their enemies; and many particular persons were carried captive at other times. But never had there been any such thing as the destruction of the whole land, the sanctuary, and the city

of Jerusalem, and all the cities and villages of the land, and carrying the whole body of the people out of their own land into a country many hundred miles distant, and leaving the land of Canaan empty of God's visible people. The ark had once forsaken the tabernacle of Shiloh, and was carried captive into the land of the Philistines; but never had there been any such thing as the burning the sanctuary, and utterly destroying the ark, and carrying away all the sacred vessels and utensils, and breaking up all their stated worship in the land, and the land's lying waste and empty for so many years together. How lively are those things set forth in the Lamentations of Jeremiah!

The work of redemption was promoted by this remarkable dispensation in these following ways.

i. It finally cured that nation of their itch after idolatry. The Prophet Isaiah, speaking of the setting up of the kingdom of Christ (*Isa.* 2:18), speaks of the abolishing of idolatry as one thing that should be done to this end: 'And the idols he shall utterly abolish.' When the time was drawing near that God would abolish heathen idolatry through the greater part of the known world, as he did by the preaching of the gospel after Christ came, it pleased him first to abolish heathenism among his own people; and he did it now by their captivity in Babylon; a presage of that abolishing of idols that God was about to bring to pass by Christ through so great a part of the heathen world.

This nation that was addicted to idolatry before for so many ages, of which nothing would cure them, not all the reproofs, and warnings, and corrections, that they had, and all the judgments God inflicted on them for it, yet now were finally cured; so that however some might fall into this sin afterwards, as they did about the time of Antiochus's persecution, yet the nation, as a nation, never showed any hankering after this sin any more. This was a remarkable and wonderful change in that people, and directly promoted the work of redemption, as it was a great advancement of the interest of religion.

ii. It was one thing that prepared the way for Christ's coming, and setting up the glorious dispensation of the gospel, as it took away many of those things wherein consisted the glory of the Jewish dispensation. In order to introduce the glorious dispensation of the gospel, the external glory of the Jewish church must be diminished, as we observed before. This the Babylonish captivity did many ways; it brought the people very low.

First, it removed the temporal diadem of the house of David away from them, that is, the supreme and independent government of themselves. It took away the crown and diadem from the nation. The time now approaching when Christ, the great and everlasting king of his church, was to reign, it was time for the typical kings to withdraw. As God said by Ezekiel (21:26-27), 'Remove the diadem, and take off the crown . . . it shall be no more, until he come whose right it is.' The Jews henceforward were always dependent on the governing power of other nations, until Christ came, for near six hundred years, except about ninety years, during which they maintained a sort of independence by continual wars under the dominion of the Maccabees and their posterity.

Again, by the captivity, the glory and magnificence of the temple was taken away, and the temple that was built afterwards, was nothing in comparison with it. Thus it was meet that, when the time drew nigh that the glorious antitype of the temple should appear, the typical temple should have its glory withdrawn.

Again, another thing that they lost by the captivity was the two tables of the testimony delivered to Moses, written with the finger of God; the two tables on which God with his own finger wrote the ten commandments on Mount Sinai. These seem to have been preserved in the ark until the captivity. They were in the ark when Solomon placed it in the temple (*1 Kings* 8:9). There was nothing in the ark, save the two tables of stone, which Moses put there at Horeb. And we have no reason to suppose anything other than that they remained there as long as that temple stood. But the Jews speak of these as finally lost at that time, though the same commandments were preserved in the book of the law. These tables also were withdrawn on the approach of their antitype.

Again, another thing that was lost that the Jews had before, was the Urim and Thummim. This is evident by Ezra 2:63: 'And the Tirshatha said unto them, that they should not eat of the most holy things, until there should stand up a priest with Urim and with Thummim.' And we have no account that this was ever restored, but the ancient writings of the Jews say the contrary. What this Urim and Thummim was, I shall not now inquire; but only observe that it was something by which the high priest inquired of God, and received immediate answers from him, or by which God gave forth immediate oracles on particular occasions. This was now withdrawn, the time approaching when Christ, the antitype of the Urim and Thummim, the great Word and Oracle of God, was to come.

Another thing that the ancient Jews say was wanting in the second temple, was the Shechinah, or cloud of glory over the mercy seat. This was promised to be in the tabernacle: 'For I will appear in the cloud upon the mercy seat' (*Lev.* 16:2). And we read elsewhere of the cloud of glory descending into the tabernacle (*Exod.* 40:35), and so we do likewise with respect to Solomon's temple. But we have no account that this cloud of glory was in the second temple. And the ancient accounts of the Jews say that there was no such thing in the second temple. This was needless in the second temple, considering that God had promised that he would fill this temple with glory another way, namely, by Christ's coming into it; which was afterwards fulfilled. 'I will shake all nations, and the desire of all nations shall come, and I will fill this house with glory, saith the LORD of hosts' (*Hag.* 2:7).

Another thing that the Jews, in their ancient writings, mention as being now withdrawn was the fire from heaven on the altar. When Moses built the tabernacle and altar in the wilderness, and the first sacrifices were offered on it, fire came down from heaven, and consumed the burnt offering, as in Leviticus 9:24; and so again, when Solomon built the temple, and offered the first sacrifices, as you may see in 2 Chronicles 7:1. And this fire was never to go out, but with the greatest care to be kept alive, as God commanded, 'The fire shall ever be burning upon the altar: it shall never go out' (*Lev.* 6:13). And there is no reason to suppose the fire in Solomon's time ever went out until the temple was destroyed by the Babylonians. But then it was extinguished, and never was restored. We have no account of its being given on the building of the second temple, as we have at the building of the tabernacle and first temple. But the Jews, after their return, were forced to make use of their common fire instead of it, according to the ancient tradition of the Jews. Thus the lights of the Old Testament go out on the approach of the glorious Sun of righteousness.

iii. The captivity into Babylon was the occasion of another thing which did afterwards much promote the setting up of Christ's kingdom in the world, and that was the dispersion of the Jews through the greater part of the known world, before the coming of Christ. For the whole nation being carried away far out of their own land, and continuing in a state of captivity for so long a time, they got them possessions, and built them houses, and settled themselves in the land of their captivity, agreeable to the direction that Jeremiah gave them, in the letter he wrote to them in Jeremiah 29. And therefore, when Cyrus gave them liberty to return to the land where they had formerly dwelt, many of them never returned; they were not willing to leave their settlements and possessions there, to go into a desolate country, many hundred miles distant, which none but the old men among them had ever seen; and therefore they were but few, but a small number, that returned, as we see in the accounts we have in the books of Ezra and Nehemiah. Great numbers tarried behind, though they still retained the same religion with those that returned, so far as it could be practised in a foreign land. Those messengers that we read of in Zechariah 7, that came to inquire of the priests and prophets in Jerusalem, Sherezer and Regem-melech, are supposed to be messengers sent from the Jews that remained still in Babylon.

Those Jews that remained still in that country were soon, by the great changes that happened in the world, dispersed thence into all the adjacent countries. And hence we find that in Esther's time, which was after the return from the captivity, the Jews were a people that were dispersed throughout all parts of the vast Persian empire, which extended from India to Ethiopia, as you may see: 'And Haman said unto king Ahasuerus, There is a certain people scattered abroad, and dispersed among the people in all the provinces of thy kingdom' (*Esther* 3:8). And so they continued dispersed until Christ came, and until the apostles went forth to preach the gospel. But yet these dispersed Jews retained their religion in this dispersion. Their captivity, as I said before, thoroughly cured them of their idolatry; and it was their manner for as many of them as could from time to time to go up to the land of Judea, to Jerusalem at their great feasts. Hence we read in Acts 2 that at the time of the great feast of Pentecost there were Jews abiding at Jerusalem out of every nation under heaven. These were

Jews come up from all countries where they were dispersed, to worship at that feast. And hence we find, in the history of the Acts of the Apostles, that wherever the apostles went preaching through the world, they found Jews. They came to such a city, and to such a city, and went into the synagogue of the Jews.

Antiochus the Great, about two hundred years before Christ, on a certain occasion transplanted two thousand families of Jews from the country about Babylon into Asia Minor; and so they and their posterity, many of them, settled in Pontus, Galatia, Phrygia, Pamphylia, and in Ephesus; and from thence settled in Athens, and Corinth, and Rome. Whence came those synagogues in the places that the Apostle Paul preached in.

Now, this dispersion of the Jews through the world before Christ came, did many ways prepare the way for his coming, and setting up his kingdom in the world.

One way was that this was a means of raising a general expectation of the Messiah through the world about the time that he actually came. For the Jews, wherever they were dispersed, carried the holy Scriptures with them, and so the prophecies of the Messiah. And being conversant with the nations among whom they lived, they, by that means, became acquainted with these prophecies, and with the expectations of the Jews of their glorious Messiah. By this means, the birth of such a glorious person in Judea about that time began to be the general expectation of the nations of the world, as appears by the writings of the learned men of the heathen that lived about that time which are still extant, particularly Virgil, the famous poet that lived in Italy a little before Christ was born. He has a poem about the expectation of a great prince that was to be born, and the happy times of righteousness and peace that he was to introduce, some of it very much in the language of the prophet Isaiah.

Another way that this dispersed state of the Jews prepared the way for Christ was that it showed the necessity of abolishing the Jewish dispensation, and introducing a new dispensation of the covenant of grace. It showed the necessity of abolishing the ceremonial law, and the old Jewish worship; for, by the dispersion, the observance of that ceremonial law became impracticable even by the Jews themselves.

The ceremonial law was adapted to the state of a people dwelling together in the same land where the city that God had chosen was; where the temple was, the only place where they might offer sacrifices; and where it was lawful for their priests and Levites to officiate, where they were to bring their first fruits, and where their cities of refuge and the like were. But the Jews, by this dispersion, lived, many of them, in other lands, more than a thousand miles distant, when Christ came; which made the observance of their laws of sacrifices, and the like, impracticable. And though their forefathers might be to blame in not going up to the land of Judea when they were permitted by Cyrus, yet the case was now, as to many of them at least, become impracticable; which showed the necessity of introducing a new dispensation, that should be fitted, not only to one particular land, but to the general circumstances and use of all nations of the world.

Again, another way that this dispersion of the Jews through the world prepared the way for the setting up of the kingdom of Christ in the world was that it contributed to making the facts concerning Jesus Christ publicly known through the world. For, as I observed before, the Jews that lived in other countries used frequently to go up to Jerusalem at their three great feasts which were from year to year; and so, by this means, they could not but become acquainted with the news of the wonderful things that Christ did in that land. We find that they were present at, and took great notice of, that great miracle of raising Lazarus, which excited the curiosity of those foreign Jews that came up to the feast of the Passover to see Jesus, as you may see in John 12:19-21. These Greeks were foreign Jews and proselytes, as is evident by their coming to worship at the feast of the Passover. The Jews that lived abroad among the Greeks, and spoke their language, were called Greeks, or Hellenists. They are called Grecians in Acts 6:1. The Grecians here spoken of were not Gentile Christians, for this was before the calling of the Gentiles.

By the same means, the Jews that went up from other countries became acquainted with Christ's crucifixion. Thus the disciples, going to Emmaus, say to Christ, when they did not know him, 'Art thou only a stranger in Jerusalem, and hast not known the things which have come to pass there in these days?' (*Luke* 24:18), plainly intimating, that the things concerning Jesus were so publicly known to all men that it was wonderful to find any man unacquainted with them. And so afterwards they became acquainted with the news of his resurrection; and when they went home again into their own countries, they carried the news with them, and so made these facts public through the world, as they had made the prophecies of them public before.

After this, those foreign Jews that came to Jerusalem, took great notice of the pouring out of the Spirit at Pentecost, and the wonderful effects of it; and many of them were converted by it, namely, Parthians, Medes, Elamites, and the dwellers in Mesopotamia, and in Egypt, and the parts of Libya about Cyrene, and the strangers of Rome, Jews and proselytes, Cretes and Arabians. And so they did not only carry back the news of the facts of Christianity, but Christianity itself, into their own countries with them; which contributed much to the spreading of it through the world.

Again, another way that the dispersion of the Jews contributed to the setting up of the gospel kingdom in the world was, that it opened a door for the introduction of the apostles in all places where they came to preach the gospel. For almost in all places where they came to preach the gospel they found Jews and synagogues of the Jews, where the holy Scriptures were wont to be read and the true God worshipped. This was a great advantage to the apostles in their spreading of the gospel through the world. For their way was, into whatever city they came, first to go into the synagogue of the Jews (they being people of the same nation), and there to preach the gospel unto them. And hereby their coming, and their new doctrine, was taken notice of by their Gentile neighbours, whose curiosity excited them to hear what they had to say; which became a fair occasion to the apostles to preach the gospel to them.

It appears that it was thus by the account we have of things in the Acts of the Apostles. And these Gentiles having been before, many of them, prepared in some measure, by the knowledge they had of the Jews' religion, and of their worship of one God, and of their prophecies, and expectation of a Messiah, which knowledge they derived from the Jews who had long been their neighbours, this opened the door for the gospel to have access to them. And the work of the apostles with them was doubtless much easier than if they never had heard any thing before of any expectation of such a person as the apostles preached, or any thing about the worship of one only true God.

In so many ways did the Babylonish captivity greatly prepare the way for Christ's coming.

2. The next particular that I would take notice of is, the addition made to the canon of Scripture in the time of the captivity, in those two remarkable portions of Scripture, the prophecies of Ezekiel and Daniel. Christ appeared to each of these prophets in the form of that nature which he was afterwards to take upon him. The prophet Ezekiel gives an account of his thus appearing to him repeatedly, as in Ezekiel 1:26:

'And above the firmament that was over their heads was the likeness of a throne, as the appearance of a sapphire stone: and upon the likeness of the throne was the likeness as the appearance of a man above upon it'; and so chapter 8:1-2.

So Christ appeared to the prophet Daniel: 'There stood before me as the appearance of a man. And I heard a man's voice between the banks of Ulai, which called, and said, Gabriel, make this man to understand the vision' (*Dan.* 8:15-16). There are several things that make it evident that this was Christ which I cannot now stop to mention particularly. So Christ appeared again as a man to this prophet, 'Then I lifted up mine eyes and looked, and behold, a certain man clothed in linen, whose loins were girded with fine gold of Uphaz: his body also was like the beryl, and his face as the appearance of lightning, and his eyes as lamps of fire, and his arms and his feet like in colour to polished brass, and the voice of his words like the voice of a multitude' (*Dan* 10:5-6). Comparing this vision with that of the Apostle John in the first chapter of Revelation, makes it manifest that it was Christ. And the prophet Daniel, in the historical part of his book, gives an account of a very remarkable appearance of Christ in Nebuchadnezzar's furnace, with Shadrach, Meshach, and Abednego. We have the account of it in the third chapter. In verse 25, Christ is said to be like the Son of God; and it is manifest that he appeared in the form of man: 'Lo, I see four men loose . . . and the form of the fourth is like the Son of God.'

Christ did not only here appear in the form of the human nature, but he appeared in a furnace, saving those persons who believed on him from that furnace; by which is represented to us how Christ, by coming himself into the furnace of God's wrath, saves those that believe in him from that furnace, so that it has no power on them; and the wrath of God never reaches or touches them so much as to singe the hair of their head.

These two prophets, in many respects, were more particular concerning the coming of Christ and his glorious gospel kingdom than any of the prophets had been before. They both mention those three great overturnings of the world that should be before he came. Ezekiel is particular in several places concerning the coming of Christ. The prophet Daniel is more particular in foretelling the time of the coming of Christ than ever any prophet had been before. In the ninth chapter of his prophecy he foretold that it should be seventy weeks, that is, seventy weeks of years, or seventy times seven years, or four hundred and ninety years, from the decree to rebuild and restore the state of the Jews until the Messiah should be crucified, which must be reckoned from the commission given to Ezra by Artaxerxes, which we have an account of in the seventh chapter of Ezra; whereby the very particular time of Christ's crucifixion was pointed out, which never had been before.

The prophet Ezekiel is very particular in the mystical description of the gospel church in his account of his vision of the temple and city in the latter part of his prophecy. The Prophet Daniel points out the order of particular events that should come to pass relating to the Christian church after Christ was come, such as the rise of Antichrist, and the continuance of his reign, and his fall, and the glory that should follow.

Thus does gospel light still increase the nearer we come to the time of Christ's birth.

3. The next particular I would mention is, the destruction of Babylon and the overthrow of the Chaldean empire by Cyrus. The destruction of Babylon was in that night in which Belshazzar the king, and the city in general, was drowned in a drunken festival which they kept to their gods. Then Daniel was called to read the handwriting on the wall, Daniel 5:30.

And it was brought about in such a manner as wonderfully to show the hand of God and remarkably to fulfil his Word by his prophets, which I cannot now stop particularly to relate. Now that great city which had long been an enemy to the city of God, his Jerusalem, was destroyed, though it had stood ever since the first building of Babel, which was about seventeen hundred years. If the check that was put to the building of this city at its beginning, whereby they were prevented from carrying of it to that extent and magnificence that they intended – I say, if this promoted the work of redemption, as I have before shown it did, much more did this destruction of it.

It was a remarkable instance of God's vengeance on the enemies of his redeemed church, for God brought this destruction on Babylon for the injuries they did to his children, as is often set forth in the prophets. It also promoted the work of redemption since thereby God's people that were held captive by them were set at liberty to return to their own land to rebuild Jerusalem. And therefore Cyrus, who did it, is called God's shepherd therein (*Isa.* 44:28; 45:1). And these are over and above those ways wherein the setting up and overthrowing of the four monarchies of the world did promote the work of redemption, which have been before observed.

4. What next followed this was the return of the Jews to their own land and the rebuilding of Jerusalem and the temple. Cyrus, as soon as he had destroyed the Babylonish empire and erected the Persian empire on its ruins, made a decree in favour of the Jews, that they might return to their own land and rebuild their city and temple. This return of the Jews out of the Babylonish captivity is, next to the redemption out of Egypt, the most remarkable of all the Old Testament redemptions, and most insisted on in Scripture as a type of the great redemption of Jesus Christ. It was under the hand of

one of the legal ancestors of Christ, namely, Zerubbabel, the son of Shealtiel, whose Babylonish name was Sheshbazzar. He was the governor of the Jews, and their leader in their first return out of captivity and, together with Joshua the son of Josedech, the high priest, had the chief hand in rebuilding the temple. This redemption was brought about by the hand of Zerubbabel and Joshua the priest, as the redemption out of Egypt was brought about by the hand of Moses and Aaron.

The return out of the captivity was a remarkable dispensation of providence. It was remarkable that the heart of a heathen prince, as Cyrus was, should be so inclined to favour such a design as he did, not only in giving the people liberty to return and rebuild the city and temple, but in giving charge that they should be helped with silver and gold, and with goods, and with beasts, as we read in Ezra 1:4.

And afterwards God wonderfully inclined the heart of Darius to further the building of the house of God with his own tribute money, and by commanding their bitter enemies, the Samaritans, who had been striving to hinder them, to help them without fail, by furnishing them with all that they needed in order to it, and to supply them day by day; making a decree, that whosoever failed of it, timber should be pulled down out of his house, and he hanged thereon, and his house made a dunghill; as we have an account of in Ezra 6.

And after this God inclined the heart of Artaxerxes, another king of Persia, to promote the work of preserving the state of the Jews by his ample commission to Ezra, which we have an account of in Ezra 7, helping them abundantly with silver and gold of his own bounty, and offering more, as should be needful, out of the king's treasure house, and commanding his treasurers beyond the river Euphrates to give more, as should be needed, unto a hundred talents of silver, a hundred measures of wheat, a hundred baths of wine, and a hundred baths of oil, and salt without prescribing how much;

and giving leave to establish magistrates in the land, freeing the priests of toll, tribute and custom, and other things, which render this decree and commission by Artaxerxes the most full and ample in the Jews' favour of any that at any time had been given for the restoring of Jerusalem. Therefore, in Daniel's prophecy, this is called the decree for restoring and building Jerusalem; and hence the seventy weeks are dated.

And then, after this, another favourable commission was granted by the king of Persia to Nehemiah, which we have an account of in Nehemiah 2.

It was remarkable that the hearts of heathen princes should be so inclined. It was the effect of the power of him who hath the hearts of kings in his hands and turneth them whithersoever he will; and it was a remarkable instance of his favour to his people.

Another remarkable circumstance of this restitution of the state of the Jews to their own land was that it was accomplished against so much opposition of their bitter and indefatigable enemies the Samaritans, who, for a long time together, with all the malice and craft they could exercise, opposed the Jews in this affair and sought their destruction, at one time by Bishlam, Mithridath, Tabeel, Rehum and Shimshai, as in Ezra 4, and then by Tatnai, Shetharboznai, and their companions, as in Ezra 5, and afterwards by Sanballat and Tobiah, as we read in the book of Nehemiah.

We have shown before how the settlement of the people in this land in Joshua's time promoted the work of redemption. On the same accounts does their restitution belong to the same work. The resettlement of the Jews in the land of Canaan belongs to this work, as it was a necessary means of preserving the Jewish church and dispensation in being until Christ should come. If it had not been for this restoration of the Jewish church and temple and worship, the people had remained without any temple and land of their own, to be as it were their headquarters, a place of worship, habitation, and resort. The whole constitution which God had done so much to establish would have been in danger of utterly failing, long before that six hundred had been out, which was from about the time of the captivity until Christ. And so all that preparation which God had been making for the coming of Christ, from the time of Abraham, would have been in vain. Now that very temple was built that God would fill with glory by Christ's coming into it, as the Prophets Haggai and Zechariah told the Jews, to encourage them in building it.

5. The next particular I would observe, is the addition made to the canon of the Scriptures soon after the captivity by the Prophets Haggai and Zechariah, who were prophets sent to encourage the people in their work of rebuilding the city and temple. And the main argument they make use of to that end is the approach of the time of the coming of Christ. Haggai foretold that Christ should be of Zerubbabel's legal posterity (*Hag.* 2:23). This seems to be the last and most particular revelation of the descent of Christ until the angel Gabriel was sent to reveal it to his mother Mary.

6. The next thing I would take notice of was the pouring out of the Spirit of God that accompanied the ministry of Ezra the priest after the captivity. That there was such a pouring out of the Spirit of God is manifest by many things in the books of Ezra and Nehemiah. Presently after Ezra came up from Babylon, with the ample commission which Artaxerxes gave him, whence Daniel's seventy weeks began, he set himself to reform the vices and corruptions he found among the Jews; and his great success in it we have an account of in Ezra 10; so that there appeared a very general and great mourning of the congregation of Israel for their sins, which was accompanied with a solemn covenant that the people entered into with

God. This was followed with a great and general reformation, as we have there an account.

And the people about the same time, with great zeal, earnestness and reverence, gathered themselves together to hear the Word of God read by Ezra, and gave diligent attention while Ezra and the other priests preached to them, by reading and expounding the law, and were greatly affected in the hearing of it. They wept when they heard the words of the law, and set themselves to observe the law, and kept the feast of tabernacles, as the Scripture observes, after such a manner as it had not been kept since the days of Joshua the son of Nun, as we read in Nehemiah 8. And after this, having separated themselves from all strangers, they solemnly observed a fast by hearing the Word of God, confessing their sins, and renewing their covenant with God. They manifested their sincerity in that transaction by actually reforming many abuses in religion and morals, as we learn from Nehemiah 9 and the following chapters.

It is observable that it has been God's manner in every remarkable new establishment of the state of his visible church to give a remarkable outpouring of his Spirit. So it was on the first establishment of the church of the Jews at their first coming into Canaan under Joshua, as has been observed; and so it was now in this second settlement of the church in the same land in the time of Ezra; and so it was on the first establishment of the Christian church after Christ's resurrection.

God wisely and graciously laid the foundation of those establishments in a work of his Holy Spirit, for the lasting benefit of the state of his church, thenceforward continued in those establishments. And this pouring out of the Spirit of God was a final cure of that nation of that particular sin which just before they especially run into, namely, intermarrying with the Gentiles; for however inclined to it they were before, they ever after showed an aversion to it.

7. Ezra added to the canon of the Scriptures. He wrote the book of Ezra; and he is supposed to have written the two books of Chronicles, at least to have compiled them, if he was not the author of the materials or all the parts of these writings. That these books were written, or compiled and completed, after the captivity, the things contained in the books themselves make manifest, for the genealogies contained therein are brought down below the captivity, as in 1 Chronicles 3:17, etc. We have there an account of the posterity of Jehoiachin for several successive generations. And there is mention in these books of his captivity in Babylon as of a thing past, and of things that were done on the return of the Jews after the captivity, as you may see in 1 Chronicles 9. The chapter is mostly filled up with an account of things that came to pass after the captivity in Babylon, as may be seen by comparing it with what is said in the books of Ezra and Nehemiah. And that Ezra was the person that compiled these books is probable by this, that they conclude with words that we know are from Ezra's history. The last two verses are Ezra's words in the history he gives in the first two verses of his book.

8. Ezra is supposed to have collected all the books of which the holy Scriptures did then consist and disposed them in their proper order. Ezra is often spoken of as a noted and eminent scribe of the law of God, and the canon of Scripture in his time was manifestly under his special care. The Jews, from the first accounts we have from them, have always held that the canon of Scripture, so much of it as was then extant, was collected and orderly disposed and settled by Ezra; and from him they have delivered it down in the order in which he disposed it until Christ's time, when the Christian church received it from them and have delivered it down to our times. And the truth of this is allowed as undoubted by divines in general.

9. The work of redemption was carried on and promoted in this period, by greatly multiplying the copies of the law, and appointing the constant public reading of them in all the cities of Israel in their synagogues. It is evident that, before the captivity, there were but few copies of the law. There was the original, laid up beside the ark; and the kings were required to write out a copy of the law for their use, and the law was required to be read to the whole congregation of Israel once every seventh year. We have no account of any other stated public reading of the law before the captivity but this. And it is manifest by several things that might be mentioned that copies of the law were exceeding rare before the captivity.

But after the captivity, the constant reading of the law was set up in every synagogue throughout the land. First, they began with reading the law, and then they proceeded to establish the constant reading of the other books of the Old Testament. And lessons were read out of the Old Testament, as made up of both the law and the other parts of the Scripture then extant, in all the synagogues which were set up in every city and wherever the Jews dwelt in any considerable number, as our meeting houses are. Thus we find it was in Christ's and the apostles' time, 'Moses of old time hath in every city them that preach him, being read in the synagogues every sabbath day' (*Acts* 15: 21). This custom is universally supposed, both by Jews and Christians, to be begun by Ezra. There were doubtless public assemblies before the captivity in Babylon. They used to assemble at the temple at their great feasts, and were directed, when at a loss about any thing in the law, to go to the priest for instruction. And they used also to resort to the prophets' houses. And we read of synagogues in the land before (*Psa.* 74:8). But it is not supposed that they had copies of the law for constant public reading and expounding through the land before as afterwards. This was one great means of their being preserved from idolatry.

10. The next thing I would mention is God's remarkably preserving the church and nation of the Jews when they were in imminent danger of being universally destroyed by Haman. We have the story in the book of Esther, with which you are acquainted. The series of providences was very wonderful in preventing this destruction. Esther was doubtless born for this end, to be the instrument of this remarkable preservation.

11. After this the canon of Scripture was further added to in the books of Nehemiah and Esther, the one by Nehemiah himself, and whether the other was written by Nehemiah or Mordecai or Malachi is not of importance for us to know, for it is one of those books that were always admitted and received as a part of their canon by the Jews, being among the books that the Jews called their Scriptures in Christ's time, and as such approved by him. For Christ does often in his speeches to the Jews manifestly approve and confirm those books which amongst them went by the name of the Scriptures, as might be easily shown if there were time for it.

12. After this the canon of the Old Testament was completed and sealed by Malachi. The manner of his concluding his prophecy seems to imply that they were to expect no more prophecies and no more written revelations from God, until Christ should come. For in the last chapter he prophesies of Christ's coming: 'But unto you that fear my name, shall the Sun of righteousness arise with healing in his wings; and ye shall go forth and grow up as calves of the stall. And ye shall tread down the wicked; for they shall be as ashes under the soles of your feet, in the day that I shall do this, saith the LORD of hosts' (*Mal.* 4:2-3). Then we read in verse 4, 'Remember ye the law of Moses my servant, which I commanded unto him in Horeb for all Israel, with the statutes and judgments', that is, 'Remember and improve what ye have; keep close to that

written rule you have, as expecting no more additions to it, until the night of the Old Testament is over, and the Sun of righteousness shall at length arise.'

13. Soon after this, the spirit of prophecy ceased among that people until the time of the New Testament. Thus the Old Testament light, the stars of the long night, began apace to hide their heads, the time of the Sun of righteousness now drawing nigh. We before observed how the kings of the house of David ceased before the true King and Head of the church came; and how the cloud of glory withdrew before Christ, the brightness of the Father's glory, appeared; and so as to several other things. And now at last the spirit of prophecy ceased. The time of the great Prophet of God was now so nigh that it was time for the typical prophets to be silent and shut their mouths.

We have now gone through the time that we have any historical account of in the writings of the Old Testament, and the last thing that was mentioned, by which the work of redemption was promoted, was the ceasing of the spirit of prophecy. I now proceed to show how the work of redemption was carried on through the remaining times that were before Christ, in which we have not that thread of Scripture history to guide us that we have had hitherto. But we have these three things to guide us: the prophecies of the Old Testament; human histories of those times; and some occasional mention made and evidence given of some things which happened in those times in the New Testament. Therefore,

14. The next particular that I shall mention under this period is the destruction of the Persian empire and setting up of the Grecian empire by Alexander. This came to pass about sixty or seventy years after the times wherein the Prophet

Malachi is supposed to have prophesied, and about three hundred and thirty years before Christ. This was the third overturning of the world that came to pass in this period, and was greater and more remarkable than either of the foregoing. It was very remarkable on account of the suddenness of that conquest of the world which Alexander made, and the greatness of the empire which he set up, which much exceeded all the foregoing in its extent.

This event is much spoken of in the prophecies of Daniel. This empire is represented by the third kingdom of brass in Daniel's interpretation of Nebuchadnezzar's dream in Daniel 2. In Daniel's vision of the four beasts it is represented by the third beast that was like a leopard and that had on his back four wings of a fowl, to represent the swiftness of its conquest (chapter 7); and it is more particularly represented by the he-goat in chapter 8 which came from the west on the face of the whole earth and touched not the ground, to represent how swiftly Alexander over-ran the world. The angel himself expressly interprets this he-goat to signify the king of Grecia: 'The rough goat is the king of Grecia: and the great horn that is between his eyes is the first king [that is, Alexander himself] (*Dan.* 8:21).

After Alexander had conquered the world, he soon died. His dominion did not descend to his posterity, but four of his principal captains divided his empire between them, as it there follows: 'Now that being broken, whereas four stood up for it, four kingdoms shall stand up out of the nation, but not in his power.' This you may also see in Daniel 11. The angel, after foretelling the Persian empire, then proceeds to foretell of Alexander: 'And a mighty king shall stand up, that shall rule with great dominion, and do according to his will' (*Dan.* 11:3). And then he foretells, in the fourth verse, of the dividing of his kingdom between his four captains: 'And when he shall stand up, his kingdom shall be broken, and shall be divided toward the four winds of heaven; and not to his posterity, nor according to his dominion which he ruled: for his kingdom shall be plucked up, even for others besides those.' Of these four captains, two had kingdoms which were next to Judea. One had Egypt and the neighbouring countries on the south of Judea, and the other had Syria and the neighbouring countries north of Judea; and these two are those that are called the kings of the north and of the south in Daniel 11.

Now, this setting up of the Grecian empire did greatly prepare the way for Christ's coming and the setting up of his kingdom in the world. Besides those ways common to the other overturnings of the world in this period that have been already mentioned there is one peculiar to this revolution which I would take notice of which did remarkably promote the work of redemption. That was that it made the Greek language common in the world. To have one common language understood and used through the greater part of the world was a thing that did greatly prepare the way for the setting up of Christ's kingdom. This gave advantage for spreading the gospel from one nation to another, and so through all nations, with vastly greater ease, than if every nation had a distinct language and did not understand each other.

For though some of the first preachers of the gospel had the gift of languages, so that they could preach in any language, yet all had not this particular gift; and they that had, could not exercise it when they would, but only at special seasons when the Spirit of God was pleased to inspire them in this way. And the church in different parts of the world, as the churches of Jerusalem, Antioch, Galatia, Corinth, and others, which were in countries distant one from another, could not have had that communication one with another, which we have an account of in the book of Acts if they had had no common language. So it was before the Grecian empire was set up. But after this, many in all these countries well understood the same language, namely, the Greek language; which wonderfully opened the door for mutual communication between those churches, so far separated one from another.

And again, the making the Greek language common through so great a part of the world, did wonderfully make way for the setting up of the kingdom of Christ because it was the language in which the New Testament was to be originally written. The apostles propagated the gospel through many scores of nations; and if they could not have understood the Bible any otherwise than as it was translated into so many languages, it would have rendered the spreading of the gospel vastly more difficult. But, by the Greek language being made common to all, they all understood the New Testament of Jesus Christ in the language in which the apostles and evangelists originally wrote it; so that as soon as ever it was written by its original penmen, it immediately lay open to the world in a language that was commonly understood everywhere, as there was no language that was so commonly understood in the world in Christ's and the apostles' times as the Greek. The cause of this was the setting up of the Grecian empire in the world.

15. The next thing I shall take notice of is the translating of the Scriptures of the Old Testament into a language that was commonly understood by the Gentiles. The translation that I here speak of is that into the Greek language commonly called the Septuagint, or the translation of the Seventy. This is supposed to have been made about fifty or sixty years after Alexander's conquering the world. This is the first translation that ever was made of the Scriptures that we have any credible account of. The canon of the Old Testament had been completed by the prophet Malachi only about a hundred and

twenty years before in its original; and hitherto the Scriptures had remained locked up from all other nations but the Jews in the Hebrew tongue, which was understood by no other nation. But now it was translated into the Greek language, which, as we observed, was a language that was commonly understood by the nations of the world.

This translation of the Old Testament is still extant. It is commonly in the hands of learned men in these days, and is made great use of by them. The Jews have many fables about the occasion and manner of this translation, but the truth of the case is supposed to be this, that multitudes of the Jews living in other parts of the world besides Judea, and being born and bred among the Greeks, Greek became their common language and they no longer understood the original Hebrew. Therefore they procured the Scriptures to be translated for their use into the Greek language; and so henceforward the Jews in all countries except Judea were wont in their synagogues to make use of this translation instead of the Hebrew.

This translation of the Scriptures into a language commonly understood through the world, prepared the way for Christ's coming, and setting up his kingdom in the world, and afterwards did greatly promote it. For as the apostles went preaching through the world they made great use of the Scriptures of the Old Testament, and especially of the prophecies concerning Christ that were contained in them. And by means of this translation, and by the Jews being scattered everywhere, they had the Scriptures at hand in a language that was understood by the Gentiles. And they did principally make use of this translation in their preaching and writings wherever they went, as is evident by this, that in all the innumerable quotations that are made out of the Old Testament in their writings in the New Testament, they are almost everywhere in the very words of the Septuagint. The sense is the same as it is in the original Hebrew; but very often the words are different, as all that are acquainted with their Bibles know. When the apostles in their epistles and the evangelists in their histories cite passages out of the Old Testament, it is very often in different words from what we have in the Old Testament, as all know. But yet these citations are almost universally in the very words of the Septuagint version, as may be seen by comparing them together, they being both written in the same language. This makes it evident that the apostles, in their preaching and writings, commonly made use of this translation.

So this very translation was that which was principally used in Christian churches through most nations of the world for several hundred years after Christ.

16. The next thing is the wonderful preservation of the church when it was imminently threatened and persecuted under the Grecian empire.

The first time they were threatened was by Alexander himself. When he was besieging the city of Tyre he sent to the Jews for assistance and supplies for his army. They refused, out of a conscientious regard to their oath to the king of Persia. Whereupon he, being a man of a very furious spirit, agreeable to the Scripture representation of the rough he-goat, marched against them, with a design to cut them off. But the priests went out to meet him in their priestly garments and when he met them, God wonderfully turned his heart to spare them, and favour them, much as he did the heart of Esau when he met Jacob.

After this, one of the kings of Egypt, a successor of one of Alexander's four captains, entertained a design of destroying the nation of the Jews, but was remarkably and wonderfully prevented by a stronger interposition of Heaven for their preservation.

But the most wonderful preservation of them all in this period was under the cruel persecution of Antiochus Epiphanes, king of Syria, and successor of another of Alexander's four captains. The Jews were at that time subject to the power of Antiochus, and he, being enraged against them, long strove to his utmost utterly to destroy them and root them out; at least all of them that would not forsake their religion and worship his idols. And he did indeed in a great measure waste the country and depopulate the city of Jerusalem. And he profaned the temple by setting up his idols in some parts of it and persecuted the people with insatiable cruelty; so that we have no account of any persecution like his before. Many of the particular circumstances of this persecution would be very affecting, if I had time to insist on them. This cruel persecution began about an hundred and seventy years before Christ. It is much spoken of in the prophecy of Daniel, as you may see in Daniel 8:9-25 and 11:31-88, and is thought to be referred to in the New Testament, in Hebrews 11:36-38.

Antiochus intended not only to extirpate the Jewish religion, but, as far as in him lay, the very nation; and particularly laboured to the utmost to destroy all copies of the law. And considering how weak they were, in comparison with a king of such vast dominion, the providence of God appears very wonderful in defeating his design.

Many times the Jews seemed to be on the very brink of ruin, and just ready to be wholly swallowed up. Their enemies often thought themselves sure of obtaining their purpose. They once came against the people with a mighty army, and with a design of killing all, except the women and children, and of selling these for slaves; and they were so confident of obtaining their purpose, and others of purchasing, that above a thousand merchants came with the army with money in their hands to buy the slaves that should be sold. But God wonderfully stirred up and assisted one Judas, and successors of his called the Maccabees, who, with a small handful in comparison, vanquished their enemies time after time, and delivered their nation. This was foretold by Daniel (11:32). Speaking of Antiochus's persecution, he says, 'And such as do wickedly against the covenant, shall he corrupt by flatteries: but the people that do know their God, shall be strong, and do exploits.' God afterwards brought this Antiochus to a fearful, miserable end by a loathsome disease, under dreadful torments of body and horrors of mind; which was foretold in these words, 'Yet he shall come to his end, and none shall help him' (*Dan.* 11:45). After his death there were attempts still to destroy the church of God, but God baffled them all.

17. The next thing to be taken notice of is the destruction of the Grecian empire and the setting up of the Roman empire. This was the fourth overturning of the world in this period. And though it was brought to pass more gradually than the setting up of the Grecian empire, yet it far exceeded that, and was much the greatest and largest temporal monarchy that ever was in the world; so that the Roman empire was commonly called *all the world*; as it is in Luke 2:1: 'There went out a decree from Caesar Augustus, that all the world should be taxed', that is, all the Roman empire.

This empire is spoken of as much the strongest and greatest of any of the four: 'And the fourth kingdom shall be strong as iron; forasmuch as iron breaketh in pieces, and subdueth all things: and as iron that breaketh all these, shall it break in pieces and bruise' (*Dan.* 2:40). So also, Daniel 7:7, 19, 23. The time that the Romans first conquered and brought under the land of Judea was between sixty and seventy years before Christ was born. And soon after this, the Roman empire was established in its greatest extent, and the world continued subject to this empire henceforward until Christ came, and many hundred years afterwards.

The nations of the world being united in one monarchy when Christ came, and when the apostles went forth to preach the gospel, did greatly prepare the way for the spreading of the gospel and the setting up of Christ's kingdom in the world. For the world being thus subject to one government opened a communication from nation to nation, and so opportunity was given for the swifter propagating of the gospel through the world. Thus we find it to be now: if any thing prevails in the English nation, the communication is quick from one part of the nation to another, throughout all parts that are subject to the English government, much easier and quicker than to other nations which are not subject to the English government and have little to do with them. There are innumerable difficulties in travelling through different nations that are under different independent governments which do not exist in travelling through different parts of the same realm, or different dominions of the same prince. So the world being under one government, the government of the Romans, in Christ's and the apostles' times, facilitated the apostles' travelling, and the spreading of the gospel through the world.

18. About the same time learning and philosophy were risen to their greatest height in the heathen world. The time of learning's flourishing in the heathen world was principally in this period. Almost all the famous philosophers that we have an account of among the heathen were after the captivity in Babylon. Almost all the wise men of Greece and Rome flourished in this time. These philosophers, many of them, were indeed men of great temporal wisdom; and that which they in general chiefly professed to make their business was to inquire wherein man's chief happiness lay, and the way in which men might obtain happiness. They seemed earnestly to busy themselves in this inquiry, and wrote multitudes of

books about it, many of which are still extant. And they were exceedingly divided in their opinions about it. There have been reckoned up several hundreds of different opinions that they had concerning it. Thus they wearied themselves in vain and wandered in the dark, not having the glorious gospel to guide them. God was pleased to suffer men to do the utmost that they could with human wisdom, and to try the extent of their own understandings to find out the way to happiness, before the true light came to enlighten the world; before he sent the great Prophet to lead men in the right way to happiness.

God suffered these great philosophers to try what they could do for six hundred years together; and then it proved, by the events of so long a time, that all they could do was in vain. The world did not become wiser, better, or happier under their instructions, but grew more and more foolish, wicked, and miserable. He suffered their wisdom and philosophy to come to the greatest height before Christ came that it might be seen how far reason and philosophy could go in their highest ascent, that the necessity of a divine teacher might appear before Christ came. And God was pleased to make foolish the wisdom of this world, to show men the folly of their best wisdom by the doctrines of his glorious gospel, which were above the reach of all their philosophy. See 1 Corinthians 1:19-21.

And after God had showed the vanity of human learning, when set up in the room of the gospel, God was pleased to make it subservient to the purposes of Christ's kingdom, as an handmaid to divine revelation; and so the prevailing of learning in the world before Christ came made way for his coming both these ways, namely, so that thereby the vanity of human wisdom was shown, and the necessity of the gospel appeared; and also so that hereby an handmaid was prepared to the gospel. The Apostle Paul made use of it in this way. He was famed for his much learning, as you may see from Acts 26:24, and was skilled in the learning not only of the Jews but also of the philosophers, which he improved to the purposes of the gospel, as you may see in his disputing with the philosophers at Athens, Acts 17:22–31. He knew how to accommodate himself in his discourses to learned men, as appears by this discourse of his, and also how to improve what he had read in their writings, as when he here cites their own poets. Now Dionysius, a philosopher, was converted by him, and, as ecclesiastical history informs us, made a great instrument of promoting the gospel. And there were many others in that and the following ages who were eminently useful by their human learning in promoting the interests of Christ's kingdom.

19. Just before Christ was born, the Roman empire was raised to its greatest height and also settled in peace. About twenty-four years before Christ was born Augustus Caesar, the first Roman emperor, began to rule as emperor of the world. Until then the Roman empire had of a long time been a commonwealth under the government of the senate; but then it became an absolute monarchy. This Augustus Caesar, as he was the first, so he was the greatest, of all the Roman emperors and reigned in the greatest glory. Thus the power of the heathen world, which was Satan's visible kingdom, was raised to its greatest height, after it had been rising higher and higher, and strengthening itself more and more from the days of Solomon to this day, which was about a thousand years. Now it appeared at a greater height than ever it appeared from the first beginning of Satan's heathenish kingdom, which was probably about the time of the building of Babel. Now the heathen world was in its greatest glory for strength, wealth, and learning.

God did two things to prepare the way for Christ's coming, wherein he took a contrary method from that which human wisdom would have taken. He brought his own visible people very low and made them weak; but the heathen, that were his enemies, he exalted to the greatest height, for the more glorious triumph of the cross of Christ. With a small number in their greatest weakness, he conquered his enemies in their greatest glory. Thus Christ triumphed over principalities and powers in his cross.

Augustus Caesar had been for many years establishing the state of the Roman empire, subduing his enemies in one part and another, until the very year that Christ was born. Then, all his enemies being subdued, his dominion over the world seemed to be settled in its greatest glory. All was established in peace; in token whereof the Romans shut the temple of Janus, which was an established symbol among them of there being universal peace throughout the Roman empire. This universal peace, which was begun that year that Christ was born, lasted twelve years, until the year that Christ disputed with doctors in the temple.

Thus the world, after it had been, as it were, in a continual convulsion for so many hundred years together, like the four winds striving together on the tumultuous raging ocean, whence arose those four great monarchies, being now established in the greatest height of the fourth and last monarchy, and settled in quietness: now all things are ready for the birth of Christ. This remarkable universal peace after so many ages of tumult and war was a fit prelude for the ushering of the glorious Prince of Peace into the world.

Thus I have gone through the first grand period of the whole space between the Fall of man and the end of the world, namely, that from the Fall to the time of the incarnation of Christ; and I have shown the truth of the first proposition, *That from the Fall of man to the incarnation of Christ, God was doing those things that were preparatory to Christ's coming, and were forerunners of it.*

IMPROVEMENT
❦

B efore I proceed to the next proposition, I would make some few remarks, by way of improvement, upon what has been said under this proposition.

1. From what has been said, we may strongly argue that Jesus of Nazareth is indeed the Son of God and the Saviour of the world; and so that the Christian religion is the true religion, seeing that Christ is the very Person so evidently pointed at in all the great dispensations of divine providence from the very Fall of man, and was so undoubtedly in so many instances foretold from age to age, and shadowed forth in a vast variety of types and figures.

If we seriously consider the course of things from the beginning, and observe the motions of all the great wheels of providence from one age to another, we shall discern that they all tend hither. They are all as so many lines, whose course, if observed and accurately followed, will be found in every case to centre here. It is so very plain in many things, that it would argue stupidity to deny it. This therefore is undeniable, that this Person is a divine Person sent from God that came into the world with his commission and authority to do his work and to declare his mind. The great Governor of the world, in all his great works before and since the Flood, to Jews and Gentiles, down to the time of Christ's birth, has declared it.

It cannot be any vain imagination, but a plain and evident truth, that that Person that was born at Bethlehem, and dwelt at Nazareth, and at Capernaum, and was crucified without the gates of Jerusalem, must be the great Messiah, or anointed of God. And blessed are all they that believe in and confess him, and miserable are all they that deny him. This shows the unreasonableness of the Deists who deny revealed religion, and of the Jews who deny that this Jesus is the Messiah foretold and promised to their fathers.

Here it may be some persons may be ready to object and say that it may be that some subtle, cunning men contrived this history, and these prophecies, so that they should all point to Jesus Christ on purpose to confirm it, that he is the Messiah. To such it may be replied, How could such a thing be contrived by cunning men to point to Jesus Christ, long before he ever was born? How could they know that ever any such Person would be born? And how could their craft and subtlety help them to foresee and point at an event that was to come to pass many ages afterwards? For no fact can be more evident, than that the Jews had those writings long before Christ was born, as they have them still, in great veneration, wherever they are, in all their dispersions through the world; and they would never have received such a contrivance from Christians, to point to and confirm Jesus to be the Messiah, whom they always denied to be the Messiah; and much less would they have been made to believe that they always had had those books in their hands when they were first made and imposed upon them.

2. What has been said affords a strong argument for the divine authority of the books of the Old Testament, from that admirable harmony there is in them, whereby they all point to the same thing. For we may see by what has been said, how all the parts of the Old Testament, though written by so many different penmen, and in ages distant one from another, do all harmonize one with another. All agree in one, and all centre in the same thing, and that a future thing: an event which it was impossible any one of them should know but by divine revelation, even the future coming of Christ. This is most evident and manifest in them, as appears by what has been said.

Now, if the Old Testament was not inspired by God, what account can be given of such an agreement? For if these books were only human writings, written without any divine direction, then none of these penmen knew that there would come such a person as Jesus Christ into the world. His coming was only a mere figment of their own brain. If so, how happened it that this figment of theirs came to pass? How came a vain imagination of theirs, which they foretold without any manner of ground for their prediction, to be so exactly fulfilled? And especially, how did they come all to agree in it, all pointing to exactly the same thing, though many of them lived so many hundred years distant one from another?

This admirable consent and agreement in a future event is therefore a clear and certain evidence of the divine authority of those writings.

3. Hence we may learn what a weak and ignorant objection it is that some make against some parts of the Old Testament's being the Word of God, that they consist so much of histories of the wars and civil transactions of the kings and people of the nation of the Jews. Some say, We find here among the books of a particular nation histories which they kept of the state of their nation, from one age to another; histories of their kings and rulers, histories of their wars with the neighbouring nations, and histories of the changes that happened from time to time in their state and government; and so we find that other nations used to keep histories of their public affairs as well as they; and, why then should we think that these histories which the Jews kept are the Word of God, more than those of other people?

But what has been said, shows the folly and vanity of such an objection. For hereby it appears that the case of these histories is very different from that of all other histories. This history alone gives us an account of the first original of all things; and this history alone deduces things down in a wonderful series from that original, giving an idea of the grand scheme of divine providence, as tending to its great end. And, together with the doctrines and prophecies contained in it, the same book gives a view of the whole series of the great events of divine providence, from the first original to the last end and consummation of all things, giving an excellent and glorious account of the wise and holy designs of the Governor of the world in all.

No common history has such penmen as this history, which was all written by men who came with evident signs and testimonies of their being prophets of the most high God, immediately inspired.

And the histories that were written, as we have seen from what has been said under this proposition, do all contain those great events of providence, by which it appears how God has been carrying on the glorious divine work of redemption from age to age. Though they are histories, yet they are no less full of divine instruction, and those things that show forth Christ and his glorious gospel, than other parts of the holy Scriptures which are not historical.

To object against a book's being divine merely because it is historical is a poor objection; just as if that could not be the Word of God which gives an account of what is past; or as though it were not reasonable to suppose that God, in a revelation he should give mankind, would give us any relation of the dispensations of his own providence. If it be so, it must be because his works are not worthy to be related; it must be because the scheme of his government, and series of his dispensations towards his church, and towards the world that he has made, whereby he has ordered and disposed it from age to age, is not worthy that any record should be kept of it.

The objection that is made, that it is a common thing for nations and kingdoms to write histories and keep records of their wars, and the revolutions that come to pass in their territories, is so far from being a weighty objection against the historical part of Scripture, as though it were not the Word of God, that it is a strong argument in favour of it. For if reason and the light of nature teaches all civilized nations to keep records of the events of their human government, and the series of their administrations, and to publish histories for the information of others, how much more may we expect that God would give the world a record of the dispensations of his divine government, which doubtless is infinitely more worthy of a history for our information? If wise kings have taken care that there should be good histories written of the nations over which they have reigned, shall we think it incredible, that Jesus Christ should take care that his church, which is his nation, his peculiar people, should have in their hands a certain infallible history of their nation, and of his government of them?

If it had not been for the history of the Old Testament, how woefully should we have been left in the dark about many things which the church of God needs to know! How ignorant should we have been of God's dealings towards mankind, and towards his church, from the beginning! We would have been wholly in the dark about the creation of the world, the Fall of man, the first rise and continued progress of the dispensations of grace towards fallen mankind! And we should have known nothing how God at first set up a church in the world, and how it was preserved; after what manner he governed it from the beginning; how the light of the gospel first began to dawn in the world; how it increased, and how things were preparing for the coming of Christ.

If we are Christians, we belong to that building of God that has been the subject of our discourse from this text; but if it had not been for the history of the Old Testament, we should never have known what was the first occasion of God's going about this building, and how the foundation of it was laid at first, and how it has gone on from the beginning. The times of the history of the Old Testament are mostly times that no other history reaches up to; and therefore, if God had not taken care to give and preserve an account of these things for us, we should have been wholly without them.

Those that object against the authority of the Old Testament history of the nation of the Jews may as well make an objection against Moses's account of the creation, that it is historical; for, in the other, we have a history of a work no less important, namely, the work of redemption. Yea, this is a far greater and more glorious work, as we observed before; that if it be inquired which of the two works, the work of creation or the work of providence, is greater, it must be answered, the work of providence; but the work of redemption is the greatest of the works of providence.

And let those who make this objection consider what part of the Old Testament history can be spared without making a great breach in that thread or series of events by which this glorious work had been carried on. This leads me to observe,

4. That, from what has been said, we may see much of the wisdom of God in the composition of the Scriptures of the Old Testament, that is, in the parts of which it consists. By what has been said, we may see that God hath wisely given us such revelations in the Old Testament as we needed. Let us briefly take a view of the several parts of it, and of the need there was of them.

Thus it was necessary that we should have some account of the creation of the world, and of our first parents, and their primitive state, and of the Fall, and a brief account of the old world, and of the degeneracy of it, and of the universal deluge, and some account of the origin of nations after this destruction of mankind.

It seems necessary that there should be some account of the succession of the church of God from the beginning; and seeing God suffered all the world to degenerate, and only took one nation to be his people, to preserve the true worship and religion until the Saviour of the world should come, that in them the world might gradually be prepared for that great light, and those wonderful things that he was to be the author of, and that they might be a typical nation, and that in them God might shadow forth and teach, as under a veil, all future glorious things of the gospel; it was therefore necessary that we should have some account of this thing, how it was first done by the calling of Abraham, and by their being bond-slaves in Egypt, and how they were brought to Canaan. It was necessary that we should have some account of the revelation which God made of himself to that people, in giving their law, and in the appointment of their typical worship, and those things wherein the gospel is veiled, and of the forming of that people, both as to their civil and ecclesiastical state.

It seems exceeding necessary that we should have some account of their being actually brought to Canaan, the country that was their promised land, and where they always dwelt. It seems very necessary that we should have a history of the successors of the church of Israel, and of those providences of God towards them, which were most considerable and fullest of gospel mystery. It seems necessary that we should have some account of the highest promised external glory of that nation under David and Solomon, and that we should have a very particular account of David, whose history is so full of the gospel, and so necessary in order to introduce the gospel into the world, and in whom began the race of their kings; and that we should have some account of the building of the temple, which was also full of gospel mystery.

And it is a matter of great consequence, that we should have some account of Israel's dividing from Judah, and of the ten tribes' captivity and utter rejection, and a brief account why, and therefore a brief history of them until that time. It is necessary that we should have an account of the succession of the kings of Judah, and of the church, until their captivity into Babylon; and that we should have some account of their return from their captivity, and re-settlement in their own land, and of the origin of the last state that the church was in before Christ came.

A little consideration will convince every one that all these things were necessary, and that none of them could be spared; and in general that it was necessary that we should have a history of God's church until such times as are within the reach of human histories; and it was of vast importance that we should have an inspired history of those times of the Jew-ish church, wherein there was kept up a more extraordinary intercourse between God and them, and while he used to dwell among them as it were visibly, revealing himself by the Shechina, by Urim and Thummim, and by prophecy, and so more immediately to order their affairs. And it was necessary that we should have some account of the great dispensations of God in prophecy, which were to be after the finishing of inspired history; and so it was exceeding suitable and needful that there should be a number of prophets raised who should foretell the coming of the Son of God, and the nature and glory of his kingdom, to be as so many harbingers to make way for him, and that their prophecies should remain in the church.

It was also a matter of great consequence that the church should have a book of divine songs given by inspiration from God, wherein there should be a lively representation of the true spirit of devotion, of faith, hope, and divine love, joy, resignation, humility, obedience, repentance, etc., and also that we should have from God such books of moral instruc-tions as we have in Proverbs and Ecclesiastes, relating to the affairs and state of mankind, and the concerns of human life, containing rules of true wisdom and prudence for our conduct in all circumstances; and that we should have particularly a song representing the great love between Christ and his spouse the church, particularly adapted to the disposition and holy affections of a true Christian soul towards Christ, and representing his grace and marvellous love to, and delight in, his people; as we have in Solomon's Song.

And it was especially important that we should have a book to teach us how to conduct ourselves under affliction, seeing the church of God here is in a militant state, and God's people do through much tribulation enter into the kingdom of heaven; and the church is for so long a time under trouble, and meets with such exceedingly fiery trials, and extreme sufferings, before her time of peace and rest in the latter ages of the world shall come: therefore God has given us a book most proper in these circumstances, even the book of Job, written upon occasion of the afflictions of a particular saint, and was probably at first given to the church in Egypt under her afflictions there: and is made use of by the Apostle to comfort Christians under persecutors. 'Ye have heard of the patience of Job, and have seen the end of the Lord; that the Lord is very pitiful, and of tender mercy' (*James* 5:11). God was also pleased, in this book of Job, to give some view of the ancient divinity before the giving of the law.

Thus, from this brief review, I think it appears, that every part of the Scriptures of the Old Testament is very useful and necessary, and no part of it can be spared, without loss to the church. And therefore, as I said, the wisdom of God is conspicuous in ordering that the Scriptures of the Old Testament should consist of those very books of which they do consist.

Before I dismiss this particular, I would add that it is very observable that the history of the Old Testament is large and particular where the great affair of redemption required it; as where there was most done towards this work, and most to typify Christ, and to prepare the way for him. Thus it is very large and particular in the history of Abraham and the other patriarchs; but very short in the account we have of the time which the children of Israel spent in Egypt. So again it is large in the account of the redemption out of Egypt, and the first settling of the affairs of the Jewish church and nation in Moses' and Joshua's time; but much shorter in the account of the times of the Judges. So again, it is large and particular in the account of David's and Solomon's times, and then very short in the history of the ensuing reigns. Thus the accounts are large or short, just as there is more or less of the affair of redemption to be seen in them.

5. From what has been said, we may see, that Christ and his redemption are the great subjects of the whole Bible. Concerning the New Testament, the matter is plain; and by what has been said on this subject hitherto, it appears to be so also with respect to the Old Testament.

Christ and his redemption is the great subject of the prophecies of the Old Testament, as has been shown. It has also been shown, that he is the great subject of the songs of the Old Testament; and the moral rules and precepts are all given in subordination to him.

And Christ and his redemption are also the great subject of the history of the Old Testament from the beginning all along; and even the history of the creation is brought in as an introduction to the history of redemption that immediately follows it.

The whole book, both Old Testament and New, is filled up with the gospel; only with this difference, that the Old Testament contains the gospel under a veil, but the New contains it unveiled, so that we may see the glory of the Lord with open face.

6. By what has been said, we may see the usefulness and excellency of the Old Testament. Some are ready to look on the Old Testament as being, as it were, out of date, and as if we in these days of the gospel have but little to do with it; which is a very great mistake, arising from want of observing the nature and design of the Old Testament, which, if it were observed, would appear full of the gospel of Christ, and would in an excellent manner illustrate and confirm the glorious doctrines and promises of the New Testament.

Those parts of the Old Testament which are commonly looked upon as containing the least divine instruction are as it were mines and treasures of gospel knowledge; and the reason why they are thought to contain so little is, because persons do but superficially read them. The treasures which are hid underneath are not observed. They only look on the top of the ground, and so suddenly pass a judgment that there is nothing there. But they never dig into the mine. If they did, they would find it richly stored with silver and gold, and would be abundantly requited for their pains.

What has been said may show us what a precious treasure God has committed into our hands, in that he has given us the Bible. How little do most persons consider how much they enjoy in that they have the possession of that holy book the Bible, which they have in their hands, and may converse with it as they please. What an excellent book is this, and how far exceeding all human writings, that reveals God to us, and gives us a view of the grand design and glorious scheme of providence from the beginning of the world, either in history or prophecy; that reveals the great Redeemer and his glorious redemption, and the various steps by which God accomplishes it from the first foundation to the top stone!

Shall we prize a history which gives us a clear account of some great earthly prince, or mighty warrior, as of Alexander the Great, or Julius Caesar, or the Duke of Marlborough? And shall we not prize the history that God gives us of the glorious kingdom of his Son Jesus Christ, the Prince and Saviour, and of the wars and other great transactions of that King of kings, and Lord of armies, the Lord mighty in battle: the history of the things which he has wrought for the redemption of his chosen people?

7. What has been said, may make us sensible how much most persons are to blame for their inattentive, unobservant way of reading the Scriptures. How much do the Scriptures contain, if it were but observed! The Bible is the most comprehensive book in the world. But, what will all this signify to us, if we read it without observing what is the drift of the Holy Ghost in it? The Psalmist begs of God, 'Open thou mine eyes, that I may behold wondrous things out of thy law' (*Psa.* 119:18). The Scriptures are full of wondrous things.

Those histories which are commonly read as if they were only histories of the private concerns of such and such particular persons, such as the histories of Abraham, Isaac, and Jacob, and Joseph, and the history of Ruth, and the histories of particular lawgivers and princes, as the history of Joshua and the Judges, and David, and the Israelitish princes, are accounts of vastly greater things, things of greater importance, and more extensive concernment, than they that read them are commonly aware of.

The histories of Scripture are commonly read as if they were stories written only to entertain men's fancies, and to while away their leisure hours, when the infinitely great things contained or pointed at in them are passed over and never taken notice of. Whatever treasures the Scriptures contain, we shall be never the better for them if we do not observe them. He that has a Bible, and does not observe what is contained in it, is like a man who has a box full of silver and gold and does not know it, does not observe that it is any thing more than a vessel filled with common stones. As long as it is thus with him, he will be never the better for his treasure: for he that knows not that he has a treasure will never make use of what he has, and so might as well be without it. He who has plenty of the choicest food stored up in his house, and does not know it, will never taste what he has, and will be as likely to starve as if his house were empty.

8. What has been said may show us how great a person Jesus Christ is, and how great an errand he came into the world upon, seeing there was so much done to prepare the way for his coming. God had been doing nothing else but prepare the way for his coming, and doing the work which he had to do in the world, through all ages of the world from the very beginning.

If we had notice of a certain stranger's being about to come into a country, and should observe that a great preparation was made for his coming, that many months were taken up in it, and great things were done, many great alterations were made in the state of the whole country, and that many hands were employed, and persons of great note were engaged in making preparation for the coming of this person, and the whole country was overturned, and all the affairs and concerns of the country were ordered so as to be subservient to the design of entertaining that person when he should come, it would be natural for us to think with ourselves, Why, surely, this person is some extraordinary person indeed, and it is some very great business that he is coming upon.

How great a person then must he be, for whose coming into the world the great God of heaven and earth, and Governor of all things, spent four thousand years in preparing the way, going about it soon after the world was created, and from age to age doing great things, bringing mighty events to pass, accomplishing wonders without number, often overturning the world in order to it, and causing every thing in the state of mankind, and all revolutions and changes in the habitable world from generation to generation, to be subservient to this great design? Surely this must be some great and extraordinary person indeed, and a great work indeed it must needs be that he is coming about.

We read in Matthew 21:8-10 that, when Christ was coming into Jerusalem, and the multitudes ran before him and cut down branches of palm trees, and strewed them in the way, and others spread their garments in the way, and cried, 'Hosannah to the son of David', that the whole city was moved, saying, 'Who is this?' They wondered who that extraordinary person should be, that there should be such an ado made on the occasion of his coming into the city, and to prepare the way before him.

But if we consider what has been said on this subject, what great things were done in all ages to prepare the way for Christ's coming into the world, and how the world was often overturned to make way for it, much more may we cry out, 'Who is this? What great person is this?' And say (as in Psalm 24: 8,10), 'Who is this king of glory?', that God should show such respect, and put such vast honour upon him. Surely this person is honourable indeed in God's eyes, and greatly beloved of him; and surely it is a great errand upon which he is sent into the world!

PERIOD 2

❦

FROM THE INCARNATION
OF CHRIST TO HIS
RESURRECTION

Having shown how the work of redemption was carried on through the first period, from the Fall of man to the incarnation of Christ, I come now to the second period, namely, the time of Christ's humiliation, or the space from the incarnation of Christ to his resurrection. And this is the most remarkable article of time that ever was or ever will be. Though it was but between thirty and forty years, yet more was done in it than had been done from the beginning of the world to that time. We have observed that all that had been done from the Fall to the incarnation of Christ was only preparatory for what was done now. And it may also be observed, that all that was done before the beginning of time, in the eternal counsels of God, and that eternal transaction there was between the Persons of the Trinity, chiefly respected this period. We therefore now proceed to consider the second proposition, namely,

THAT DURING THE TIME OF CHRIST'S HUMILIATION, FROM HIS INCARNATION TO HIS RESURRECTION, THE PURCHASE OF REDEMPTION WAS MADE.

Though there were many things done in the affair of redemption from the Fall of man to this time, though millions of sacrifices had been offered up, yet nothing was done to purchase redemption before Christ's incarnation: no part of the purchase was made, no part of the price was offered until now.

But as soon as Christ was incarnate, then the purchase began immediately without any delay. And the whole time of Christ's humiliation, from the morning that Christ began to be incarnate, until the morning that he rose from the dead, was taken up in this purchase. And then the purchase was entirely and completely finished. As nothing was done before Christ's incarnation, so nothing was done after his resurrection, to purchase redemption for men. Nor will there ever be any thing more done to all eternity. But that very moment that the human nature of Christ ceased to remain under the power of death, the utmost farthing was paid of the price of the salvation of every one of the elect.

But for the more orderly and regular consideration of the great things done by our Redeemer to purchase redemption for us, I would speak:

1. Of Christ's becoming incarnate to capacitate himself for this purchase, and

2. Of the purchase itself.

PART 1

✎❀❧

CHRIST'S INCARNATION

First, I would consider Christ's coming into the world, or his taking upon him our nature to put himself in a capacity to purchase redemption for us. Christ became incarnate, or, which is the same thing, became man, to put himself in a capacity for working out our redemption; for though Christ, as God, was infinitely sufficient for the work, yet, as to his being in an immediate capacity for it, it was needful that he should be not only God but man.

If Christ had remained only in the divine nature he would not have been in a capacity to have purchased our salvation, not from any imperfection of the divine nature, but by reason of its absolute and infinite perfection; for Christ, merely as God, was not capable either of that obedience or of that suffering that was needful. The divine nature is not capable of suffering; for it is infinitely above all suffering. Neither is it capable of obedience to that law that was given to man. It is as impossible that one who is only God should obey the law that was given to man as it is that he should suffer man's punishment.

And it was necessary not only that Christ should take upon him a created nature but that he should take upon him *our* nature. It would not have sufficed for us for Christ to have become an angel, and to have obeyed and suffered in the angelic nature. But it was necessary that he should become a man, and that upon three accounts.

[199]

1. It was needful to answer the law that that nature should obey the law to which the law was given. Man's law could not be answered but by being obeyed by man. God insisted upon it, that the law which he had given to man should be honoured and submitted to, and fulfilled by the nature of man, otherwise the law could not be answered for men. The words that were spoken, Thou shalt not eat thereof, Thou shalt, or Thou shalt not do thus or thus, were spoken to the race of mankind, to the human nature; and therefore the human nature must fulfil them.

2. It was needful to answer the law that the nature that sinned should die. These words, 'Thou shalt surely die', respect the human nature. The same nature to which the command was given was the nature to which the threatening was directed.

3. God saw meet that the same world which was the stage of man's Fall and ruin should also be the stage of his redemption. We read often of his coming into the world to save sinners and of God's sending him into the world for this purpose. It was needful that he should come into this sinful, miserable, undone world, to restore and save it. In order to man's recovery, it was needful that he should come down to man, to the world that was man's proper habitation, and that he should tabernacle with us: 'The Word was made flesh, and dwelt among us' (*John* 1:14).

Concerning the incarnation of Christ, I would observe, these following things:

1. THE INCARNATION ITSELF, in which especially two things are to be considered, namely:

i.   *His conception*, which was in the womb of one of the race of mankind, whereby he became truly the Son of man, as he was often called. He was one of the posterity of Adam, and a child of Abraham, and a son of David, according to God's promise. But his conception was not in the way of ordinary generation, but by the power of the Holy Ghost. Christ was formed in the womb of the virgin, of the substance of her body, by the power of the Spirit of God. So that he was the immediate son of the woman, but not the immediate son of any male whatsoever; and so he was the seed of the woman, and the son of a virgin, one that had never known man.

ii.   *His birth.* Though the conception of Christ was supernatural, yet after he was conceived, and so the incarnation of Christ begun, his human nature was gradually perfected in the womb of the virgin, in a way of natural progress; and so his birth was in the way of nature. But his conception being supernatural, by the power of the Holy Ghost, he was both conceived and born without sin.

2.   ITS TIME. The second thing I would observe concerning the incarnation of Christ is the fullness of the time in which it was accomplished. It was after things had been preparing for it from the very first Fall of mankind, and when all things were ready. It came to pass at a time which, in infinite wisdom, was the most fit and proper: 'But when the fulness of time was come, God sent forth his Son, made of a woman, made under the law' (*Gal.* 4:4).

It was now the most proper time on every account. Any time before the Flood would not have been so fit a time. For then the mischief and ruin that the Fall brought on mankind was not so fully seen. The curse did not so fully come on the earth before the Flood, as it did afterwards; for though the ground was cursed in a great measure before, yet it pleased

God that the curse should once, before the restoration by Christ, be executed in a universal destruction, as it were, of the very form of the earth, that the dire effects of the Fall might once in such a way be seen before the recovery by Christ. Though mankind were mortal before the flood, yet their lives were the greater part of a thousand years in length, a kind of immortality in comparison with what the life of man is now. It pleased God that that curse, 'Dust thou art, and unto dust shalt thou return', should have its full accomplishment and be executed in its greatest degree on mankind before the Redeemer came to purchase never-ending life for man.

It would not have been so fit a time for Christ to come after the Flood but before Moses's time; for until then mankind were not so universally apostatized from the true God; they were not fallen universally into heathenish darkness; and so the need of Christ, the Light of the world, was not so evident; and the woeful consequence of the Fall with respect to man's mortality was not so fully manifest until then; for man's life was not so shortened as to be reduced to the present standard until about Moses's time.

It was most fit that the time of the Messiah's coming should not be until many ages after Moses's time; until all nations but the children of Israel had lain long in heathenish darkness; that the remedilessness of their disease might, by long experience, be seen, and so the absolute necessity of the heavenly physician, before he came.

Another reason why Christ did not come soon after the Flood probably was, that the earth might be full of people, that Christ might have the more extensive kingdom, and that the effects of his light and power and grace might be glorified, and that his victory over Satan might be attended with the more glory in the multitude of his conquests. It was also needful that the coming of Christ should be many ages after Moses that the church might be prepared which was formed by Moses for his coming, by the Messiah's being long prefigured, and by his being many ways foretold, and by his being long expected.

It was not proper that Christ should come before the Babylonish captivity because Satan's kingdom was not then come to the height. The heathen world before that consisted of lesser kingdoms. But God saw meet that the Messiah should come in the time of one of the four great monarchies of the world. Nor was it proper that he should come in the time of the Babylonish monarchy; for it was God's will, that several general monarchies should follow one another, and that the coming of the Messiah should be in the time of the last, which appeared above them all. The Persian monarchy, by overcoming the Babylonian, appeared above it: and so the Grecian, by overcoming the Persian, appeared above that; and for the same reason, the Roman above the Grecian. Now it was the will of God, that his Son should make his appearance in the world in the time of this greatest and strongest monarchy, which was Satan's visible kingdom in the world, that, by overcoming this, he might visibly overcome Satan's kingdom in its greatest strength and glory, and so obtain the more complete triumph over Satan himself.

Again it was not proper that Christ should come before the Babylonish captivity for, before that, we have not histories of the state of the heathen world to give us an idea of the need of a Saviour. And besides, before that, learning did not much flourish, and so there had not been an opportunity to show the insufficiency of human learning and wisdom to reform and save mankind. Again, before that, the Jews were not dispersed over the world, as they were afterwards; and so things were not prepared in this respect for the coming of Christ. The necessity of abolishing the Jewish dispensation was not then so apparent as it was afterwards, by reason of the dispersion of the Jews; neither was the way prepared for the propagation of the gospel as it was afterwards by the same dispersion. Many other things might be mentioned by which it would appear that no other time before that very time in which Christ did come would have been proper for his appearing in the world to purchase the redemption of men.

3. ITS GREATNESS. The next thing that I would observe concerning the incarnation of Christ is the greatness of this event. Christ's incarnation was a greater and more wonderful thing than ever had come to pass; and there has been but one that has ever come to pass which was greater, and that was the death of Christ, which was afterwards. But Christ's incarnation was a greater thing than had ever come to pass before. The creation of the world was a very great thing, but not so great a thing as the incarnation of Christ. It was a great thing for God to make the creature, but not so great as for God, as for the Creator himself, to become a creature. We have spoken of many great things that were accomplished from one age to another in the ages between the Fall of man and the incarnation of Christ, but God's becoming man was a greater thing than they all. When Christ was born, the greatest Person was born that ever was or ever will be born.

4. ITS CIRCUMSTANCES. What I would next observe concerning the incarnation of Christ are the remarkable circumstances of it, such as his being born of a virgin that was a pious holy person but poor, as appeared by her offering at her purification: 'And to offer a sacrifice according to that which is said in the law of the Lord, a pair of turtle doves or two young pigeons' (*Luke* 2:24). Which refers to Leviticus 5:7: 'And if he be not able to bring a lamb, then he shall bring two turtle doves, or two young pigeons.' And this poor virgin was espoused to a husband who was a poor man. Though they

were both of the royal family of David, the most honourable family, and Joseph was the rightful heir to the crown, yet the family was reduced to a very low state; which is represented by the tabernacle of David's being fallen or broken down, 'In that day will I raise up the tabernacle of David that is fallen, and close up the breaches thereof, and I will raise up his ruins, and I will build it as in the days of old' (*Amos* 9:11).

He was born in the town of Bethlehem, as was foretold; and there was a very remarkable providence of God to bring about the fulfilment of this prophecy, the taxing of all the world by Augustus Caesar, as in Luke 2. He was born in a very low condition, even in a stable, and laid in a manger.

5. ITS CONCOMITANTS. I would observe the concomitants of this great event, or the remarkable events with which it was attended.

i. The first thing I would take notice of that attended the incarnation of Christ, was *the return of the Spirit*; which indeed began a little before the incarnation of Christ, but yet was given on occasion of that, as it was to reveal either his birth or the birth of his forerunner, John the Baptist. I have before observed how the spirit of prophecy ceased not long after the book of Malachi was written. From about the same time visions and immediate revelations ceased also. But now, on this occasion, they are granted anew, and the Spirit in these operations returns again.

The first instance of this restoration that we have any account of is in the vision of Zacharias, the father of John the Baptist, which we read of in the first chapter of Luke. The next is in the vision which the virgin Mary had, of which we read also in the same chapter. The third is in the vision which Joseph had, of which we read in the first chapter of Matthew. In the next place, the Spirit was given to Elisabeth (*Luke*

1:41). Next to Mary, as appears by her song (*Luke* 1:46-55). Then to Zacharias again, verse 64. Then the Spirit was sent to the shepherds, of which we have an account in Luke 2:9. Then to Simeon (*Luke* 2:25). Then to Anna, verse 36. Then to the wise men in the east. Then to Joseph again, directing him to flee into Egypt, and after that directing his return.

ii. The next concomitant of Christ's incarnation that I would observe is *the great notice that was taken of it* in heaven and on earth. How it was noticed by the glorious inhabitants of the heavenly world appears by their joyful songs on this occasion, heard by the shepherds in the night. This was the greatest event of providence that ever the angels had beheld. We read of their singing praises when they saw the formation of this lower world: 'When the morning stars sang together, and all the sons of God shouted for joy' (*Job* 38: 7). And as they sang praises then, so they do now, on this much greater occasion of the birth of the Son of God, who is the Creator of the world.

The glorious angels had all along expected this event. They had taken great notice of the prophecies and promises of these things all along, for we are told that the angels desire to look into the affairs of redemption (*1 Pet.* 1:12). They had all along been the ministers of Christ in this affair of redemption, in all the several steps of it down from the very Fall of man. So we read, that they were employed in God's dealings with Abraham, and in his dealings with Jacob, and in his dealings with the Israelites from time to time. And doubtless they had long joyfully expected the coming of Christ; but now they see it accomplished, and therefore greatly rejoice, and sing praises on this occasion.

Notice was taken of it by some among the Jews; as particularly by Elisabeth and the virgin Mary before the birth of Christ; not to mention by John the Baptist before he was born, when he leaped in his mother's womb, as it were for joy, at the voice of the salutation of Mary. But Elisabeth and Mary do most joyfully praise God together when they meet with Christ and his forerunner in their wombs, and the Holy Spirit in their souls. And afterwards what joyful notice is taken of this event by the shepherds, and by those holy persons Zacharias and Simeon and Anna! How do they praise God on this occasion! Thus the church of God in heaven and the church on earth do, as it were, unite in their joy and praise on this occasion.

Notice was taken of it by the Gentiles, which appears in the wise men of the east. Great part of the universe does, as it were, take a joyful notice of the incarnation of Christ. Heaven takes notice of it, and the inhabitants sing for joy. This lower world, the world of mankind, does also take notice of it in both parts of it, Jews and Gentiles. It pleased God to put honour on his Son, by wonderfully stirring up some of the wisest of the Gentiles to come a long journey to see and worship the Son of God at his birth, being led by a miraculous star, signifying the birth of that glorious Person who is the bright and morning star, going before, and leading them to the very place where the young child was.

Some think they were instructed by the prophecy of Balaam, who dwelt in the eastern parts, and foretold Christ's coming as a star that should rise out of Jacob. Or they might be instructed by that general expectation there was of the Messiah's coming about that time, before spoken of, from the notice they had of it by the prophecies the Jews had of him in their dispersions in all parts of the world at that time.

iii. The next concomitant of the birth of Christ was *his circumcision*. But this may more properly be spoken of under another head, and so I will not insist upon it now.

iv. The next concomitant was *his first coming into the second temple*, which was his being brought thither when an infant, on occasion of the purification of the blessed virgin. We read, 'The desire of all nations shall come: and I will fill this house [or temple] with glory' (*Hag.* 2:7). And in Malachi 3:1, 'The Lord, whom ye seek, shall suddenly come to his temple, even the messenger of the covenant.' And now was the first instance of the fulfilment of these prophecies.

v. The last concomitant I shall mention is *the sceptre's departing from Judah* in the death of Herod the Great. The sceptre had never totally departed from Judah until now. Judah's sceptre was greatly diminished in the revolt of the ten tribes in Jeroboam's time; and the sceptre departed from Israel or Ephraim at the time of the captivity of the ten tribes by Shalmaneser. But yet the sceptre remained in the tribe of Judah under the kings of the house of David. And when the tribes of Judah and Benjamin were carried captive by Nebuchadnezzar, the sceptre of Judah ceased for a little while, until the return from the captivity under Cyrus: and then, though they were not an independent government, as they had been before, but owed fealty to the kings of Persia, yet their governor was of themselves, who had the power of life and death, and they were governed by their own laws; and so Judah had a lawgiver from between his feet during the Persian and Grecian monarchies.

Towards the latter part of the Grecian monarchy, the people were governed by kings of their own, of the race of the Maccabees, for the greater part of an hundred years; and after that they were subdued by the Romans. But yet the Romans suffered them to be governed by their own laws, and to have a king of their own, Herod the Great, who reigned about forty years, and governed with proper kingly authority, only paying homage to the Romans. But presently after Christ was born he died, as we have an account, Matthew 2:19, and Archelaus succeeded him; but was soon put down by the Roman Emperor; and then the sceptre departed from Judah. There were no more temporal kings of Judah after that, neither had that people their governors from the midst of themselves after that, but were ruled by a Roman governor sent among them; and they ceased any more to have the power of life and death among themselves. Hence the Jews say to Pilate, 'It is not lawful for us to put any man to death' (*John* 18:31). Thus the sceptre departed from Judah when Shiloh came.

PART 2

❧❧❧

CHRIST'S PURCHASE OF
REDEMPTION

Having thus considered Christ's coming into the world, and his taking on him our nature, to put himself in a capacity for the purchase of redemption, I come now, secondly, to speak of the purchase itself. And in speaking of this, I would:

1. Show what is intended by the purchase of redemption.

2. Observe some things in general concerning those things by which this purchase was made.

3. Consider in order those things which Christ did and suffered by which that purchase was made.

1. I would show what is here intended by *Christ purchasing redemption*. There are two things that are intended by it, namely, his *satisfaction* and his *merit*. All is done by the price that Christ lays down. But the price that Christ lays down does two things: i. it pays our debt, and so it *satisfies*; ii. by its intrinsic value, and by the agreement between the Father and the Son, it procures a title for us to happiness, and so it *merits*. The satisfaction of Christ is to free us from misery, and the merit of Christ is to purchase happiness for us.

The word *purchase*, as it is used with respect to the purchase of Christ, is taken either more strictly or more largely. It is oftentimes used more strictly, to signify only the merit of Christ; and sometimes more largely, to signify both his satisfaction and merit.

Indeed most of the words which are used in this affair have various significations. Thus sometimes divines use *merit* in this affair for the whole price that Christ offered, both satisfactory and also positively meritorious. And so the word *satisfaction* is sometimes used, not only for his propitiation, but also for his meritorious obedience. For in some sense, not only suffering the penalty but positively obeying is needful to satisfy the law. The reason of this various use of these terms seems to be that satisfaction and merit do not differ so much really as relatively. They both consist in paying a valuable price, a price of infinite value. But that price, as it respects a debt to be paid, is called satisfaction; and as it respects a positive good to be obtained, it is called merit. The difference between paying a debt, and making a positive purchase is more relative than it is essential. He who lays down a price to pay a debt does in some sense make a purchase: he purchases liberty from the obligation. And he who lays down a price to purchase a good does as it were make satisfaction: he satisfies the conditional demands of him to whom he pays it. This may suffice concerning what is meant by the purchase of Christ.

2. I now proceed to some general observations concerning *those things by which this purchase was made.*

i.   Here I would observe that, whatever in Christ had the nature of satisfaction, it was by virtue of the suffering or humiliation that was in it. But whatever had the nature of merit, it was by virtue of the obedience or righteousness that was in it. The satisfaction of Christ consists in his answering the demands of the law on man, which were consequent on the breach of the law. These were answered by suffering the penalty of the law. The merit of Christ consists in what he did to answer the demands of the law, which were prior to man's breach of the law, or to fulfil what the law demanded before man sinned, which was obedience.

The satisfaction or propitiation of Christ consists either in his suffering evil, or his being subject to abasement. For Christ did not only make satisfaction by proper suffering but by whatever had the nature of humiliation, and abasement of circumstances. Thus Christ made satisfaction for sin, by continuing under the power of death, while he lay buried in the grave, though neither his body nor soul properly endured any suffering after he was dead. Whatever Christ was subject to, that was the judicial fruit of sin, and had the nature of satisfaction for sin. But not only proper suffering but all abasement and depression of the state and circumstances of mankind below its primitive honour and dignity, such as his body's remaining under death, and body and soul remaining separate, and other things that might be mentioned, are the judicial fruits of sin. And all that Christ did in his state of humiliation that had the nature of obedience or moral virtue or goodness in it, in one respect or another had the nature of merit in it, and was part of the price with which he purchased happiness for the elect.

ii. I would observe that both Christ's satisfaction for sin, and also his meriting happiness by his righteousness, were carried on through the whole time of his humiliation. Christ's satisfaction for sin was not only by his last sufferings, though it was principally by them, but all his sufferings, and all the humiliation that he was subject to from the first moment of his incarnation to his resurrection, were propitiatory or satisfactory. Christ's satisfaction was chiefly by his death, because his sufferings and humiliation in that were greatest. But all his other sufferings, and all his other humiliation, all along had the nature of satisfaction. So had the mean circumstances in which he was born. His being born in such a low condition, was to make satisfaction for sin. His being born of a poor virgin, in a stable, and his being laid in a manger; his taking the human nature upon him in its low state, and under those infirmities brought upon it by the Fall; his being born in the form of sinful flesh, had the nature of satisfaction.

So all his sufferings in his infancy and childhood, and all that labour, and contempt, and reproach, and temptation, and difficulty of any kind, or that he suffered through the whole course of his life, was of a propitiatory and satisfactory nature.

And so his purchase of happiness by his righteousness was also carried on through the whole time of his humiliation until his resurrection; not only in that obedience he performed through the course of his life, but also in the obedience he performed in laying down his life.

iii. It was by the same things that Christ hath satisfied God's justice, and also purchased eternal happiness. This satisfaction and purchase of Christ were not only both carried on through the whole time of Christ's humiliation, but they were both carried on by the same things. He did not make satisfaction by some things that he did, and then work out a righteousness by other different things. In the same acts by which he wrought out righteousness, he also made satisfaction, but only taken in a different relation. One and the same act of Christ, considered with respect to the obedience there was in it, was part of his righteousness, and purchased heaven: but considered with respect to the self denial and difficulty and humiliation with which he performed it, had the nature of satisfaction for sin, and procured our pardon. Thus his going about doing good, preaching the gospel, and teaching his disciples, was a part of his righteousness, and purchase of heaven, as it was done in obedience to the Father; and the same was a part of his satisfaction, as he did it with great labour, trouble, and weariness, and under great temptations, exposing himself hereby to reproach and contempt.

So his laying down his life had the nature of satisfaction to God's offended justice, considered as his bearing our punishment in our stead; but considered as an act of obedience to God, who had given him this command, that he should lay down his life for sinners, it was a part of his righteousness, and purchase of heaven, and as much the principal part of his righteousness as it was the principal part of his satisfaction. And so to instance in his circumcision, what he suffered in that had the nature of satisfaction: the blood that was shed in his circumcision was propitiatory blood; but, as it was a conformity to the law of Moses, it was part of his meritorious righteousness. Though it was not properly the act of his human nature, he being an infant, yet, it being what the human nature was the subject of, and being the act of that Person, it was accepted as an act of his obedience, as our Mediator.

And so even his being born in such a low condition had the nature of satisfaction, by reason of the humiliation that was in it, and also of righteousness, as it was the act of his Person in obedience to the Father, and what the human nature was the subject of, and what the will of the human nature did acquiesce in, though there was no act of the will of the human nature prior to it. These things may suffice to have observed in general concerning the purchase Christ made of redemption.

3. I now proceed *to speak more particularly of those things which Christ did and was the subject of during the time of his*

humiliation whereby this purchase was made. And the nature of the purchase of Christ, as it has been explained, leads us to consider these things under a twofold view, namely,

   i. With respect to his righteousness which appeared in them.

  ii. With respect to the sufferings and humiliation that he was subject to in them in our stead.

   i. I will consider the things that passed during the time of Christ's humiliation, *with respect to the obedience and righteousness that he exercised in them.* And this is subject to a threefold distribution. I shall therefore consider his obedience,

  a. With respect to the laws which he obeyed.
  b. With respect to the different stages of his life in which he performed it.
  c. With respect to the virtues he exercised in his obedience.

  a. The first distribution of the acts of Christ's righteousness is *with respect to the laws which Christ obeyed* in that righteousness which he performed.

But here it must be observed in general that all the precepts which Christ obeyed may be reduced to one law, and that is that which the apostle calls the law of works (*Rom.* 3:27). Every command that Christ obeyed may be reduced to that great and everlasting law of God that is contained in the covenant of works, that eternal rule of right which God had established between himself and mankind. Christ came into the world to fulfil and answer the covenant of works, that is, the covenant that is to stand for ever as a rule of judgment. That was the covenant that we had broken, and that was the covenant that must be fulfilled.

This law of works indeed includes all the laws of God which ever have been given to mankind, for it is a general rule of the law of works, and indeed of the law of nature, that God is to be obeyed, and that he must be submitted to in whatever positive precept he is pleased to give us. It is a rule of the law of works that men should obey their earthly parents; and it is certainly as much a rule of the same law that we should obey our heavenly Father. So the law of works requires obedience to all positive commands of God. It required Adam's obedience to the positive command not to eat of the forbidden fruit; and it required obedience of the Jews to all the positive commands of their institution. When God commanded Jonah to arise and go to Nineveh, the law of works required him to obey; and so it required Christ's obedience to all the positive commands which God gave him.

But, more particularly, the commands of God which Christ obeyed were of three kinds: they were such as he was subject to merely as man, or such as he was subject to as he was a Jew, or such as he was subject to purely as Mediator.

He obeyed those commands which he was subject to *merely as man*; and they were the commands of the moral law, which was the same with that which was given at Mount Sinai, written in two tables of stone, which are obligatory on mankind of all nations and all ages of the world.

He obeyed all those laws he was subject to *as he was a Jew*. Thus he was subject to the ceremonial law, and was conformed to it. He was conformed to it in his being circumcised the eighth day; and he strictly obeyed it in going up to Jerusalem to the temple three times a year, at least after he was come to the age of twelve years, which seems to have been the age when the males began to go up to the temple. And so Christ constantly attended the service of the temple and of the synagogues. To this head of his obedience to the law that he was subject to as a Jew may be reduced his submission to John's baptism. For it was a special command to the Jews to go forth to John the Baptist and be baptized of him; and therefore Christ, being a Jew, was subject to this command. And therefore, when he came to be baptized of John, and John objected, that he had more need to come to him to be baptized of him, he gives this reason for it, that it was needful that he should do it, that he might fulfil all righteousness (*Matt.* 3:13–15).

Another law that Christ was subject to was *the mediatorial law*, which contained those commands of God to which he was subject, not merely as man, nor yet as a Jew, but which related purely to his mediatorial office. Such were the commands which the Father gave him, to teach such doctrines, to preach the gospel, to work such miracles, to call such disciples, to appoint such ordinances, and finally to lay down his life: for he did all these things in obedience to commands he had received of the Father, as he often tells us. And these commands he was not subject to merely as man, for they did not belong to other men; nor yet was he subject to them as a Jew, for they were no part of the Mosaic law; but they were commands that he had received of the Father that purely respected the work he was to do in the world in his mediatorial office.

And it is to be observed that Christ's righteousness by which he merited heaven for himself and all who believe in him consists principally in his obedience to this mediatorial law, for in fulfilling this law consisted his chief work and business in the world. The history of the evangelists is chiefly taken up in giving an account of his obedience to this law: and this part of his obedience was that which was attended with the greatest difficulty of all; and therefore his obedience in it was most meritorious.

What Christ had to do in the world by virtue of his being Mediator, was infinitely more difficult than what he had to do merely as a man, or as a Jew. To his obedience to this mediatorial law belongs his going through his last sufferings, beginning with his agony in the garden, and ending with his resurrection.

As the obedience of the first Adam, wherein his righteousness would have consisted if he had stood, would have mainly consisted, not in his obedience to the moral law, to which he was subject merely as man, but in his obedience to that special law that he was subject to as moral head and surety of mankind – the command of abstaining from the tree of knowledge of good and evil – so the obedience of the second Adam, wherein his righteousness consists, lies mainly, not in his obedience to the law that he was subject to merely as man, but in his obedience to that special law which he was subject to in his office as Mediator and surety for man.

Before I proceed to the next distribution of Christ's righteousness, I would observe three things concerning Christ's obedience to these laws.

1. He performed that obedience to them which was *in every respect perfect*. It was universal as to the kinds of laws that he was subject to. He obeyed each of these three laws. And it was universal with respect to every individual precept contained in these laws and perfect as to each command. It was perfect as to positive transgressions avoided, for he never transgressed in one instance; he was guilty of no sin of commission. It was perfect with respect to the work commanded, for he perfected the whole work that each command required and never was guilty of any sin of omission. And it was perfect with respect to the principle from which he obeyed; his heart was perfect, his principles were wholly right, there was no corruption in his heart. And it was perfect with respect to the ends he acted for, for he never had any by-ends but aimed perfectly at such ends as the law of God required. And it was perfect with respect to the manner of performance; every circumstance of each act was perfectly conformed to the

command. And it was perfect with respect to the degree of the performance; he acted wholly up to the rule. And it was perfect with respect to the constancy of obedience; he did not only perfectly obey sometimes but constantly, without any interruption. And it was perfect with respect to perseverance; he held out in perfect obedience to the very end, through all the changes he passed through, and all the trials that were before him.

The meritoriousness of Christ's obedience, depends on the perfection of it. If it had failed in any instance of perfection, it could not have been meritorious; for imperfect obedience is not accepted as any obedience at all in the sight of the law of works, which was that law that Christ was subject to; for that is not accepted as an obedience to a law that does not answer that law.

2. The next thing I would observe of Christ's obedience is that it was performed *through the greatest trials and temptations* that ever any obedience was. His obedience was attended with the greatest difficulties and most extreme abasement and sufferings that ever any obedience was. This was another thing that rendered it more meritorious and thankworthy. To obey another when his commands are easy is not so worthy as it is to obey when it cannot be done without great difficulty.

3. He performed this obedience *with infinite respect to God, and the honour of his law*. The obedience he performed was with infinitely greater love to God and regard to his authority, than the angels perform their obedience with. The angels perform their obedience with that love which is perfect, with sinless perfection. But Christ performed his obedience with much greater love than the angels do theirs, even infinite love; for though the human nature of Christ was not capable

of love absolutely infinite, yet Christ's obedience that was performed in that human nature is not to be looked upon as merely the obedience of the human nature, but the obedience of his Person, as God-man; and there was infinite love of the Person of Christ manifest in that obedience. And this, together with the infinite dignity of the Person that obeyed, rendered his obedience infinitely meritorious.

b. The second distribution of the acts of Christ's obedience is with respect to the different parts of his life wherein they were performed. And in this respect they may be divided into those which were performed in private life and those which were performed in his public ministry.

As to those acts he performed *during his private life*, he was perfectly obedient in his childhood. He infinitely differed from other children who, as soon as they begin to act, begin to sin and rebel. He was subject to his earthly parents, though he was Lord of all (*Luke* 2:51). He was found about his Father's business at twelve years of age in the temple (*Luke* 2:42). He then began that work that he had to do in fulfilment of the mediatorial law which the Father had given him. He continued his private life for about thirty years, dwelling at Nazareth in the house of his reputed father Joseph, where he served God in a private capacity, and in following a mechanical trade, the business of a carpenter.

As to those acts which he performed *during his public ministry*, these began when he was about thirty years of age and continued for the last three years and a half of his life. Most of the history of the evangelists is taken up in giving an account of what passed during these three years and a half; so is all the history of the Evangelist Matthew, excepting the first two chapters. So is the whole of the history of the Evangelist Mark; it begins and ends with it. And so also is all the gospel of John, and all the gospel of Luke, excepting the first two chapters. A further exception is what we find in the evangelists concerning the ministry of John the Baptist. Christ's first appearing in his public ministry is often called his coming in Scripture. Thus John speaks of Christ's coming as what is yet to be, though he had been born long before.

Concerning *the public ministry of Christ*, I would observe the following things: the forerunner of it; the manner of his first entering upon it; the works in which he was employed during the course of it; and the manner of his finishing it.

The *forerunner* of Christ's coming in his public ministry was John the Baptist: he came preaching repentance for the remission of sins, to make way for Christ's coming, agreeable to the prophecies of him (*Isa.* 40:3-5; *Matt.* 4:5-6). It is supposed that John the Baptist began his ministry about three years and a half before Christ, so that John's ministry and Christ's put together made seven years, which was the last of Daniel's weeks; and this time is intended in Daniel 9:27: 'He will confirm the covenant with many for one week.' Christ came in the midst of this week, namely, in the beginning of the last half of it, or the last three years and a half, as Daniel foretold in the verse just now quoted: 'And in the midst of the week he shall cause the sacrifice and the oblation to cease.'

John the Baptist's ministry consisted principally in preaching the law to awaken men and convince them of sin, to prepare men for the coming of Christ to comfort them, as the law is to prepare the heart for the entertainment of the gospel.

A very remarkable outpouring of the Spirit of God attended John's ministry. The effect of it was that Jerusalem, and all Judea, and all the region round about Jordan, were awakened, convinced, went out to him, and submitted to his baptism, confessing their sins. John is spoken of as the greatest of all the prophets who came before Christ: 'Among those that are born of women, there hath not risen a greater than John the Baptist' (*Matt.* 11:11); that is, he had the most honourable office. He was as the morning star, which is the harbinger of the approaching day and forerunner of the rising sun. The other prophets were stars that were to give light in the night; but we have heard how those stars went out on the approach of the gospel day. Now, the coming of Christ being very nigh, the morning star comes before him, the brightest of all the stars, as John the Baptist was the greatest of all the prophets.

And when Christ came in his public ministry, the light of that morning star decreased too; as we see, when the sun rises it diminishes the light of the morning star. So John the Baptist says of himself, 'He must increase, but I must decrease' (*John* 3:30). And soon after Christ began his public ministry, John the Baptist was put to death, as the morning star is visible a little while after the sun is risen yet soon goes out.

The next thing to be taken notice of is *Christ's entrance on his public ministry*. This was by baptism, followed with the temptation in the wilderness. His baptism was, as it were, his solemn inauguration, by which he entered on his ministry; and was attended with his being anointed with the Holy Ghost, in a solemn and visible manner, the Holy Ghost descending upon him in a visible shape like a dove, attended with a voice from heaven, saying, 'This is my beloved Son, in whom I am well pleased' (*Matt.* 3:17).

After this he was led by the devil into the wilderness. Satan made a violent onset upon him at his first entrance on his work, and now he had a remarkable trial of his obedience. But he got the victory. He who had such success with the first Adam had none with the second.

I would take notice of *the work in which Christ was employed during his ministry*. And here there are three things chiefly to be taken notice of, namely, his *preaching*, his *working miracles*, and his *calling and appointing disciples* and ministers of his kingdom.

1. *His preaching the gospel.* A great part of the work of his public ministry consisted in this, and much of that obedience by which he purchased salvation for us was in his speaking those things which the Father commanded him. He more clearly and abundantly revealed the mind and will of God, than ever it had been revealed before. He came from the bosom of the Father, and perfectly knew his mind, and was in the best capacity to reveal it. As the sun, as soon as it is risen, begins to shine, so Christ, as soon as he came into his public ministry, began to enlighten the world with his doctrine. As the law was given at Mount Sinai, so Christ delivered his evangelical doctrine, full of blessings, and not curses, to a multitude on a mountain, as we have an account of in Matthew 5–7.

When he preached he did not teach as the scribes, but he taught as one having authority, so that his bearers were astonished at his doctrine. He did not reveal the mind and will of God in the style in which the prophets used to preach, as not speaking their own words, but the words of another, using such a style as this, 'Thus saith the LORD'; but Christ spoke in such a style as this, 'I say unto you', thus or thus; 'Verily, verily, I say unto you'. He delivered his doctrines, not only as the doctrines of God the Father, but as his own doctrines. He gave forth his commands, not as the prophets were wont to do, as God's commands, but as his own commands. He spoke in such a style as this, 'This is my commandment' (*John* 15:12). 'Ye are my friends, if ye do whatsoever I command you' (verse 14).

2. Another thing that Christ was employed in during the course of his ministry, was *working miracles.* Concerning these we may observe several things:

Their multitude. Besides particular instances, we often have an account of multitudes coming at once with diseases and his healing them.

They were *works of mercy.* In them was displayed not only his infinite power and greatness, but his infinite mercy and goodness. He went about doing good, healing the sick, restoring sight to the blind, hearing to the deaf, and the proper use of their limbs to the lame and halt; feeding the hungry, cleansing the leprous, and raising the dead.

They were almost all of them such as had been spoken of as *the peculiar works of God* in the Old Testament. So with respect to stilling the sea, 'He maketh the storm a calm, so that the waves thereof are still' (*Psa.* 107:29). So as to walking on the sea in a storm, 'Which alone . . . treadeth upon the waves of the sea' (*Job* 9:8). So as to casting out devils, 'Thou brakest the heads of leviathan in pieces' (*Psa.* 74:14). So as to feeding a multitude in a wilderness, 'Who fed thee in the wilderness with manna' (*Deut.* 8:16). So as to telling man's thoughts, 'Lo, he that . . . declareth unto man what is his thought . . . the LORD, The God of hosts, is his name' (*Amos* 4:13). So as to raising the dead, 'Unto GOD the Lord belong the issues from death' (*Psa.* 68:20). So as to opening the eyes of the blind, 'The LORD openeth the eyes of the blind' (*Psa.* 146:8). So as to healing the sick, 'Who healeth all thy diseases' (*Psa.* 103:3). So as to lifting up those who are bowed together, 'The LORD raiseth them that are bowed down' (*Psa.* 146:8).

They were in general such works as were *images of the great work which he came to work on man's heart*; representing that inward, spiritual cleansing, healing, renovation, and resurrection, which all his redeemed are the subjects of.

He wrought them in such a manner as to show that he did them *by his own power,* and not by the power of another, as the other prophets did. They were wont to work all their miracles in the name of the Lord; but Christ wrought in his own name. Moses was forbidden to enter into Canaan because he seemed by his speech to assume the honour of working only one miracle to himself. Nor did Christ work miracles as the apostles did, who wrought them all in the name of Christ; but he wrought them in his own name, and by his own authority and will. Thus, saith he, 'I will; be thou clean' (*Matt.*8:3). And in the same strain he put the question, 'Believe ye that I am able to do this?' (*Matt.* 9:28).

3. Another thing that Christ did in the course of his ministry was to *call his disciples*. He called many disciples. There were many that he employed as ministers. He sent seventy disciples at one time in this work; but there were twelve that he set apart as apostles who were the grand ministers of his kingdom and, as it were, the twelve foundations of his church (see Revelation 21:14). These were the main instruments of setting up his kingdom in the world and therefore shall sit on twelve thrones, judging the twelve tribes of Israel.

I would also observe *how he finished his ministry*. And this was,

1. In giving his dying counsels to his disciples, and all that should be his disciples, which we have recorded particularly in John 14-16.

2. In instituting a solemn memorial of his death. This he did in instituting the sacrament of the Lord's supper, wherein we have a representation of his body broken and of his blood shed.

3. In offering up himself, as God's high priest, a sacrifice to God, which he did in his last sufferings. This act he did as God's minister, as God's anointed priest; and it was the greatest act of his public ministry, the greatest act of his obedience, by which he purchased heaven for believers. The priests of old used to do many other things as God's ministers; but then were they in the highest execution of their office when they were actually offering sacrifice on the altar. So the greatest thing that Christ did in the execution of his priestly office, and the greatest thing that he ever did, and the greatest thing

that ever was done, was the offering up himself a sacrifice to God. Herein he was the antitype of all that had been done by all the priests, in all their sacrifices and offerings, from the beginning of the world.

c. The third distribution of the acts by which Christ purchased redemption regards the virtues that Christ exercised and manifested in them. And here I would observe that Christ, in doing the work that he had to do here in the world for our redemption, exercised every possible virtue and grace. Indeed there are some particular virtues that sinful man may have that were not in Christ, not from any want or defect of virtue, but because his virtue was perfect and without defect. Such is the virtue of repentance, and brokenness of heart for sin, and mortification, and denying of lust. Those virtues were not in Christ, because he had no sin of his own to repent of, nor any lust to deny. But all virtues which do not presuppose sin were in him, and that in a higher degree than ever they were in any other man, or any mere creature. Every virtue in him was perfect. Virtue itself was greater in him than in any other; and it was under greater advantages to shine in him than in any other. Strict virtue shines most when most tried; but never any virtue had such trials as Christ's had.

The virtues that Christ exercised in the work he did may be divided into three sorts, namely, the virtues which more immediately respect God, those which immediately respect himself, and those which immediately respect men.

1. *Those virtues which more immediately respect God* appeared in Christ in the work that he did for our redemption. There appeared in him a holy fear and reverence towards God the Father. Christ had a greater trial of his virtue in this respect than any other had, from the honourableness of his Person. This was the temptation of the angels that fell, to cast off their worship of God and reverence of his majesty, since

they were beings of such exalted dignity and worthiness themselves. But Christ was infinitely more worthy and honourable
than they, for he was the eternal Son of God, and his Person
was equal to the Person of God the Father; and yet, as he had
taken on him the office of Mediator, and the nature of man,
he was full of reverence towards God. He had obeyed him in
the most reverential manner time after time. So he manifested
a wonderful love towards God. The angels give great testimonies of their love towards God, in their constancy and agility
in doing the will of God; and many saints have given great
testimonies of their love, who, from love to God, have
endured great labours and sufferings. But none ever gave such
testimonies of love to God as Christ has given; none ever performed such a labour of love as he, and suffered so much from
love to God. So he manifested the most wonderful submission
to the will of God. Never was any one's submission so tried as
his was. So he manifested the most wonderful spirit of obedience that ever was manifested.

2. In this work he most wonderfully manifested *those
virtues which more immediately respected himself*; as particularly humility, patience and contempt of the world. Christ,
though he was the most excellent and honourable of all men,
yet was the most humble; yea, he was the most humble of all
creatures. No angel or man ever equalled him in humility,
though he was the highest of all creatures in dignity and honourableness. Christ would have been under the greatest
temptations to pride, if it had been possible for any thing to
be a temptation to him. The temptation of the angels that fell
was the dignity of their nature, and the honourableness of
their circumstances; but Christ was infinitely more honourable than they. The human nature of Christ was so honoured
as to be in the same Person with the eternal Son of God, who
was equal with God; and yet that human nature was not at all
lifted up with pride. Nor was the man Christ Jesus at all lifted

up with pride with all those wonderful works which he wrought, of healing the sick, curing the blind, lame, and maimed, and raising the dead. And though he knew that God had appointed him to be the king over heaven and earth, angels and men, as he says, 'All things are delivered unto me of my Father' (*Matt.* 11: 27); though he knew he was such an infinitely honourable Person, and thought it not robbery to be equal with God; and though he knew he was the heir of God the Father's kingdom; yet such was his humility that he did not disdain to be abased and depressed down into lower and viler circumstances and sufferings than ever any other elect creature was; so that he became least of all, and lowest of all.

The proper trial and evidence of humility is stooping or complying with those acts or circumstances, when called to it, which are very low and contain great abasement. But none ever stooped so low as Christ, if we consider either the infinite height that he stooped from or the great depth to which he stooped. Such was high humility that, though he knew his infinite worthiness of honour, and of being honoured ten thousand times as much as the highest prince on earth, or angel in heaven; yet he did not think it too much when called to it to be bound as a cursed malefactor, and to become the laughing-stock and spitting-stock of the vilest of men, and to be crowned with thorns, and to have a mock robe put upon him, and to be crucified like a slave and malefactor, and as one of the meanest and worst of vagabonds and miscreants, and an accursed enemy of God and men who was not fit to live on the earth. And this was not for himself, but for some of the meanest and vilest of creatures, some of those accursed wretches that crucified him. Was not this a wonderful manifestation of humility, when he cheerfully and most freely submitted to this abasement?

And how did his patience shine forth under all the terrible sufferings which he endured, when he was dumb and opened not his mouth, but went as a lamb to the slaughter, and was like a patient lamb under all the sufferings he endured from first to last!

And what contempt of the glory of this world was there when he rather chose this contempt and meanness and suffering than to wear a temporal crown and be invested with the external glories of an earthly prince, as the multitude often solicited him!

3. Christ, in the work which he wrought out, in a wonderful manner exercised *those virtues which more immediately respect other men*. And these may be summed up under two heads, namely, meekness, and love.

Christ's *meekness* was his humble calmness of spirit under the provocations that he met with. None ever met with so great provocations as he did. The greatness of provocation lies in two things: in the degree of opposition by which the provocation is given; and in the degree of the unreasonableness of that opposition, or in its being very causeless, and without reason, and the great degree of obligation to the contrary. Now, if we consider both these things, no man ever met with such provocations as Christ did, when he was upon earth.

If we consider how much he was hated, what abuses he suffered from the vilest of men, how great his sufferings from men were, and how spiteful and how contemptuous they were, in offering him these abuses; and also consider how causeless and unreasonable these abuses were, how undeserving he was of them, and how much deserving of the contrary, namely, of love, and honour, and good treatment at their hands: I say, if we consider these things, no man ever met with a thousandth part of the provocation that Christ met with from men: and yet how meek was he under all! How composed and quiet his spirit! How far from being in a ruffle and tumult! When he was reviled, he reviled not again; and as a sheep before her shearers is dumb, so he opened not his mouth. No appearance was there of a revengeful spirit. On the contrary, what a spirit of forgiveness did he exhibit, so that he fervently and effectually prayed for their forgiveness, when they were in the highest act of provocation that ever they perpetrated, namely, nailing him to the cross, 'Father, forgive them, for they know not what they do' (*Luke* 23:34).

And never did there appear such an instance of *love* to men. Christ's love to men that he showed when on earth, and especially in going through his last sufferings and offering up his life and soul under those sufferings, which was his greatest act of love, was far beyond all parallel. There have been very remarkable manifestations of love in some of the saints, as in the Apostle Paul, the Apostle John, and others; but the love to men that Christ showed when on earth, as much exceeded the love of all other men as the ocean exceeds a small stream.

And it is to be observed, that all the virtues which appeared in Christ shone brightest in the close of his life, under the trials he met with then. Eminent virtue always shows brightest in the fire. Pure gold shows its purity chiefly in the furnace. It was chiefly under those trials which Christ underwent in the close of his life that his love to God, his honour of God's majesty, his regard to the honour of his law, his spirit of obedience, his humility, contempt of the world, patience, meekness, and spirit of forgiveness towards men appeared. Indeed every thing that Christ did to work out redemption for us appears mainly in the close of his life. Here mainly is his satisfaction for sin, and here chiefly is his merit of eternal life for sinners, and here chiefly appears the brightness of his example which he hath set us to follow.

Thus we have taken a brief view of the things whereby the purchase of redemption was made with respect to his righteousness that appeared in them.

ii. I proceed now to take a view of them *with respect to the satisfaction that he thereby made for sin,* or the sufferings and humiliation that he was the subject of in them on our account. And here,

a. He was subject to uncommon humiliation and sufferings *in his infancy.* He was born to the end that he might die; and therefore he did, as it were, begin to die as soon as he was born. His mother suffered in an uncommon manner in bearing him. When her travail came upon her, it is said, 'There was no room for them in the inn' (*Luke* 2:7). She was forced to betake herself to a stable; and therefore Christ was born in the place of the bringing forth of beasts. Thus he suffered in his birth, as though he had been meaner and viler than a man and not possessed of the dignity of the human nature, but had been of the rank of the brute creatures. And we may conclude that his mother's circumstances in other respects were proportionably strait and difficult, and that she was destitute of the conveniences necessary for so young an infant which others were wont to have; for want of which the new born babe without doubt suffered much.

And besides, he was persecuted in his infancy. They began to seek his life as soon as he was born. Herod, the chief man of the land, was so engaged to kill him, that, in order to it, he killed all the children in Bethlehem, and in all the coasts thereof, from two years old and under. And Christ suffered banishment in his infancy, was driven out of his native country into Egypt; and without doubt suffered much by being carried so long a journey, when he was so young, into a strange country.

b. Christ was subject to great humiliation in his private life at Nazareth. He there led a servile obscure life in a mean laborious occupation; for he is called not only the carpenter's son, but the carpenter: 'Is not this the carpenter . . . the brother of James, and Joses, and of Juda, and Simon?' (*Mark* 6:3). He, by hard labour, earned his bread before he ate it, and so suffered that curse which God pronounced on Adam, 'In the sweat of thy face shalt thou eat bread' (*Gen.* 3:19).

Let us consider how great a degree of humiliation the glorious Son of God, the Creator of heaven and earth, was subject to in this, that for about thirty years he should live a private obscure life among labouring men, and all this while be overlooked, and not taken notice of in the world as more than other common labourers. Christ's humiliation in some respects was greater in private life than in the time of his public ministry. There were many manifestations of his glory in the Word he preached, and the great miracles he wrought; but the first thirty years of his life he spent among mean ordinary men, as it were in silence, without those manifestations of his glory, or any thing to make him to be taken notice of more than any ordinary mechanic, but only the spotless purity and eminent holiness of his life. And that was in a great measure hid in obscurity, so that he was little taken notice of until after his baptism.

c. Christ was the subject of great humiliation and suffering *during his public life*, from his baptism until the night wherein he was betrayed. As particularly,

1. He suffered great *poverty*, so that he had not 'where to lay his head' (*Matt.* 8:20), and commonly used to lodge abroad in the open air, for want of a shelter to betake himself to; as you will see is manifest, if you compare the following places together, which I shall but name to you: Matthew 8:20; John 18:1-2; Luke 21:37; Luke 22:39. So that what was spoken of Christ in Song of Solomon 5:2, 'My head is filled with dew, and my locks with the drops of the night', was literally fulfilled. And through his poverty he doubtless was often

pinched with hunger, and thirst, and cold. We read in Matthew 4:2 that he was an hungered; and so again in Matthew 21:18. His mother and natural relations were poor, and not able to help him; and he was maintained by the charity of some of his disciples while he lived. So we read in Luke 8, at the beginning, of certain women that followed him, and ministered to him of their substance. He was so poor, that he was not able to pay the tribute that was demanded of him, without the miraculous coming of a fish to bring him the money out of the sea in his mouth (*Matt.* 17:27). And when he ate at his last passover it was not at his own charge but at the charge of another, as appears by Luke 22:7–13.

And from his poverty he had no grave of his own to be buried in. It was the manner of the Jews, unless they were very poor and were not able, to prepare themselves a sepulchre while they lived. But Christ had no land of his own, though he was possessor of heaven and earth; and therefore was buried by Joseph of Arimathea's charity, and in his tomb which he had prepared for himself.

2. He suffered great *hatred and reproach*. He was despised and rejected of men. He was by most esteemed a poor insignificant person; one of little account, slighted for his low parentage, and his mean city Nazareth. He was reproached as a glutton and drunkard, a friend of publicans and sinners; was called a deceiver of the people; sometimes was called a madman, and a Samaritan, and one possessed with a devil (*John* 7:20; 8:48; 10: 20). He was called a blasphemer, and was accounted by many a wizard, or one that wrought miracles by the black art and by communication with Beelzebub.

They excommunicated him, and agreed to excommunicate any man that should own him, as in John 9:22. They wished him dead, and were continually seeking to murder him, sometimes by force, and sometimes by craft. They often took up stones to stone him, and once led him to the brow of a hill, intending to throw him down the precipice, to dash him in pieces against the rocks.

He was thus hated and reproached by his own visible people, 'He came to his own, and his own received him not' (*John* 1:11). And he was principally despised and hated by those who were in chief repute, and were their greatest men. And the hatred wherewith he was hated was general. Into whatever part of the land he went, he met with hatred and contempt. He met with these in Capernaum, and when he went to Jericho, when he went to Jerusalem, which was the holy city, when he went to the temple to worship, and also in Nazareth, his own city, and among his own relations, and his old neighbours.

3. He suffered the buffetings of Satan in an uncommon manner. We read of one time in particular, when he had a long conflict with the devil, when he was in the wilderness forty days, with nothing but wild beasts and devils; and was so exposed to the devil's power, that he was bodily carried about by him from place to place, while he was otherwise in a very suffering state. And so much for the humiliation and suffering of Christ's public life, from his baptism to the night wherein he was betrayed.

d. I come now to his *last humiliation and sufferings*, from the evening of the night wherein he was betrayed to his resurrection. And here was his greatest humiliation and suffering, by which principally he made satisfaction to the justice of God for the sins of men. First, his life was sold by one of his own disciples for thirty pieces of silver, which was the price of the life of a servant, as you may see in Exodus 21:32. Then he was in that dreadful agony in the garden. There came such a dismal gloom upon his soul, that he began to be sorrowful and very heavy, said his soul was exceeding sorrowful, even unto death, and was sore amazed. So violent was the agony of his soul, as to force the blood through the pores of his skin; so that while his soul was overwhelmed with amazing sorrow, his body was all clotted with blood. The disciples, who used to be as his friends and family, at this time, above all, appeared cold towards him, and unconcerned for him, at the same time that his Father's face was hid from him.

Judas, to whom Christ had been so very merciful, and treated as one of his family or familiar friends, comes and betrays him in the most deceitful, treacherous manner. The officers and soldiers apprehend and bind him; his disciples forsake him and flee; his own best friends do not stand by him to comfort him, in this time of his distress. He is led away as a malefactor to appear before the priests and scribes, his venomous, mortal enemies, that they might sit as his judges, who sat up all night to have the pleasure of insulting him, now they had got him into their hands. But because they aimed at nothing short of his life, they set themselves to find some colour to put him to death, and seek for witnesses against him. When none appeared, they set some to bear false witness; and when their witness did not agree together, then they go to examining him, to catch something out of his own mouth.

They hoped he would say that he was the Son of God, and then they thought they should have enough. But because they see they are not likely to obtain it, they then try to force him to say it by adjuring him in the name of God to say whether he was or not: and when he confessed that he was, then they supposed they had enough; and then it was a time of rejoicing with them, which they show, by falling upon Christ, and spitting in his face, and blindfolding him, and striking him in the face with the palms of their hands, and then bidding him prophesy who it was that struck him; thus ridiculing him for pretending to be a prophet. And the very servants have a hand in the sport, 'And the servants did strike him with the palms of their hands' (*Mark* 14:65).

During the sufferings of that night, Peter, one of the chief of his own disciples, instead of standing by him to comfort him, appears ashamed to own him, and denies and renounces him with oaths and curses. And after the chief priests and elders had finished the night in so shamefully abusing him, when the morning was come, which was the morning of the most wonderful day that ever was, they led him away to Pilate, to be condemned to death by him, because they had not the power of life and death in their own hands.

He is brought before Pilate's judgment seat, and there the priests and elders accuse him as a traitor. And when Pilate, upon examining into the matter, declared he found no fault in him, the Jews were but the more fierce and violent to have him condemned. Upon which Pilate, after clearing him, very unjustly brings him upon a second trial; and then, not finding any thing against him, acquits him again. Pilate treats him as a poor worthless fellow; but is ashamed on so little pretence to condemn him as a traitor.

And then he was sent to Herod to be tried by him, and was brought before Herod's judgment seat; and his enemies followed, and virulently accused him before Herod. Herod does not condemn him as a traitor, or one that would set up for a king, but looks upon him as Pilate did, as a poor worthless creature, not worthy to be taken notice of, and does but make a mere laugh of the Jews' accusing him as a dangerous person to Caesar, as one that was in danger of setting up to be a king against him; and therefore in derision dresses him up in a mock robe and makes sport of him, and sends him back through the streets of Jerusalem to Pilate with the mock robe on.

Then the Jews prefer Barabbas before him, and are instant and violent with loud voices to Pilate, to crucify him. So Pilate, after he had cleared him twice, and Herod once, very unrighteously brings him on trial the third time, to try if he could not find something against him sufficient to crucify him. Christ was stripped and scourged; thus he gave his back to the smiter. After that, though Pilate still declared that he found no fault in him, yet so unjust was he that, for fear of the Jews, he delivered Christ to be crucified. But before they execute the sentence, his spiteful and cruel enemies take the pleasure of another spell of mocking him; they get round him, and make a set business of it.

They stripped him, and put on him a scarlet robe, and a reed in his hand, and a crown of thorns on his head. Both Jews and Roman soldiers were united in the transaction; they bow the knee before him, and in derision cry, 'Hail, king of the Jews!' They spit upon him also, and take the reed out of his hand, and smite him on the head. After this, they led him away to crucify him, and made him carry his own cross, until he sunk under it, his strength being spent; and then they laid it on one Simon, a Cyrenian.

At length, being come to Mount Calvary, they execute the sentence which Pilate had so unrighteously pronounced. They nail him to his cross by his hands and feet, then raise it erect, and fix one end in the ground, he being still suspended on it by the nails which pierced his hands and feet. And now Christ's sufferings are come to the extremity. Now the cup, which he so earnestly prayed that it might pass from him, is come, and he must, he does drink it.

In those days crucifixion was the most tormenting kind of death by which any were wont to be executed. There was no death wherein the person expired so much of mere torment. And hence the Roman word, which signifies torment, is taken from this kind of death. And besides what our Lord endured in his excruciating death in his body, he endured vastly more in his soul. Now was that travail of his soul, of which we read in the prophet; now it pleased God to bruise him, and to put him to grief; now he poured out his soul unto death, as in Isaiah 53. And if the mere forethought of this cup made him sweat blood, how much more dreadful and excruciating must the drinking of it have been! Many martyrs have endured much in their bodies, while their souls have been joyful, and have sung for joy, whereby they have been supported under the sufferings of their outward man, and have triumphed over them. But this was not the case with Christ; he had no such support; but his sufferings were chiefly those of the mind, though the other were extremely great. In his crucifixion Christ did not sweat blood, as he had before, because his blood had vent otherwise, and not because his agony was now not so great. But though he did not sweat blood, yet such was the suffering of his soul, that probably it rent his vitals, as seems probable by this, that, when his side was pierced, there came forth blood and water. And so here was a kind of literal fulfil-ment of that in Psalm 22:14, 'I am poured out like water . . . my heart is like wax; it is melted in the midst of my bowels.'

Now, under all these sufferings, the Jews still mocked him; and wagging their heads said, 'Thou that destroyest the tem-ple, and buildest it in three days, save thyself: if thou be the Son of God, come down from the cross.' And even the chief priests, scribes, and elders, joined in the cry, saying, 'He saved others, himself he cannot save.' And probably the devil at the same time tormented him to the utmost of his power; and hence it is said, 'This is your hour, and the power of darkness' (*Luke* 22:53).

Under these sufferings, Christ having cried out once and again with a loud voice, at last he said, 'It is finished', and bowed his head, and gave up the ghost (*John* 19:30). And thus was finished the greatest and most wonderful thing that ever was done. Now the angels beheld the most wonderful sight that ever they saw. Now was accomplished the main thing that had been pointed at by the various institutions of the ceremonial law, and by all the typical dispensations, and by all the sacrifices from the beginning of the world.

Christ being thus brought under the power of death, continued under it until the morning of next day but one; and then was finished that great work, the purchase of our redemption, for which such great preparation had been made from the beginning of the world. Then was finished all that was required in order to satisfy the threatenings of the law, and all that was necessary in order to satisfy divine justice; then the utmost that vindictive justice demanded, even the whole debt, was paid. Then was finished the whole of the purchase of eternal life. And now there is no need of any thing more to be done towards a purchase of salvation for sinners; nor has ever any thing been done since, nor will any thing more be done for ever and ever.

IMPROVEMENT

I n surveying the history of redemption, from the Fall of man
to the end of the world we have now shown how this work
was carried on through the two former of the three main
periods into which this whole space of time was divided,
namely, from the Fall to the incarnation of Christ, and from
thence to the end of the time of Christ's humiliation; and
have particularly explained how in the first of these periods
God prepared the way for Christ's appearing and purchasing
redemption; and how, in the second period, that purchase was
made and finished. I would now make some improvement of
what has been said on both these subjects considered
conjunctly. And this I would do,

1. In a use of reproof.
2. In a use of encouragement.

1. REPROOF

I begin with a use of reproof; a reproof of three things:
    i.   Of unbelief.
    ii. Of self righteousness.
    iii. Of a careless neglect of the salvation of Christ.

i. If it be as we have heard, how greatly do these things
reprove those who *do not believe in but reject the Lord Jesus
Christ*, all those who do not heartily receive him! Persons may
receive him in profession, and carry well outwardly towards
him, and may wish that they had some of those benefits that
Christ has purchased, and yet their hearts not receive Christ.
They may be hearty in nothing that they do towards Christ;

they may have no high esteem of Christ, nor any sincere honour or respect to Christ. They may never have opened the door of their heart to Christ, but have kept him shut out all their days, ever since they first heard of Christ, and his salvation has been offered to them. Though their hearts have been opened to others, their doors flung wide open to them, and they have had free admittance at all times, and have been embraced and made much of, and the best room in their hearts has been given them, and the throne of their hearts has been allowed them – yet Christ has always been shut out, and they have been deaf to all his knocks and calls. They never could find an inclination of heart to receive him, nor would they ever trust in him.

Let me now call upon you with whom it is thus, to consider how great your sin in thus rejecting Jesus Christ appears to be from those things that have been said. You slight the glorious Person for whose coming God made such great preparation in such a series of wonderful providences from the beginning of the world, and whom, after all things were made ready, God sent into the world, bringing to pass a thing before unknown, namely, the union of the divine nature with the human in one Person.

You have been guilty of slighting that great Saviour who, after such preparation, actually accomplished the purchase of redemption; and who, after he had spent three or four and thirty years in poverty, labour, and contempt, in purchasing redemption, at last finished the purchase by closing his life under such extreme sufferings as you have heard; and so by his death, and continuing for a time under the power of death, completed the whole. This is the Person you reject and despise. You make light of all the glory of his Person, and of all the glorious love of God the Father in sending him into the world, and all his wonderful love appearing in the whole of this affair. That precious stone that God hath laid in Zion for a foundation in such a manner, and by such wonderful works as you have heard, is a stone set at nought by you.

Sinners sometimes are ready to wonder why the sin of unbelief should be looked upon as such a great sin. But if you consider what you have heard, how can you wonder? If it be so, that this Saviour is so great a Saviour, and this work so great a work, and such great things have been done in order to it, truly there is no cause of wonder that the sin of unbelief, or the rejection of this Saviour, is spoken of in Scripture as such a dreadful sin, so provoking to God, and as that which brings greater guilt than the sins of the worst of the heathen, who never heard of those things, nor have had this Saviour offered to them.

ii. What has been said, affords matter of reproof to those who, instead of believing in Christ, *trust in themselves for salvation*. It is a common thing with men to take it upon themselves to purchase salvation for themselves, and so to do that great work which Christ came into the world to do. Are there none such here who trust in their prayers, and their good conversations, and the pains they take in religion, and the reformation of their lives, and in their self denial, to recommend them to God, to make some atonement for their past sins, and to draw the heart of God to them?

Consider three things:

a. *How great a thing that is which you take upon you.* You take upon you to do the work of the great Saviour of the world. You trust in your own doings to appease God for your sins, and to incline the heart of God to you. Though you are poor, worthless, vile, polluted worms of the dust; yet so arrogant are you, that you take upon you that very work that the only begotten Son of God did when upon earth, and that he became man to capacitate himself for, and in order to which God spent four thousand years in all the great dispensations of his providence in the government of the world, aiming chiefly at this, to make way for Christ's coming to do this work. This is the work that you take upon yourself, and foolishly think yourself sufficient for it; as though your prayers and other performances were excellent enough for this purpose.

Consider how vain is the thought which you entertain of yourself. How must such arrogance appear in the sight of Christ, whom it cost so much to make a purchase of salvation, when it was not to be obtained even by him, so great and glorious a Person, at a cheaper rate than his wading through a sea of blood, and passing through the midst of the furnace of God's wrath! And how vain must your arrogance appear in the sight of God, when he sees you imagining yourself sufficient, and your worthless, polluted performances excellent enough for the accomplishing of that work of his own Son, to prepare the way for which he was employed in ordering all the great affairs of the world for so many ages!

b. If there be ground for you to trust, as you do, in your own righteousness, then *all that Christ did to purchase salvation when on earth, and all that God did from the first Fall of man to that time to prepare the way for it, is in vain.* Your self righteousness charges God with the greatest folly, as though he has done all things in vain, even so much in vain, that he has done all this to bring about an accomplishment of that which you alone, a little worm, with your poor polluted prayers, and the little pains you take in religion, mingled with all that hypocrisy and filthiness, are sufficient to accomplish for yourself without Christ's help. For if you can appease God's anger, and can commend yourself to God by these means, then you have no need of Christ, but he is dead in vain: 'If righteousness come by the law, then Christ is dead in vain' (*Gal.* 2:21).

If you can do this by your prayers and good works, Christ might have spared his pains; he might have spared his blood; he might have kept within the bosom of his Father, without coming down into this evil world to be despised, reproached, and persecuted to death; and God needed not have busied himself, as he did for four thousand years together causing so many changes in the state of the world all that while, in order to the bringing about of that which you, little as you are, can accomplish in a few days, only with the trouble of a few sighs, and groans, and prayers, and some other religious performances. Consider with yourself what greater folly could you have devised to charge upon God than this, to do all those things before and after Christ came into the world so needlessly; when, instead of all this, he might have called you forth, and committed the business to you, which you think you can do so easily.

Alas! how blind are natural men! How sottish are the thoughts they have of things! And especially, how vain are the thoughts which they have of themselves! How ignorant of their own littleness and pollution! How do they exalt themselves up to heaven! What great things do they assume to themselves!

c. You that trust to your own righteousness, *arrogate to yourselves the honour of the greatest thing that ever God himself did*; not only as if you were sufficient to perform divine works, and to accomplish some of the great works of God; but such is your pride and vanity, that you are not content without taking upon you to do the very greatest work that ever God himself wrought, even the work of redemption. You see by what has been said, how God has subordinated all his other works to this work of redemption. You see how God's works of providence are greater than his works of creation, and that all God's works of providence, from the beginning of the generations of men, were in order to this, to make way for the purchasing of redemption. But this is what you take upon yourself. To take on yourself to work out redemption, is a greater thing than if you had taken it upon you to create a world. Consider with yourself what a figure you, a poor worm, would make, if you should seriously go about to create such a world as God did, should swell in your own conceit of yourself, should deck yourself with majesty, pretend to speak the word of power, and call a universe out of nothing, intending to go on in order, and say, 'Let there be light; Let there be a firmament,' etc.

But then consider, that in attempting to work out redemption yourself, you attempt a greater thing than this, and are serious in it, and will not be beat off from it, but strive in it, and are full of the thought of yourself that you are sufficient for it, and always big with hopes of accomplishing it.

You take upon you to do the very greatest and most difficult part of this work, namely, to purchase redemption. Christ can accomplish other parts of this work without cost, without any trouble and difficulty; but this part cost him his life, as well as innumerable pains and labours, with very great ignominy and contempt besides. Yet this is that part which self-righteous persons go about to accomplish for themselves. If all the angels in heaven had been sufficient for this work, would God have set himself to effect such things as he did in order to it, before he sent his Son into the world? And, would he ever have sent his own Son, the great Creator and God of the angels, into the world, to have done and suffered such things?

What self-righteous persons take to themselves, is the same work that Christ was engaged in when he was in his agony and bloody sweat, and when he died on the cross, which was the greatest thing that ever the eyes of angels beheld. This, great as it is, they imagine they can do the same that Christ accomplished by it. Their self-righteousness does, in effect, charge Christ's offering up himself in these sufferings as the greatest instance of folly that ever men or angels saw, instead of being the most glorious display of the divine wisdom and grace that ever was seen. Yea, self-righteousness makes all that Christ did through the whole course of his life, and all that he said and suffered through that whole time, and his incarnation itself, and not only so, but all that God had been doing in the great dispensations of his providence from the beginning of the world to that time, as all nothing but a scene of the most wild, and extreme, and transcendent folly.

Is it any wonder, then, that a self-righteous spirit is so represented in Scripture, and spoken of, as that which is most fatal to the souls of men? And is it any wonder that Christ is represented in Scripture as being so provoked with the Pharisees and others, who trusted in themselves that they were righteous, and were proud of their goodness, and thought that their own performances were a valuable price of God's favour and love?

Let persons hence be warned against a self-righteous spirit. You that are seeking your salvation, and taking pains in religion, take heed to yourselves that you do not trust in what you do; that you do not harbour any such thoughts; that God now, seeing how much you are reformed, how you take pains in religion, and how you are sometimes affected, will be pacified towards you with respect to your sins, and on account of it will not be so angry for your former sins; and that you shall gain on him by such things, and draw his heart to show you mercy; or at least that God ought to accept of what you do, so as to be inclined by it in some measure to have mercy on you. If you entertain this thought that God is obliged to do it, and does not act justly if he refuse to regard your prayers and pains, and so quarrel with God, and complain of him for not doing so, this shows what your opinion is of your own righteousness, namely, that it is a valuable price of salvation, and ought to be accepted of God as such. Such complaining of God and quarrelling with him for not taking more notice of your righteousness plainly shows that you are guilty of all that arrogance that has been spoken of, thinking yourself sufficient to offer the price of your own salvation.

iii. What has been said on this subject, affords matter of reproof to those who *carelessly neglect the salvation of Christ*; such as live a senseless kind of life, neglecting the business of religion and their own souls for the present, not taking any course to get an interest in Christ, or what he has done and suffered, or any part in that glorious salvation he has purchased by that price, but rather have their minds taken up about the gains of the world, or about the vanities and pleasures of youth, and so make light of what they hear from time to time of Christ's salvation that they do not at present so much as seek after it. Let me here apply myself to you in some expostulatory interrogations.

a. Shall so many prophets, and kings, and righteous men, have their minds so much taken up with the prospect, that the purchase of salvation was to be wrought out in ages long after their death, and will you neglect it *when actually accomplished?* You have heard what great account the church in all ages made of the future redemption of Christ, how joyfully they expected it, how they spoke of it, how they studied and searched into these things, how they sang joyful songs and had their hearts greatly engaged about it, and yet never expected to see it done, and did not expect that it would be accomplished until many ages after their death (*1 Pet.* 1:10-12).

How much did Isaiah and Daniel, and other prophets, speak concerning this redemption! And how much were their hearts engaged and their attention and study fixed upon it! How was David's mind taken up in this subject! He declared that it was all his salvation, and all his desire (*2 Sam.* 23:5). How did he employ his voice and harp in celebrating it, and the glorious display of divine grace therein exhibited! And all this although they beheld it not as yet accomplished, but saw that it was to be brought to pass so long a time after their day. And before this, how did Abraham and the other patriarchs rejoice in the prospect of Christ's day, and the redemption which he was to purchase! And even the saints before the Flood were affected and elated in the expectation of this glorious event, though it was then so long future, and it was so very faintly and obscurely revealed to them.

Now these things are declared to you as actually fulfilled. The church now has seen accomplished all those great things which they so joyfully prophesied of, and you are abundantly shown how those things were accomplished: 'Verily I say unto you, that many prophets and righteous men have desired to see those things which ye see, and have not seen; and to hear those things which ye hear, and have not heard them' (*Matt.* 13:17).

And yet, when these things are thus abundantly set before you as already accomplished, how do you slight them! How light do you make of them! How little are they taken notice of by you! How unconcerned are you about them, following other things, and not so much as feeling any interest in them! Indeed your sin is extremely aggravated in the sight of God. God has put you under great advantages for your eternal salvation, far greater than those saints of old enjoyed. He has put you under a more glorious dispensation; has given you a more clear revelation of Christ and his salvation, and yet you neglect all these advantages, and go on in a careless course of life, as though nothing had been done, no such proposals and offers had been made to you.

b. Have the angels been so engaged about this salvation which is by Christ, ever since the Fall of man, *though they are not immediately concerned in it*, and will you who need it, and have it offered to you, be so careless about it? You have heard how the angels at first were subjected to Christ as Mediator, and how they have all along been ministering spirits to him in this affair. In all the great dispensation which you have heard of from the beginning of the world they have been active and as a flame of fire in this affair, being most diligently employed as ministering spirits to minister to Christ in this great affair of man's redemption.

And when Christ came, how engaged were their minds! They came to Zacharias, to inform him of the coming of Christ's forerunner. They came to the virgin Mary to inform her of the approaching birth of Christ. They came to Joseph to warn him of the danger which threatened the newborn Saviour and to point out to him the means of safety. And how were their minds engaged at the time of the birth of Christ! The whole multitude of the heavenly host sang praises upon the occasion, saying, 'Glory to God in the highest, and on earth peace, good will towards men.'

And afterwards, from time to time, they ministered to Christ when on earth. They did so at the time of his temptation, at the time of his agony in the garden, at his resurrection, and at his ascension. All these things show that they were greatly engaged in this affair. And the Scripture informs us that they pry into these things: 'Which things the angels desire to look into' (*1 Pet.* 1:12). And how are they represented in the Revelation as being employed in heaven in singing praises to him that sitteth on the throne, and to the Lamb!

Now, shall these take so much notice of this redemption and of the Purchaser, who need it not for themselves and have no immediate concern or interest in it or offer of it, and will you, to whom it is offered and who are in such extreme necessity of it, neglect and take no notice of it?

c. Was it worth Christ's while to labour so hard and do and suffer so much to procure this salvation, and is it not worth your while to be at some labour in seeking it? Was it a thing of so great importance, that salvation should be procured for sinners as that it was worthy to lie with such weight on the mind of Christ as to induce him to become man, and to suffer such contempt and labour, and even death itself, in order to procure it – though he stood in need of nothing, though he was like to gain no addition to his eternal happiness, though he could get nothing by those that he saved, though he did not need them – was it of such importance that sinners should be saved, that he might properly be induced to submit to such humiliation and suffering, and yet is it not worth while for you, who are one of those miserable sinners that need this salvation and must perish eternally without it, to take earnest pains to obtain an interest in it after it is procured, and all things are ready?

d. Shall the great God be so concerned about this salvation, as so often to overturn the world to make way for it; and when all is done, is it not worth your seeking after? How has the Lord of heaven and earth been, as it were, engaged about this affair! What great, what wonderful things has he done from one age to another, removing kings, and setting up kings, raising up a great number of prophets, separating a distinct nation from the rest of the world, overturning one nation and kingdom, and another, and often overturning the state of the world, and so has continued bringing about one change and revolution after another for forty centuries in succession, to make way for the procuring of this salvation! And when he has done all, and when, at the close of these ages, the great

Saviour comes, and, becoming incarnate, and passing through a long series of reproach and suffering, and then suffering all the waves and billows of God's wrath for men's sins, insomuch that they overwhelmed his soul, after all these things done to procure salvation for sinners, is it not worthy of your so much as taking notice of it or being concerned about it, though you are those persons who need this salvation, but that it should be thrown by and made nothing of in comparison with worldly gain, or gay clothing, or youthful diversions, or other such trifling things?

Oh, that you who live negligent of this salvation would consider what you do! What you have heard from this subject may show you what reason there is in that exclamation of the Apostle, 'How shall we escape, if we neglect so great salvation?' (*Heb.* 2:3), and in that, 'Behold, ye despisers, and wonder, and perish: for I work a work in your days, a work which you shall in no wise believe, though a man declare it unto you' (*Acts* 13:41). God looks on such as you as great enemies of the cross of Christ, and adversaries and despisers of all the glory of this great work.

And if God has made such account of the glory of salvation as to destroy many nations and so often to overturn all nations, to prepare the way for the glory of his Son in this affair, how little account will he make of the lives and souls of ten thousand such opposers and despisers as you that continue impenitent, in comparison of that glory, when he shall hereafter come and find that your welfare stands in the way of that glory? Why, surely you shall be dashed to pieces as a potter's vessel, and trodden down as the mire of the streets. God may, through wonderful patience, bear with hardened careless sinners for a while, but he will not long bear with such despisers of his dear Son and his great salvation, the glory of which he has had so much at heart, but will utterly consume them without remedy or mercy.

2. ENCOURAGEMENT

I will conclude with a second use, of encouragement to burdened souls to put their trust in Christ for salvation. To all such as are not careless and negligent, but do make seeking an interest in Christ their main business, being sensible in some measure of their necessity of an interest in him, being afraid of the wrath to come: to such what has been said on this subject holds forth great matter of encouragement to come and venture their souls on the Lord Jesus Christ. And as motives proper to excite you so to do, let me lead you to consider two things in particular.

i. *The completeness of the purchase which has been made.* As you have heard, this work of purchasing salvation was wholly finished during the time of Christ's humiliation. When Christ rose from the dead, and was exalted from that abasement to which he submitted for our salvation, the purchase of eternal life was completely made, so that there was no need of any thing more to be done in order to it. But now the servants were sent forth with the message which we have account of in Matthew 22:4, 'Behold, I have prepared my dinner: my oxen and my fatlings are killed, and all things are ready: come unto the marriage.'

Therefore, all things being ready, are your sins many and great? Here is enough done by Christ to procure their pardon. There is no need of any righteousness of yours to obtain your pardon and justification. No, you may come freely, without money and without price. Since therefore there is such a free and gracious invitation given you, come. Come naked as you are; come as a poor condemned criminal; come and cast yourself down at Christ's feet, as one justly condemned, and utterly helpless in yourself. Here is a complete salvation wrought out by Christ, and through him offered to you. Come, therefore, accept of it, and be saved.

ii. *For Christ to reject one that thus comes to him would be to frustrate all those great things which you have heard that God brought to pass* from the Fall of man to the incarnation of Christ. It would also frustrate all that Christ did and suffered while on earth. Yea, it would frustrate the incarnation of Christ itself, and all the great things done in preparation for his incarnation. For all these things were for that end, that those might be saved who should come to Christ.

Therefore you may be sure Christ will not be backward in saving those who come to him and trust in him, for he has no desire to frustrate himself in his own work. It cost him too dear for that. Neither will God the Father refuse you, for he has no desire to frustrate himself in all that he did for so many hundreds and thousands of years to prepare the way for the salvation of sinners by Christ. Come, therefore; hearken to the sweet and earnest calls of Christ to your soul. Do as he invites, and as he commands you, 'Come unto me, all ye that labour, and are heavy laden, and I will give you rest. Take my yoke upon you, and learn of me . . . and ye shall find rest unto your souls. For my yoke is easy, and my burden is light' (*Matt.* 11:28-30).

PERIOD 3

❧❀❧

FROM THE RESURRECTION
OF CHRIST TO THE END
OF THE WORLD

I n discoursing on this subject, we have already shown how
the work of redemption was carried on through the first
two of the three periods into which we divided the whole
space of time from the Fall to the end of the world. We are
now come to the third and last period, beginning with
Christ's resurrection, and reaching to the end of the world,
and would now show how this work was also carried on
through this period, from this proposition:

THAT THE SPACE OF TIME FROM THE END OF CHRIST'S
HUMILIATION TO THE END OF THE WORLD IS ALL TAKEN UP IN
BRINGING ABOUT THE GREAT EFFECT OR SUCCESS OF CHRIST'S
PURCHASE.

Not but that there were great effects and glorious success of
Christ's purchase of redemption before, even from the beginning of the generations of men. But all that success of Christ's
redemption which was before, was only preparatory, and was
by way of anticipation, as some few fruits are gathered before
the harvest. There was no more success before Christ came
than God saw needful to prepare the way for his coming. The
proper time of the success or effect of Christ's purchase of

redemption is after the purchase has been made, as the proper time for the world to enjoy the light of the sun is the day time, after the sun is risen, though we may have some small matter of it reflected from the moon and planets before. And even the success of Christ's redemption while he himself was on earth, was very small in comparison of what it was after the conclusion of his humiliation.

But Christ having finished that greatest and most difficult of all works, the work of the purchase of redemption, now is come the time for obtaining the end of it, the glorious effect of it. This is the next work he goes about. Having gone through the whole course of his sufferings and humiliation, there is an end to all things of that nature: he is never to suffer any more. But now is the time for him to obtain the joy that was set before him. Having made his soul an offering for sin, now is the time for him to see his seed, and to have a portion divided to him with the great, and to divide the spoil with the strong.

One design of Christ in what he did in his humiliation, was to lay a foundation for the overthrow of Satan's kingdom; and now is come the time to effect it, as Christ, a little before his crucifixion, said, 'Now is the judgment of this world; now shall the prince of this world be cast out' (*John* 12:31). Another design was, to gather together in one all things in Christ. Now is come the time for this also: 'And I, if I be lifted up from the earth, will draw all men unto me' (*John* 12:32); which is agreeable to Jacob's prophecy of Christ, that when Shiloh should come, to him should the gathering of the people be (*Gen.* 49:10). Another design is the salvation of the elect. Now when his sufferings are finished, and his humiliation is perfected, the time is come for that also: 'Though he were a Son, yet learned he obedience by the things which he suffered: and being made perfect, he became the author of eternal salvation unto all them that obey him' (*Heb.* 5:8-9).

[256]

Another design was to accomplish by these things great glory to the persons of the Trinity. Now also is come the time for that: 'Father, the hour is come; glorify thy Son, that thy Son also may glorify thee' (*John* 17:1). Another design was the glory of the saints. Now is the time also for this: 'As thou hast given him power over all flesh, that he should give eternal life to as many as thou hast given him' (*John* 17: 2). And all the dispensations of God's providence henceforward, even to the final consummation of all things, are to give Christ his reward, and fulfil his end in what he did and suffered upon earth, and to fulfil the joy that was set before him.

INTRODUCTION

❧⚜❧

B efore I enter on the consideration of any particular things accomplished in this period, I would briefly observe some things in general concerning it; and particularly how the times of this period are represented in Scripture.

1. The times of this period, for the most part, are those which in the Old Testament are called *the latter days*. We often, in the prophets of the Old Testament, read of such and such things that should come to pass in *the latter days*, and sometimes in *the last days*. Now these expressions of the prophets are most commonly to be understood of the times of the period that we are now upon. They are called the latter days and the last days because this is the last period of the series of God's providences on earth, the last period of that great work of providence, the work of redemption; which is as it were the sum of God's works of providence, the time wherein the church is under the last dispensation of the covenant of grace that ever it will be under on earth.

2. The whole time of this period is sometimes in Scripture called *the end of the world*; for example, 'Now all these things happened unto them for ensamples: and they are written for our admonition, upon whom the ends of the world are come' (*1 Cor.* 10:11). And the Apostle, in this expression of the end of the world, means the whole of the gospel day, from the birth of Christ to the finishing of the day of judgment: 'But now once in the end of the world hath he appeared to put away sin by the sacrifice of himself' (*Heb.* 9:26).

This space of time may well be called the end of the world; for this whole time is taken up in bringing things to their great end and issue, to that great issue that God had been preparing the way for, in all the great dispensations of providence, from the first Fall of man to this time. Before, things were in a kind of preparatory state; but now they are in a finishing state. It is the winding up of things which is all this while accomplishing. An end is now brought to the former carnal state of things, which by degrees vanishes, and a spiritual state begins to be established, and to be established more and more.

First, an end is brought to the former state of the church, which may be called its worldly state, the state wherein it was subject to carnal ordinances, and the rudiments of the world; and then an end is brought to the Jewish state, in the destruction of their city and country; and then, after that, an end is brought to the old heathen empire in Constantine's time; which is another and further degree of the winding up and finishing of the world; and the next step is the finishing of Satan's visible kingdom in the world, upon the fall of Antichrist, and the calling of the Jews; and last will come the destruction of the outward frame of the world itself, at the conclusion of the day of judgment.

But the world is all this while as it were a-finishing, though it comes to an end by several steps and degrees. Heaven and earth began to shake, in order to a dissolution, according to the prophecy of Haggai, before Christ came, that so only those things that cannot be shaken may remain, that is, that those things that are to come to an end may come to an end, and that only those things may remain which are to remain to all eternity.

So, in the first place, the carnal ordinances of the Jewish worship came to an end, to make way for the establishment of that spiritual worship, the worship of the heart, which is to endure to all eternity: 'Jesus saith unto her, Woman, believe me, the hour cometh, when ye shall neither in this mountain, nor yet at Jerusalem, worship the Father . . . But the hour cometh, and now is, when the true worshippers shall worship the Father in spirit and in truth: for the Father seeketh such to worship him' (*John* 4:21,23). This is one instance of the temporary world's coming to an end, and the eternal world's beginning.

And then, after that, the outward temple, and the outward city Jerusalem, came to an end, to give place to the setting up of the spiritual temple and the spiritual city, which are to last to eternity; which is another instance of removing those things which are ready to vanish away, that those things which cannot be shaken may remain.

And then, after that, the old heathen empire comes to an end, to make way for the empire of Christ, which shall last to all eternity; which is another step of bringing the temporal world to an end, and of the beginning of the world to come, which is an eternal world.

And after that, upon the fall of Antichrist, an end is put to Satan's visible kingdom on earth, to establish Christ's kingdom, which is an eternal kingdom; as the prophet Daniel says, 'And the kingdom and dominion, and the greatness of the kingdom under the whole heaven, shall be given to the people of the saints of the Most High, whose kingdom is an everlasting kingdom, and all dominions shall serve and obey him' (*Dan.* 7:27); which is another instance of the ending of the temporary world, and the beginning of the eternal one. And then, lastly, the very frame of this corruptible world shall come to an end, to make way for the church to dwell in another dwelling place, which shall last to eternity; which is the last instance of the same thing.

Because the world is thus coming to an end by various steps and degrees, the Apostle perhaps uses this expression, that the *ends* of the world are come on us; not *the end* but *the ends*, of the plural number, as though the world has several endings one after another.

The gospel dispensation is the last state of things in the world; and this state is a finishing state: it is all spent in finishing things off which before had been preparing, or abolishing things which before had stood. It is all spent as it were in summing things up, and bringing them to their issues, and their proper fulfilment. Now all the old types are fulfilled, and all the prophecies of all the prophets from the beginning of the world shall be accomplished in this period.

3. That state of things which is attained in the events of this period is called *a new heaven and a new earth*: 'For behold, I create new heavens, and a new earth: and the former shall not be remembered, nor come into mind. But be ye glad and rejoice for ever in that which I create: for, behold, I create Jerusalem a rejoicing, and her people a joy' (*Isa.* 65:17-18). And Isaiah 66:22: 'For as the new heavens and the new earth, which I will make, shall remain before me . . . so shall your seed and your name remain.' See also Isaiah 51:16.

As the former state of things, or the old world, by one step after another, is through this period coming to an end, so the new state of things, or the new world, which is a spiritual world, is beginning and setting up. The heaven and earth which are corruptible are shaking, that the new heavens and new earth, which cannot be shaken, may be established and remain.

In consequence of each of these finishings of the old state of things, there is a new beginning of a new and eternal state of things. So was that which accompanied the destruction of Jerusalem, which was an establishing of the spiritual Jerusalem instead of the literal. So with respect to the destruction of the old heathen empire, and all the other endings of the old state of things, until at length the very outward frame of the old world itself shall come to an end; and the church shall dwell in a world new to it, or to a great part of it, even heaven, which will be a new habitation; and then shall the utmost be accomplished that is meant by *the new heavens and the new earth.* See Revelation 21:1.

The end of God's creating the world was to prepare a kingdom for his Son, (for he is appointed heir of the world) and that he might have the possession of it, and a kingdom in it, which should remain to all eternity. So that, so far forth as the kingdom of Christ is set up in the world, so far is the world brought to its end, and the eternal state of things set up. So far are all the great changes and revolutions of the ages of the world brought to their everlasting issue, and all things come to their ultimate period. So far are the waters of the long channel of divine providence, which has so many branches, and so many windings and turnings, emptied out into their proper ocean, which they have been seeking from the beginning and head of their course, and so are come to their rest. So far as Christ's kingdom is established in the world, so far are things wound up and settled in their everlasting state, and a period put to the course of things in this changeable world; so far are the first heavens and the first earth come to an end, and the new heavens and the new earth, the everlasting heavens and earth, established in their room.

This leads me to observe:

4. That the state of things which is attained by the events of this period is what is so often called *the kingdom of heaven,* or *the kingdom of God.* We very often read in the New Testament of the kingdom of heaven. John the Baptist preached that the kingdom of heaven was at hand; and so did Christ, and his disciples after him; referring to something that the Jews in those days expected, and very much talked of, which they called by that name. They seem to have taken their expectation and the name chiefly from that prophecy of Daniel in

Nebuchadnezzar's dream, 'And in the days of these kings shall the God of heaven set up a kingdom' (*Dan.* 2:44); together with that in Daniel 7:13-14.

Now this *kingdom of heaven* is that evangelical state of things in his church, and in the world, wherein consists the success of Christ's redemption in this period. There had been often great kingdoms set up before, which were earthly kingdoms, as the Babylonish, the Persian, the Grecian, and the Roman monarchies. But Christ came to set up the last kingdom, which is not an earthly kingdom, but a heavenly, and so is the kingdom of heaven: 'My kingdom is not of this world' (*John* 18:36). This is the kingdom of which Christ speaks, 'I appoint unto you a kingdom, as my Father hath appointed unto me' (*Luke* 22:29).

This kingdom began soon after Christ's resurrection, and was accomplished in various steps from that time to the end of the world. Sometimes by the kingdom of heaven is meant that spiritual state of the church which began soon after Christ's resurrection; sometimes that more perfect state of the church which shall obtain after the downfall of Antichrist; and sometimes that glorious and blessed state to which the church shall be received at the day of judgment. So the Apostle, speaking of the resurrection, says, 'This I say, brethren, that flesh and blood cannot inherit the kingdom of God' (*1 Cor.* 15:50).

Under this head I would observe several things particularly, for the clearer understanding of what the Scripture says concerning this period.

i. The setting up of the kingdom of Christ is chiefly accomplished by four successive great events, each of which is in Scripture called Christ's *coming in his kingdom*. The whole success of Christ's redemption is comprehended in one word, namely, his setting up his kingdom. This is chiefly done by four great successive dispensations of providence; and every one of them is represented in Scripture as Christ's coming in his kingdom.

The first is Christ's appearing in those wonderful dispensations of providence in the apostles' days, in setting up his kingdom, and destroying the enemies of his kingdom, which ended in the destruction of Jerusalem. This is called Christ's coming in his kingdom: 'Verily I say unto you, There be some standing here, which shall not taste of death till they see the Son of Man coming in his kingdom' (*Matt.* 16:28). And so it is represented in Matthew 24.

The second is that which was accomplished in Constantine's time, in the destruction of the heathen Roman empire. This is represented as Christ's coming, and is compared to his coming to judgment in the 6th chapter of Revelation at the latter end.

The third is that which is to be accomplished at the destruction of Antichrist. This also is represented as Christ's coming in his kingdom in the 7th chapter of Daniel, and in other places, as I may possibly show hereafter, when I come to speak of it.

The fourth and last is his coming to the last judgment, which is the event principally signified in Scripture by Christ's coming in his kingdom.

ii. I would observe that each of the three former of these is a lively image or type of the fourth and last, namely, Christ's coming to the final judgment, as the principal dispensations of providence before Christ's first coming were types of that first coming. As Christ's last coming to judgment is accompanied with a resurrection of the dead, so is each of the three foregoing with a spiritual resurrection. That coming of Christ which ended in the destruction of Jerusalem, was preceded by a glorious spiritual resurrection of souls in the calling of the

Gentiles, and bringing home such multitudes of souls to Christ by the preaching of the gospel. So Christ's coming in Constantine's time, was accompanied with a glorious spiritual resurrection of the greater part of the known world, in a restoration of it to a visible church state, from a state of heathenism. So Christ's coming at the destruction of Antichrist, will be attended with a spiritual resurrection of the church after it had been long as it were dead, in the times of Antichrist. This is called *the first resurrection* in the 20th chapter of Revelation.

Again, as Christ in the last judgment will gloriously manifest himself, coming in the glory of his Father, so in each of the three foregoing events, Christ gloriously manifested himself in sending judgments upon his enemies, and in showing grace and favour to his church; and as the last coming of Christ will be attended with a literal gathering together of the elect from the four winds of heaven, so were each of the preceding attended with a spiritual gathering in of the elect. As this gathering together of the elect will be effected by God's angels, with a great sound of a trumpet, as in Matthew 24:31, so were each of the preceding spiritual ingatherings effected by the trumpet of the gospel, sounded by the ministers of Christ. As there shall precede the last appearance of Christ, a time of great degeneracy and wickedness, so this has been, or will be, the case with each of the other appearances. Before each of them is a time of great opposition to the church: before the first, by the Jews, in their persecutions that we read of in the New Testament; before the second, in Constantine's time, by the heathen, in several successive persecutions raised by the Roman emperors against the Christians; before the third, by Antichrist; and before the last, by Gog and Magog, as described in the Revelation.

By each of these comings of Christ, God works a glorious deliverance for his church. Each of them is accompanied with a glorious advancement of the state of the church. The first, which ended in the destruction of Jerusalem, was attended with bringing the church into the glorious state of the gospel, a glorious state of the church very much prophesied of old, whereby the church was advanced into far more glorious circumstances than it was in before under the Jewish dispensation. The second, which was in Constantine's time, was accompanied with an advancement of the church into a state of liberty from persecution, and the countenance of civil authority, and triumph over their heathen persecutors. The third, which shall be at the downfall of Antichrist, will be accompanied with an advancement of the church into that state of the glorious prevalence of truth, liberty, peace, and joy, that we so often read of in the prophetical parts of Scripture. The last will be attended with the advancement of the church to consummate glory in both soul and body in heaven.

Each of these comings of Christ is accompanied with a terrible destruction of the wicked, and the enemies of the church: the first, with the destruction of the persecuting Jews, which was amazingly terrible; the second, with dreadful judgments on the heathen persecutors of the church, of which more hereafter; the third, with the awful destruction of Antichrist, the most cruel and bitter enemy that ever the church had; the fourth, with divine wrath and vengeance on all the ungodly.

Further, there is in each of these comings of Christ an ending of the old heavens and the old earth, and a beginning of new heavens and a new earth; or an end of a temporal state of things, and a beginning of an eternal state.

iii. I would observe, that each of those four great dispensations which are represented as Christ's coming in his kingdom, are but so many steps and degrees of the accomplishment of one event. They are not the setting up of so many distinct kingdoms of Christ; they are all of them only several degrees of the accomplishment of that one event prophesied of, 'And I saw in the night visions, and behold, one like the Son of man, came with the clouds of heaven, and came to the Ancient of days, and they brought him near before him. And there was given him dominion, and glory, and a kingdom, that all people, nations, and languages, should serve him: his dominion is an everlasting dominion, and his kingdom that which shall not be destroyed' (*Dan.* 7: 13-14). This is what the Jews expected, and called 'the coming of the kingdom of heaven'; and what John the Baptist and Christ had respect to when they said, 'The kingdom of heaven is at hand.' This great event is gradually accomplished, or is accomplished by several steps. Those four great events which have been mentioned, were several steps towards the accomplishment of this grand event.

When Christ came with the preaching of the apostles, to set up his kingdom in the world, which dispensation ended with the destruction of Jerusalem, then it was accomplished in a glorious degree; when the heathen empire was destroyed in Constantine's time, it was fulfilled in a further degree; when Antichrist shall be destroyed, it will be accomplished in a yet higher degree; but when the end of the world is come, then will it be accomplished in its most perfect degree of all; then it will be finally and completely accomplished. And because these four great events are but images one of another, and the three former but types of the last, and since they are all only several steps of the accomplishment of the same thing; hence we find them all from time to time prophesied of under one, as they are in the prophecies of Daniel, and as they are in the 24th chapter of Matthew, where some things seem more applicable to one of them, and others to another.

iv. I would observe that, as there are several steps of the accomplishment of the kingdom of Christ, so in each one of them the event is accomplished in a further degree than in the foregoing. That in the time of Constantine was a greater and further accomplishment of the kingdom of Christ, than that which ended in the destruction of Jerusalem; that which shall be at the fall of Antichrist, will be a further accomplishment of the same thing, than that which took place in the time of Constantine; and so on with regard to each: so that the kingdom of Christ is gradually prevailing and growing by these several great steps of its fulfilment, from the time of Christ's resurrection, to the end of the world.

v. And lastly, it may be observed, that the great providences of God between these four great events are to make way for the kingdom and glory of Christ in the great event following. Those dispensations of providence which were towards the church of God and the world before the destruction of the heathen empire in the time of Constantine seem all to have been to make way for the glory of Christ and the happiness of the church in that event. And so the great providences of God which are after that until the destruction of Antichrist, and the beginning of the glorious times of the church which follow, seem all to be to prepare the way for the greater glory of Christ and his church in that event; and the providences of God which shall be after that to the end of the world seem to be for the greater manifestation of Christ's glory at the end of the world, and in the consummation of all things.

Thus I thought it needful to observe these things in general concerning this last period of the series of God's providence, before I take notice of the particular providences by which the work of redemption is carried on through this period, in their order; and before I do that, I will also briefly answer the enquiry, Why the setting up of Christ's kingdom after his humiliation should be so gradual, by so many steps that are so long in accomplishing, since God could easily have finished it at once?

Though it would be presumption in us to pretend to declare all the ends of God in this, yet doubtless much of the wisdom of God may be seen in it by us; and particularly in these two things.

1. In this way *the glory of God's wisdom, in the manner of doing this, is more visible to the observation of creatures.* If it had been done at once, in an instant, or in a very short time, there would not have been such opportunities for creatures to perceive and observe the particular steps of divine wisdom, as when the work is gradually accomplished, and one effect of his wisdom is held forth to observation after another. It is wisely determined of God to accomplish his great design by a wonderful and long series of events, that the glory of his wisdom may be displayed in the whole series, and that the glory of his perfections may be seen, appearing, as it were, by parts, and in particular successive manifestations: for if all that glory which appears in all these events had been manifested at once, it would have been too much for us, and more than we at once could take notice of; it would have dazzled our eyes, and overpowered our sight.

2. *Satan is more gloriously triumphed over.* God could easily, by an act of almighty power, at once have crushed Satan. But by giving him time to use his utmost subtlety to hinder the success of what Christ had done and suffered, he is not defeated merely by surprise, but has large opportunity to ply his utmost power and subtlety again and again, to strengthen his own interest all that he can by the work of many ages. Thus God destroys and confounds him, and sets up Christ's kingdom time after time, in spite of all his subtle machinations and great works, and by every step advances it still higher and higher, until at length it is fully set up, and

Satan perfectly and eternally vanquished in the end of all things.

I now proceed to take notice of the particular events whereby, from the end of Christ's humiliation to the end of the world, the success of Christ's purchase has been or shall be accomplished.

1. I would take notice of those things whereby Christ was put into an immediate capacity for accomplishing the end of his purchase.

2. I would show how he obtained or accomplished that success.

PART 1

❧❧❧

CHRIST'S RESURRECTION
AND ASCENSION

I would take notice, first, of those things by which Christ was put into a capacity for accomplishing the end of his purchase. And they are two things, namely, his *resurrection*, and his *ascension*. As we observed before, the incarnation of Christ was necessary in order to Christ's being in a near capacity for the purchase of redemption; so the resurrection and ascension of Christ were requisite, in order to his accomplishing the success of his purchase.

1. *His Resurrection.* It was necessary, in order to Christ's obtaining the end and effect of his purchase of redemption, that he should rise from the dead. For God the Father had committed the whole affair of redemption, not only the purchasing of it, but the bestowing of the blessings purchased, to his Son, that he should not only purchase it as priest, but actually bring it about as king; and that he should do this as God-man. For God the Father would have nothing to do with fallen man, in a way of mercy, but by a Mediator. But in order that Christ might carry on the work of redemption, and accomplish the success of his own purchase as God-man, it was necessary that he should be alive, and so that he should rise from the dead. Therefore Christ, after he had finished this purchase by death, and by continuing for a time under the power of death, rises from the dead, to fulfil the end of his

purchase, and himself to bring about that for which he died; for this matter God the Father had committed unto him, that he might, as Lord of all, manage all to his own purposes: 'For to this end Christ both died, and rose, and revived, that he might be Lord both of the dead and living' (*Rom.* 14:9).

Indeed Christ's resurrection, and so his ascension, was part of the success of what Christ did and suffered in his humiliation. For though Christ did not properly purchase redemption for himself, yet he purchased eternal life and glory for himself by what he did and suffered; and this eternal life and glory was given him as a reward of what he did and suffered. 'He humbled himself, and became obedient unto death, even the death of the cross. Wherefore God also hath highly exalted him' (*Phil.* 2:8-9). And it may be looked upon as part of the success of Christ's purchase, if it be considered that Christ did not rise as a private person, but as the head of the elect church; so that they did, as it were, all rise with him. Christ was justified in his resurrection, that is, God acquitted and discharged him hereby, as having done and suffered enough for the sins of all the elect.

'Who was delivered for our offences, and raised again for our justification' (*Rom.* 4: 25). And God put him in possession of eternal life, as the head of the church, as a sure earnest that they should follow. For when Christ rose from the dead, that was the beginning of eternal life in him. His life before his death was a mortal life, a temporal life; but his life after his resurrection was an eternal life: 'Knowing that Christ being raised from the dead, dieth no more; death hath no more dominion over him' (*Rom.* 6:9). 'I am he that liveth, and was dead; and behold, I am alive for evermore, Amen' (*Rev.* 1:18). But he was put in possession of this eternal life, as the Head of the body; and took possession of it, not only to enjoy himself, but to bestow on all who believe in him: so that the whole church, as it were, rises in him. And now he who lately suffered so much, after this is to suffer no more for ever, but to enter into eternal glory God the Father neither expects nor desires any more suffering.

This resurrection of Christ is the most joyful event that ever came to pass; because hereby Christ rested from the great and difficult work of purchasing redemption, and received God's testimony, that it was finished.

The death of Christ was the greatest and most wonderful event that ever came to pass; but that has a great deal in it that is sorrowful. But by the resurrection of Christ, that sorrow is turned into joy. The head of the whole church, in that great event, enters on the possession of eternal life; and the whole church is, as it were, 'begotten again to a lively hope' (*1 Pet.* 1:3). Weeping had continued for a night, but now joy cometh in the morning, the most joyful morning that ever was. This is the day of the reigning of the head of the church, and all the church reigns with him. This is spoken of as a day which was worthy to be commemorated with the greatest joy of all days. 'This is the day which the Lord hath made, we will rejoice and be glad in it' (*Psa.* 118:24). And therefore this above all other days is appointed for the day of the church's spiritual rejoicing to the end of the world, to be weekly sanctified, as their day of holy rest and joy, that the church therein may rest and rejoice with her head. And as the third chapter of Genesis is the most sorrowful chapter in the Bible, so those chapters in the evangelists that give an account of the resurrection of Christ may be looked upon as the most joyful chapters of all the Bible; for those chapters give an account of the finishing of the purchase of redemption, and the beginning of the glory of the head of the church, as the greatest seal and earnest of the eternal glory of all the rest.

It is further to be observed, that the day of the gospel most properly begins with the resurrection of Christ. Until Christ rose from the dead, the Old Testament dispensation

remained; but now it ceases, all being fulfilled that was shadowed forth in the typical ordinances of that dispensation, so
that here most properly is the end of the Old Testament
night. And Christ rising from the grave with joy and glory,
was as the joyful bridegroom of the church, as a glorious con-
queror to subdue their enemies under their feet; or was like
the sun rising as it were from under the earth, after a long
night of darkness, and coming forth as a bridegroom, prepared as a strong man to run his race, appearing in joyful
light to enlighten the world. Now that joyful and excellent
dispensation begins, that glorious dispensation, of which the
prophets prophesied so much; now the gospel sun is risen in
glory and 'with healing in his wings', that those who fear
God's name, may 'go forth, and grow up as calves of the
stall'.

2. *Christ's Ascension into Heaven.* In this I would include
his sitting at the right hand of God. For Christ's ascension
and sitting at the right hand of God can scarcely be looked
upon as two distinct things; for ascension was nothing else,
but ascending to God's right hand. It was his coming to sit
down at his Father's right hand in glory. This was another
thing whereby Christ was put into a capacity for the accomplishing the effect of his purchase, as one that comes to be a
deliverer of a people as their king, in order to it, and that he
may be under the best capacity for it, is first installed in his
throne. We are told, that Christ was exalted for this end, that
he might accomplish the success of his redemption: 'Him
hath God exalted with his right hand to be a Prince and a
Saviour, for to give repentance unto Israel, and forgiveness of
sins' (*Acts* 5:31).

Christ's ascension into heaven was, as it were, his solemn
enthronement, whereby the Father did set him upon the
throne, and invest him with the glory of his kingdom which

he had purchased for himself, that he might thereby obtain the success of his redemption in conquering all his enemies. 'Sit thou at my right hand, until I make thine enemies thy footstool' (*Psa.* 110:1). Christ entered into heaven in order to obtain the success of his purchase, as the high priest of old, after he had offered sacrifice, entered into the holy of holies with the blood of the sacrifice, in order to obtain the success of the sacrifice which he had offered. See Hebrews 9:12. He entered into heaven, there to make intercession for his people, to plead the sacrifice which he had made in order to the success of it (*Heb.* 7:25).

And as he ascended into heaven, God the Father did in a visible manner set him on the throne as king of the universe. He then put the angels all under him, and subjected heaven and earth under him, that he might govern them for the good of the people for whom he had died (*Eph.* 1:20–22).

And as Christ rose from the dead, so he ascended into heaven as the head of the body and forerunner of all the church; and so they, as it were, ascend with him, as well as rise with him: so that we are both raised up together, and made to sit together in heavenly places in Christ (*Eph.* 2:6).

The day of Christ's ascension into heaven was doubtless a joyful, glorious day in heaven. And as heaven received Christ, the God-man, as its king, so doubtless it received a great accession of glory and happiness, far beyond what it had before. So that the times in both parts of the church, both that part which is in heaven, and also that which is on earth, are become more glorious since Christ's humiliation than before.

So much for those things whereby Christ was put into the best capacity for obtaining the success of redemption.

PART 2

❧❀❧

CHRIST'S ACCOMPLISHMENT IN GRACE AND GLORY

I now proceed to show how he accomplished this success. And here I would observe, that this success consists in two things, namely, either in Grace or in Glory. That success which consists in the former is to be seen in those works of God which are wrought during those ages of the church wherein the church is continued under the outward means of Grace. That success which consists in the latter of these, Glory, has its chief accomplishment at the day of judgment.

SECTION 1

SUCCESS ACCOMPLISHED BY GOD'S GRACE HERE

I would first consider the former kind of success, consisting in God's grace here; which mainly appears in the works of God during the time that the Christian church continues under the means of grace; which is from Christ's resurrection to his appearing in the clouds of heaven to judgment; which includes the three former of those great events of providence before mentioned, which are called Christ's coming in his kingdom. In speaking of this success, I would:

1. Mention those things by which the means of this success were established after Christ's resurrection; and

2. Consider the success itself.

1. I would consider those dispensations of providence by which the means of this success were established after Christ's resurrection.

i. *The abolishing of the Jewish dispensation.* This indeed was gradually done, but it began from the time of Christ's resurrection, in which the abolition of it is founded. This was the first thing done towards bringing the former state of the world to an end. This is to be looked upon as the great means of the success of Christ's redemption. For the Jewish dispensation was not fitted for more than one nation; it was not fitted for the practice of the world in general, or for a church of God dwelling in all parts of the world; nor would it have been in any wise practicable by them. It would have been impossible for men living in all parts of the world to go to Jerusalem three times a year, as was prescribed in that constitution.

When therefore God had a design of enlarging his church, as he did after Christ's resurrection, it was necessary that this dispensation should be abolished. If it had been continued, it would have been a great block and hindrance to the enlargement of the church. And besides, their ceremonial law, by reason of its burdensomeness, and the great peculiarity of some of its rites, was as it were a wall of partition, and was the ground of enmity between the Jews and Gentiles, and would have kept the Gentiles from complying with the true religion. This wall therefore was broken down to make way for the more extensive success of the gospel (see *Eph.* 2:14–15).

ii. The next thing in order of time seems to be *the appointment of the Christian Sabbath.* For though this was gradually established in the Christian church, yet those things by which the revelation of God's mind and will was made, began on the day of Christ's resurrection, by his appearing then to his disciples (*John* 20:19), and was afterwards confirmed by his appearing from time to time on that day rather than any other (*John* 20: 26) and by his sending down the Holy Spirit so remarkably on that day (*Acts* 2:1), and afterwards in directing that public assemblies and the public worship of Christians should be on that day, which may be concluded from Acts 20:7, 1 Corinthians 16:1-2 and Revelation 1:10. And so the day of the week on which Christ rose from the dead, that joyful day, is appointed to be the day of the church's holy rejoicing to the end of the world, and the day of their stated public worship. And this is a very great and principal means of the success which the gospel has had in the world.

iii. The next thing was *Christ's appointment of the gospel ministry*, and commissioning and sending forth his apostles to teach and baptize all nations. Of these things we have an account in Matthew 28:19-20: 'Go ye, therefore, and teach all nations, baptizing them in the name of the Father, and of the Son, and of the Holy Ghost; teaching them to observe all things whatsoever I have commanded you: and lo, I am with you alway, even unto the end of the world.' There were three things done by this one instruction and commission of Christ to his apostles, namely:

a. The appointment of the office of the gospel ministry. For this commission which Christ gives to his apostles, in the most essential parts of it, belongs to all ministers; and the apostles, by virtue of it, were ministers or elders of the church.

b. There is something peculiar in this commission of the apostles, to go forth from one nation to another, preaching the gospel in all the world. The apostles had something above what belonged to their ordinary character as ministers; they had an extraordinary power of teaching and ruling, which extended to all the churches; and not only all the churches which then were, but all that should be to the end of the world by their ministry. And so the apostles were, as it were, in subordination to Christ, made foundations of the Christian church (see *Eph.* 2:20 and *Rev.* 21:14).

c. There is an appointment of Christian baptism. This ordinance indeed had a beginning before; John the Baptist and Christ both baptized. But now especially by this institution is it established as an ordinance to be upheld in the Christian church to the end of the world. The ordinance of the Lord's supper had been established before, just before Christ's crucifixion.

iv. The next thing to be observed is *the enduing of the apostles, and others, with extraordinary and miraculous gifts of the Holy Ghost*, such as the gift of tongues, the gift of healing, of prophecy, etc. The Spirit of God was poured out in great abundance in this respect; so that not only ministers but a very great part of the Christians through the world were endued with them, both old and young; not only officers and more honourable persons, but the meaner sort of people, servants and handmaids, were commonly endued with them, agreeable to Joel's prophecy (*Joel* 2:28-29), of which the Apostle Peter takes notice, that it is accomplished in this dispensation (*Acts* 2:11).

How wonderful a dispensation was this! Under the Old Testament only a few had such honours put upon them by God. Moses wished that all the Lord's people were prophets (*Num.* 11:29), whereas Joshua thought it much that Eldad and Medad prophesied. But now we find the wish of Moses fulfilled. And this continued in a very considerable degree to the end of the apostolic age, or the first hundred years after the birth of Christ, which is therefore called the age of miracles.

This was a great means of the success of the gospel in that age, and of establishing the Christian church in all parts of the world; and not only in that age, but in all ages to the end of the world: for Christianity being by this means established through so great a part of the known world by miracles, it was after that more easily continued by tradition; and then, by means of these extraordinary gifts of the Holy Ghost, the apostles, and others, were enabled to write the New Testament, to be an infallible rule of faith and manners to the church to the end of the world. And furthermore, these miracles stand recorded in those writings as a standing proof and evidence of the truth of the Christian religion to all ages.

v. The next thing I would observe is *the revealing of those glorious doctrines of the gospel fully and plainly*, which had under the Old Testament been obscurely revealed. The doctrine of Christ's satisfaction and righteousness, his ascension and glory, and the way of salvation, under the Old Testament were, in a great measure, hid under the veil of types and shadows and more obscure revelations, as Moses put a veil on his face to hide the shining of it. But now the veil of the temple is rent from the top to the bottom; and Christ, the antitype of Moses, shines. The shining of his face is without a veil (*2 Cor.* 3:12-13,18). Now these glorious mysteries are plainly revealed which were in a great measure kept secret from the foundation of the world (*Eph.* 3:3-5), 'According to the revelation of the mystery, which was kept secret since the world began, but now is made manifest' (*Rom.* 16:25); 'Even the mystery which hath been hid from ages and from generations, but now is made manifest to his saints' (*Col.* 1:26).

Thus the Sun of Righteousness, after it is risen from under the earth, begins to shine forth clearly, and not only by a dim reflection as it did before. Christ, before his death, revealed many things more clearly than ever they had been revealed in the Old Testament; but the great mysteries of Christ's redemption, and reconciliation by his death, and justification by his righteousness, were not so plainly revealed before Christ's resurrection. Christ gave this reason for it, that he would not put new wine into old bottles; and it was gradually done after Christ's resurrection.

In all likelihood, Christ much more clearly instructed them personally after his resurrection, and before his ascension; as we read that he continued with them forty days, speaking of the things pertaining to the kingdom (*Acts* 1:3), and that 'he opened their understandings, that they might understand the scriptures' (*Luke* 24:45). But the clear revelation of these things was principally after the pouring out of the Spirit on the day of Pentecost, agreeable to Christ's promise, 'I have yet many things to say unto you, but ye cannot bear them now. Howbeit, when he, the Spirit of truth, is come, he will guide you into all truth' (*John* 16:12-13). This clear revelation of the mysteries of the gospel, as they are delivered, we have chiefly through the hands of the Apostle Paul, by whose writings a child may come to know more of the doctrines of the gospel, in many respects, than the greatest prophets knew under the darkness of the Old Testament. Thus we see how the light of the gospel, which began to dawn immediately after the Fall, and gradually grew and increased through all the ages of the Old Testament, as we observed as we went along, is now come to the light of perfect day, and the brightness of the sun shining forth in his unveiled glory.

vi. The next thing that I would observe, is *the appointment of the office of deacons in the Christian church*, which we have an account of in the sixth chapter of the Acts, to take care for the outward supply of the members of Christ's church, and the exercise of that great Christian virtue of charity.

vii. *The calling, and qualifying, and sending of the Apostle Paul.* This was begun in his conversion as he was going to Damascus, and was one of the greatest means of the success of Christ's redemption that followed for this success was more by the labours, preaching, and writings of this apostle than all the other apostles put together. For, as he says, he 'laboured more abundantly than they all' (*1 Cor.* 15:10); so his success was more abundant than that of them all. As he was the apostle of the Gentiles, so it was mainly by his ministry that the Gentiles were called, and the gospel spread through the world; and our nation, and the other nations of Europe, have the gospel among them chiefly through his means; and he was more employed by the Holy Ghost in revealing the glorious doctrines of the gospel by his writings, for the use of the church in all ages than all the other apostles taken together.

viii. The next thing I would observe is *the institution of ecclesiastical councils*, for deciding controversies, and ordering the affairs of the church of Christ, of which we have an account in the fifteenth chapter of Acts.

ix. The last thing I shall mention under this head is *the committing of the New Testament to writing.* This was all written after the resurrection of Christ; and all written either by the apostles or by the evangelists, who were companions of the apostles. All the New Testament was written by the apostles themselves, excepting what was written by Mark and Luke, namely, the gospels of Mark and Luke, and the book of the Acts of the Apostles. He that wrote the gospel of Mark is supposed to be he whose mother was Mary, in whose house they were praying for Peter when he, brought out of prison by the angel, came and knocked at the door: 'And when he had considered the thing, he came to the house of Mary the mother of John, whose surname was Mark, where many were gathered together, praying' (*Acts* 12: 12).

He was the companion of the apostles Barnabas and Saul: 'And Barnabas determined to take with them John, whose surname was Mark' (*Acts* 15:37). He was Barnabas's sister's son, and seems sometimes to have been a companion of the Apostle Paul: 'Aristarchus, my fellow prisoner, saluteth you, and Marcus, sister's son to Barnabas; touching whom ye received commandment: if he come unto you, receive him' (*Col.* 4:10).

The apostles seem to have made great account of him, as appears by those places, and also by Acts 12:25: 'And Barnabas and Saul returned from Jerusalem, and took with them John, whose surname was Mark'; and Acts 13:5: 'And when they were at Salamis, they preached the word of God in the synagogues of the Jews; and they had also John to their minister'; and 2 Timothy 4:11: 'Only Luke is with me: take Mark and bring him with thee; for he is profitable to me for the ministry.'

This Luke, who wrote the gospel of Luke and the book of Acts, was a great companion of the Apostle Paul. He is spoken of as being with him in the last-mentioned place, and speaks of himself as accompanying him in his travels in the history of the Acts; and therefore he speaks in the first person plural, when speaking of Paul's travels, saying, *We* went to such and such a place; *We* set sail; *We* launched from such a place; and landed at such a place. He was greatly beloved by the Apostle Paul: he is that beloved physician spoken of in Colossians 4:14. The Apostle ranks Mark and Luke among his fellow labourers: 'Marcus, Aristarchus, Demas, Lucas, my fellow labourers' (*Philem.* 24).

The rest of the books were all written by the apostles themselves. The books of the New Testament are either historical, or doctrinal, or prophetical. The historical books are the writings of the four evangelists, giving us the history of Christ, and his purchase of redemption, and his resurrection and ascension; and the Acts of the Apostles, giving an account of the great things by which the Christian church was first established and propagated. The doctrinal books are the epistles. These, most of them, we have from the great Apostle Paul. And we have one prophetical book, which takes place after the end of the history of the whole Bible, and gives an account of the great events which were to come to pass by which the work of redemption was to be carried on to the end of the world.

All these books are supposed to have been written before the destruction of Jerusalem, excepting those which were written by the Apostle John, who lived the longest of all the apostles, and wrote what he wrote after the destruction of Jerusalem, as is supposed. And to this beloved disciple it was that Christ revealed those wonderful things which were to come to pass in his church to the end of time; and he was the person that put the finishing hand to the canon of the Scriptures, and sealed the whole of it. So that now the canon of Scripture, that great and standing written rule, which was begun about Moses's time, is completed and settled, and a curse denounced against him that adds any thing to it, or diminishes any thing from it. And so all things are established and completed which relate to the appointed means of grace. All the stated means of grace were finished in the apostolical age, or before the death of the Apostle John, and are to remain unaltered to the day of judgment.

Thus far we have considered those things by which the means of grace were given and established in the Christian church.

2. The other thing proposed relating to the success of Christ's redemption during the church's continuance under means of grace was to show how this success was carried on, which is what I would now proceed to do.

And here it is worthy to be remembered that the Christian church, during its continuance under the means of grace, is in two very different states.

1. *In a suffering, afflicted, persecuted state*, as, for the most part it is, from the resurrection of Christ until the fall of Antichrist.

2. *In a state of peace and prosperity*, which is the state that the church, for the most part, is to be in after the fall of Antichrist.

First, I would show how the success of Christ's redemption is carried on during the continuance of the church's suffering state, from the resurrection of Christ to the fall of Antichrist. This space of time, for the most part, is a state of the church's sufferings, and is so represented in Scripture. Indeed God is pleased, out of love and pity to his elect, to grant many intermissions of the church's sufferings during this time, whereby the days of tribulation are, as it were, shortened. But from Christ's resurrection until the fall of Antichrist is the appointed day of Zion's troubles. During this space of time, for the most part, some part or other of the church is under persecution; and great part of the time the whole church, or at least the generality of God's people, have been persecuted.

For the first three hundred years after Christ, the church was for the most part in a state of great affliction, the object of reproach and persecution, first by the Jews, and then by the heathen. After this, from the beginning of Constantine's time, the church had rest and prosperity for a little while, which is represented in Revelation 7 at the beginning, by the angel's holding the four winds for a little while. But presently after, the church again suffered persecution from the Arians; and after that, Antichrist rose, and the church was driven away into the wilderness, and was kept down in obscurity, and contempt, and suffering for a long time, under Antichrist, before the Reformation by Luther and others. And since the Reformation, the church's persecutions have been beyond all that ever were before.

And though some parts of God's church sometimes have had rest, yet to this day, for the most part, the true church is very much kept under by its enemies, and some parts of it under grievous persecution; and so we may expect it will continue until the fall of Antichrist; and then will come the appointed day of the church's prosperity on earth, the set time in which God will favour Zion, the time when the saints shall not be kept under by wicked men, as it has been hitherto; but wherein they shall be uppermost, and shall 'reign on earth', as it is said (*Rev.* 5:10). 'And the kingdom shall be given to the people of the saints of the Most High' (*Dan.* 7:27).

This suffering state of the church is in Scripture represented as a state of the church's travail (*John* 16:20-21; *Rev.* 12:1-2). What the church is in travail striving to bring forth during this time is that glory and prosperity of the church which shall be after the fall of Antichrist, and then shall she bring forth her child.

This is a long time of the church's trouble and affliction, and is so spoken of in Scripture, though it be spoken of as being but for a little season, in comparison of the eternal prosperity of the church. Hence the church, under the long continuance of this affliction, cries out, as in Revelaion 6:10, 'How long, O Lord, holy and true, dost thou not judge and avenge our blood on them that dwell on the earth?' And we are told, that 'white robes were given unto every one of them;

and it was said unto them, that they should rest yet for a little season, until their fellow servants also, and their brethren, that should be killed as they were, should be fulfilled.' So, 'How long shall it be to the end of these wonders?' (*Dan.* 12: 6). It is to be observed that, during the time of these sufferings of the church, the main instrument of their sufferings has been the Roman government. Her afflictions have almost all along been from Rome. That is therefore in the New Testament called Babylon; because, just as of old the troubles of the city Jerusalem were mainly from that adverse city Babylon, so the troubles of the Christian church, the spiritual Jerusalem, during the long time of its tribulation, is mainly from Rome. Before the time of Constantine, the troubles of the Christian church were from heathen Rome; since that time, its troubles have been mainly from Antichristian Rome. And as of old, the captivity of the Jews ceased on the destruction of Babylon, so the time of the trouble of the Christian church will cease with the destruction of the church of Rome, that spiritual Babylon.

In showing how the success of Christ's redemption is carried on, during this time of the church's tribulation, I would show:

1. How it was carried on until the destruction of Jerusalem, with which ended the first great dispensation of providence which is called Christ's coming in his kingdom.

2. How it was carried on from thence to the destruction of the heathen empire in the time of Constantine, which is the second dispensation called Christ's coming.

3. How it was carried on from thence to the destruction of Antichrist, when will be accomplished the third great event called Christ's coming, and with which the days of the church's tribulation and travail end.

1. I would show how the success of Christ's purchase of redemption was carried on *from Christ's resurrection to the destruction of Jerusalem.* In speaking of this, I would take notice, i. of *the success itself;* ii. of *the opposition made against it* by the enemies of it; and iii. of *the terrible judgments of God* on those enemies.

i. I would observe *the success itself.* Soon after Christ had finished the purchase of redemption, and was gone into heaven, and entered into the holy of holies with his own blood, there began a glorious success of what he had done and suffered. Having undermined the foundation of Satan's kingdom, it began to fall apace. Swiftly did it hasten to ruin in the world, which might well be compared to Satan's falling like lightning from heaven. Satan before had exalted his throne very high in this world, even to the very stars of heaven, reigning with great glory in his heathen Roman empire: but never before had he such a downfall as he had soon after Christ's ascension. He had, we may suppose, been very lately triumphing in a supposed victory, having brought about the death of Christ, which he doubtless gloried in as the greatest feat that ever he did; and probably imagined he had totally defeated God's design by him. But he was quickly made sensible that he had only been ruining his own kingdom, when he saw it tumbling so fast so soon after, as a consequence of the death of Christ. For Christ, by his death, having purchased the Holy Spirit, and having ascended, and received the promise of the Spirit, he poured it forth abundantly for the conversion of thousands and millions of souls.

Never had Christ's kingdom been so set up in the world. There probably were more souls converted in the age of the apostles than had been before from the beginning of the world until that time. Thus God so soon began gloriously to accomplish his promise to his Son, wherein he had promised that he should see his seed, and that the pleasure of the Lord should prosper in his hand, if he should make his soul an offering for sin. And,

a. Here is to be observed the success which the gospel had *among the Jews*, for God first began with them. He, being about to reject the main body of that people, first calls in his elect from among them, before he forsook them, to turn to the Gentiles. It was so in former great and dreadful judgments of God on that nation. The bulk of them were destroyed, and only a remnant saved, or reformed. So it was in the rejection of the ten tribes, long before this rejection: the bulk of the ten tribes were rejected, when they left the true worship of God in Jeroboam's time, and afterwards more fully in Ahab's time. But yet there was a remnant of them that God reserved. A number left their possessions in these tribes, and went and settled in the tribes of Judah and Benjamin. And afterwards there were seven thousand in Ahab's time, who had not bowed the knee to Baal. And so, in the captivity in Babylon, only a remnant of them ever returned to their own land. And so now again, by far the greater part of the people were rejected entirely, but some few were saved. And therefore the Holy Ghost compares this reservation of a number that were converted by the preaching of the apostles, to those former remnants: 'Esaias also crieth concerning Israel, Though the number of the children of Israel be as the sand of the sea, a remnant shall be saved' (*Rom.* 9:27). See Isaiah 10:22.

The glorious success of the gospel among the Jews after Christ's ascension, began by the pouring out of the Spirit upon the day of Pentecost, of which we read in Acts 2. So wonderful was this pouring out of the Spirit, and so remarkable and swift the effect of it, that we read of three thousand who were converted to the Christian faith in one day (*Acts* 2:41). And probably the greater part of these were savingly converted.

And after this, we read of God's adding to the church daily such as should be saved, verse 47. And soon after, we read, that the number of them were about five thousand. Thus were not only a multitude converted, but the church was then eminent in piety, as appears by Acts 2:46-47 and Acts 4:32.

Thus the Christian church was first of all of the nation of Israel; and therefore, when the Gentiles were called, they were but as it were added to Israel, to the seed of Abraham. They were added to the Christian church of Israel, as the proselytes of old were to the Mosaic church of Israel; and so were, as it were, only grafted on the stock of Abraham, and were not a distinct tree; for they are all still the seed of Abraham and Israel; as Ruth the Moabitess, and Uriah the Hittite, and other proselytes of old, were the same people, and ranked as the seed of Israel.

So the Christian church at first began at Jerusalem, and from thence was propagated to all nations; so that this church of Jerusalem was the church that was, as it were, the mother of all other churches in the world, agreeable to the prophecy, 'Out of Zion shall go forth the law, and the word of the Lord from Jerusalem: and he shall judge among the nations, and rebuke many people' (*Isa.* 2:3-4). So that the whole church of God is still God's Jerusalem. They are his spiritual Jerusalem and are, as it were, only added to the church which was begun in the literal Jerusalem.

After this, we read of many thousands of Jews that believed in Jerusalem (*Acts* 21:20). And so we read of multitudes of Jews who were converted in other cities of Judea; and not only so, but even in other parts of the world. For wherever the apostles went, if there were any Jews there, their manner was, first to go into the synagogues of the Jews, and preach the gospel to them, and many in one place and another believed, as in Damascus and Antioch, and many other places that we read of in the Acts of the Apostles.

In this pouring out of the Spirit, which began at the Pentecost following Christ's ascension, began that first great dispensation which is called Christ's coming in his kingdom. Christ's coming thus in a spiritual manner for the glorious setting up of his kingdom in the world, is represented by Christ himself as his coming down from heaven, whither he had ascended (*John* 14:18). There Christ, having spoken of his ascension, says, 'I will not leave you comfortless; I will come unto you', speaking of his coming by the coming of the Comforter, the Spirit of truth. And in verse 28: 'Ye have heard how I said unto you, I go away, and come again unto you.' And thus the apostles began to see the kingdom of heaven come with power, as he promised they should (*Mark* 9:1).

b. What is next to be observed is the success of the gospel *among the Samaritans*. After the success of the gospel had been so gloriously begun among the Jews proper, the Spirit of God was next wonderfully poured out on the Samaritans, who were not Jews by nation, but the posterity of those whom the king of Assyria removed from different parts of his dominions and settled in the land that was inhabited by the ten tribes whom he carried captive. But yet they had received the five books of Moses, and practised most of the rites of the law of Moses, and so were a sort of mongrel Jews. We do not find them reckoned as Gentiles in the New Testament: for the calling of the Gentiles is spoken of as a new thing after this, beginning with the conversion of Cornelius. But yet it was an instance of making that a people that were no people, for they had corrupted the religion which Moses commanded, and did not go up to Jerusalem to worship, but had another temple of their own in Mount Gerizim, which is the mountain of which the woman of Samaria speaks, when she says, 'Our fathers worshipped in this mountain.' Christ there does not approve of their separation from the Jews, but tells the woman of

Samaria, that they worshipped they knew not what, and that salvation is of the Jews. But now salvation is brought from the Jews to them by the preaching of Philip (except that before Christ had some success among them) with whose preaching there was a glorious pouring out of the Spirit of God in the city of Samaria. We are told that the people 'believed Philip preaching the things concerning the kingdom of God, and the name of Jesus Christ, [and] were baptized, both men and women'; and that 'there was great joy in that city' (*Acts* 8:8 and 12).

Thus Christ had a glorious harvest in Samaria; which is what Christ seems to have had respect to in what he said to his disciples at Jacob's well three or four years before on the occasion of the people of Samaria's appearing at a distance in the fields coming to the place where Christ was, at the instigation of the woman of Samaria. On that occasion, he bids his disciples lift up their eyes to the fields, for that they were white to the harvest (*John* 4: 35-36). The disposition which the people of Samaria showed towards Christ and his gospel showed that they were ripe for the harvest. But now the harvest is come by Philip's preaching. There used to be a most bitter enmity between the Jews and Samaritans; but now, by their conversion, the Christian Jews and Samaritans are all happily united; for in Christ Jesus is neither Jew nor Samaritan, but Christ is all in all. This was a glorious instance of the wolf's dwelling with the lamb, and the leopard's lying down with the kid.

c. The next thing to be observed is the success there was of the gospel in calling *the Gentiles*. This was a great and glorious dispensation of divine providence, much spoken of in the prophecies of the Old Testament, and spoken of by the apostles, time after time, as a most glorious event of Christ's redemption. This was begun in the conversion of Cornelius and his family, greatly to the admiration of Peter, who was used as the instrument of it, and of those who were with him, and of those who were informed of it; as you may see, Acts 10 and 11. And the next instance of it that we have any account of, was in the conversion of great numbers of Gentiles in Cyprus, and Cyrene, and Antioch, by the disciples that were scattered abroad by the persecution which arose about Stephen, as we have an account in Acts 11:19-21. And presently, upon this, the disciples began to be called Christians first at Antioch (*Acts* 19:26).

And after this vast multitudes of Gentiles were converted in many different parts of the world, chiefly by the ministry of the Apostle Paul, a glorious pouring out of the Spirit accompanying his preaching in one place and another. Multitudes flocked into the church of Christ in a great number of cities where the Apostle came. So the number of the members of the Christian church that were Gentiles soon far exceeded the number of its Jewish members; yea, so that in less than ten years' time after Paul was sent forth from Antioch to preach to the Gentiles, it was said of him and his companions, that they had turned the world upside down: 'These that have turned the world upside down are come hither also' (*Acts* 17:6).

But the most remarkable pouring out of the Spirit in a particular city that we have any account of in the New Testament, seems to be that in the city of Ephesus, which was a very great city. Of this we have an account in Acts 19. There was also a very extraordinary ingathering of souls at Corinth, one of the greatest cities in all Greece.

And after this, many were converted in Rome, the chief city of all the world; and the gospel was propagated into all parts of the Roman empire. Thus the gospel sun, which had lately risen on the Jews, now rose upon, and began to enlighten, the heathen world, after they had continued in gross heathenish darkness for so many ages.

This was a great thing, and a new thing, such as never had been before. All nations but the Jews, and a few who had at one time and another joined with them, had been rejected from about Moses' time. The Gentile world had been covered over with the thick darkness of idolatry; but now, at the joyful, glorious sound of the gospel, they began in all parts to forsake their old idols and to abhor them, and to cast them to the moles and to the bats, and to learn to worship the true God, and to trust in his Son Jesus Christ; and God owned them for his people.

Those who had so long been afar off, were made nigh by the blood of Christ. Men were changed from being heathenish and brutish, to be the children of God; were called out of Satan's kingdom of darkness, and brought into God's marvellous light; and in almost all countries throughout the known world there were assemblies of the people of God; joyful praises were sung to the true God, and Jesus Christ the glorious Redeemer. Now that great building which God began soon after the Fall of man rises gloriously, not in the same manner that it had done in former ages, but in quite a new manner. Now Daniel's prophecies concerning the last kingdom, which should succeed the four heathenish monarchies, begins to be fulfilled. Now the stone cut out of the mountain without hands began to smite the image on its feet, and to break it in pieces, and to grow great, and to make great advances towards filling the earth; and now God gathers together the elect from the four winds of heaven, by the preaching of the apostles and other ministers, the angels of the Christian church, sent forth with the great sound of the gospel trumpet, before the destruction of Jerusalem, agreeable to what Christ foretold (*Matt.* 24:31).

This was the success of Christ's purchase, during this first period of the Christian church, which terminated in the destruction of Jerusalem.

ii. I would proceed now, in the second place, to take notice of *the opposition which was made to this success of Christ's purchase* by the enemies of it. Satan, who lately was so ready to triumph and exult, as though he had gained the victory in putting Christ to death, now finding himself fallen into the pit which he had digged, and finding his kingdom falling so fast, and seeing Christ's kingdom make such amazing progress, such as never had been before, we may conclude he was filled with the greatest confusion and astonishment, and hell seemed to be effectually alarmed by it to make the most violent opposition against it.

And, first, the devil stirred up the Jews, who had before crucified Christ, to persecute the church; for it is observable, that the persecution which the church suffered during this period was mostly from the Jews. Thus we read in the Acts how, when, at Jerusalem, the Holy Ghost was poured out at Pentecost, the Jews mocked and said, 'These men are full of new wine'; and how the scribes and Pharisees, and the captain of the temple, were alarmed and bestirred themselves to oppose and persecute the apostles, and first apprehended and threatened them, and afterwards imprisoned and beat them; and breathing out threatenings and slaughter against the disciples of the Lord, they stoned Stephen in a tumultuous rage. They were not content to persecute those that they could find in Judea but sent abroad to Damascus and other places, to persecute all that they could find everywhere. Herod, who was chief among them, stretched forth his hands to vex the church, and killed James with the sword, and proceeded to take Peter also, and cast him into prison.

So in other countries we find that, almost wherever the apostles came, the Jews opposed the gospel in a most malignant manner, contradicting and blaspheming. How many things did the blessed Apostle Paul suffer at their hands in one place and another! How violent and bloodthirsty did they show themselves towards him, when he came to bring alms to his nation! In this persecution and cruelty was fulfilled the saying of Christ, 'Behold, I send you prophets, and wise men, and scribes: and some of them ye shall kill and crucify; and some of them shall ye scourge in your synagogues, and persecute them from city to city' (*Matt.* 23:34).

iii. I proceed to take notice of the *judgments which were executed* on those enemies of Christ, the persecuting Jews.

a. The bulk of the people were given up to judicial blindness of mind and hardness of heart. Christ denounced such a woe upon them in the days of his flesh, as Matthew 13:14-15. This curse was also denounced on them by the Apostle Paul, Acts 28:25-27, and under this curse, under this judicial blindness and hardness, they remain to this very day, having been subject to it for about seventeen hundred years. This is the most awful instance of such a judgment, and they the monuments of God's terrible vengeance, of any people that ever were. That they should continue from generation to generation so obstinately to reject Christ that it is a very rare thing that any one of them is converted to the Christian faith, though their own Scriptures of the Old Testament, which they acknowledge, are so full of plain testimonies against them, is a remarkable evidence of their being dreadfully left of God.

b. They were rejected and cast off from being any longer God's visible people. They were broken off from the stock of Abraham, and since then have no more been reputed his seed than the Ishmaelites or Edomites, who are as much his natural seed as they. The greater part of the two tribes were now cast off, as the ten tribes had been before, and another people were taken in their room, agreeable to the predictions of their own prophets: 'They have moved me to jealousy with that which is not God; they have provoked me to anger with their vanities; and I will move them to jealousy with those which are not a people, I will provoke them to anger with a foolish nation' (*Deut.* 32:21). And, 'I am sought of them that asked not for me; I am found of them that sought me not' (*Isa.* 65:1). They were visibly rejected and cast off by God's directing his apostles to turn away from them, and let them alone: 'Then Paul and Barnabas waxed bold, and said, It was necessary that the word of God should first have been spoken to you: but seeing ye put it from you, and judge yourselves unworthy of everlasting life, lo, we turn to the Gentiles: for so hath the Lord commanded us' (*Acts* 13:46-47). See also Acts 18:6 and 28:28.

Thus far we have had the Scripture history to guide us; henceforward we shall have the guidance only of two things, Scripture prophecy, and God's providence, as related in human histories.

c. The third and last judgment of God on those enemies of the success of the gospel which I shall mention is the terrible destruction of their city and country by the Romans. They had great warnings and many means used with them before this destruction. First, John the Baptist warned them, and told them that the axe was laid at the root of the tree; and that every tree which should not bring forth good fruit should be hewn down and cast into the fire. Then Christ warned them very particularly, and told them of their approaching destruction, and at the thoughts of it wept over them. And then the apostles after Christ's ascension abundantly warned them. But they proved obstinate, and went on in their opposition to Christ and his church, and in their bitter persecuting practices. Their so malignantly persecuting the Apostle Paul, of which we have an account towards the end of the Acts of the

Apostles, is supposed to have been not more than seven or eight years before their destruction.

And after this God was pleased to give them one more very remarkable warning by the Apostle Paul, in his epistle to the Hebrews, which is an epistle written to that nation of the Jews, as is supposed, about four years before their destruction, wherein the plainest and clearest arguments are set before them from their own law, and from their prophets, for whom they professed such a regard, to prove that Christ Jesus must be the Son of God, and that all their law pointed to him and typified him, and that their Jewish dispensation must needs have now ceased. For, though the epistle was more immediately directed to the Christian Hebrews, yet the matter of the epistle plainly shows that the apostle intended it for the use and conviction of the unbelieving Jews, and in this epistle, he mentions particularly the approaching destruction, 'So much the more, as ye see the day approaching' (*Heb.* 10:25); and in verse 27, he speaks of the approaching judgment and fiery indignation which should devour the adversaries.

But, the generality of them refusing to receive conviction, God soon destroyed them with such terrible circumstances as the destruction of no country or city since the foundation of the world can parallel, agreeable to what Christ foretold, 'For then shall be tribulation, such as was not from the beginning of the world to this time, no, nor ever shall be' (*Matt.* 24:21) . The first destruction of Jerusalem by the Babylonians was very terrible, as it is in a most affecting manner described by the prophet Jeremiah, in his Lamentations; but this was nothing to the dreadful misery and wrath which they suffered in this destruction.

God, as Christ foretold, brought on them all the righteous blood that had been shed from the foundation of the world. Thus the enemies of Christ are made his footstool after his ascension, agreeable to God's promise in Psalm 110, and

Christ rules them with a rod of iron. The briars and thorns set themselves against him in battle, but he went through them; he burned them together.

This destruction of Jerusalem was in all respects agreeable to what Christ had foretold of it in Matthew 24, as appears by the account which Josephus gives of it, who was then present, and who was one of the Jews, having a share in the calamity, and writing the history of their destruction. Many circumstances of this destruction resembled the destruction of the wicked at the day of judgment, by his account. It was accompanied with many fearful sights in the heavens, and with a separation of the righteous from the wicked. Their city and temple were burnt and razed to the ground, and the ground on which the city stood was ploughed; and so one stone was not left upon another (*Matt.* 24:2).

The people had ceased for the most part to be an independent government after the Babylonish captivity, but the sceptre entirely departed from Judah on the death of Archelaus, when Judea was made a Roman province. After this, they were cast off from being the people of God; but now their very city and land were utterly destroyed, and they carried away from it; and so they have continued in their dispersions through the world for now above sixteen hundred years.

Thus there was a final end put to the Old Testament world. All was finished with a kind of day of judgment, in which the people of God were saved, and his enemies terribly destroyed. Thus does he who was so lately mocked, despised, and spit upon by these Jews, and whose followers they so malignantly persecuted, appear gloriously exalted over his enemies.

2. I would now show how this success was carried on from that time until *the destruction of the heathen empire in the time of Constantine the Great*, the second great event which is in Scripture compared to Christ's coming to judgment.

Jerusalem was destroyed about the year of our Lord 68, and so before that generation passed away which was contemporary with Christ; and it was about thirty-five years after Christ's death. The destruction of the heathen empire under Constantine was about 260 years after this. In showing how the success of the gospel was carried on through this time, I would take notice of the opposition made against it by the Roman Empire, of how the work of the gospel went on, notwithstanding all that opposition, of the peculiar circumstances of tribulation and distress that the church was in just before their deliverance by Constantine, and of the great revolution in Constantine's time.

i. I would briefly show what *opposition* was made against the gospel, and the kingdom of Christ, by the Roman Empire. The opposition that was made to the gospel by the heathen Roman Empire was mainly after the destruction of Jerusalem, though their opposition began before. The opposition that was before the destruction of Jerusalem was mainly by the Jews. But when Jerusalem was destroyed, the Jews were put out of a capacity of much troubling the church. Now therefore the devil turns his hand elsewhere, and uses other instruments. The opposition which was made in the Roman Empire against the kingdom of Christ, was chiefly of two kinds.

a. They employed all their *learning, philosophy and wit* in opposing it. Christ came into the world in an age wherein learning and philosophy were at their height in the Roman Empire. This was employed to the utmost against the kingdom of Christ. The gospel, which held forth a crucified Saviour, was not at all agreeable to the notions of the philosophers. The Christian scheme of trusting in such a crucified Redeemer, appeared foolish and ridiculous to them. Greece was a country the most famous for learning of any in the Roman Empire; but the apostle observes that the doctrine of

Christ crucified appeared foolishness to the Greeks (*1 Cor.* 1:23), and therefore the wise men and philosophers opposed the gospel with all the wit they had. We have a specimen of their manner of opposing, in the story we have of their treatment of the Apostle Paul at Athens, which was a city that had been for many ages the chief seat of philosophers of any in the whole world. We read in Acts 17:18 that the philosphers of the Epicureans and Stoics encountered him saying, 'What will this babbler say? . . . He seemeth to be a setter forth of strange gods.' So they were wont to deride and ridicule Christianity.

And after the destruction of Jerusalem, several of these philosophers published books against it, the chief of whom were Celsus and Porphyry. These wrote books against the Christian religion with a great deal of virulence and contempt, much after the manner that the Deists of the present age oppose and ridicule Christianity. Something of their writings yet remains. As great enemies and despisers as they were of the Christian religion, they never denied the facts recorded of Christ and his apostles in the New Testament, particularly the miracles which they wrought, but allowed them. They lived too near the times wherein these miracles were wrought to deny them, for they were so publicly done, and so lately, that neither Jews nor heathens in those days appeared to deny them; but they ascribed them to the power of magic.

b. The authority of the Roman Empire employed all its *strength*, time after time, to persecute and, if possible, root out, Christianity. This they did in ten general successive persecutions. We have heretofore observed that Christ came into the world when the strength of heathen dominion and authority was the greatest that ever it was under the Roman monarchy, the greatest and strongest human monarchy that ever was on earth. All the strength of this monarchy was employed for a long time to oppose and persecute the Christian church and if possible to destroy it in ten successive attempts, called *the ten heathen persecutions.*

The *first* of these, which was the persecution under Nero, was a little before the destruction of Jerusalem, in which the apostle Peter was crucified, and the apostle Paul beheaded, soon after he wrote his second epistle to Timothy. When he wrote that epistle, he was a prisoner at Rome under Nero, and says, 'I am now ready to be offered, and the time of my departure is at hand. I have fought a good fight, I have finished my course, I have kept the faith' (*2 Tim.* 4:6-7). And there were many thousands of other Christians slain in that persecution. The other nine persecutions were all after the destruction of Jerusalem. Some of these were very terrible indeed, and far exceeded the first persecution under Nero. One emperor after another set himself with the utmost rage to root out the Christian church from the earth, that there should not be so much as the name of Christian left in the world. Thousands, yea millions, were put to cruel deaths in these persecutions, for they spared neither sex nor age.

In the *second* general persecution (under Domitian), that which was next after the destruction of Jerusalem, the apostle John was banished to the isle of Patmos, where he had those visions of which he has given an account in the Revelation. Under that persecution it was reckoned that about forty thousand suffered martydom, which yet was nothing to what were put to death under some succeeding persecutions. Ten thousand suffered that one kind of cruel death, crucifixion, in the *third* persecution under the emperor Adrian. Under the *fourth* persecution, which began about the year of Christ 162, many suffered martydom in England, the land of our forefathers, where Christianity had been planted, it is supposed, in the days of the apostles. And in the later persecutions the Roman emperors, being vexed at the frustration of their predecessors, who were not able to extirpate Christianity or hinder its progress, were enraged to be the more violent in their attempts.

Thus a great part of the first three hundred years after Christ were spent in violent and cruel persecutions of the church by the Roman powers. Satan was very unwilling to let go his hold of so great a part of the world, and every way the chief part of it, as the countries contained in the Roman Empire were, of which he had had quiet possession for so many ages; and therefore, when he saw it going so fast out of his hands, he bestirred himself to his utmost. All hell was, as it were, raised against it to oppose it with its utmost power.

Satan thus exerting himself by the power of the heathen Roman Empire is called in Scripture the great red dragon, having seven heads and ten horns, fighting against the woman clothed with the sun (*Rev.* 12). And the terrible conflict there was between the church of Christ and the powers of the heathen empire before Constantine's time is there, in verse 7, represented by the war between Michael and his angels and the dragon and his angels: 'And there was war in heaven: Michael and his angels fought against the dragon; and the dragon fought and his angels.'

ii. I would take notice of what *success* the gospel had in the world before the time of Constantine, notwithstanding all this opposition. Though the learning and power of the Roman empire were so great, and both were employed to the utmost against Christianity to put a stop to it and to root it out for so long a time and in so many repeated attempts, yet all was in vain. They could neither root it out, nor put a stop to it. But still, in spite of all that they could do, the kingdom of Christ wonderfully prevailed, and Satan's heathen kingdom mouldered and consumed away before it, agreeable to the words of the text, 'The moth shall eat them up like a garment, and the worm shall eat them like wool.' And it was very observable that, for the most part, the more they persecuted the church, the more it increased; insomuch that it became a common saying, 'The blood of the martyrs is the seed of the church.'

Herein the church of Christ proved to be like a palm tree; of which it is remarked, that the greater the weight that is laid upon it, or hung to its branches, the more it grows and flourishes; on which account probably the church is compared to a palm tree in Song of Solomon 7:7: 'This thy stature is like to a palm tree.'

Justin Martyr, an eminent father in the Christian church who lived in the age next after the apostles, in some writings of his which are yet extant, says that in his days there was no part of mankind, whether Greeks or barbarians, or by what name so ever they were called, even the most rude and unpolished nations, where prayers and thanksgivings were not made to the great Creator of the world, through the name of the crucified Jesus. Tertullian, another eminent father in the Christian church, who lived in the beginning of the following age, testifies that in his day the Christian religion had extended itself to the utmost bounds of the then known world, in which he reckons Britain, the country of our forefathers. He thence demonstrates that the kingdom of Christ was then more extensive than any of the four great monarchies, and moreover says that, though the Christians were as strangers of no long standing, yet they had filled all places of the Roman dominions, their cities, islands, castles, corporations, councils, armies, tribes, the palace, senate, and courts of judicature; only they had left to the heathen their temples; and that if they should all agree to retire out of the Roman Empire, the world would be amazed at the solitude and desolation that would ensue upon it, there would be so few left; and that the Christians were enough to be able easily to defend themselves, if they were disposed to rise up in arms against the heathen magistrates.

[305]

And Pliny, a heathen who lived in those days, says that multitudes of each sex, of every age and quality, were become Christians. This superstition, says he, having infected and overrun not the city only but towns and countries, the temples and sacrifices are generally desolate and forsaken.

And it was remarked by both heathen and Christian writers in those days that the famous heathen oracles in their temples, where princes and others for many past ages had been wont to inquire and receive answers with an audible voice from their gods, which were indeed answers from the devil – I say, those oracles were now silenced and struck dumb, and gave no more answers. And particularly the oracle at Delphos, which was the most famous heathen oracle in the whole world, which both Greeks and Romans used to consult, began to cease to give any answers, even from the birth of Christ: and the false deity who was worshipped, and used to give answers from his oracle in that temple, being once inquired of, Why he did not now give answers as he was wont to do? made this reply, as several heathen historians who lived about those times relate, There is an Hebrew boy, says he, who is king of the gods, who has commanded me to leave this house, and be gone to hell, and therefore you are to expect no more answers.

And many of the heathen writers who lived about that time, speak much of the oracles being silenced, as a thing at which they wondered, not knowing what the cause should be. Plutarch, a heathen writer of those times, wrote a particular treatise about it, which is still extant. And Porphyry, one of the heathen writers before mentioned, who opposed the Christian religion, in his writings has these words: 'It is no wonder if the city for these so many years has been overrun with sickness, Esculapius, and the rest of the gods, having withdrawn their converse with men; for since Jesus began to be worshipped, no man has received any public help or benefit by the gods.'

Thus did the kingdom of Christ prevail against the kingdom of Satan.

iii. I now proceed to take notice of the peculiar circumstances of *tribulation and distress* just before Constantine the Great came to the throne. This distress they suffered under the *tenth* heathen persecution, which, as it was the last, so it was by far the heaviest, and most severe. The church before this, after the ceasing of the *ninth* persecution, had enjoyed a time of quietness for about forty years together; but, abusing their liberty, they began to grow cold and lifeless in religion, and carnal contentions prevailed among them; by which they offended God to suffer this dreadful trial to come upon them. And Satan, having lost ground so much, notwithstanding all his attempts, now seemed to bestir himself with more than ordinary rage. Those who were then in authority set themselves with the utmost violence to root out Christianity, by burning all Bibles, and destroying all Christians; and therefore they did not stand to try or convict them in a formal process, but fell upon them wherever they could; sometimes setting fire to houses where multitudes of them were assembled, and burning them all together; and at other times slaughtering multitudes together, so that sometimes their persecutors were quite spent with the labour of killing and tormenting them. And in some populous places, so many were slain together that the blood ran like torrents. It is related, that seventeen thousand martyrs were slain in one month's time; and that during the continuance of this persecution, in the province of Egypt alone, no less than 144,000 Christians died by the violence of their persecutors, besides 700,000 that died through the fatigues of banishment, or the public works to which they were condemned.

This persecution lasted for ten years together; and as it exceeded all foregoing persecutions in the number of martyrs, so it exceeded them in the variety and multitude of inventions of torture and cruelty. Some authors, who lived at that time, say they were innumerable, and exceed all account and expression.

This persecution in particular was very severe in England; it is that which was foretold in Revelation 6:9–10: 'And when he had opened the fifth seal, I saw under the altar the souls of them that were slain for the word of God, and for the testimony which they held. And they cried with a loud voice, saying, How long, O Lord, holy and true, dost thou not judge and avenge our blood on them that dwell on the earth ?'

And at the end of the ten years during which this persecution continued, the heathen persecutors thought they had finished their work, and boasted that they had utterly destroyed the name and superstition of the Christians, and had restored and propagated the worship of the gods.

Thus it was the darkest time with the Christian church just before the break of day. They were brought to the greatest extremity just before God appeared for their glorious deliverance, as the bondage of the Israelites in Egypt was the most severe and cruel just before their deliverance by the hand of Moses. Their enemies thought they had swallowed them up just before their destruction, as it was with Pharaoh and his host, when they had hemmed in the children of Israel at the Red Sea.

iv. I come now, in the fourth place, to the *great revolution* which was in the world in the days of Constantine, which was in many respects like Christ's appearing in the clouds of heaven to save his people and judge the world. The people of Rome, being weary of the government of those tyrants to whom they had lately been subject, sent to Constantine, who was then in the city of York in England, to come and take the throne. He was encouraged, as is said, by a vision of a pillar of light in the heavens, in the form of a cross, in the sight of his whole army, with this inscription, Εν τουτω νικα, In this overcome; and the night following, by Christ's appearing to him in a dream with the same cross in his hand, who directed him to make a cross like that to be his royal standard, that his army might fight under that banner, and assured him that he should overcome. Accordingly he did, and overcame his enemies, and took possession of the imperial throne. He embraced the Christian religion and was the first Christian emperor that ever reigned. He came to the throne about 320 years after Christ. There are several things which I would take notice of which attended or immediately followed Constantine's coming to the throne.

a. The Christian church was thereby wholly delivered from persecution. Now the day of her deliverance came after such a dark night of affliction. Weeping had continued for a night, but now deliverance and joy came in the morning. Now God appeared to judge his people, and repented himself for his servants, when he saw their power was gone, and that there was none shut up or left. Christians had no persecutions now to fear. Their persecutors now were all put down, and their rulers were, some of them, Christians like themselves.

b. God now appeared to execute terrible judgments on their enemies. Remarkable are the accounts which history gives us of the fearful ends to which the heathen emperors, and princes, and generals, and captains, and other great men came who had exerted themselves in persecuting the Christians; dying miserably, one and another, under exquisite torments of body, and horrors of conscience, with a most visible hand of God upon them. So that what now came to pass might very fitly be compared to their hiding themselves in the dens and rocks of the mountains.

c. Heathenism now was in a great measure abolished throughout the Roman Empire. Images were now destroyed, and heathen temples pulled down. Images of gold and silver were melted down, and coined into money. Some of the chief of their idols, which were curiously wrought, were brought to Constantinople, and there drawn with ropes up and down the streets for the people to behold and laugh at. The heathen priests were dispersed and banished.

d. The Christian church was brought into a state of great peace and prosperity. Now all heathen magistrates were put down, and only Christians were advanced to places of authority all over the Empire. They had now Christian presidents, Christian governors, Christian judges and officers, instead of their old heathenish ones. Constantine set himself to put honour upon Christian bishops or ministers, and to build and adorn churches; and now large and beautiful Christian churches were erected in all parts of the world, instead of the old heathen temples.

This revolution was the greatest revolution and change in the face of things that ever came to pass in the world since the Flood. Satan, the prince of darkness, that king and god of the heathen world, was cast out. The roaring lion was conquered by the Lamb of God, in the strongest dominion that ever he had, even the Roman Empire. This was a remarkable accomplishment of Jeremiah 10:11: 'The gods that have not made the heavens and the earth, even they shall perish from the earth, and from under these heavens.' The chief part of the world was now brought utterly to cast off their old gods and their old religion, to which they had been accustomed much longer than any of their histories give an account of. They had been accustomed to worship the gods so long that they knew not any beginning of it. It was formerly spoken of as a thing unknown for a nation to change their gods (*Jer.* 2:11), but now the greater part of the nations of the known world were brought to cast off all their former gods. That multitude of gods that they worshipped were all forsaken. Thousands of them were cast away for the worship of the true God, and Christ the only Saviour: and there was a most remarkable fulfilment of that in Isaiah 2:17–18: 'And the loftiness of man shall be bowed down, and the haughtiness of men shall be made low: and the LORD alone shall be exalted in that day. And the idols he shall utterly abolish.' And since that it has come to pass that those gods that were once so famous in the world, as Jupiter, and Saturn, and Minerva, and Juno, etc., are only heard of as things which were of old. They have no temples, no altars, no worshippers, and have not had for many hundred years.

Now is come the end of the old heathen world in the principal part of it, the Roman Empire. And this great revolution and change of the state, of the world, with that terrible destruction of the great men who had been persecutors, is compared in Revelation 6 to the end of the world, and Christ's coming to judgment; and is what is most immediately signified under the sixth seal, which followed upon the souls under the altar crying, 'How long, O Lord, holy and true, dost thou not avenge our blood on them that dwell on the earth?' This vision of the sixth seal, by the general consent of divines and expositors, has respect to this downfall of the heathen Roman Empire, though it has a more remote respect to the day of judgment, of which this was a type. The day of judgment cannot be what is immediately intended, because we have an account of many events which were to come to pass under the seventh seal, and so were to follow after those of the sixth seal.

What came to pass now is also represented by the devil's being cast out of heaven to the earth. In his great strength and glory, in that mighty Roman Empire, he had as it were exalted his throne up to heaven. But now he fell like lightning from heaven, and was confined to the earth. His kingdom was confined to the meaner and more barbarous nations, or to the lower parts of the world of mankind. This is the event foretold: 'And the great dragon was cast out, that old serpent, called the Devil, and Satan, which deceiveth the whole world: he was cast out into the earth, and his angels were cast out with him' (*Rev.* 12:9). Satan tempted Christ, and promised to give him the glory of the kingdoms of the world; but now he is obliged to give it to him even against his will.

This was a glorious fulfilment of that promise which God made to his Son: 'Therefore will I divide him a portion with the great, and he shall divide the spoil with the strong; because he hath poured out his soul unto death: and he was numbered with the transgressors, and he bare the sin of many, and made intercession for the transgressors' (*Isa.* 53:12). This was a great fulfilment of the prophecies of the Old Testament concerning the glorious time of the gospel, and particularly of the prophecies of Daniel. Now the kingdom of heaven was come in a glorious degree. It pleased the Lord God of heaven to set up a kingdom on the ruins of Satan's kingdom. And such success is there of the purchase of Christ's redemption, and such honour does the Father put upon Christ for the disgrace he suffered when on earth. And now see to what a height that glorious building is erected, which had been building ever since the Fall.

INFERENCE: From what has been said of the success of the gospel from Christ's ascension to the time of Constantine, we may deduce a strong argument of the truth of the Christian religion, and that the gospel of Jesus Christ is really from God. This wonderful success of it which has been spoken of, and the circumstances of it which have been mentioned, are a strong argument of it several ways.

1. We may gather from what has been said that it is the gospel, and that only, which has actually been the means of bringing the world to the knowledge of the true God. That those are no gods whom the heathen worshipped, and that there is but one only God, is what, now since the gospel has so taught us, we can see to be truth by our own reason. It is plainly agreeable to the light of nature. It can be easily shown by reason to be demonstrably true. The very Deists themselves acknowledge that it can be demonstrated, that there is one God, and but one, who has made and governs the world. But now it is evident that it is the gospel, and that only, which has actually been the means of bringing men to the knowledge of this truth. It was not the instructions of philosophers. They tried in vain: 'The world by wisdom knew not God.' Until the gospel and the holy Scriptures came abroad in the world, all the world lay in ignorance of the true God, and in the greatest darkness with respect to the things of religion, embracing the absurdest opinions and practices, which all civilized nations now acknowledge to be childish fooleries. And so they lay one age after another, and nothing proved effectual to enlighten them. The light of nature, and their own reason, and all the wisdom of learned men, signified nothing until the Scriptures came. But when these came abroad, they were successful to bring the world to an acknowledgment of the one only true God, and to worship and serve him.

And hence it is that all that part of the world which now does own one only true God, Christians, Jews, Mahometans, and even Deists too, originally came by the knowledge of him. It is owing to this that they are not in general at this day left in heathenish darkness. They have it all, first of all, either immediately from the Scriptures, or by tradition from their fathers, who had it first from the Scriptures. And doubtless those who now despise the Scriptures, and boast of the strength of their own reason, as being sufficient to lead into the knowledge of the one true God, if the gospel had never come abroad in the world to enlighten their forefathers, would have been as sottish and brutish idolators as the world in general was before the gospel came abroad. The Mahometans, who own but one true God, at first borrowed the notion from the Scriptures; for the first Mahometans had been educated in the Christian religion, and apostatized from it. And this is evidential, that the Scriptures were designed of God to be the proper means to bring the world to the knowledge of himself, rather than human reason, or any thing else.

For it is unreasonable to suppose that the gospel, and that only, which God never designed as the proper means for obtaining this effect, should actually obtain it, after human reason, which he designed as the proper means, had been tried for a great many ages without any effect. If the Scriptures be not the Word of God, then they are nothing but darkness and delusion, yea, the greatest delusion that ever was. Now, is it reasonable to suppose that God in his providence would make use of falsehood and delusion, and that only, to bring the world to the knowledge of himself, and that no part of it should be brought to the knowledge of him any other way?

2. The gospel's prevailing as it did against such powerful opposition, plainly shows the hand of God. The Roman government, that did so violently set itself to hinder the success of the gospel, and to subdue the church of Christ, was the most powerful human government that ever was in the world; and not only so, but they seemed as it were to have the church in their hands. The Christians were mostly their subjects, under their command, and never took up arms to defend themselves. They did not gather together and stand in their own defence; they armed themselves with nothing but patience, and such like spiritual weapons; and yet this mighty

power could not conquer them; but, on the contrary, Christianity conquered them. The Roman Empire had subdued the world; they had subdued many mighty and potent kingdoms; they subdued the Grecian monarchy, when they were not their subjects, and made the utmost resistance: and yet they could not conquer the church which was in their hands; but, on the contrary, were subdued, and finally triumphed over by the church.

3. No other sufficient cause can possibly be assigned of this propagation of the gospel but only God's own power. Nothing else can be devised as the reason of it but this. There was certainly some reason. Here was a great and wonderful effect, the most remarkable change that ever was in the face of the world of mankind since the Flood; and this effect was not without some cause. Now, what other cause can be devised but only the divine power?

It was not the outward strength of the instruments which were employed in it. At first, the gospel was preached only by a few fishermen, who were without power and worldly interest to support them. It was not their craft and policy that produced this wonderful effect; for they were poor illiterate men. It was not the agreeableness of the story they had to tell to the notions and principles of mankind. This was no pleasant fable. A crucified God and Saviour was to the Jews a stumbling block, and to the Greeks foolishness. It was not the agreeableness of their doctrines to the dispositions of men, for nothing is more contrary to the corruptions of men than the pure doctrines of the gospel. This effect therefore can have proceeded from no other cause than the power and agency of God. And if it was the power of God that was exercised to cause the gospel to prevail, then the gospel is his Word; for surely God does not use his almighty power to promote a mere imposture and delusion.

4. This success is agreeable to what Christ and his apostles foretold. 'Upon this rock I will build my church; and the gates of hell shall not prevail against it' (*Matt.* 16:18). 'Verily, verily, I say unto you, Except a corn of wheat fall into the ground and die, it abideth alone: but if it die, it bringeth forth much fruit' (*John* 12:24). And, 'Now is the judgment of this world: now shall the prince of this world be cast out. And I, if I be lifted up from the earth, will draw all men unto me' (*John* 12:31-32). 'When he (the Comforter) is come, he will reprove the world of sin, of righteousness, and of judgment . . . because the prince of this world is judged' (*John* 16:8, 11).

So the Apostle Paul, in 1 Corinthians 1:21, 28, declares: 'After that in the wisdom of God the world by wisdom knew not God, it pleased God by the foolishness of preaching to save them that believe'; and that 'God hath chosen the foolish things of the world to confound the wise; and God hath chosen the weak things of the world to confound the things which are mighty; and base things of the world, and things which are despised . . . and things which are not, to bring to nought things that are'. If any man foretells a thing, very likely in itself to come to pass, from causes which can be foreseen, it is no great argument of a revelation from God: but when a thing is foretold which is very unlikely ever to come to pass, is entirely contrary to the common course of things, and yet it does come to pass just agreeable to the prediction, this is a strong argument that the prediction was from God.

Thus the consideration of the manner of the propagation and success of the gospel during the time which has been spoken of, affords great evidence that the Scriptures are the Word of God.

3. I am now to show how the success of Christ's redemption is carried on *from the time of the overthrow of the heathen Roman Empire in the time of Constantine the Great,*

until the fall of Antichrist, and the destruction of Satan's visible kingdom on earth, which is the third great dispensation which is in Scripture compared to Christ's coming to judgment. This is a period wherein many great and wonderful things are brought to pass. Herein is contained a long series of wonders of divine providence towards the Christian church. The greater part of the book of Revelation is taken up in foretelling the events of this period.

The success of Christ's purchase of redemption in this period appears mainly at the close of it, when Antichrist comes to fall, when there will be a far more glorious success of the gospel than ever was before; and that long series of events which are before seem to be only to prepare the way for it. And in order to a more clear view of the great works of God in accomplishing the success of Christ's redemption, and our seeing the glory of them it will be necessary, as we have done in the foregoing periods, to consider not only the success itself, but the opposition made to it, and the great works of Satan in this period against the church and kingdom of Christ.

And therefore, in taking a view of this period, I would take notice of events which may be referred to either of these heads, namely, either to the head of Satan's opposition to the success of Christ's redemption, or to the head of the success of Christ's redemption. And for the more orderly consideration of the events of this period, I would divide it into these four parts:

The *first* reaching from the destruction of the heathen empire to the rise of Antichrist;

The *second*, from the rise of Antichrist to the Reformation in Luther's time;

The *third*, from thence to the present time;

The *fourth*, from the present time, until Antichrist is fallen, and Satan's visible kingdom on earth is destroyed.

i. I would consider the events of the first part of this period, reaching *from the destruction of the heathen empire to the rise of Antichrist.* And here, first, I would take notice of the opposition of Satan made in this space of time to the church: and, secondly, the success that the gospel had in it.

a. *The opposition.* Satan being cast out of his old heathen empire, the great red dragon, after so sore a conflict with Michael and his angels for the greater part of three hundred years, being at last entirely routed and vanquished, so that no place was found anymore in heaven for him, but he was cast down, as it were, from heaven to the earth; yet does not give over his opposition to the woman, the church of Christ, concerning which all this conflict has been. But he is still in a rage, and renews his attempts, and has recourse to new devices against the church. The serpent, after he is cast out of heaven to the earth, casts out of his mouth water as a flood, to cause the woman to be carried away of the flood. The opposition that he made to the church of Christ before the rise of Antichrist was principally of two sorts. It was either by corrupting the church of Christ with heresies, or by new endeavours to restore Paganism.

I would observe, that after the destruction of the heathen Roman Empire, Satan infested the church with *heresies.* Though there had been so glorious a work of God in delivering the church from her heathen persecutors, and overthrowing the heathen empire, yet, the days of the church's travail not being ended, and the set time of her prosperity not being yet come, as being what was to succeed the fall of Antichrist, therefore the peace and prosperity which the church enjoyed in Constantine's time was but very short. It was a respite, which gave the church a time of peace and silence, as it were for half an hour, wherein the four angels held the four winds from blowing, until the servants of God should be sealed in their foreheads. But the church soon began to be greatly infested with heresies. The two principal, and those which did most infest the church, were the *Arian* and *Pelagian* heresies.

The *Arians* began soon after Constantine came to the throne. They denied the doctrine of the Trinity, and the divinity of Christ and the Holy Ghost, and maintained that they were but mere creatures. This heresy increased more and more in the church, and prevailed like a flood, which threatened to overflow all, and entirely to carry away the church, insomuch that before that age was out, that is, before the fourth century after Christ was finished, the greater part of the Christian church were become Arians. There were some emperors, the successors of Constantine, who were Arians; so that the Arians, being the prevailing party, and having the civil authority on their side, did raise a great persecution against the true church of Christ. This heresy might well be compared to a flood out of the mouth of the serpent, which threatened to overthrow all, and quite carry away the woman.

The *Pelagian heresy* arose in the beginning of the next century. It began by one Pelagius, who was born in Britain. His British name was Morgan. He denied original sin, and the influence of the Spirit of God in conversion, and held the power of free will, and many other things of like tendency. This heresy did for a while greatly infest the church. Pelagius' principal antagonist, who wrote in defence of the orthodox faith, was Augustine.

The other kind of opposition which Satan made against the church, was in his *endeavours to restore Paganism.* His first attempt to restore it in the Roman Empire was by Julian the Apostate. Julian was nephew to Constantine the Great. When Constantine died, he left his empire to his three sons; and when they were dead, Julian the Apostate reigned in their stead. He had been a professed Christian; but he fell from

Christianity, and turned Pagan; and therefore is called the Apostate. When he came to the throne, he used his utmost endeavours to overthrow the Christian church and set up Paganism again in the Empire. He put down the Christian magistrates and set up heathens in their room. He rebuilt the heathen temples and set up the heathen worship in the Empire, and became a most notorious persecutor of the Christians, and, as is thought, against his own light. He used to call Christ, by way of reproach, *the Galilean*. He was killed with a lance in his wars with the Persians. When he saw that he was mortally wounded, he took a handful of his blood, and threw it up towards heaven, crying out, 'Thou hast overcome, O Galilean.' He is commonly thought by divines to have committed the unpardonable sin.

Another way that Satan attempted to restore Paganism in the Roman Empire, was by the invasions and conquests of heathen nations. For in this space of time that we are upon the Goths and Vandals, and other heathen barbarous nations that dwelt in the north of the Roman Empire, invaded the Empire and obtained great conquests, and even overran the Empire. In the fifth century they took the city of Rome, and finally subdued and conquered and took possession of the Western Empire, as it was called, or the western half of the Empire, and divided it amongst them. They divided it into ten kingdoms, with which began the ten horns of the beast; for we are told, that the ten horns are ten kings who should rise in the latter part of the Roman Empire. These are also represented by the ten toes of Nebuchadnezzar's image. The invasion and conquests of these heathen nations are supposed to be foretold in Revelation 8, in what came to pass under the sounding of the first four trumpets. Now these nations who now took possession of the Western Empire were heathens; so that by their means heathenism was again for a while restored after it had been rooted out.

So much for the opposition of Satan against the success of the gospel during this space before the rise of Antichrist.

b. I proceed to show what *success* there was of the gospel in this space, notwithstanding this opposition.

I would observe, that the opposition of Satan in those things was baffled. Though the dragon cast out of his mouth such a flood after the woman to carry her away, yet he could not obtain his design; but the earth helped the woman, and opened her mouth, and swallowed up the flood which the dragon cast out of his mouth. These heresies, which for a while so much prevailed, yet after a while dwindled away, and orthodoxy was again restored, and his attempt by Julian was baffled at his death.

The gospel, during this space of time, was further propagated amongst many barbarous heathen nations in the confines of the Roman Empire. In the time of Constantine there was a considerable propagation of the gospel in the East Indies, chiefly by the ministry of one Frumentius. Great numbers of the Iberians, a heathen people, were converted to Christianity by a Christian woman of eminent piety whom they had taken captive. And some account is given of several other barbarous nations who were not within the Roman Empire, that great numbers of them were brought to receive the gospel by the teaching and examples of captives whom they had taken in war. And after this, about the year of Christ 372, the gospel was propagated among the barbarous people that dwelt in Arabia, as it was also among some of the northern nations. In particular a prince of the country of the Goths about this time became Christian, and a great number of his people with him. Towards the latter end of this century, the gospel was also further propagated among the Persians, and also the Scythians, a barbarous people that the apostle mentions in Colossians 3:11.

And after this, about the year 430, there was a remarkable conversion of a heathen people called the Burgundians to the Christian faith. About the same time, in this age, the gospel began to be propagated in Ireland; and the Irish, who until now had been heathen, began to receive the Christian faith. About the same time it was further propagated among some barbarous people in Scotland, and also in some other places. In the next century to this, one Zathus, a heathen king, who ruled over a people called the Colchians, was brought to renounce his heathenism, and to embrace the Christian religion. Several other barbarous nations are recorded to have renounced heathenism and embraced Christianity about this time which I do not have time to mention.

Thus I have briefly considered the principal events of providence which concern the success of the gospel of Christ from Constantine to the rise of Antichrist.

ii. I come now to the second part of the time from Constantine to the destruction of Antichrist, namely, that which reaches *from the rise of Antichrist to the Reformation* by Luther and others. And this is the darkest and most dismal day that ever the Christian church saw, and probably the darkest that ever it will see. The time of the church's affliction and persecution, as was observed before, is from Christ's resurrection until the destruction of Antichrist, except that the day is, as it were, shortened by some intermissions and times of respite, which God gives for the elect's sake. But this time, from the rise of Antichrist until the Reformation, was a space wherein the Christian church was in its greatest depth of depression, and its darkest time of all. The true church in this space was for many hundred years in a state of great obscurity, like the woman in the wilderness. Indeed she was almost hid from sight and observation. In speaking of the events of this space of time, I would take notice of the great machinations and works of the devil against the kingdom of Christ during this time, and of how the church of Christ was upheld during this time.

a. I would take notice of the great works of the devil against the kingdom of Christ during this time. Satan had done great things against the Christian church before, but had been baffled once and again. Michael and his angels had obtained a glorious victory. How terrible was his opposition during the continuance of the heathen empire; and how glorious was Christ's victory and triumph over him in the time of Constantine! It pleased God now to prepare the way for a yet more glorious victory over him, to suffer him to renew his strength, and to do the utmost that his power and subtilty can help him to; and therefore he suffers him to have a long time to lay his schemes, and to establish his interest, and make his matters strong; and suffers him to carry his designs a great length indeed, almost to the swallowing up of his church; and to exercise a high, and proud, and almost uncontrolled dominion in the world, a long time before Christ finally conquers, and subdues, and utterly ruins his visible kingdom on earth, as he will do in the time of the destruction of Antichrist: thus gloriously triumphing over him after he has done the utmost that his power and subtilty can extend to, and showing that he is above him, after he has dealt most proudly, and lifted himself highest of all.

The two great works of the devil which he in this space of time wrought against the kingdom of Christ, are his creating his Antichristian and Mahometan kingdoms, which have been, and still are, two kingdoms of great extent and strength, both together swallowing up the ancient Roman Empire; the kingdom of Antichrist swallowing up the Western Empire, and Satan's Mahometan kingdom the Eastern Empire. As the Scriptures in the book of Revelation represent it, it is in the destruction of these that the glorious victory of Christ, at the introduction of the glorious times of the church, will mainly consist. And here let us briefly observe how Satan erects and maintains these two great kingdoms of his in opposition to the kingdom of Christ.

With respect to *the kingdom of Antichrist*, this seems to be the masterpiece of all the contrivances of the devil against the kingdom of Christ, and is evidently so spoken of in Scripture, and therefore Antichrist is the man of sin, or *that* man of sin (*2 Thess.* 2:3), which he is called emphatically, as though he were so eminently. So he is called Antichrist, which signifies the opponent or adversary of Christ. Not that he is the only opponent of Christ; there were many others besides him. The Apostle John observes, that in his days there were many Antichrists. But yet this is called *the* Antichrist, as though there were none but he, because he was so eminently and above all others. So this contrivance of the devil, is called the mystery of iniquity (*2 Thess.* 2:7). And we find no enemy of Christ one half so much spoken of in the prophecies of Revelation as this. And the destruction of no enemy is spoken of as so glorious and happy for the church. The craft and subtilty of the devil above all appears in this work of his, as might be shown, were it not that it would consume too much time.

This is a contrivance of the devil to turn the ministry of the Christian church into a ministry of the devil, and to turn these angels of the churches into fallen angels, and so into devils. And in the tyranny, and superstition, and idolatry, and persecution, which he sets up, he contrives to make an image of ancient Paganism, and more than to restore what was lost in the Empire by the overthrow of Paganism in the time of Constantine, so that by these means the head of the beast, which was wounded unto death in Constantine, has his deadly wound healed in Antichrist (*Rev.* 13:3). And the dragon that formerly reigned in the heathen Roman Empire, being cast out thence, after the beast with seven heads and ten horns rises up out of the sea, he gives him his power and seat and great authority; and all the world wonders after the beast.

I am far from pretending to determine the time when the reign of Antichrist began, which is a point that has been so much controverted among divines and expositors. It is certain that the 1260 days, or years, which are so often in Scripture mentioned as the time of the continuance of Antichrist's reign, did not commence before the year of Christ 479, because, if they did, they would have ended, and Antichrist would have fallen before now. But I shall not pretend to determine precisely how long it was after this that that period began. The rise of Antichrist was gradual. The Christian church corrupted itself in many things soon after Constantine's time, growing more and more superstitious in its worship, by degrees bringing in many ceremonies into the worship of God, until at length they brought in the worship of saints, and set up images in their churches, and the clergy in general, and especially the bishop of Rome, assumed more and more authority to himself.

In the primitive times he was only a minister of a congregation; then a standing moderator of a presbytery; then a diocesan bishop; then a metropolitan, which is equivalent to an archbishop; then he was a patriarch, then afterwards he claimed the power of universal bishop over the whole Christian church through the world, wherein he was opposed for a while, but afterwards was confirmed in it by the civil power of the Emperor in the year 606. After that he claimed the power of a temporal prince; and so was wont to carry two swords, to signify that both the temporal and spiritual power was his; and claimed more and more authority, until at length he, as Christ's vicegerent on earth, claimed the very same power that Christ would have, if he was present on earth, and reigned on his throne, or the same power that belongs to God, and used to be called God on earth; and used to be submitted to by all the princes of Christendom.

He claimed power to crown princes, and to degrade them at his pleasure. This power was owned and it came to that, that kings and emperors used to kiss his feet. The emperors were wont to receive their crowns at his hands and princes were wont to dread the displeasure of the Pope as they would dread a thunderbolt from heaven; for if the Pope was pleased to excommunicate a prince, all his subjects were at once freed from their allegiance to him; yea, and obliged not to own him any more, on pain of excommunication. And not only so, but any man might kill him wherever he found him. And further, the Pope was believed to have power to damn men at pleasure, for whoever died under his excommunication was looked upon as certainly damned. And several emperors were actually deposed, and ejected, and died miserably by his means: and if the people of any state or kingdom did not please him, he had power to lay that state or kingdom under an interdict, which was a sentence pronounced by the Pope against that state or kingdom, whereby all sacred administrations among them could have no validity. There could be no valid baptism, or sacraments, or prayers, or preaching or pardons, until that interdict was taken off; so that that people remained, in their apprehension, in a miserable, damnable state, and therefore dreaded it as they would a storm of fire and brimstone from heaven. And in order to execute his wrath on a prince or people with whom the Pope was displeased, other princes must also be put to a great deal of trouble and expense.

And as the Pope and his clergy robbed the people of their ecclesiastical and civil liberties and privileges, so they also robbed them of their estates, and drained all Christendom of their money, and engrossed the most of their riches into their own coffers, by their vast revenues, besides pay for pardons and indulgences, baptisms and extreme unctions, deliverance out of purgatory, and a hundred other things. See how well this agrees with the prophecies in 2 Thessalonians 2:3-4, Daniel 7:20-21 and Revelation 13:6-7; 17:3-4.

During this time also superstition and ignorance more and more prevailed. The holy Scriptures by degrees were taken out of the hands of the laity, the better to promote the unscriptural and wicked designs of the Pope and the clergy; and instead of promoting knowledge among the people, they industriously promoted ignorance. It was a received maxim among them that ignorance is the mother of devotion; and so great was the darkness of those times that learning was almost extinct in the world. The very priests themselves, most of them, were barbarously ignorant as to any commendable learning, or any other knowledge, than their hellish craft in oppressing and tyrannizing over the souls of the people.

The superstition and wickedness of the church of Rome kept growing worse and worse until the very time of the Reformation, and the whole Christian world were led away into this great defection, excepting the remains of the Christian church in the Eastern Empire that had not been utterly overthrown by the Turks, as the Greek Church, and some others, which were also sunk into great darkness and gross superstition, excepting also those few that were the people of God, who are represented by the woman in the wilderness, and God's two witnesses, of which more hereafter.

This is one of those two great kingdoms which the devil in this period erected in opposition to the kingdom of Christ, and was the greatest and chief. I come now to speak of the other, the second, which is in many respects like unto it, namely, his Mahometan kingdom.

This is another great kingdom of mighty power and vast extent, set up by Satan against the kingdom of Christ. He set this up in the Eastern Empire, as he did that of Antichrist in the Western.

Mahomet was born in the year of Christ 570, in Arabia. When he was about forty years of age he began to give forth that he was the great prophet of God, and began to teach his new invented religion, of which he was to be worshipped as the head next under God. He published his Koran, which he pretended he received from the angel Gabriel; and being a subtle, crafty man, and possessed of considerable wealth, and living among a people who were very ignorant, and greatly divided in their opinions of religious matters, by subtlety and fair promises of a sensual paradise he gained a number to be his followers, and set up for their prince, and propagated his religion by the sword, and made it meritorious of paradise to fight for him. By this means his party grew and went on fighting until they conquered and brought over neighbouring countries; and so his party gradually grew until they overran a great part of the world. First, the Saracens who were some of his followers, and were a people of the country of Arabia, where Mahomet lived, about the year 700, began dreadfully to waste the Roman Empire. They overran a great many countries belonging to the Empire, and continued their conquests for a long time. These are supposed to be meant by the 'locusts' that we read of in Revelation 9.

And then after this the Turks, who were originally another people, different from the Saracens, but were followers of Mahomet, conquered all the Eastern Empire. They began their empire about the year of Christ 1296, and began to invade Europe in 1300, and took Constantinople, and so became masters of all the Eastern Empire in the year 1453, which is near three hundred years ago. And thus all those cities and countries where were those famous churches of old that we read of in the New Testament, as Jerusalem, Antioch, Ephesus, Corinth, etc. now all became subject to the Turks. And they took possession of Constantinople, which was named after Constantine the Great, being made by him the head city of the Roman Empire, whereas Rome had been until then. These are supposed to be prophesied of by the 'horsemen' in Revelation 9, from verse 15. And the remains of the Christians that are in those parts of the world, who are mostly of the Greek Church, are in miserable slavery under these Turks, treated with a great deal of barbarity and cruelty, and are become mostly very ignorant and superstitious. Thus I have shown what great works of Satan were wrought during this space of time in opposition to the kingdom of Christ.

b. I come now to show how the church of Christ was upheld through this dark time. And here it is to be observed that, towards the former part of this space of time, some of the nations of Christendom held out a long time before they complied with the corruptions and usurpations of the church of Rome. Though all the world wondered after the beast, yet all nations did not fall in at once. Many of the principal corruptions of the church of Rome were brought in with a great deal of struggle and opposition; and particularly, when the Pope gave out that he was universal bishop; many churches greatly opposed him in it; and it was a long time before they would yield to his exorbitant claims. And so, when the worship of images was first brought into the churches, there were many who greatly opposed it, and long held out against it. And so with respect to other corruptions of the church of Rome. Those people that dwelt nearer to the city of Rome complied sooner, but some that were more remote, were a long time before they could be induced to put their necks under the yoke. And particularly ecclesiastical history gives an account that it was so with a great part of the churches in England, Scotland and France, who retained the ancient purity of doctrine and worship much longer than many others who were nearer the chief seat of Antichrist. In every age of this dark time there appeared particular persons in all parts of Christendom who bore a testimony against the corruptions and tyranny of the church of Rome. There is no one age of Antichrist, even in the darkest times of all, but ecclesiastical historians mention a great many by name who manifested an abhorrence of the Pope and his idolatrous worship and pleaded for the ancient purity of doctrine and worship. God was pleased to maintain an uninterrupted succession of witnesses through the whole time in Germany, France, Britain and other countries. Historians mention these by name and give an account of the testimony which they held. Many of them were private persons, and many of them ministers, and some magistrates, and persons of great distinction. And there were numbers in every age who were persecuted and put to death for this testimony.

Besides these particular persons dispersed here and there, there was a certain people called the Waldenses who lived separate from all the rest of the world, who kept themselves pure, and constantly bore a testimony against the church of Rome through all this dark time. The place where they dwelt was the Vaudois, or the five valleys of Piedmont, a very mountainous country, between Italy and France. The place where they lived was compassed about with those exceeding high mountains called the Alps which were almost impassable. The passage over these mountainous desert countries was so difficult that the valleys where this people dwelt were almost inaccessible. There this people lived for many ages, as it were alone, in a state of separation from all the world, having very little to do with any other people. And there they served God in the ancient purity of his worship, and never submitted to the church of Rome. This place in this desert mountainous country probably was the place especially meant in Revelation 12:6 as the place prepared of God for the woman, that they should feed her there during the reign of Antichrist.

Some of the Popish writers themselves own that that people never submitted to the church of Rome. One of the Popish writers, speaking of the Waldenses, says, 'The heresy of the Waldenses is the oldest heresy in the world.' It is supposed that this people first betook themselves to this desert secret place among the mountains, to hide themselves from the severity of the heathen persecutions which were before Constantine the Great. And thus the woman fled into the wilderness from the face of the serpent (*Rev.* 12:6). And so, 'To the woman were given two wings of a great eagle, that she might fly into the wilderness, into her place: where she is nourished for a time, and times, and half a time, from the face of the serpent' (*Rev.* 12:14). And the people being settled there, their posterity continued there from age to age afterwards; and being, as it were, by natural walls, as well as by God's grace, separated from the rest of the world, never partook of the overflowing corruption.

These especially were those virgins who were not defiled with the rest of women, or when other women prostituted themselves and were defiled; but they kept themselves pure for Christ alone. They followed the Lamb, their spiritual husband, whithersoever he went. They followed him into this hideous wilderness (*Rev.* 14:4-5). Their doctrine and their worship, as there still remain accounts of them, appear to be the same with the Protestant doctrine and worship; and by the confession of Popish writers, they were a people remarkable for the strictness of their lives, for charity and other Christian virtues. They lived in external poverty in this hideous country; but they chose this rather than to comply with the great corruptions of the rest of the world.

They living in so secret a place it was a long time before they seem to have been much taken notice of by the Romanists; but at last, falling under observation, mighty armies went out against them, and fell upon them with insatiable cruelty, barbarously massacring and putting to death men, women, and children, with all imaginable tortures; and so continued persecuting them with but little intermission for several hundred years. By this means many of them were driven out of their old habitations in the valleys of Piedmont and fled into all parts of Europe, carrying with them their doctrine, to which many were brought over. So their persecutors could not by all their cruelties extirpate the church of God, so fulfilling his word that 'the gates of hell should not prevail against it'.

Towards the latter part of this dark time, several noted divines openly appeared to defend the truth and bear testimony against the corruptions of the church of Rome. They had many followers. The first and principal of these was a certain English divine, *John Wycliffe*, who appeared about one hundred and forty years before the Reformation and strenuously opposed the Popish religion, teaching the same doctrine that the Reformers afterwards did, and having many followers in England. He was hotly persecuted in his lifetime, yet died in peace; and after he was buried his bones were dug up by his persecutors and burnt. His followers remained in considerable numbers in England until the Reformation, and were cruelly persecuted, and multitudes put to death for their religion. Wycliffe had many disciples, not only in England, but in other parts of Europe whither his books were carried, and particularly in Bohemia, among whom were two eminent divines, *John Huss*, and *Jerome*, a divine belonging to Prague, the chief city of Bohemia. These strenuously opposed the church of Rome, and had many who adhered to them. They were both burnt by the Papists for their doctrine; and their followers in Bohemia were cruelly persecuted, but never extirpated until the Reformation.

iii. Thus having gone through this dark time of the church which is the second part of the space from Constantine the

Great to the destruction of Antichrist, I come now, to the third part, namely, *that which begins with the Reformation and reaches to the present time.* And here I would speak of the Reformation itself, of the opposition which the devil has made to the Reformed church, of the success there has lately been of the gospel in one place and another, and of the state of things now in the world with regard to the church of Christ, and the success of his purchase.

a. Here the first thing to be taken notice of is the *Reformation.* This was begun about two hundred and twenty years ago, first in Saxony in Germany by the preaching of Martin Luther. He was stirred in his spirit to see the horrid practices of the Popish clergy and, having set himself diligently to enquire after truth, by the study of the holy Scriptures and the writings of the ancient fathers of the church, very openly and boldly decried the corruptions and usurpations of the Romish church in his preaching and writings. He had soon a great number that fell in with him, among whom was the Elector of Saxony, the sovereign prince of the country to which he belonged. This greatly alarmed the church of Rome; and it did as it were rally all its force to oppose him and his doctrine, and fierce wars and persecutions were raised against it. But yet it went on by the labours of Luther and Melancthon in Germany, and Zuinglius in Switzerland, and other eminent divines who were contemporary with Luther and fell in with him; and particularly Calvin, who appeared somewhat after the beginning of the Reformation but was one of the most eminent Reformers.

Many of the princes of Germany soon fell in with the Reformed religion, and many other states and kingdoms in Europe, as England, Scotland, Sweden, Denmark, Norway, a great part of France, Poland, Lithuania, Switzerland, and the Low Countries. So that it is thought that heretofore about half Christendom were of the Protestant religion, though, since, the Papists have gained ground, so that the Protestants now have not so great a proportion.

Thus God began gloriously to revive his church again and advance the kingdom of his Son, after such a dismal night of darkness as had been before from the rise of Antichrist to that time. There had been many endeavours used by the witnesses for the truth for a reformation before. But now, when God's appointed time was come, his work was begun and went on with a swift and wonderful progress. Antichrist, who had been rising higher and higher from his very first beginning until that time, was swiftly and suddenly brought down, fell half way towards utter ruin, and never has been able to rise again to his former height. A certain recent expositor, Mr Lowman, who explains the first five vials in Revelation 16 with greater probability perhaps than any who went before him, explains the fifth vial, which was poured out on the seat of the beast, as what came to pass in the Reformation, explaining the four preceding vials of certain great judgments God brought on the Popish dominions before the Reformation. It is said in Revelation 16:10-11 that 'the fifth angel poured out his vial on the seat of the beast', in the original, the throne of the beast, 'and his kingdom was full of darkness; and they gnawed their tongues for pain, and blasphemed the God of heaven because of their pains and their sores, and repented not of their deeds'. He poured out his vial upon the throne of the beast, that is, on the authority and dominion of the Pope; so the word 'throne' is often used in Scripture; see 1 Kings 1:37: 'As the LORD hath been with my lord the king, even so be he with Solomon, and make his throne greater than the throne of my lord king David', that is, make his dominion and authority greater and his kingdom more glorious.

But now, in the Reformation, the vials of God's wrath were poured out on the throne of the beast. His throne was terribly shaken and diminished. The Pope's authority and dominion were greatly diminished, in both extent and degree. He lost, as was said before, about half his dominions. And besides, since the Reformation, the Pope has lost great part of that authority, even in the Popish dominions, which he had before. He is not regarded, and his power is dreaded in no measure as it was wont to be.

The powers of Europe have learned not to put their necks under the Pope's feet, as formerly they were wont to do. So that he is as a lion that has lost his teeth, in comparison of what he was once. And when the Pope and his clergy, enraged to see their authority so diminished at the Reformation, laid their heads together and joined their forces to destroy the Reformation, their policy, which was wont to serve them so well, failed; and they found their kingdom full of darkness, so that they could do nothing, any more than the Egyptians, who rose not from their seats for three days. The Reformed church was defended as Lot and the angels were in Sodom, by smiting the Sodomites with darkness or blindness, that they could not find the door.

God then fulfilled what is said in Job 5:11–15, 'To set up on high those that be low; that those which mourn may be exalted to safety. He disappointeth the devices of the crafty, so that their hands cannot perform their enterprise. He taketh the wise in their own craftiness: and the counsel of the froward is carried headlong. They meet with darkness in the day time, and grope in the noon day as in the night. But he saveth the poor from the sword, from their mouth, and from the hand of the mighty.'

Those proud enemies of God's people being so disappointed, and finding themselves so unable to uphold their own dominion and authority, this made them as it were to gnaw their tongues for pain, or bite their tongues for mere rage.

b. I proceed therefore to show what *opposition* has been made to this success of Christ's purchase by the Reformation by Satan and his adherents; observing, as we go along, how far they have been baffled, and how far they have been successful.

This opposition has been principally made by a general council of the church of Rome; by secret plots and devices; by open wars and invasions; by cruel oppression and persecution; and by bringing in corrupt opinions.

The first opposition that I shall take notice of is that which was made by the clergy of the church of Rome uniting together in a general council. This was the famous *Council of Trent* which the Pope called a little while after the Reformation. In that council, there met together six cardinals, thirty-two archbishops, two hundred and twenty-eight bishops, besides innumerable others of the Romish clergy. This council, in all their sittings, including the times of intermission between their sittings, was held for twenty-five years together. Their main business all this while was to concert measures for establishing the church of Rome against the Reformers, and for destroying the Reformation. But it proved that they were not able to perform their enterprise. The Reformed church, notwithstanding their holding so great a council, and for so long a time together against it, remained, and remains still. So that the counsel of the froward is carried headlong, and their kingdom is full of darkness, and they weary themselves to find the door.

Thus the church of Rome, instead of repenting of their deeds, when such clear light was held forth to them by Luther and other servants of God, the Reformers, does by general agreement in council, persist in their vile corruption and wickedness, and obstinate opposition to the kingdom of Christ. The doctrines and practices of the church of Rome, which were chiefly condemned by the Reformed, were confirmed by the decrees of their council; and the corruptions, in many respects, were carried higher than ever before. They uttered blasphemous reproaches and curses against the Reformed religion, and all the Reformed church was excommunicated and anathematized by them. And so, according to the prophecy, they 'blasphemed God'. Thus God hardened their hearts, intending to destroy them.

The Papists have often endeavoured to overthrow the Reformation by *secret plots and conspiracies*. So there were many plots against the life of Luther. The Papists contrived to dispatch him, and to put him out of their way; and he, as he was a very bold man, often very much exposed himself in the cause of Christ: but yet they were wonderfully prevented from hurting him, and he at last died in his bed in peace. And so there have been from time to time innumerable schemes secretly laid for the overthrow of the Protestant religion.

Among these that which seems most considerable and most likely to have taken effect was in the time of King James II of England, which is within the memory of many of us. There was at that time a strong conspiracy between the King of England and Louis XIV of France, who were both Papists, to extirpate the *Northern Heresy*, as they called the Protestant religion, not only out of England, but out of all Europe; and had laid their schemes so that they seemed to be almost sure of their purpose. They looked upon it that if the Reformed religion were suppressed in the British realms and in the Netherlands, which were the strongest part and chief defence of the Protestant interest, they should have easy work with the rest. And just as their matters seemed to be come to a head, and their enterprise ripe for execution, God, in his providence, suddenly dashed all their schemes in pieces by the Revolution, at the coming in of King William and Queen Mary. By this all their designs were at an end; and the Protestant interest was more strongly established by the crown of Great Britain being transferred to the Protestant house of

Hanover, and a Papist being, by the constitution of the nation, for ever rendered incapable of wearing the crown. Thus they groped in darkness at noonday as in the night, and their hands could not perform their enterprise. Their kingdom was full of darkness, and they gnawed their tongues for pain.

After this, there was a deep design laid to bring the same thing to pass in the latter end of Queen Anne's reign by the bringing in of the Popish Pretender. This was no less suddenly and totally baffled by divine providence, as all the plots against the Reformation by bringing in a Pretender have been from time to time.

The Reformation has often been opposed by *open wars and invasions*. So in the beginning of the Reformation the Emperor of Germany, to suppress the Reformation, declared war with the Duke of Saxony, and the principal men who favoured and received Luther's doctrine. But they could not obtain their end; they could not suppress the Reformation. For the same end, the King of Spain maintained a long war with Holland and the Low Countries in the century before last. But those cruel wars issued greatly to the disadvantage of the Romish church as they occasioned the setting up of one of the most powerful Protestant states in Europe which, next to Great Britain, is the chief bastion of the Protestant religion. And the design of the Spanish invasion of England in Queen Elizabeth's time was to suppress and root out the Reformed religion; and therefore they brought in their fleet all manner of instruments of cruelty wherewith to torture the Protestants who would not renounce the Protestant religion. But their design was totally baffled, and their mighty fleet in a great measure ruined.

Satan has opposed the Reformation with *cruel persecutions*. The persecutions with which the Protestants in one kingdom and another have been persecuted by the church of

Rome have in many respects been far beyond any of the heathen persecutions which were before Constantine the Great, and beyond all that ever were before. So that Antichrist has proved the greatest and cruellest enemy to the church of Christ that ever was in the world, in this, as well as in all other respects; agreeable to the description given of the church of Rome: 'And I saw the woman drunken with the blood of the saints, and with the blood of the martyrs of Jesus' (*Rev.* 17:6). And, 'And in her was found the blood of prophets, and of saints, and of all that were slain upon the earth' (*Rev.* 18:24).

The heathen persecutions had been very dreadful. But now persecution by the church of Rome was improved and studied and cultivated as an art or science. Such ways of afflicting and tormenting were found out as are beyond the thought and invention of ordinary men, or men who are unstudied in those things, and beyond the invention of all former ages. And that persecution might be managed the more effectually, there were certain societies of men established in various parts of the Popish dominions whose business it should be to study and improve and practise persecution in its highest perfection, which are called the courts of inquisition. A reading of the particular histories of the Romish persecution and their courts of inquisition will give that idea which a few words cannot express.

When the Reformation began, the beast with seven heads and ten horns began to rage in a dreadful manner. After the Reformation, the church of Rome renewed its persecution of the poor Waldenses, and great multitudes of them were cruelly tortured and put to death. Soon after the Reformation, there were terrible persecutions in various parts of Germany, and especially in Bohemia, which lasted for thirty years together, in which so much blood was shed for the sake of religion that a certain writer compares it to the plenty of waters of the great rivers of Germany. The countries of

Poland, Lithuania and Hungary were in like manner deluged with Protestant blood.

By means of these and other cruel persecutions, the Protestant religion was in a great measure suppressed in Bohemia, the Palatinate and Hungary, which before were Protestant countries. Thus was fulfilled what was foretold of the little horn, 'And of the ten horns that were in his head, and of the other which came up, and before whom three fell, even of that horn that had eyes, and a mouth that spake very great things, whose look was more stout than his fellows. I beheld, and the same horn made war with the saints, and prevailed against them' (*Dan.* 7:20-21). And what was foretold of the beast having seven heads and ten horns, 'And it was given unto him to make war with the saints, and to overcome them: and power was given him over all kindreds, and tongues, and nations' (*Rev.* 13:7).

Also Holland and the other Low Countries were for many years a scene of nothing but the most affecting and amazing cruelties, being deluged with the blood of Protestants, under the merciless hands of the Spaniards, to whom they were then in subjection. But in this persecution the devil in a great measure failed of his purpose, as it issued in a great part of the Netherlands casting off the Spanish yoke, and setting up a wealthy and powerful Protestant state, to the great defence of the Protestant cause ever since.

France is another country which since the Reformation has been, perhaps in some respects more than any other country, a scene of dreadful cruelties suffered by Protestants. After many cruelties had been exercised towards them in that kingdom, a persecution was begun in the year 1571, in the reign of Charles IX. It began with a cruel massacre wherein seventy thousand Protestants were slain in a few days' time, as the King boasted. And in all this persecution, he slew, as is supposed, three hundred thousand martyrs. And it is reckoned that about this time, within thirty years, there were martyred in this kingdom, for the Protestant religion, thirty-nine princes, one hundred and forty-eight counts, two hundred and thirty-four barons, 147,518 gentlemen, and 760,000 of the common people.

But all these persecutions were, for exquisite cruelty, far exceeded by those which followed in the reign of Louis XIV. These indeed are supposed to exceed all others that ever have been. Being long continued, by reason of the long reign of that king, they almost wholly extirpated the Protestant religion out of that kingdom, where there had been before a multitude of famous Protestant churches all over the kingdom. Thus it was given to the beast to make war with the saints, and to overcome them.

There was also a terrible persecution in England in Queen Mary's time, wherein great numbers in all parts of the kingdom were burnt alive. And after this, though the Protestant religion has been for the most part established by law in England, yet there have been very severe persecutions by the high churchmen, who sympathize in many things with the Papists. Such a persecution was that which occasioned our forefathers to flee from their native country, and to come and settle in this land, which was then a hideous howling wilderness. And these persecutions were continued with little intermission until King William came to the throne.

Scotland has also been the scene, for many years together, of cruelties and blood by the hands of high churchmen, such as came very little short of the Popish persecution in Queen Mary's days, and in many things much exceeded it, which continued until they were delivered by King William.

Ireland also has been as it were overwhelmed with Protestant blood. In the days of King Charles I above two hundred thousand Protestants were cruelly murdered in that kingdom in a few days. The Papists, by a secret agreement, rose all over the kingdom at an appointed time, intending to kill every Protestant in the kingdom at once.

Besides these, there have been very cruel persecutions in Italy, Spain, and other places, which I shall not take time to relate.

Thus did the devil, and his great minister Antichrist, rage with such violence and cruelty against the church of Christ; and thus did the whore of Babylon make herself drunk with the blood of the saints and martyrs of Jesus; and thus, by these persecutions, the Protestant church has been much diminished. Yet with all have they not been able to prevail; but still the Protestant church is upheld, and Christ fulfils his promise, that 'the gates of hell shall not prevail against' his church.

The last kind of opposition that Satan has made to the Reformation is by *corrupt opinions*. Satan has opposed the light of the gospel which shone forth in the Reformation with many corrupt opinions which he has brought in and propagated in the world.

The first opposition of this kind was by raising up the sect of the *Anabaptists*, which began about four or five years after the Reformation itself began. This sect, as it first appeared in Germany, were vastly more extravagant than the present Anabaptists are in England. They held a great many exceedingly corrupt opinions. One tenet of theirs was that there ought to be no civil authority, and so that it was lawful to rebel against civil authority. And on this principle, they refused to submit to magistrates, or any human laws; and gathered together in vast armies, to defend themselves against their civil rulers, and put all Germany into an uproar, and so kept it for some time.

The next opposition of this kind to the Reformation was that which was made by *enthusiasts*. Those are called enthusiasts who falsely pretend to be inspired by the Holy Ghost as the prophets were. These began in Germany about ten years after Luther began the Reformation; and there arose various sects of them who were exceedingly wild and extravagant. The followers of these are the Quakers in England, and other parts of the British dominions.

The next to these were the *Socinians*, who had their beginning chiefly in Poland, by the teaching of two men; the name of the one was Laelius Socinus, of the other, Faustus Socinus. They held that Christ was a mere man, and denied Christ's satisfaction, and most of the fundamental doctrines of the Christian religion. Their heresy has since been greatly propagated among Protestants in Poland, Germany, Holland, England, and other places.

After these arose the *Arminians*. These first appeared in Holland about 130 years ago. They take their name from a Dutchman whose name was Jacobus Van Harmin, which, turned into Latin, is called Jacobus Arminius; and from his name the whole sect are called Arminians. This Jacobus Arminius was first a minister at Amsterdam, and then a professor of divinity in the university of Leiden. He had many followers in Holland. There was upon this a synod of all the Reformed churches called together, who met at Dort in Holland. The Synod of Dort condemned the Arminians; but yet they spread and prevailed. They began to prevail in England in the reign of Charles I, especially in the Church of England. The Church of England divines before that were almost universally Calvinists, but since that, Arminianism has gradually more and more prevailed, until they are become almost universally Arminians. And not only so, but Arminianism has greatly prevailed among the Dissenters, and has spread greatly in New England, as well as Old.

Since this, *Arianism* has been revived. As I told you before, Arianism, a little after Constantine's time, almost swallowed up the Christian world, like a flood out of the mouth of the serpent which threatened to swallow up the woman. And of late years, this heresy has been revived in England, and greatly prevails there, both in the Church of England, and among Dissenters. These hold that Christ is but a mere creature, though they grant that he is the greatest of all creatures.

Another thing which has of late exceedingly prevailed among Protestants, and especially in England, is *Deism*. The Deists wholly cast off the Christian religion, and are professed infidels. They are not like the heretics, Arians, Socinians, and others, who own the Scriptures to be the Word of God, and hold the Christian religion to be the true religion, but only deny these and these fundamental doctrines of the Christian religion: they deny the whole Christian religion. Indeed they own the being of God; but deny that Christ was the Son of God, and say he was a mere cheat; and so they say all the prophets and apostles were: and they deny the whole Scripture. They deny that any of it is the Word of God. They deny any revealed religion, or any Word of God at all; and say, that God has given mankind no other light to walk by but their own reason. These sentiments and opinions our nation, which is the principal nation of the Reformation, is very much overrun with, and they prevail more and more.

Thus much concerning the opposition that Satan has made against the Reformation.

c. I proceed now to show what *success* the gospel has more lately had, or what success it has had in these later times of the Reformed church. This success may be reduced to these three heads: Reformation in doctrine and worship in countries called Christian; Propagation of the gospel among the heathen; Revival of religion in the power and practice of it.

As to the first, namely, *reformation in doctrine*, the most considerable success of the gospel that has been of late of this kind has been in the empire of Muscovy, which is a country of vast extent. The people of this country, so many of them as call themselves Christians, professed to be of the Greek Church; but were barbarously ignorant, and very superstitious, until of late years. Their late emperor, Peter the Great, who reigned until within these twenty years, set himself to reform the people of his dominions, and took great pains to bring them out of their darkness, and to have them instructed in religion. And to that end, he set up schools of learning, and ordered the Bible to be printed in the language of the country, and made a law that every family should keep the holy Scriptures in their houses, and that every person should be able to read the same, and that no person should be allowed to marry until they were able to read the Scriptures. He also reformed the churches of his country in many of their superstitions, whereby the religion professed and practised in Muscovy is much nearer to that of the Protestants than formerly it used to be. This emperor gave great encouragement to the exercise of the Protestant religion in his dominions. And since that Muscovy has become a land of light, in comparison of what it was before. Wonderful alterations have been brought about in the face of religion for the better within these fifty years past.

As to the second kind of success which the gospel has lately had, namely, its *propagation among the heathen*, I would take notice of three things:

The propagation there has been of the gospel among the heathen here in *America*. This American continent on which we live, which is a very great part of the world, and, together with its neighbouring seas adjoining, takes up one side of the globe, was wholly unknown to all Christian nations until these latter times. It was not known that there was any such part of the world, though it was very full of people: and therefore here the devil had the people that inhabited this part of the world as it were secure to himself, out of the reach of the light of the gospel, and so out of the way of molestation in his dominion over them. And here the many nations of Indians worshipped him as God from age to age, while the gospel was confined to the opposite side of the globe. It is probably supposed, from some remaining accounts of things, that the occasion of the first peopling of America was this, that the devil being alarmed and surprised by the wonderful success of the gospel which there was the first three hundred years after Christ, and by the downfall of the heathen empire in the time of Constantine, and seeing the gospel spread so fast, and fearing that his heathenish kingdom would be wholly overthrown through the world, led away a people from the other continent into America, that they might be quite out of the reach of the gospel, that here he might quietly possess them, and reign over them as their god. It is what many writers give an account of, that some of the nations of Indians, when the Europeans first came into America, had a tradition among them, that their god first led them into this continent, and went before them in an ark.

Whether this was so or not, yet it is certain that the devil did here quietly enjoy his dominion over the poor nations of Indians for many ages. But in later times God has sent the gospel into these parts of the world, and now the Christian church is set up here in New England, and in other parts of America, where before had been nothing but the grossest heathenish darkness. A great part of America is now full of Bibles, and full of at least the form of the worship of the true God and Jesus Christ, where the name of Christ before had not been heard of for many ages, if at all. And though there has been but a small propagation of the gospel among the heathen here, in comparison of what were to be wished for, yet there has been something worthy to be taken notice of. There was something remarkable in the first times of New England, and something remarkable has appeared of late here, and in other parts of America among many Indians, of an inclination to be instructed in the Christian religion.

And however small the propagation of the gospel among the heathen here in America has been hitherto, yet I think we may well look upon the discovery of so great a part of the world as America, and bringing the gospel into it, as one thing by which divine providence is preparing the way for the future glorious times of the church, when Satan's kingdom shall be overthrown, not only throughout the Roman Empire, but throughout the whole habitable globe, on every side, and on all its continents.

When those times come, then doubtless the gospel, which is already brought over into America, shall have glorious success, and all the inhabitants of this new discovered world shall become subjects of the kingdom of Christ, as well as all the other ends of the earth: and in all probability providence has so ordered it that the mariner's compass, which is an invention of later times, whereby men are enabled to sail over the widest ocean, when before they durst not venture far from land, should prove a preparation for what God intends to bring to pass in the glorious times of the church, namely, the sending forth the gospel wherever any of the children of men dwell, how far so ever off, and however separated by wide oceans from those parts of the world which are already Christianized.

There has of late years been a very considerable propagation of the gospel among the heathen in the dominions of *Muscovy.* I have already observed the reformation which there has lately been among those who are called Christians there, but I now speak of the heathen. A great part of the vast dominions of the Emperor of Muscovy are gross heathens. The greater part of Great Tartary, a heathen country, has in later times been brought under the Muscovite government; and there have been of late great numbers of those heathen who have renounced their heathenism and have embraced the Christian religion.

There has been lately a very considerable propagation of the Christian religion among the heathen in the *East Indies*. Particularly, many in a country in the East Indies called Malabar, have been brought over to the Christian Protestant religion, chiefly by the labours of certain missionaries sent thither to instruct them by the King of Denmark, who have brought over many heathens to the Christian faith, and have set up schools among them, and a printing press to print Bibles and other books for their instruction, in their own language, with great success.

The last kind of success which there has lately been of the gospel which I shall take notice of is the revivals of the power and practice of religion which have lately been. And here I shall take notice of but two instances.

There has not long since been a remarkable revival of the power and practice of religion in *Saxony* in Germany, through the endeavours of an eminent divine there whose name was August Hermann Francke, professor of divinity at Halle in Saxony, who, being a person of eminent charity, the great work that God wrought by him began with his setting on foot a charitable design. It began only with his placing an alms box at his study door, into which some poor mites were thrown, whereby books were bought for the instruction of the poor. And God was pleased so wonderfully to smile on his design and so to pour out a spirit of charity on people there on that occasion, that with their charity he was enabled in a little time to erect public schools for the instruction of poor children, and an orphan house for the supply and instruction of the poor; so that at last it came to pass that near five hundred children were maintained and instructed in learning and piety by the charity of others; and the number continued to increase more and more for many years, and until the last account I have seen. This was accompanied with a wonderful reformation and revival of religion, and a spirit of piety, in the city and university of Halle; and thus it continued. Which also had great influence in many other places in Germany. Their example seemed remarkably to stir up multitudes to their imitation.

Another thing, which it would be ungrateful in us not to take notice of, is that remarkable pouring out of the Spirit of God which has been of late in this part of *New England*, of which we, in this town, have had such a share. But it is needless for me particularly to describe it, it being what you have so lately been eye witnesses to, and I hope multitudes of you sensible of the benefit of.

Thus I have mentioned the more remarkable instances of the success which the gospel has lately had in the world.

d. I proceed now to the last thing that was proposed to be considered relating to the success of Christ's redemption during this space, namely, *what the state of things is now* in the world with regard to the church of Christ, and the success of Christ's purchase. And this I would do by showing how things are now compared with the first times of the Reformation. And I would show wherein the state of things is altered for the worse, and how it is altered for the better.

The state of things is altered from what it was in the beginning of the Reformation for the worse in these respects:

The Reformed church is much diminished. The Reformation, in the former times of it, as was observed before, was supposed to take place through one half of Christendom, excepting the Greek Church, so that there were as many Protestants as Papists. But now it is not so. The Protestant church is much diminished. Heretofore there have been multitudes of Protestants in France; many famous Protestant churches were all over that country, who used to meet together in synods, and maintain a very regular discipline; and great part of that kingdom were Protestants. The Protestant church of

France was a great part of the glory of the Reformation. But now it is far otherwise. This church is all broken to pieces and scattered. The Protestant religion is almost wholly rooted out of that kingdom by the cruel persecutions which have been there, and there are now but very few Protestant assemblies in all that kingdom. The Protestant interest is also greatly diminished in Germany. There were several sovereign princes there formerly who were Protestants whose successors are now Papists; as, particularly, the Elector Palatine, and the Elector of Saxony. The Kingdom of Bohemia was formerly a Protestant kingdom, but is now in the hands of the Papists. Also Hungary was formerly a Protestant country, but the Protestants there have been greatly reduced, and in a great measure subdued, by the persecutions that have been there. And the Protestant interest has no way remarkably gained ground of late of the church of Rome.

Another thing wherein the state of things is altered for the worse from what was in the former times of the Reformation is *the prevailing of licentiousness* in principles and opinions. There is not now that spirit of orthodoxy which there was then. There is very little appearance of zeal for the mysterious and spiritual doctrines of Christianity; and they never were so ridiculed, and had in contempt, as they are in the present age, and especially in England, the principal kingdom of the Reformation. In this kingdom, those principles, on which the power of godliness depends, are in a great measure exploded, and Arianism, Socinianism, Arminianism and Deism are the things which prevail, and carry almost all before them. And particularly history gives no account of any age wherein there was so great an apostasy of those who had been brought up under the light of the gospel to infidelity. Never was there such a casting off of the Christian and all revealed religion; never any age wherein was so much scoffing at and ridiculing the gospel of Christ, by those who have been brought up under gospel light, nor any thing like it, as there is at this day.

Another thing wherein things are altered for the worse is that there is *much less of the prevalency of the power of godliness* than there was at the beginning of the Reformation. There was a glorious outpouring of the Spirit of God that accompanied the first Reformation, not only to convert multitudes in so short a time from Popery to the true religion, but to turn many to God and true godliness. Religion gloriously flourished in one country and another, as most remarkably appeared in those times of terrible persecution which have already been spoken of. But now there is an exceeding great decay of vital piety; yea, it seems to be despised, called enthusiasm, whimsy, and fanaticism. Those who are truly religious are commonly looked upon to be crack-brained and beside their right mind; and vice and profaneness dreadfully prevail, like a flood which threatens to bear down all before it.

But I proceed now to show in what respect things are altered for the better from what they were in the first Reformation.

The power and influence of the Pope is much diminished. Although, since the former times of the Reformation, he has gained ground in extent of dominion, yet he has lost in degree of influence. The vial which in the beginning of the Reformation was poured out on the throne of the beast, to the great diminishing of his power and authority in the world, has continued running ever since. The Pope, soon after the Reformation, became less regarded by the princes of Europe than he had been before; and so he has been since less and less. Many of the Popish princes themselves seem now to regard him very little more than they think will serve their own designs; of which there have been several remarkable proofs and instances of late.

There is *far less persecution* now than there was in the first times of the Reformation. You have heard already how dreadfully persecution raged in the former times of the Reformation; and there is something of it still. Some parts of the Protestant church are at this day under persecution, and so probably will be until the day of the church's suffering and travail is at an end, which will not be until the fall of Antichrist. But it is now in no measure as it was heretofore. There does not seem to be the same spirit of persecution prevailing. It is become more out of fashion, even among the Popish princes. The wickedness of the enemies of Christ, and the opposition against his cause, seem to run in another channel. The humour now is to despise and laugh at all religion; and there seems to be a spirit of indifferency about it. However, so far the state of things is better than it has been that there is so much less of persecution.

There is *a great increase of learning.* In the dark times of Popery before the Reformation, learning was so far decayed that the world seemed to be overrun with barbarous ignorance. Their very priests were many of them grossly ignorant. Learning began to revive with the Reformation, which was owing very much to the art of printing, which was invented a little before the Reformation; and since that, learning has increased more and more, and at this day is undoubtedly raised to vastly a greater height than ever it was before: and though no good use is made of it by the greater part of learned men, yet the increase of learning in itself is a thing to be rejoiced in, because it is a good, and if duly applied, an excellent handmaid to divinity, and is a talent which, if God gives men a heart, affords them a great advantage to do great things for the advancement of the kingdom of Christ, and the good of the souls of men. That learning and knowledge should greatly increase before the glorious times, seems to be foretold: 'But thou, O Daniel, shut up the words, and seal the book, even to the time of the end: many shall run to and fro, and knowledge shall be increased' (*Dan.* 12:4). And however little is applied to the advancement of religion, yet we may hope that the days are approaching wherein God will make great use of it for the advancement of the kingdom of Christ.

God in his providence now seems to be acting over again the same part which he did a little before Christ came. The age wherein Christ came into the world was an age wherein learning greatly prevailed, and was at a greater height than ever it had been before; and yet wickedness never prevailed more than then. God was pleased to suffer human learning to come to such a height before he sent forth the gospel into the world that the world might see the insufficiency of all their own wisdom for obtaining the knowledge of God, without the gospel of Christ, and the teachings of his Spirit; and then, 'after that, in the wisdom of God, the world by wisdom knew not God, it pleased God, by the foolishness of preaching, to save them that believe'. And when the gospel came to prevail first without the help of man's wisdom, then God was pleased to make use of learning as a handmaid. So now learning is at a great height at this day in the world, far beyond what it was in the age when Christ appeared; and now the world, by their learning and wisdom, do not know God; and they seem to wander in darkness, are miserably deluded, stumble and fall in matters of religion, as in midnight darkness. Trusting to their learning, they grope in the day time as in the night. Learned men are exceedingly divided in their opinions concerning the matters of religion and run into all manner of corrupt opinions and pernicious and foolish errors. They scorn to submit their reason to divine revelation, to believe anything that is above their comprehension; and so, being wise in their own eyes, they become fools, and even vain in their imaginations, and turn the truth of God into a lie, and their foolish hearts are darkened. See Romans 1:21.

But yet, when God has sufficiently shown men the insufficiency of human wisdom and learning for the purposes of religion, and when the appointed time comes for that glorious outpouring of the Spirit of God, when he will himself by his own immediate influence enlighten men's minds, then may we hope that God will make use of the great increase of learning as an handmaid to religion, as a means of the glorious advancement of the kingdom of his Son. Then shall human learning be subservient to the understanding of the Scriptures, and to a clear explanation and a glorious defence of the doctrines of Christianity. And there is no doubt to be made of it, that God in his providence has of late given the world the art of printing, and such a great increase of learning, to prepare for what he designs to accomplish for his church in the approaching days of its prosperity. And thus the wealth of the wicked is laid up for the just, agreeable to Proverbs 13:22.

Having now shown how the work of redemption has been carried on from the Fall of man to the present time, before I proceed any further, I would make some APPLICATION.

1. From what has been said, we may see great evidence of the truth of the Christian religion, and that the Scriptures are the Word of God. There are three arguments of this which I shall take notice of, which may be drawn from what has been said.

i. It may be argued from that violent and inveterate *opposition* there has always appeared of the wickedness of the world against this religion. The religion that the church of God has professed from the first founding of the church after the Fall to this time has always been the same. Though the dispensations have been altered, yet the religion which the church has professed has always, as to its essentials, been the same. The church of God, from the beginning, has been one society. The Christian church which has been since Christ's ascension is manifestly the same society continued with the church that was before Christ came. The Christian church is grafted on their root. They are built on the same foundation. The revelation on which both have depended, is essentially the same, for as the Christian church is built on the holy Scriptures, so was the Jewish church, though now the Scriptures be enlarged by the addition of the New Testament; but still it is essentially the same revelation with that which was given in the Old Testament, only the subjects of divine revelation are now more clearly revealed in the New Testament than they were in the Old. But the sum and substance of both the Old Testament and New is Christ and his redemption. The religion of the church of Israel was essentially the same religion with that of the Christian church, as evidently appears from what has been said.

The ground work of the religion of the church of God, both before and since Christ has appeared, is the same great scheme of redemption by the Son of God; and so the church that was before the Israelitish church was still the same society, and it was essentially the same religion that was professed and practised in it. Thus it was from Noah to Abraham, and thus it was before the Flood. And this society of men that is called the church has always been built on the foundation of those revelations which we have in the Scriptures, which have always been essentially the same, though gradually increasing. The church before the Flood was built on the foundation of those revelations of Christ which were given to Adam, Abel, and Enoch, of which we have an account in the former chapters of Genesis, and others of the like import. The church after the Flood was built on the foundation of the revelations made to Noah and Abraham, to Melchisedec, Isaac, and Jacob, to Joseph, Job, and other holy men of whom we have an account in the Scriptures, or other revelations that were to the same purpose. And after this the church depended on the

Scriptures themselves as they gradually increased. So that the church of God has always been built on the foundations of divine revelation, and always on those revelations that were essentially the same and which are summarily comprehended in the holy Scriptures; and ever since about Moses' time the church has been built on the Scriptures themselves.

So the opposition which has been made to the church of God in all ages has always been against the same religion and the same revelation. Now therefore the violent and perpetual opposition that has ever been made by the corruption and wickedness of mankind against this church is a strong argument of the truth of this religion, and this revelation upon which the church has always been built. Contraries are well argued one from another. We may well and safely argue that a thing is good according to the degree of opposition in which it stands to evil, or the degree in which evil opposes it and is an enemy to it. We may well argue that a thing is light by the great enmity which darkness has to it. Now it is evident by the things which you have heard concerning the church of Christ and that holy religion of Jesus Christ which it has professed that the wickedness of the world has had a perpetual hatred to it and has made most violent opposition against it.

That the church of God has always met with great opposition in the world, none can deny. This is plain by profane history, as far as that reaches; and before that, divine history gives us the same account. The church of God, and its religion and worship, began to be opposed in Cain's and Abel's time, and was so when the earth was filled with violence in Noah's time. And after this, how was the church opposed in Egypt! And how was the church of Israel always hated by the nations round about, agreeable to that in Jeremiah 12:9, 'Mine heritage is unto me as a speckled bird, the birds round about are against her.' And after the Babylonish captivity, how was this church persecuted by Antiochus Epiphanes and others! How was Christ persecuted when he was on earth! And how were the apostles and other Christians persecuted by the Jews before the destruction of Jerusalem by the Romans! How violent were that people against the church! And how dreadful was the opposition of the heathen world against the Christian church after this, before Constantine! How great was their spite against the true religion! And since that, how yet more violent, spiteful and cruel has been the opposition of Antichrist against the church!

There is no other such instance of opposition. History gives no account of any other body of men that have been so hated, and so maliciously and insatiably pursued and persecuted, nor anything like it. No other religion ever was so maligned age after age. The nations of other professions have enjoyed their religions in peace and quietness, however they have differed from their neighbours. One nation has worshipped one sort of gods, and others another, without molesting or disturbing one another about it. All the spite and opposition has been against this religion which the church of Christ has professed. All other religions have seemed to show an implacable enmity to this; and men have seemed to have, from one age to another, such a spite against it that they have seemed as though they could never satisfy their cruelty. They put their invention upon the rack to find out torments that should be cruel enough, and yet, after all, never seemed to be satisfied. Their thirst has never been satisfied with blood.

So that this is out of doubt, that this religion, and these Scriptures, have always been malignantly opposed in the world. The only question that remains is, What it is that has made this opposition, and whether it has been good or bad? Whether it be the wickedness and corruption of the world, or not, that has done this? But of this there can be no greater doubt than of the other, if we consider how causeless this cruelty has always been, who the opposers have been, and the manner in which they have opposed. The opposition has chiefly been from heathenism and Popery, which things certainly are evil. They are both of them very evil, and the fruits of the blindness, corruption, and wickedness of men, as the very Deists themselves confess. The light of nature shows that the religion of heathens, consisting in the worship of idols, and sacrificing their children to them, and in obscene and abominable rites and ceremonies, is wickedness. And the superstitions, and idolatries, and usurpations, of the church of Rome, are no less contrary to the light of nature. By this it appears that this opposition which has been made against the church of God, has been made by wicked men. And with regard to the opposition of the Jews in Christ's and the apostles' times, it was in a most corrupt time of that nation, when the people were generally become exceeding wicked, as some of the Jewish writers themselves, as Josephus and others who lived about that time, do expressly say. And that it has been mere wickedness that has made this opposition is manifest from the manner of opposition, the extreme violence, injustice, and cruelty, with which the church of God has been treated. It seems to show the hand of malignant infernal spirits in it.

Now, what reason can be assigned why the corruption and wickedness of the world should so implacably set itself against this religion of Jesus Christ, and against the Scriptures, but only that they are contrary to wickedness, and consequently are good and holy? Why should the enemies of Christ, for so many thousand years together, manifest such a mortal hatred of this religion, but only that it is the cause of God? If the Scriptures be not the Word of God, and the religion of the church of Christ be not the true religion, then it must follow that it is a most wicked religion; nothing but a pack of lies and abominable delusions, invented by the enemies of God themselves. And if this were so, it is not likely that the enemies of

God, and the wickedness of the world, would have main-tained such a perpetual and implacable enmity against it.

ii. It is a great argument that the Christian church and its religion is from God, that *it has been upheld* hitherto through all the opposition and dangers it has passed through. That the church of God and the true religion, which has been so con-tinually and violently opposed, with so many endeavours to overthrow it, and which has so often been brought to the brink of ruin and almost swallowed up through the greatest part of six thousand years, has yet been upheld, does most remarkably show the hand of God in favour of the church. If we consider it, it will appear one of the greatest wonders and miracles that ever came to pass. There is nothing else like it upon the face of the earth. There is no other society of men that has stood as the church has. As to the old world which was before the Flood, that was overthrown by a deluge of waters; but yet the church of God was preserved. Satan's visible kingdom on earth was then once entirely overthrown; but the visible kingdom of Christ never has been overthrown. All those ancient human kingdoms and monarchies of which we read, and which have been in former ages, are long since come to an end. Those kingdoms of which we read in the Old Testament, of the Moabites, the Ammonites, the Edomites, etc., are all long ago come to an end. Those four great monar-chies of the world have been overthrown one after another. The great empire of proud Babylon was overthrown by the Persians; and then the Persian empire was overthrown by the Greeks; after this the Grecian empire was overthrown by the Romans; and, finally, the Roman empire fell a sacrifice to various barbarous nations.

Here is a remarkable fulfilment of the words of the text with respect to other things, even the greatest and most glori-ous of them: they have all grown old, and have vanished away;

'the moth has eaten them up like a garment, and the worm has eaten them like wool' (*Isa.* 51:8), but yet God's church remains.

Never were there so many and so potent endeavours to destroy any thing else as there have been to destroy the church. Other kingdoms and societies of men which have appeared to be ten times as strong as the church of God have been destroyed with a hundredth part of the opposition which the church of God has met with. This shows that it is God who has been the Protector of the church. For it is most plain that it has not upheld itself by its own strength. For the most part it has been a very weak society. They have been a little flock. So they were of old. The children of Israel were but a small handful of people, in comparison of the many who often sought their overthrow. And so in Christ's time, and in the beginning of the Christian church after Christ's resurrection, they were but a remnant, whereas the whole multitude of the Jewish nation were against them. And so in the beginning of the Gentile church, they were but a small number in comparison with the heathen, who sought their overthrow. And so in the dark times of Antichrist, before the Reformation, they were but a handful; and yet their enemies could not overthrow them.

And it has commonly been so, that the enemies of the church have not only had the greatest number on their side, but they have had the strength on their side in other respects. They have commonly had all the civil authority on their side. So it was in Egypt: the civil authority was on the side of the Egyptians, and the church were only their slaves, and were in their hands; and yet they could not overthrow them. And so it was in the time of the persecution of Antiochus Epiphanes: the authority was all on the side of the persecutors, and the church was under their dominion; and yet all their cruelty could not extirpate it. And so it was afterwards in the time of the heathen Roman government. And so it was in the time of Julian the Apostate, who did his utmost to overthrow the Christian church and to restore heathenism. And so it has been for the most part since the rise of Antichrist: for a great many ages. The civil authority was all on the side of Antichrist, and the church seemed to be in their hands.

And not only has the strength of the enemies of the church been greater than the strength of the church, but ordinarily the church has not used what strength they have had in their own defence, but have committed themselves wholly to God. So it was in the time of the Jewish persecutions before the destruction of Jerusalem by the Romans; and so it was in the time of the heathen persecutors before Constantine. The Christians did not only not rise up in arms to defend themselves, but they did not pretend to make any forcible resistance to their heathen persecutors. So it has for the most part been under the Popish persecutors, and yet they have never been able to overthrow the church of God; but it stands to this very day.

And this is still the more exceeding wonderful, if we consider how often the church has been brought to the brink of ruin, and the case seemed to be desperate, and all hope gone, and they seemed to be swallowed up. In the time of the old world, when wickedness so prevailed as that but one family was left, yet God wonderfully appeared and overthrew the wicked world with a Flood and preserved his church. And so at the Red Sea, when Pharaoh and his host thought they were quite sure of their prey; yet God appeared, and destroyed them, and delivered his church. And so was it from time to time in the church of Israel, as has been shown. So under the tenth and last heathen persecution, their persecutors boasted that now they had done the business for the Christians, and had overthrown the Christian church; yet in the midst of their triumph, the Christian church rises out of the dust and prevails, and the heathen empire totally falls before it. So when the Christian church seemed ready to be swallowed up by the Arian heresy; so when Antichrist rose and prevailed, and all the world wondered after the beast, and the church for many hundred years was reduced to such a small number, and seemed to be hidden, and the power of the world was engaged to destroy those little remainders of the church; yet they could never fully accomplish their design, and at last God wonderfully revived his church in the time of the Reformation, and made it to stand as it were on its feet in the sight of its enemies, and raised it out of their reach. And so since, when the Popish powers have plotted the overthrow of the Reformed church, and have seemed just about to bring their matters to a conclusion, and to finish their design, then God has wonderfully appeared for the deliverance of his church, as it was in the time of the Revolution by King William. And so it has been from time to time. Presently after the darkest times of the church, God has made his church most gloriously to flourish.

If such a preservation of the church of God, from the beginning of the world hitherto, attended with such circumstances, is not sufficient to shew a divine hand in favour of it, what can be devised that would be sufficient? But if this be from the divine hand, then God owns the church, and owns her religion, and owns that revelation and those Scriptures on which she is built; and so it will follow that their religion is the true religion, or God's religion, and that the Scriptures, which they make their rule, are his Word.

iii. We may draw this further argument for the divine authority of the Scriptures from what has been said, namely, that God has so *fulfilled those things which are foretold in the Scriptures.* I have already observed, as I went along, how the prophecies of Scripture were fulfilled. I shall now therefore single out but two instances of the fulfilment of Scripture prophecy.

a. One is in *preserving his church from being ruined*. I have just now shown what an evidence this is of the divine authority of the Scriptures, in itself considered. I now speak of it as a fulfilment of Scripture prophecy. This is abundantly foretold and promised in the Scriptures, as particularly in the text: there it is foretold that other things shall fail, other kingdoms and monarchies which set themselves in opposition shall come to nothing: 'The moth shall eat them up like a garment, and the worm shall eat them like wool.' And so it has in fact come to pass. But it is here foretold that God's covenant mercy to his church shall continue forever; and so it hath hitherto proved, though now it be so many ages since, and though the church has passed through so many dangers. The same is promised: 'No weapon that is formed against thee, shall prosper; and every tongue that shall rise against thee in judgment, thou shalt condemn' (*Isa*. 54:17). And again: 'But Zion said, The LORD hath forsaken me, and my Lord hath forgotten me. Can a woman forget her sucking child, that she should not have compassion on the son of her womb? yea, they may forget, yet will I not forget thee. Behold, I have graven thee upon the palms of my hands; thy walls are continually before me' (*Isa*. 49:14-16). The same is promised again in Isaiah 59:21, Isaiah 43:1-2 and Zechariah 12:2-3. So Christ promises the same when he says, 'Upon this rock I will build my church; and the gates of hell shall not prevail against it.'

Now if this be not from God, and the Scriptures be not the Word of God, and the church of Christ built on the foundation of this Word be not of God, how could the persons who foretold this know it? For if the church were not of God, it was a very unlikely thing ever to come to pass. For they foretold the great opposition, and the great dangers, and also foretold that other kingdoms should come to nought, and

[363]

that the church should often be almost swallowed up, as it were easy to show, and yet foretold that the church should remain. Now, how could they foresee so unlikely a thing but by divine inspiration?

b. The other remarkable instance which I shall mention of the fulfilment of Scripture prophecy, is in *fulfilling what is foretold concerning Antichrist*, a certain great opposer of Christ and his kingdom. And the way that this Antichrist should arise is foretold, namely, not among the heathen, or those nations that never professed Christianity; but that he should arise by the apostasy and falling away of the Christian church into a corrupt state: 'For that day shall not come, except there come a falling away first, and that man of sin be revealed, the son of perdition' (*2 Thess.* 2:3). And it is prophesied, that this Antichrist, or man of sin, should be one that should set himself up in the temple or visible church of God, pretending to be vested with the power of God himself, as head of the church, as in the same chapter, verse 4. And all this is exactly come to pass in the church of Rome. Again, it is intimated, that the rise of Antichrist should be gradual, as in that chapter, verse 7: 'For the mystery of iniquity doth already work: only he who now letteth will let, until he be taken out of the way.' This also came to pass.

Again, it is prophesied of such a great and mighty enemy of the Christian church that he should be a great prince or monarch of the Roman Empire. So he is represented as a horn of the fourth beast in Daniel, or fourth kingdom or monarchy upon earth, as the angel himself explains it, as you may see of the little horn in Daniel 7. This also came to pass. Yea, it is prophesied that the seat of this great prince, or pretended vicar of God, and head of his church, should be in the city of Rome itself. In Revelation 17 it is said expressly, that the spiritual whore, or false church, should have her seat on seven mountains or hills: 'The seven heads are seven mountains, on which the woman sitteth' (*Rev.* 17:9). And in the last verse of the chapter, it is said expressly, 'The woman which thou sawest, is that great city, which reigneth over the kings of the earth', which it is certain was at that time the city of Rome. This prophecy also has come to pass in the church of Rome.

Further, it was prophesied, that this Antichrist should reign over peoples, and multitudes, and nations, and tongues (*Rev.* 17:15) and that all the world should wonder after the beast (*Rev.* 13:3). This also came to pass in the church of Rome. It was foretold that this Antichrist should be eminent and remarkable for the sin of pride, pretending to great things, and assuming very much to himself, as in the forementioned place in Thessalonians, that he should exalt himself above all that is called God, or that is worshipped. So in Revelation 13:5, 'And there was given unto him a mouth speaking great things, and blasphemies.' In Daniel 7:20, the little horn is said to have a mouth speaking very great things and his look to be more stout than his fellows. This also came to pass in the Pope, and the church of Rome. It was also prophesied that Antichrist should be an exceeding cruel persecutor (*Dan.* 7:21). The same horn made war with the saints, and prevailed against them: 'And it was given unto him to make war with the saints, and to overcome them' (*Rev.* 13: 7). 'And I saw the woman drunken with the blood of the saints, and with the blood of the martyrs of Jesus' (*Rev.* 17:6). This also came to pass in the church of Rome. It was foretold that Antichrist should excel in craft and policy: 'In this horn were eyes like the eyes of a man' (*Dan.* 7:8). And verse 20, 'Even of that horn that had eyes.' This also came to pass in the church of Rome. It was foretold that the kings of Christendom should be subject to Antichrist: 'And the ten horns which thou sawest are ten kings, which have received no kingdom as yet;

but receive power as kings one hour with the beast. These have one mind, and shall give their power and strength unto the beast' (*Rev.* 17:12-13). This also came to pass with respect to the Romish church. It was foretold that he should perform pretended miracles and lying wonders: 'Whose coming is after the working of Satan with all power and signs and lying wonders' (*2 Thess.* 2:9). 'And he doth great wonders, so that he maketh fire come down from heaven on the earth, in the sight of men, and deceiveth them that dwell on the earth by the means of those miracles which he had power to do in the sight of the beast' (*Rev.* 13:13-14). This also came to pass in the church of Rome. Fire coming down from heaven, seems to have reference to their excommunications, which were dreaded like fire from heaven.

It was foretold that he should forbid to marry, and command to abstain from meats: 'Forbidding to marry, and commanding to abstain from meats, which God had created to be received with thanksgiving' (*1 Tim.* 4:3). This also is exactly fulfilled in the church of Rome. It was foretold that he should be very rich, and arrive at a great degree of earthly splendour and glory: 'And the woman was arrayed in purple and scarlet colour, and decked with gold and precious stones and pearls, having a golden cup in her hand' (*Rev.* 17:4). And also chapter 18, verses 7, 12, 13 and 16. This also is come to pass with respect to the church of Rome. It was foretold that he should forbid any to buy or sell but those that had his mark: 'And that no man might buy or sell, save he that had the mark, or the name of the beast, or the number of his name' (*Rev.* 13:17). This also is fulfilled in the church of Rome. It was foretold that he should sell the souls of men (*Rev.* 18:13), where, in enumerating the articles of his merchandise, the souls of men are mentioned as one. This also is exactly fulfilled in the same church. It was foretold, that Antichrist would not suffer the bodies of God's people to be put into graves: 'And their dead bodies shall lie in the street of the great city . . . and they . . . shall not suffer their dead bodies to be put in graves' (*Rev.* 11:8-9). This also has literally come to pass with respect to the church of Rome. I might mention many other things which were foretold of Antichrist, or that great enemy of the church so often spoken of in Scripture, and show that they were fulfilled most exactly in the Pope and the church of Rome.

How strong an argument is this that the Scriptures are the Word of God!

2. But I come now to a second inference; which is this: from what has been said, we may learn what the spirit of true Christians is, namely, a spirit of suffering. Seeing God has so ordered it in his providence that his church should for so long a time, for the greater part of so many ages, be in a suffering state, yea, and often in a state of such extreme suffering, we may conclude that the spirit of the true church is a suffering spirit, otherwise God never would have ordered so much suffering for her; for doubtless God accommodates the state and circumstances of the church to the spirit that he has given her. No wonder therefore that Christ so much inculcated upon his disciples that it was necessary that, if any would be his disciples, they must deny themselves and take up their cross and follow him.

And we may argue that the spirit of the true church of Christ is a suffering spirit by the spirit the church has shown and exercised under her sufferings. She has actually, under those persecutions through which she has passed, rather chosen to undergo those dreadful torments and to sell all for the pearl of great price, to suffer all that her bitterest enemies could afflict, than to renounce Christ and his religion. History furnishes us with a great number of remarkable instances and sets in view a great cloud of witnesses. This abundantly confirms the necessity of being of a spirit to sell all for Christ, to renounce our own ease, our own worldly profit and honour, and our all, for him, and for the gospel.

Let us inquire, whether we are of such a spirit. How does it prove upon trial? Does it prove in fact that we are willing to deny ourselves, and renounce our own worldly interest, and to pass through the trials to which we are called in providence? Alas, how small are our trials, compared with those of many of our fellow Christians in former ages! And I would on this occasion apply what is said in Jeremiah 12:5, 'If thou hast run with the footmen, and they have wearied thee, then how canst thou contend with horses?' If you have not been able to endure the light trials to which you have been called in this age, and in this land, how would you be able to endure the far greater trials to which the church has been called in former ages? Every true Christian has the spirit of a martyr, and would suffer as a martyr, if he were called to it in providence.

3. Hence we learn what great reason we have assuredly to expect the fulfilment of what yet remains to be fulfilled of things foretold in Scripture. The Scriptures foretell many great things yet to be fulfilled before the end of the world, but there seem to be great difficulties in the way. We seem at present to be very far from such a state as is foretold in the Scriptures; but we have abundant reason to expect that these things, however seemingly difficult, will yet be accomplished in their season. We see the faithfulness of God to his promises hitherto. How true has God been to his church, and remembered his mercy from generation to generation! We may say concerning what God has done hitherto for his church what Joshua said to the children of Israel, 'Not one thing hath failed of all the good things which the LORD your God spake concerning you' (*Josh.* 23:14), but all things are hitherto come to pass, agreeable to the divine prediction. This should strengthen our

faith in those promises, encourage us, and stir us up to earnest prayer to God for the accomplishment of the great and glorious things which yet remain to be fulfilled.

iv. I come now to show how the success of Christ's redemption will be carried on *from the present time until Antichrist is fallen and Satan's visible kingdom on earth is destroyed.* And with respect to this space of time, we have nothing to guide us but the prophecies of Scripture. Through most of the time from the Fall of man to the destruction of Jerusalem by the Romans we had Scripture history to guide us; and from thence to the present time we had prophecy, together with the accomplishment of it in providence as related in human histories. But henceforward we have only prophecy to guide us. And here I would pass by those things that are only conjectural, or that are surmised by some from those prophecies which are doubtful in their interpretation, and shall insist only on those things which are more clear and evident.

We know not what particular events are to come to pass before that glorious work of God's Spirit begins, by which Satan's kingdom is to be overthrown. By the consent of most divines, there are but few things, if any at all, that are foretold to be accomplished before the beginning of that glorious work of God. Some think the slaying of the witnesses (*Rev.* 11:7-8) is not yet accomplished. So divines differ with respect to the pouring out of the seven vials, of which we have an account in Revelation 16: how many are already poured out, or how many remain to be poured out; though a late expositor whom I have before mentioned to you seems to make it very plain and evident, that all are already poured out but two, namely, the sixth on the river Euphrates, and the seventh into the air. But I will not now stand to inquire what is intended by the pouring out of the sixth vial on the river Euphrates, that the way of the kings of the east may be prepared; but only would say that it seems to be something immediately preparing the way for the destruction of the spiritual Babylon, as the drying up of the river Euphrates, which ran through the midst of old Babylon, was what prepared the way of the kings of the Medes and Persians, the kings of the east, to come in under the walls and destroy that city.

But whatever this be, it does not appear that it is any thing which shall be accomplished before that work of God's Spirit is begun by which, as it goes on, Satan's visible kingdom on earth shall be utterly overthrown. And therefore I would proceed directly to consider what the Scripture reveals concerning the work of God itself by which he will bring about this great event, as being the next thing which is to be accomplished that we are certain of from the prophecies of Scripture.

And, first, I would observe two things in general concerning it. We have all reason to conclude from the Scriptures, that just before this work of God begins, it will be *a very dark time with respect to the interests of religion in the world*. It has been so before those glorious revivals of religion that have been hitherto. It was so when Christ came; it was an exceeding degenerate time among the Jews. And so it was a very dark time before the Reformation. And not only so, but it seems to be foretold in Scripture that it shall be a time of but little religion, when Christ shall come to set up his kingdom in the world. Thus when Christ spake of his coming to encourage his elect who cry to him day and night in Luke 18:8, he adds this, 'Nevertheless, when the Son of man cometh, shall he find faith on the earth?', which seems to denote a great prevalence of infidelity just before Christ's coming to avenge his suffering church. Though Christ's coming at the last judgment is not here to be excluded, yet there seems to be a special respect to his coming to deliver his church from their long continued suffering persecuted state, which is accomplished at his coming at the destruction of Antichrist. That time that the elect cry to God, as in Revelation 6:10, 'How long, O Lord, holy and true, dost thou not judge and avenge our blood on them that dwell on the earth?', and the time spoken of in Revelation 18:20: 'Rejoice over her, thou heaven, and ye holy apostles, and prophets, for God hath avenged you on her', will then be accomplished.

It is now a very dark time with respect to the interests of religion, and such a time as is prophesied of in this place, wherein there is but a little faith, and a great prevailing of infidelity on the earth. There is now a remarkable fulfilment of that in 2 Peter 3:3: 'Knowing this first, that there shall come in the last days scoffers, walking after their own lusts.' And so in Jude 17-18: 'But beloved, remember ye the words which were spoken before of the apostles of our Lord Jesus Christ; how that they told you there should be mockers in the last time, who should walk after their own ungodly lusts.' Whether the times shall be any darker still, or how much darker, before the beginning of this glorious work of God, we cannot tell.

Secondly, there is no reason from the Word of God to think any other than that *this great work of God will be wrought*, though very swiftly, yet *gradually*. As the children of Israel were gradually brought out of the Babylonish captivity, first one company, and then another, and gradually rebuilt their city and temple; and as the heathen Roman Empire was destroyed by a gradual though a very swift prevalency of the gospel, so, though there are many things which seem to hold forth as though the work of God would be exceeding swift, and many great and wonderful events should very suddenly be brought to pass, and some great parts of Satan's visible kingdom should have a very sudden fall, yet all will not be accomplished at once, as by some great miracle, as the resurrection of the dead at the end of the world will be all at once; but this is a work which will be accomplished by means, by the preaching of the gospel and the use of the ordinary means of grace, and so shall be gradually brought to pass. Some shall be converted, and be the means of the conversion of others. God's Spirit shall be poured out first to raise up instruments, and then those instruments shall be used and caused to succeed. And doubtless one nation shall be enlightened and converted after another, one false religion and false way of worship exploded after another. By the representation in Daniel 2:3-4, the stone cut out of the mountain without hands gradually grows. So Christ teaches us that the kingdom of heaven is like a grain of mustard seed, and like leaven hid in three measures of meal (*Matt.* 13:31-33). The same representation we have in Mark 4:26-28, and in the vision of the waters of the sanctuary in Ezekiel 47.

The Scriptures hold forth as though there should be several successive great and glorious events by which this work should be accomplished. The angel, speaking to the prophet Daniel of those glorious times, mentions two glorious periods, at the end of which glorious things should be accomplished: 'And from the time that the daily sacrifice shall be taken away, and the abomination that maketh desolate set up, there shall be a thousand two hundred and ninety days' (*Dan.* 12:11). But then he adds in the next verse, 'Blessed is he that waiteth, and cometh to the thousand three hundred and five and thirty days', intimating, that something very glorious should be accomplished at the end of the former period, but something much more glorious at the end of the latter.

But I now proceed to show how this glorious work shall be accomplished.

a. The Spirit of God shall be gloriously poured out for the wonderful revival and propagation of religion. This great work shall be accomplished, not by the authority of princes, nor by the wisdom of learned men, but by God's Holy Spirit: 'Not by might, nor by power, but by my Spirit, saith the LORD of hosts. Who art thou, O great mountain? Before Zerubbabel thou shalt become a plain: and he shall bring forth the headstone thereof with shoutings, crying, Grace, grace unto it' (*Zech.* 4:6-7). So the prophet Ezekiel, speaking of this great work of God, says, 'Neither will I hide my face any more from them; for I have poured out my Spirit on the house of Israel, saith the Lord GOD' (*Ezek.* 39:29). We know not where this pouring out of the Spirit shall begin, or whether in many places at once, or whether what hath already been be not some forerunner and beginning of it.

This pouring out of the Spirit of God, when it is begun, shall soon bring great multitudes to forsake that vice and wickedness which now so generally prevails, and shall cause vital religion, which is now so despised and laughed at in the world, to revive. The work of conversion shall break forth, and go on in such a manner as never has been hitherto; agreeable to what is said in Isaiah 44:3-5. God, by pouring out his Holy Spirit, will furnish men to be glorious instruments of carrying on this work. He will fill them with knowledge and wisdom and fervent zeal to promote the kingdom of Christ, and the salvation of souls, and to propagate the gospel in the world. So that the gospel shall begin to be preached with abundantly greater clearness and power than had heretofore been; for this great work of God shall be brought to pass by the preaching of the gospel, as is represented in Revelation 14:6-8, so that before Babylon falls the gospel shall be powerfully preached and propagated in the world.

This was typified of old by the sounding of the silver trumpets in Israel in the beginning of their jubilee: 'Then shalt thou cause the trumpet of the jubilee to sound on the tenth day of the seventh month; on the day of atonement shall ye make the trumpet sound throughout all your land' (*Lev.* 25:9). The glorious times which are approaching are as it were the

[373]

church's jubilee, which shall be introduced by the sounding of the silver trumpet of the gospel, as is foretold in Isaiah 27:13: 'And it shall come to pass in that day, that the great trumpet shall be blown, and they shall come which were ready to perish in the land of Assyria, and the outcasts of the land of Egypt, and shall worship the LORD in the holy mount at Jerusalem.' And there shall be a glorious pouring out of the Spirit with this clear and powerful preaching of the gospel to make it successful for reviving those holy doctrines of religion which are now chiefly ridiculed in the world, and turning many from heresy, and from Popery, and from other false religions; and also for turning many from their vice and profaneness, and for bringing vast multitudes savingly home to Christ.

That work of conversion shall go on in a wonderful manner, and spread more and more. Many shall flow together to the goodness of the Lord, and shall come as it were in flocks, one flock and multitude after another continually flowing in as in Isaiah 60:4-5, 'Lift up thine eyes round about, and see: all they gather themselves together, they come to thee: thy sons shall come from far, and thy daughters shall be nursed at thy side. Then thou shalt see and flow together.' And so verse 8: 'Who are these that fly as a cloud, and as the doves to their windows?' And as the gospel shall be preached to every tongue, and kindred, and nation, and people, before the fall of Antichrist, so we may suppose, that it will soon be gloriously successful to bring in multitudes from every nation; and it shall spread more and more with wonderful swiftness, and vast numbers shall suddenly be brought in as it were at once, as you may see in Isaiah 66:7-9.

b. This pouring out of the Spirit of God will not effect the overthrow of Satan's visible kingdom until there has first been a violent and mighty opposition made. In this the Scripture is plain that, when Christ is thus gloriously coming forth and the destruction of Antichrist is ready at hand, and Satan's kingdom begins to totter, and to appear to be imminently threatened, the powers of the kingdom of darkness will rise up and mightily exert themselves to prevent their kingdom being overthrown. Thus, after the pouring out of the sixth vial, which was to dry up the river Euphrates, to prepare the way for the destruction of spiritual Babylon, it is represented in Revelation 16 as though the powers of hell will be mightily alarmed and stir up themselves to oppose the kingdom of Christ, before the seventh and last vial shall be poured out, which shall give them a final and complete overthrow. We have an account of the pouring out of the sixth vial in verse 12. And then after this the beloved disciple informs us in the following verses that three unclean spirits like frogs shall 'go forth unto the kings of the earth and of the whole world, to gather them to the battle of that great day of God Almighty'. This seems to be the last and greatest effort of Satan to save his kingdom from being overthrown, though perhaps he may make as great an effort towards the end of the world to regain it.

When the Spirit begins to be so gloriously poured forth, and the devil sees such multitudes flocking to Christ in one nation and another, and the foundations of his kingdom daily undermining, and the pillars of it breaking, and the whole ready to come to swift and sudden destruction, it will greatly alarm all hell. Satan has ever had a dread of having his kingdom overthrown, and he has been opposing it ever since Christ's ascension, and has been doing great works to fortify his kingdom, and to prevent it, ever since the day of Constantine the Great. To this end he has set up those two mighty kingdoms of Antichrist and Mahomet, and brought in all the heresies, superstitions and corruptions, which there are in the world. But when he sees all begin to fail, it will rouse him up exceedingly. If Satan dreaded being cast out of the

Roman Empire, how much more does he dread being cast out of the whole world!

It seems as though in this last great opposition which shall be made against the church to defend the kingdom of Satan, all the forces of Antichrist and Mahometanism and heathenism will be united: all the forces of Satan's visible kingdom through the whole world of mankind. And therefore it is said, that 'spirits of devils . . . [shall] go forth unto the kings of the earth, and of the whole world, to gather them together to the battle of that great day of God Almighty' (*Rev.* 16:14). And these spirits are said to come out of the mouth of the dragon, and out of the mouth of the beast, and out of the mouth of the false prophet; that is, there shall be the spirit of Popery, and the spirit of Mahometanism, and the spirit of heathenism, all united. By the beast is meant Antichrist; by the dragon, in this book, is commonly meant the devil, as he reigns over his heathen kingdom; by the false prophet, in this book, is sometimes meant the Pope and his clergy, but here an eye seems to be had to Mahomet, whom his followers call the great prophet of God. This will be as it were the dying struggles of the old serpent, a battle wherein he will fight as one that is almost desperate.

We know not particularly in what manner this opposition shall be made. It is represented as a battle, the battle of the great day of God Almighty. There will be in some way or other a mighty struggle between Satan's kingdom and the church, and probably in all ways of opposition that can be; and doubtless great opposition by external force, wherein the princes of the world who are on the devil's side shall join hand in hand: for it is said, 'The kings of the earth are gathered together to battle' (*Rev.* 19:19). And probably withal there will be great opposition of subtle disputers and carnal reasoning, and great persecution in many places, and great opposition by virulent reproaches, and also great opposition by craft and subtlety.

The devil now doubtless will ply his skill, as well as strength, to the utmost. The devils, and those who belong to their kingdom, will everywhere be stirred up, and engaged to make a united and violent opposition against this holy religion which they see prevailing so mightily in the world.

c. But Christ and his church shall in this battle obtain a complete and entire victory over their enemies. They shall be totally routed and overthrown in this their last effort. When the powers of hell and earth are thus gathered together against Christ, and his armies shall come forth against them by his Word and Spirit to fight with them, in how august, and pompous, and glorious a manner is this coming forth of Christ and his church to this battle described (*Rev.* 19:11, etc.)! And to represent to us how great the victory should be which they should obtain, and how mighty the overthrow of their enemies, it is said that all the fowls of heaven are called together, to eat the great supper given them, of the flesh of kings, and captains, and mighty men (*Rev* 19:17-18), and then, in the following verses, we have an account of the victory and overthrow.

In this victory, the seventh vial shall be poured out. It is said of the great army that should be gathered together against Christ, 'And he gathered them together into a place called in the Hebrew tongue Armageddon', and then it is said, 'And the seventh angel poured out his vial into the air; and there came a great voice out of the temple of heaven, from the throne, saying, It is done' (*Rev.* 16:16-17). Now the business is done for Satan and his adherents. When this victory is obtained, all is in effect done. Satan's last and greatest opposition is conquered; all his measures are defeated; the pillars of his kingdom broken asunder, and will fall of course. The devil is utterly baffled and confounded, and knows not what else to do. He now sees his Antichristian, and Mahometan, and heathenish kingdoms through the world all tumbling about his ears. He and his most powerful instruments are taken captive. Now that is in effect done which the church of God had been so long waiting and hoping for, and so earnestly crying to God for, saying, 'How long, O Lord, holy and true!' Now the time is come.

The angel who set his right foot on the sea and his left foot on the earth lifted up his hand to heaven and swore by him that liveth for ever and ever, who created heaven, and all things that therein are, and the earth, and the things that therein are, and the sea, and the things which are therein, that when the seventh angel should come to sound, the time should be no longer (*Rev.* 10:5-6). And now the time is come; now the seventh trumpet sounds, and the seventh vial is poured out, both together, intimating that now all is finished as to the overthrow of Satan's visible kingdom on earth. This victory shall be by far the greatest that ever was obtained over Satan and his adherents. By this blow, with which the stone cut out of the mountain without hands shall strike the image of gold, and silver, and brass, and iron, and clay, it shall all be broken to pieces. This will be a finishing blow to the image, so that it shall become as the chaff of the summer threshing floor.

In this victory will be a most glorious display of divine power. Christ shall therein appear in the character of King of kings, and Lord of lords, as in Revelation 19:16. Now Christ shall dash his enemies, even the strongest and proudest of them, in pieces; as a potter's vessel shall they be broken to shivers. Then shall strength be shown out of weakness, and Christ shall cause his church as it were to thresh the mountains, 'Behold, I will make thee a new sharp threshing instrument having teeth: thou shalt thresh the mountains, and beat them small, and shalt make the hills as chaff' (*Isa.* 41:15). And then shall Isaiah 42:13-15 be fulfilled.

d. Consequent on this victory, Satan's visible kingdom on earth shall be destroyed. When Satan is conquered in this last battle, the church of Christ will have easy work of it; as when Joshua and the children of Israel had obtained that great victory over the five kings of the Amorites, when the sun stood still, and God sent great hailstones on their enemies, they after that went from one city to another, and burnt them with fire. They had easy work of subduing the cities and country to which they belonged. So it was also after that other great battle that Joshua had with that great multitude at the waters of Merom. So after this glorious victory of Christ and his church over their enemies, over the chief powers of Satan's kingdom, they shall destroy that kingdom in all those cities and countries to which they belonged.

After this the Word of God shall have a speedy and swift progress through the earth, as it is said that, on the pouring out of the seventh vial, 'the cities of the nations fell . . . and every island fled away, and the mountains were not found' (*Rev.* 16:19-20). When once the stone cut out of the mountain without hands had broken the image in pieces, it was easy to abolish all remains of it. The very wind will carry it away as the chaff of the summer threshing floor. Because Satan's visible kingdom on earth shall now be destroyed, therefore it is said that the seventh vial, by which this shall be done, shall be poured out into the air, which is represented in Scripture as the special seat of his kingdom; for he is called the prince of the power of the air (*Eph.* 2:2). Now is come the time for punishing leviathan that piercing serpent of which we read in Isaiah 27:1, 'In that day the LORD with his sore and great and strong sword shall punish leviathan the piercing serpent, even leviathan that crooked serpent; and he shall slay the dragon that is in the sea.'

Concerning this overthrow of Satan's visible kingdom on earth, I would show wherein this overthrow will chiefly consist, and the extent and universality of the overthrow. I shall mention the particular things in which it will consist, without pretending to determine in what order they shall come to pass, or which shall be accomplished first, or whether they shall be accomplished together.

1. Heresies, infidelity and superstition, among those who have been brought up under the light of the gospel will then be abolished. Then there will be an end to Socinianism, Arianism, Quakerism and Arminianism; and Deism, which is now so bold and confident in infidelity, shall then be crushed, and driven away, and vanish to nothing; and all shall agree in the same great and important doctrines of the gospel, agreeable to that in Zechariah 14:9, 'And the LORD shall be king over all the earth: in that day shall there be one LORD, and his name one.' Then shall be abolished all superstitious ways of worship, and all shall agree in worshipping God in his own ways: 'And I will give them one heart, and one way, that they may fear me for ever, for the good of them, and of their children after them' (*Jer.* 32:39).

2. The kingdom of Antichrist shall be utterly overthrown. His kingdom and dominion has been much brought down already by the vial poured out on his throne in the Reformation, but then it shall be utterly destroyed. Then shall be proclaimed, 'Babylon is fallen, is fallen.' When the seventh angel sounds, the 'time, times and half a time' shall be out, and 'time shall be no longer'. Then shall be accomplished concerning Antichrist the things which are written in Revelation 18 of the spiritual Babylon, that great city Rome, or the idolatrous Roman government that has for so many ages been the great enemy of the Christian church, first under heathenism, then under Popery: that proud city which titled herself up to heaven, and above God himself in her pride and haughtiness; that cruel, bloody city, shall come down to the ground. Then shall that be fulfilled, 'For he bringeth down them that dwell

on high; the lofty city he layeth it low; he layeth it low, even to the ground; he bringeth it even to the dust' (*Isa.* 26:5). She shall be thrown down with violence, like a great millstone cast into the sea, and shall be found no more at all, and shall become an habitation of devils, and the hold of every foul spirit, and a cage of every unclean and hateful bird. Now shall she be stripped of all her glory, and riches, and ornaments, and shall be cast out as an abominable branch, and shall be trodden down as the mire of the streets. All her policy and craft, in which she so abounded, shall not save her. And God shall make his people, who have been so persecuted by her, to come and put their foot on the neck of Antichrist, and he shall be their footstool. All the strength and wisdom of this great whore shall fail her, and there shall be none to help her. The kings of the earth, who before gave their power and strength to the beast, shall now hate the whore, and shall make her desolate and naked, and shall eat her flesh, and burn her with fire (*Rev.* 17:16).

3. That other great kingdom which Satan has set up in opposition to the Christian church, namely, his Mahometan kingdom, shall be utterly overthrown. The locusts and horsemen, in Revelation 9, have their appointed and limited time set them there, and the false prophet shall be taken and destroyed. And then, though Mahometanism has been so vastly propagated in the world, and is upheld by such a great empire, this smoke, which has ascended out of the bottomless pit, shall be utterly scattered before the light of that glorious day, and the Mahometan empire shall fall at the sound of the great trumpet which shall then be blown.

4. Jewish infidelity shall then be overthrown. However obstinate they have been now for above 1700 years in their rejection of Christ, and instances of the conversion of any of that nation have been so very rare ever since the destruction of Jerusalem, but they have, against the plain teachings of

their own prophets, continued to approve of the cruelty of their forefathers in crucifying Christ; yet when this day comes, the thick veil that blinds their eyes shall be removed (*2 Cor.* 3:16); and divine grace shall melt and renew their hard hearts, 'and they shall look upon me whom they have pierced, and they shall mourn for him, as one mourneth for his only son, and shall be in bitterness for him, as one that is in bitterness for his firstborn' (*Zech.* 12:10).

And then shall the house of Israel be saved. The Jews in all their dispersions shall cast away their old infidelity, and shall wonderfully have their hearts changed, and abhor themselves for their past unbelief and obstinacy; and shall flow together to the blessed Jesus, penitently, humbly, and joyfully owning him as their glorious King and only Saviour, and shall with all their hearts, as with one heart and voice, declare his praises unto other nations.

Nothing is more certainly foretold than this national conversion of the Jews is in the 11th chapter of Romans. And there are also many passages of the Old Testament which cannot be interpreted in any other sense, which I cannot now take time to mention. Besides the prophecies of the calling of the Jews, we have a remarkable seal of the fulfilment of this great event in providence, by a thing which is a kind of continual miracle, namely, their being preserved a distinct nation in such a dispersed condition for above sixteen hundred years. The world affords nothing else like it. There is undoubtedly a remarkable hand of providence in it. When they shall be called, then shall that ancient people, who were alone God's people for so long a time, be God's people again, never to be rejected more. They shall then be gathered into one fold together with the Gentiles; and so also shall the remains of the ten tribes, wherever they be, and though they have been rejected much longer than the Jews, be brought in with their brethren the Jews. The prophecies of Hosea especially seem to hold this forth, that in the future glorious times of the church both Judah and Ephraim, or Judah and the ten tribes, shall be brought in together, and shall be united as one people, as they formerly were under David and Solomon (*Hos.* 1:11, chapter 14, and other parts of his prophecy).

Though we do not know the time in which this conversion of the nation of Israel will come to pass, yet thus much we may determine by Scripture, that it will be before the glory of the Gentile part of the church shall be fully accomplished, because it is said that their coming in shall be life from the dead to the Gentiles (*Rom.* 11:12, 15).

5. Then shall also Satan's heathenish kingdom be overthrown. Gross heathenism now possesses a great part of the earth, and there are supposed to be more heathens now in the world than of all other professions taken together, Jews, Mahometans, or Christians. But then the heathen nations shall be enlightened with the glorious gospel. There will be a wonderful spirit of pity towards them, and zeal for their instruction and conversion, put into multitudes, and many shall go forth and carry the gospel unto them. Then shall the joyful sound be heard among them, and the Sun of Righteousness shall then arise with his glorious light, shining on those many vast regions of the earth that have been covered with heathenish darkness for many thousand years, many of them doubtless ever since the times of Moses and Abraham, and have lain thus long in a miserable condition under the cruel tyranny of the devil, who has all this while blinded and befooled them, and domineered over them, and made a prey of them from generation to generation. Now the glad tidings of the gospel shall sound there, and they shall be brought out of darkness into marvellous light.

It is promised that heathenism shall thus be destroyed in many places. God has said that the gods that have not made these heavens and this earth shall perish from the earth, and from under these heavens (*Jer.* 10:11), and that he will utterly abolish idols (*Isa.* 2:18).

Then shall the many nations of Africa, the nations of negroes and other heathens who chiefly fill that quarter of the world, who now seem to be in a state but little above the beasts, and in many respects much below them, be enlightened with glorious light, and delivered from all their darkness, and shall become a civil, Christian, understanding and holy people. Then shall the vast continent of America, which now in so great a part of it is covered with barbarous ignorance and cruelty, be everywhere covered with glorious gospel light and Christian love; and instead of worshipping the devil, as now they do, they shall serve God, and praises shall be sung everywhere to the Lord Jesus Christ, the blessed Saviour of the world. So may we expect it will be in that great and populous part of the world, the East Indies, which are now mostly inhabited by the worshippers of the devil; and so throughout that vast country Great Tartary. And then the kingdom of Christ will be established in those continents which have been more lately discovered towards the north and south poles, where now men differ very little from the wild beasts excepting that they worship the devil, and beasts do not. The same will be the case with respect to those countries which have never yet been discovered. Thus will be gloriously fulfilled that in Isaiah 35:1, 'The wilderness and the solitary place shall be glad for them; and the desert shall rejoice, and blossom as the rose.' See also verses 6 and 7.

Having thus shown wherein this overthrow of Satan's kingdom will consist, I come now to the other thing to be observed concerning it, namely, *its universal extent*. The visible kingdom of Satan shall be overthrown, and the kingdom of Christ set up on the ruins of it, everywhere throughout the whole habitable globe. Now shall the promise made to Abraham be fulfilled that in him and in his seed all the families of the earth should be blessed; and now Christ shall become the desire of all nations, agreeable to Haggai 2:7. Now the kingdom of Christ shall in the most strict and literal sense be extended to all nations, and the whole earth.

There are many passages of Scripture that can be understood in no other sense. What can be more universal than that in Isaiah 11:9, 'For the earth shall be full of the knowledge of the LORD, as the waters cover the sea.' As much as to say, as there is no part of the channel or cavity of the sea anywhere but what is covered with water, so there shall be no part of the world of mankind but what shall be covered with the knowledge of God. So it is foretold in Isaiah 45:22 that all the ends of the earth shall look to Christ and be saved. And to show that the words are to be understood in the most universal sense, it is said in the next verse, 'I have sworn by myself, the word is gone out of my mouth in righteousness, and shall not return, that unto me every knee shall bow, every tongue shall swear.'

So the most universal expression is used in Daniel 7:27: 'And the kingdom and dominion, and the greatness of the kingdom under the whole heaven, shall be given to the people of the saints of the most High.' You see the expression includes all under the whole heaven.

When the devil was cast out of the Roman Empire, because that was the highest and principal part of the world, and the other nations that were left were low and mean in comparison of those of that empire, it was represented as Satan's being cast out of heaven to the earth (*Rev.* 12:9), but it is represented that he shall be cast out of the earth too, and shut up in hell (*Rev.* 20:1–3). This is the greatest revolution by far that ever came to pass. Therefore it is said in Revelation 16:17–18 that, on the pouring out of the seventh vial, there was a great earthquake such as was not since men were upon earth, so mighty an earthquake and so great. And this is the third great dispensation of providence which is in Scripture compared to Christ's coming to judgment. So it is in Revelation 16:15. There, after the sixth vial, and after the devil's armies were gathered together to their great battle, and just before Christ's glorious victory over them, it is said, 'Behold I come quickly; blessed is he that watcheth, and keepeth his garments.' So it is called Christ's coming in 2 Thessalonians 2:8. Speaking of Antichrist it is said, 'And then shall that Wicked be revealed, whom the Lord shall consume with the spirit of his mouth, and shall destroy with the brightness of his coming.' See also Daniel 7:13-14, where Christ's coming to set up his kingdom on earth and to destroy Antichrist is called coming with the clouds of heaven. And this is more like Christ's last coming to judgment than any of the preceding dispensations which are so called, on these accounts:

i. That the dispensation is so much greater and more universal, and so more like the day of judgment, which respects the whole world.

ii. On account of the great spiritual resurrection there will be of the church of God accompanying it, more resembling the general resurrection at the end of the world than any other. This spiritual resurrection is the resurrection spoken of as attended with judgment (*Rev.* 20:4).

iii. Because of the terrible judgments and fearful destruction which shall now be executed on God's enemies. There will doubtless at the introducing of this dispensation be a visible and awful hand of God against blasphemers, deists, obstinate heretics, and other enemies of Christ, terribly destroying them, with remarkable tokens of wrath and vengeance; and especially will this dispensation be attended with terrible judgments on Antichrist; and the cruel persecutors who belong to the church of Rome shall in a most awful manner be destroyed. This is compared to a casting of Antichrist into the burning flame (*Dan.* 7:11) and to casting him alive into the lake that burns with fire and brimstone (*Rev.* 19:20).

Then shall this cruel persecuting church suffer those judgments from God, which shall be far more dreadful than her persecutions of the saints, agreeable to Revelation 18:6-7. The judgments which God shall execute on the enemies of the church are so great, that they are compared to God's sending great hailstones from heaven upon them, every one of the weight of a talent, as it is said on the pouring out of the seventh vial: 'And there fell upon men a great hail out of heaven, every stone about the weight of a talent: and men blasphemed God, because of the plague of the hail; for the plague thereof was exceeding great' (*Rev.* 16:21). And now shall be that treading of the wine press spoken of in Revelation 14:19-20.

iii. This shall put an end to the church's suffering state, and shall be attended with their glorious and joyful praises. The church's afflicted state is long, being continued, excepting some short intermissions, from the resurrection of Christ to this time. But now shall a final end be put to her suffering state. Indeed after this, near the end of the world, the church shall be greatly threatened; but it is said, it shall be but for a little season (*Rev.* 20:3), for as the times of the church's rest are but short, before the long day of her afflictions are at an end, so whatever affliction she may suffer after this, it will be very short. But otherwise, the day of the church's affliction and persecution shall now come to a final end. The Scriptures in many places speak of this time as the end of the suffering state of the church. So in Isaiah 51:22 God says to his church with respect to this time, 'Behold, I have taken out of thine hand the cup of trembling, even the dregs of the cup of my fury; thou shalt no more drink it again.' Then shall that be proclaimed to the church, 'Comfort ye, comfort ye my people, saith your God. Speak ye comfortably to Jerusalem, and cry unto her, that her warfare is accomplished, that her iniquity is pardoned: for she hath received of the LORD's hand double for all her sins' (*Isa.* 40:1-2). Also that in Isaiah 54:8-9 belongs to this time. And so that in Isaiah 60:20, 'The LORD shall be thine everlasting light, and the days of thy mourning shall be ended.' And also Zephaniah 3:15, 'The LORD hath taken away thy judgments, he hath cast out thine enemy: the King of Israel, even the LORD, is in the midst of thee: thou shalt not see evil any more.'

The time which had been before this, had been the church's sowing time wherein she sowed in tears and in blood; but now is her harvest, wherein she will come again rejoicing, bringing her sheaves with her. Now the time of the travail of the woman clothed with the sun is at an end: now she hath brought forth her son, for this glorious setting up of the kingdom of Christ through the world is what the church had been in travail for, with such terrible pangs, for so many ages: 'Like as a woman with child, that draweth near the time of her delivery, is in pain, and crieth out in her pangs; so have we been in thy sight, O LORD' (*Isa.* 26:17). See Isaiah 60:20 and 61:10-11.

And now the church shall forget her sorrow, since a man child is born into the world. Now succeed her joyful praise and triumph. Her praises shall then go up to God from all parts of the earth, as in Isaiah 42:10-12. And praise shall not only fill the earth, but also heaven. The church on earth, and the church in heaven shall both gloriously rejoice and praise God, as with one heart, on that occasion. Without doubt it will be a time of very distinguished joy and praise among the holy prophets and apostles, and the other saints in heaven: 'Rejoice over her, thou heaven, and ye holy apostles and prophets, for God hath avenged you on her' (*Rev.* 18:20). See how universal these praises will be in Isaiah 44:23, 'Sing, O ye heavens; for the Lord hath done it: shout, ye lower parts of the earth: break forth into singing, ye mountains, O forest, and every tree therein: for the Lord hath redeemed Jacob, and glorified himself in Israel.' See what joyful praises are sung to God on this occasion by the universal church in heaven and earth, in the beginning of Revelation 19.

v. This dispensation is above all preceding ones like Christ's coming to judgment in that it so puts an end to the former state of the world, and introduces the everlasting kingdom of Christ. Now Satan's visible kingdom shall be overthrown, after it had stood ever since the building of Babel. And the old heavens and the old earth shall in a greater measure be passed away then than before, and the new heavens and new earth set up in a far more glorious manner than ever before.

Thus I have shown how the success of Christ's purchase has been carried on through the times of the afflicted state of the Christian church, from Christ's resurrection until Antichrist is fallen and Satan's visible kingdom on earth is overthrown. Therefore I come now,

Secondly, To show how the success of redemption will be carried on through that space wherein the Christian church shall for the most part be in a state of peace and prosperity. And in order to this, I would speak

1. Of the *prosperous state of the church* through the greater part of this period.
2. Of the *great apostasy* there shall be towards the close of it: how greatly then the church shall be threatened by her enemies for a short time.

1. I would speak of the *prosperous state of the church* through the greater part of this period. And in doing this I would describe this prosperous state of the church, and say something of the duration of this state.

In general I would observe two things:

a. That this is most properly the time of the kingdom of heaven upon earth. Though the kingdom of heaven was in a degree set up soon after Christ's resurrection, and in a further degree in the time of Constantine; and though the Christian church in all ages of it is called the kingdom of heaven, yet this time that we are upon is the principal time of the kingdom of heaven upon earth, the time principally intended by the prophecies of Daniel, which speak of the kingdom of heaven, whence the Jews took the name of the kingdom of heaven.

b. Now is the principal fulfilment of all the prophecies of the Old Testament which speak of the glorious times of the gospel which shall be in the latter days. Though there has been a glorious fulfilment of those prophecies already, in the times of the apostles, and of Constantine; yet the expressions are too high to suit any other time entirely, but that which is to succeed the fall of Antichrist. This is most properly the glorious day of the gospel. Other times are only forerunners and preparatories to this: other times were the seed time, but this is the harvest. But more particularly,

i. *It will be a time of great light and knowledge.* The present days are days of darkness in comparison with those days. The light of that glorious time shall be so great that it is represented as though there should then be no night but only day; no evening nor darkness. 'And it shall come to pass in that day, that the light shall not be clear, nor dark: But it shall be one day which shall be known to the LORD, not day, nor night:

but it shall come to pass, that at evening time it shall be light' (*Zech.* 14:6-7). It is further represented as though God would then give such light to his church, that it should so much exceed the glory of the light of the sun and moon that they should be ashamed: 'Then the moon shall be confounded, and the sun ashamed, when the LORD of hosts shall reign in mount Zion, and in Jerusalem, and before his ancients gloriously' (*Isa.* 24:23).

There is a kind of veil now cast over the greater part of the world, which keeps them in darkness: but then this veil shall be destroyed: 'And he will destroy in this mountain the face of the covering cast over all people, and the veil that is spread over all nations' (*Isa.* 25:7). And then all countries and nations, even those which are now most ignorant, shall be full of light and knowledge. Great knowledge shall prevail everywhere. It may be hoped that then many of the Negroes and Indians will be divines and that excellent books will be published in Africa, in Ethiopia, in Tartary, and other countries which are now the most barbarous. And not only learned men but others of more ordinary education, shall then be very knowing in religion: 'The eyes of them that see shall not be dim, and the ears of them that hear shall hearken. The heart also of the rash shall understand knowledge' (*Isa.* 32:3-4). Knowledge then shall be very universal among all sorts of persons, agreeable to Jeremiah 31:34: 'And they shall teach no more every man his neighbour, and every man his brother, saying, Know the LORD: for they shall all know me, from the least of them unto the greatest of them.'

There shall then be a wonderful unravelling of the difficulties in the doctrines of religion, and a clearing up of seeming inconsistencies. So 'crooked things shall be made straight, and rough places shall be made plain', and darkness shall become light before God's people. Difficulties in Scripture shall then be cleared up, and wonderful things shall be discovered in the

Word of God which were never discovered before. The great discovery of those things in religion which had been before kept hid seems to be compared to removing the veil and discovering the ark of the testimony to the people, which before used to be kept in the secret part of the temple and was never seen by them. Thus at the sounding of the seventh angel, when it is proclaimed that 'the kingdoms of this world are become the kingdoms of our Lord and of his Christ', it is added that 'the temple of God was opened in heaven; and there was seen in his temple the ark of his testament' (*Rev.* 11:15, 19). So great shall be the increase of knowledge in this time that heaven shall be as it were opened to the church of God on earth.

ii. *It shall be a time of great holiness.* Now vital religion shall everywhere prevail and reign. Religion shall not be an empty profession, as it now mostly is, but holiness of heart and life shall abundantly prevail. Those times shall be an exception from what Christ says of the ordinary state of the church, namely, that there shall be but few saved; for now holiness shall become general: 'Thy people also shall be all righteous' (*Isa.* 60:21). Not that there will be none remaining in a Christless condition, but that visible wickedness shall be suppressed everywhere, and true holiness shall become general, though not universal. And it shall be a wonderful time, not only for the multitude of godly men, but for eminency of grace: 'There shall be no more thence an infant of days, nor an old man that hath not filled his days: for the child shall die an hundred years old, but the sinner being an hundred years old, shall be accursed' (*Isa.* 65:20). And, 'He that is feeble among them at that day shall be as David; and the house of David shall be as God, as the angel of the Lord before them' (*Zech.* 12:8). And holiness shall then be as it were inscribed on every thing, on all men's common business and employments, and the common utensils of life: all shall be as it were dedicated to God, and applied to holy purposes; every thing shall then be done to the glory of God: 'And her merchandise and her hire shall be holiness to the LORD' (*Isa.* 23:18). And so Zechariah 14:20-21. And as God's people then shall be eminent in holiness of heart, so they shall be also in holiness of life and practice.

iii. *It shall be a time wherein religion shall in every respect be uppermost in the world.* It shall be had in great esteem and honour. The saints have hitherto for the most part been kept under, and wicked men have governed. But now they will be uppermost. The kingdoms shall be given into the hands of the 'saints of the Most High' (*Dan.* 7:27). And they 'shall reign on the earth' (*Rev.* 5:10). 'They lived and reigned with Christ a thousand years' (*Rev.* 20:4). In that day, such persons as are eminent for true piety and religion, shall be chiefly promoted to places of trust and authority. Vital religion shall then take possession of kings' palaces and thrones; and those who are in highest advancement shall be holy men: 'And kings shall be thy nursing fathers, and their queens thy nursing mothers' (*Isa.* 49:23). Kings shall employ all their power and glory and riches for the advancement of the honour and glory of Christ, and the good of his church: 'Thou shalt also suck the milk of the Gentiles, and shalt suck the breast of kings' (*Isa.* 60:16). And the great men of the world, and the rich merchants, and others who have great wealth and influence, shall devote all to Christ and his church. 'The daughter of Tyre shall be there with a gift, even the rich among the people shall entreat thy favour' (*Psa.* 45:12).

iv. *Those will be times of great peace and love.* There shall then be universal peace and a good understanding among the nations of the world, instead of such confusion, wars, and bloodshed as have hitherto been from one age to another: 'And he shall judge among the nations, and shall rebuke many people: and they shall beat their swords into plough-shares, and their spears into pruning hooks: nation shall not lift up sword against nation, neither shall they learn war any more' (*Isa.* 2:4). So it is represented as if all instruments of war should be destroyed, as being become useless: 'He maketh wars to cease unto the end of the earth: he breaketh the bow, and cutteth the spear in sunder; he burneth the chariot in the fire' (*Psa.* 46:9). See also Zechariah 9:10. Then shall all nations dwell quietly and safely, without fear of any enemy. 'And my people shall dwell in a peaceable habitation, and in sure dwell-ings, and in quiet resting places' (*Isa.* 32:18). Also Zechariah 8:10-11.

And then shall malice, envy, wrath and revenge be sup-pressed everywhere, and peace and love shall prevail between one man and another, which is most elegantly set forth in Isaiah 11:6-10. Then shall there be peace and love between rulers and ruled. Rulers shall love their people, and with all their might seek their best good; and the people love their rul-ers, and shall joyfully submit to them, and give them that honour which is their due. And so shall there be a happy love between ministers and their people: 'And he shall turn the heart of the fathers to the children, and the heart of the chil-dren to their fathers' (*Mal.* 4:6). Then shall flourish in an eminent manner those Christian virtues of meekness, forgive-ness, long-suffering, gentleness, goodness, brotherly kindness: those excellent fruits of the Spirit. Men, in their temper and disposition, shall then be like the Lamb of God, the lovely Jesus. The body shall be conformed to the Head.

Then shall all the world be united in one amiable society. All nations, in all parts of the world, on every side of the globe, shall then be knit together in sweet harmony. All parts of God's church shall assist and promote the spiritual good of one another. A communication shall then be upheld between all parts of the world to that end; and the art of navigation, which is now applied so much to favour men's covetousness and pride, and is used so much by wicked debauched men, shall then be consecrated to God, and applied to holy uses, as we read in Isaiah 60:5-9. And it will then be a time wherein men will be abundant in expressing their love one to another, not only in words, but in deeds of charity, as we learn, 'The vile person shall be no more called liberal, nor the churl said to be bountiful' (*Isa.* 32:5), and, 'But the liberal deviseth liberal things, and by liberal things shall he stand' (*Isa.* 32:8).

v. *It will be a time of excellent order in the church of Christ.* The true government and discipline of the church will then be settled and put into practice. All the world shall then be as one church, one orderly, regular, beautiful society. And as the body shall be one, so the members shall be in beautiful proportion to each other. Then shall that be verified in Psalm 122:3, 'Jerusalem is builded as a city that is compact together.'

vi. *The church of God shall then be beautiful and glorious* on these accounts; yea it will appear in perfection of beauty: 'Arise, shine, for thy light is come, and the glory of the LORD is risen upon thee' (*Isa.* 60:1). 'He hath covered me with the robe of righteousness, as a bridegroom decketh himself with ornaments, and as a bride adorneth herself with her jewels' (*Isa.* 61:10). On these forementioned accounts, the church will then be the greatest image of heaven itself.

vii. *That will be a time of the greatest temporal prosperity.* Such a spiritual state as we have just described has a natural tendency to temporal prosperity. It has a tendency to health and long life; and that this will actually be the case is evident by Zechariah 8:4: 'Thus saith the LORD of hosts, There shall yet old men and old women dwell in the streets of Jerusalem, and every man with his staff in his hand for very age.' It has also a natural tendency to procure ease, quietness, pleasantness, and cheerfulness of mind, and also wealth, and great increase of children, as is intimated in Zechariah 8:5: 'And the streets of the city shall be full of boys and girls playing in the streets thereof.'

But further, the temporal prosperity of the people of God will also be promoted by a remarkable blessing from heaven: 'They shall build houses, and inhabit them; and they shall plant vineyards, and eat the fruit of them' (*Isa.* 65:21). And in Micah 4:4, 'But they shall sit every man under his vine and under his fig tree; and none shall make them afraid.' 'For the seed shall be prosperous; the vine shall give her fruit, and the ground shall give her increase, and the heavens shall give their dew; and I will cause the remnant of this people to possess all these things' (*Zech.* 8:12). See also Jeremiah 31:12-13 and Amos 9:13. Yea, then they shall receive all manner of tokens of God's presence, acceptance and favour: 'And it shall be to me a name of joy, a praise and an honour before all the nations of the earth, which shall hear all the good that I do unto them: and they shall fear and tremble for all the goodness and for all the prosperity that I procure unto it' (*Jer.* 33:9). Even the days of Solomon were but an image of those days, as to the temporal prosperity which shall obtain in them.

viii. *It will also be a time of great rejoicing*: 'And the ransomed of the LORD shall return, and come to Zion with songs and everlasting joy upon their heads: they shall obtain joy and gladness, and sorrow and sighing shall flee away' (*Isa.* 35:10). 'For ye shall go out with joy, and be led forth with peace: the mountains and the hills shall break forth before you into singing' (*Isa.* 55:12). 'That ye may suck, and be satisfied with the breasts of her consolations; that ye may milk out, and be delighted with the abundance of her glory' (*Isa.* 66:11). 'With joy shall ye draw water out of the wells of salvation' (*Isa.* 12:3). Then will be a time of feasting. That will be the church's glorious wedding day, so far as her wedding with Christ shall ever be upon earth: 'Let us be glad and rejoice, and give honour to him; for the marriage of the Lamb is come, and his wife hath made herself ready' (*Rev.* 19:7). And (verse 9), 'Blessed are they which are called to the marriage supper of the Lamb.'

But I come now, to say something of the *duration* of this state of the church's prosperity. On this I shall be very brief. The Scriptures everywhere represent it to be of long continuance. The former intervals of rest and prosperity, as we before observed, are represented to be but short; but the representations of this state are quite different: 'And I saw the souls of them that were beheaded for the witness of Jesus . . . and they lived and reigned with Christ a thousand years' (*Rev.* 20:4). 'Whereas thou hast been forsaken and hated, so that no man went through thee, I will make thee an eternal excellency, a joy of many generations' (*Isa.* 60:15).

This may suffice as to the prosperous state of the church through the greater part of the period from the destruction of Satan's visible kingdom in the world to Christ's appearing in the clouds of heaven to judgment.

2. I now come to speak of the *great apostasy* there should be towards the close of this period, and how eminently the church should be for a short time threatened by her enemies. And this I shall do under three particulars.

i. A little before the end of the world, there shall be a very great apostasy wherein great part of the world shall fall away from Christ and his church. It is said in Revelation 20:3 that

Satan should be cast into the bottomless pit, and shut up, and have a seal set upon him, that he should deceive the nations no more until the thousand years should be fulfilled; and that after that he must be loosed out of his prison for a little season. And accordingly we are told, in verses 7–8, that when the thousand years are expired Satan shall be loosed out of his prison and shall go forth to deceive the nations which are in the four quarters of the earth, Gog and Magog. Which seems to show that the apostasy will be very general.

The nations of the four quarters of the earth shall be deceived; and the number of those who shall now turn enemies to Christ shall be vastly great, as the army of Gog and Magog is represented in Ezekiel, and as it is said in Revelation 20:8, that the number of them is as the sand of the sea, and that they went up on the breadth of the earth, as though they were an army big enough to reach from one side of the earth to the other.

Thus after such an happy and glorious season, such a long day of light and holiness, of love and peace and joy, now it shall begin again to be a dark time. Satan shall begin to set up his dominion again in the world. This world shall again become a scene of darkness and wickedness. The bottomless pit of hell shall be opened, and devils shall come up again out of it, and a dreadful smoke shall ascend to darken the world. And the church of Christ, instead of extending to the utmost bounds of the world, as it did before, shall be reduced to narrow limits again. The world of mankind, being continued so long in a state of such great prosperity, shall now begin to abuse their prosperity, to serve their lust and corruption. This we learn from Luke 17:26, etc.

ii. Those apostates shall make great opposition to the church of God. The church shall seem to be eminently threatened with a sudden and entire overthrow by them. It is said,

Satan shall gather them together to battle, as the sand on the sea shore; 'And they went up on the breadth of the earth, and compassed the camp of the saints about, and the beloved city.' So that this beloved city shall seem just ready to be swallowed up by them; for her enemies shall not only threaten her but shall actually have gathered together against her; and not only so, but shall have besieged her, shall have compassed her about on every side.

There is nothing in the prophecy which seems to hold forth as though the church had actually fallen into their hands, as the church had fallen into the hands of Antichrist, to whom it was given to make war with the saints, and to overcome them. God will never suffer this to be again after the fall of Antichrist; for then the day of her mourning shall be ended. But the church shall seem most eminently threatened with utter and sudden destruction.

iii. Now the state of things will seem most remarkably to call for Christ's immediate appearance to judgment. For then the world shall be filled with the most aggravated wickedness that ever was. For much the greater part of the world shall have become visibly wicked and open enemies to Christ, and their wickedness shall be dreadfully aggravated by their apostasy. Before the fall of Antichrist, most of the world was full of visibly wicked men. But the greater part of these are poor heathens, who never enjoyed the light of the gospel; and others are those that have been bred up in the Mahometan or Popish darkness. But these are those that have apostatized from the Christian church, and the visible kingdom of Christ, in which they enjoyed the great light and privileges of the glorious times of the church, which shall be incomparably greater than the light and privileges which the church of God enjoys now. This apostasy will be more like the apostasy of the devils than any that ever had been before: for the devils apostatized, and turned enemies to Christ, though they enjoyed the light of heaven; and these will apostatize, and turn enemies to him, though they have enjoyed the light and privileges of the glorious times of the church. That such should turn open and avowed enemies to Christ, and should seek the ruin of his church, will cry aloud for such immediate vengeance as was executed on the devils when they fell.

The wickedness of the world will remarkably call for Christ's immediate appearing in flaming fire to take vengeance on them because of the way in which they shall manifest their wickedness, which will be by scoffing and blaspheming Christ and his holy religion; and particularly, they will scoff at the notion of Christ's coming to judgment, of which the church shall be in expectation, and of which they will warn them. For now doubtless will be another fulfilment, and the greatest fulfilment of 2 Peter 3:3-4, 'Knowing this first, that there shall come in the last days scoffers, walking after their own lusts, and saying, Where is the promise of his coming? For since the fathers fell asleep, all things continue as they were from the beginning of the creation.'

They shall be in no expectation of the coming of Christ to judgment, and shall laugh at the notion. They shall trample all such things under foot, and shall give up themselves to their lusts, or to eat and drink, and wallow in sensual delights, as though they were to be here forever. They shall despise the warnings the church shall give them of the coming of Christ to judgment, as the people of the old world despised what Noah told them of the approaching Flood, and as the people of Sodom did when Lot said to them, 'The LORD will destroy this city.' Their wickedness on this account will cry aloud to heaven for Christ's appearing in flaming fire to take vengeance of his enemies; and also because another way that they shall exercise their wickedness will be in the wicked design and violent attempt they shall be engaged in against the holy city of God, that holy city, wherein lately, and for so long a time, so much of the religion of Christ had been seen. They shall then be about to perpetrate the most horrid design against this church.

And the numerousness of the wicked that shall then be is another thing which shall especially call for Christ's coming: for the world will doubtless then be exceeding full of people, having continued so long in so great a state of prosperity, without such terrible desolating extremities, as wars, pestilences, and the like, to diminish them. And the most of this world, which shall be so populous, will be such wicked contemptuous apostates from God. Undoubtedly that will be a day wherein the world will be by far fuller of wickedness than ever before it was from the foundation of it. And if the wickedness of the old world, when men began to multiply on the earth, called for the destruction of the world by a deluge of waters, this wickedness will as much call for its destruction by a deluge of fire.

Again, the circumstances of the church at that day will also eminently call for the immediate appearing of Christ, as they will be compassed about by their blasphemous murderous enemies, just ready to be swallowed up by them. And it will be a most distressing time with the church, excepting the comfort they will have in the hope of deliverance from God: for all other help will seem to fail. The case will be come to the last extremity, and there will be an immediate need that Christ should come to their deliverance.

And though the church shall be so eminently threatened, yet so will providence order it that it shall be preserved until Christ shall appear in his immediate presence, coming in the glory of his Father with all his holy angels. And then will come the time when all the elect shall be gathered in. That work of conversion which has been carried on from the beginning of the church after the Fall through all those ages shall be carried on no more. There never shall another soul be converted. Every one of those many millions whose names were written in the book of life before the foundation of the world shall be brought in; not one soul shall be lost.

And the mystical body of Christ, which has been growing since it first began in the days of Adam, will be complete as to number of parts, having every one of its members. In this respect, the work of redemption will now be finished. And now the end for which the means of grace have been instituted shall be obtained. All that effect which was intended to be accomplished by them shall now be accomplished.

SECTION 2

SUCCESS ACCOMPLISHED
AT THE DAY OF JUDGMENT

Thus I have shown how the success of Christ's redemption has been accomplished during the continuance of the Christian church under the means of grace. We have seen what great revolutions there have been, and are to be, during this space of time; how the great wheels of providence have gone round for the accomplishment of that kind of success of Christ's purchase which consists in the bestowment of grace on the elect; and we are, in the prosecution of the subject, come to the time when all the wheels have gone round; the course of things in this state of it is finished, and all things are ripe for Christ's coming to judgment.

When I began to discourse of this third proposition, namely, that, from the resurrection of Christ to the end of the world, the whole time is taken up in procuring the success and effect of Christ's purchase of redemption, I observed that the success of Christ's purchase is of two kinds, consisting either in grace or glory; and that the success consisting in the former of these is to be seen in those works of God which are wrought during those ages that the church is continued under the means of grace; and that the success consisting in the latter will chiefly be accomplished at the day of judgment.

Having already shown how the former kind of success has been accomplished, I come now, in the second place, to the latter, that is, *that kind of success which is accomplished in the bestowment of glory on the church*, which shall chiefly be bestowed on the church at the day of judgment. And here I would mention two or three things in general concerning this kind of success of Christ's purchase.

1. How great the success of Christ's purchase is, chiefly appears in this. The success of Christ's purchase summarily consists in the salvation of the elect. But this bestowment of glory is eminently called their salvation: 'Unto them that look for him shall he appear the second time without sin unto salvation' (*Heb.* 9:28). It is called redemption, being eminently that wherein the redemption of the church consists: 'The day of redemption' (*Eph.* 4:30); 'The redemption of the purchased possession' (*Eph.* 1:14). See also Luke 21:28.

2. All that is before this, while the church is under the means of grace, is only to make way for the success which is to be accomplished in the bestowment of glory. The means of grace are to fit for glory; and God's grace itself is bestowed on the elect to make them meet for glory.

3. All those glorious things which were brought to pass for the church while under the means of grace are but images and shadows of this. So were those glorious things which were accomplished for the church in the days of Constantine the Great; and so is all that glory which is to be accomplished in the glorious times of the church which are to succeed the fall of Antichrist. As great as it is, it is all but a shadow of what will be bestowed at the day of judgment. And therefore, as I have already often observed, all those preceding glorious events by which God wrought glorious things for his church are spoken of in Scripture as images of Christ's last coming to judgment.

But I hasten more particularly to show how this kind of success of Christ's purchase is accomplished.

1. *Christ will appear in the glory of his Father, with all his holy angels, coming in the clouds of heaven.* When the world are thus revelling in their wickedness, and compassing the holy city about, just ready to destroy it, and when the church

is reduced to such a great strait, then shall the glorious Redeemer appear. He through whom this redemption has all along been carried on, he shall appear in the sight of the world; the light of his glory shall break forth; the whole world shall immediately have notice of it, and they shall lift up their eyes and behold this wonderful sight. It is said, 'Every eye shall see him' (*Rev.* 1:7). Christ shall appear, coming in his human nature, in that same body which was brought forth in a stable and laid in a manger, and which afterwards was so cruelly used and nailed to the cross.

Men shall now lift up their eyes, and see him coming in such majesty and glory as now is to us utterly inconceivable. The glory of the sun in a clear firmament will be but darkness in comparison with it; and all the glorious angels and archangels shall attend upon him, thousand thousands ministering to him, and ten thousand times ten thousand round about him. How different a Person will he then appear from what he did at his first coming, when he was as a root out of a dry ground, a poor, despised, afflicted man! How different now is his appearance, in the midst of those glorious angels, principalities, and powers in heavenly places, attending him as his ordinary servants, from what it was when in the midst of a ring of soldiers, with his mock robe and his crown of thorns, to be buffeted and spit upon, or hanging on the cross between two thieves, with a multitude of his enemies about him triumphing over him!

This sight will be a most unexpected sight to the wicked world: it will come as a cry at midnight: they shall be taken in the midst of their wickedness, and it will give them a dreadful alarm. It will at once break up their revels, their eating, and drinking, and carousing. It will put a quick end to the design of the great army that will then be compassing the camp of the saints: it will make them let drop their weapons out of their hands. The world, which will then be very full of people, most of whom will be wicked men, will then be filled with dolorous shrieking and crying; for all the kindreds of the earth shall wail because of him (*Rev.* 1:7). And where shall they hide themselves? How will the sight of that awful majesty terrify them when taken in the midst of their wickedness! Then they shall see who he is, what kind of a Person he is, whom they have mocked and scoffed at, and whose church they have been endeavouring to overthrow. This sight will change their voice. The voice of their laughter and singing, while they are marrying and giving in marriage, and the voice of their scoffing, shall be changed into hideous, yea, hellish yelling. Their countenances shall be changed from a show of carnal mirth, haughty pride, and contempt of God's people. They shall put on a show of ghastly terror and amazement; and trembling and chattering of teeth shall seize upon them.

But with respect to the saints, the church of Christ, it shall be a joyful and most glorious sight to them: for this sight will at once deliver them from all fear of their enemies, who were before compassing them about, just ready to swallow them up. Deliverance shall come in their extremity: the glorious Captain of their salvation shall appear for them, at a time when no other help appears. Then shall they lift up their heads, and their redemption shall be drawing nigh (*Luke* 21:28). And thus Christ will appear with infinite majesty, and yet at the same time they shall see infinite love in his countenance to them.

Thus to see their Redeemer coming in the clouds of heaven will fill their hearts full of gladness. Their countenances also shall be changed, but not as the countenances of the wicked, but shall be changed from being sorrowful to be exceeding joyful and triumphant. And now the work of redemption will be finished in another sense, namely, that the whole church shall be completely and eternally freed from all persecution and molestation from wicked men and devils.

2. *The last trumpet shall sound, the dead shall be raised, and the living changed.* God sent forth his angels with a great sound of a trumpet to gather together his elect from the four corners of the earth in a mystical sense before the destruction of Jerusalem; that is, he sent forth the apostles, and others, to preach the gospel all over the world. And so in a mystical sense the great trumpet was blown at the beginning of the glorious times of the church. But now the great trumpet is blown in a more literal sense, with a mighty sound, which shakes the earth. There will be a great signal given by a mighty sound, which is called the voice of the archangel, as being the angel of greatest strength (*1 Thess.* 4:16), 'For the Lord himself shall descend from heaven with a shout, with the voice of the archangel, and with the trump of God.' On the sound of the great trumpet, the dead shall be raised everywhere.

Now the number of the dead is very great. How many has death cut down since the world has stood! But then the number will be much greater after the world shall have stood so much longer, and through most of the remaining time will doubtless be much fuller of inhabitants than ever it has been. All these shall now rise from the dead. The graves shall be opened everywhere in all parts of the world, and the sea shall give up the innumerable dead that are in it (*Rev.* 20:13).

And now all the inhabitants that ever shall have been upon the face of the earth, from the beginning of the world to that time, shall all appear upon earth at once; all that ever have been of the church of God in all ages, Adam and Eve, the first parents of mankind, and Abel, and Seth, and Methuselah, and all the saints who were their contemporaries, and Noah, and Abraham, and Isaac, and Jacob, and the prophets of Israel, and the saints in the time of Antiochus Epiphanes, and all that were of the church in their times; and all the holy apostles of Jesus Christ, and all the saints of their times; and all the holy martyrs under the ten heathen persecutions; and all who belonged to the church in its wilderness state during the dark times of Antichrist; and all the holy martyrs who have suffered under the cruelty of the Popish persecutions; and all the saints of the present time; and all the saints who are here in this assembly among the rest; and all that shall be from hence to the end of the world.

Now also all the enemies of the church that have been or shall be in all the ages of the world shall appear upon the face of the earth again; all the wicked killed in the Flood, and the multitudes that died all over the world among God's professing people, or others; all that died in all the heathen nations before Christ, and all wicked heathens, and Jews, and Mahometans, and Papists that have died since; all shall come together. Sinners of all sorts; demure hypocrites, those who have the fairest and best outside, and open profane drunkards, whoremasters, heretics, deists, and all cruel persecutors, and all that have died or shall die in sin amongst us.

And at the same time that the dead are raised, the living shall be changed. The bodies of the wicked who shall then be living shall be so changed as to fit them for eternal torment without corruption; and the bodies of all the living saints shall be changed to be like Christ's glorious body (1 Cor. 15:51–53). The bodies of the saints shall be so changed as to render them forever incapable of pain or affliction or uneasiness. All that dullness and heaviness, and all that deformity, which their bodies had before shall be put off; and they shall put on strength, and beauty, and activity, and incorruptible unfading glory. And in such glory shall the bodies of all the risen saints appear.

And now the work of redemption shall be finished in another respect, namely, that all the elect shall now be actually redeemed in both soul and body. Before this, the work of redemption, as to its actual success, was but incomplete and imperfect; for only the souls of the redeemed were actually saved and glorified, excepting in some few instances: but now all the bodies of the saints shall be saved and glorified together; all the elect shall be glorified in the whole man, and the soul and body in union one with the other.

3. *Now shall the whole church of saints be caught up in the clouds to meet the Lord in the air, and all wicked men and devils shall be arraigned before the judgment seat.* When the dead saints are raised, then the whole church, consisting of all the elect through all ages, will be standing together, on the face of the earth, at least all excepting those whose bodies were glorified before; and then they shall all mount up as with wings in the air to meet Christ; for it seems that Christ, when he comes to judgment, will not come quite down to the ground, but his throne will be fixed in the air, in the region of the clouds, whence he may be seen by all that vast multitude that shall be gathered before him. The church of saints therefore shall be taken up from the earth to ascend up to their Saviour. Thus the apostle tells us that when the dead in Christ are raised, and the living changed, then those who are alive and remain, shall be caught up together with them to meet the Lord in the air, and so shall we be ever with the Lord (*1 Thess.* 4:16-17). What a wonderful sight will that be, when all the many millions of saints are seen thus mounting up from all parts of the world!

Then shall the work of redemption be finished in another respect. Then shall the whole church be perfectly and for ever delivered from this present evil world and for ever forsake this cursed ground: they shall take their everlasting leave of this earth, where they have been strangers, and which has been for the most part such a scene of their trouble and sorrow; where the devil for the most part has reigned as god, and has greatly molested them, and which has been such a scene of wickedness and abomination, where Christ their Lord has been cruelly used, and where they have been so hated, reproached and persecuted from age to age, through most of the ages of the world. They shall leave it under foot to go to Christ, and never shall set foot on it again. And there shall be an everlasting separation made between them and wicked men. Before they were mixed together, and it was impossible in many instances to determine which were which; but now all shall become visible; both saints and sinners shall appear in their true characters.

Then shall all the church be seen flocking together in the air to the place where Christ shall have fixed his throne, coming from the east and west, and north and south, to the right hand of Christ. What a mighty cloud of them will there be, when all that ever have been of the church of God, all that were before Christ, all that multitude of saints that were in the apostles' time, and all that were in the days of Constantine the Great, and all that were before and since the Reformation, and also all that great multitude of saints that shall be in all the glorious times of the church, when the whole earth shall for so many generations be full of saints, and also all that shall be then living when Christ shall come; I say, what a cloud of them will there be, when all these are seen flocking together in the region of the clouds at the right hand of Christ!

And then also the work of redemption will be finished in another respect, namely, that then the church shall all be gathered together. They all belonged to one society before, but yet were greatly separated with respect to the place of their habitation; some being in heaven, and some on earth; and those who were on earth together were separated one from another, many of them by wide oceans, and vast continents. But now they shall all be gathered together, never to be separated any more. And not only shall all the members of the church now be gathered together but all shall be gathered unto their head, into his immediate glorious presence, never to be separated from him any more. This never came to pass until now.

At the same time all wicked men and devils shall be brought before the judgment seat of Christ. These shall be gathered to the left hand of Christ, and, as it seems, will still remain upon the earth, and shall not be caught up into the air, as the saints shall be. The devil, that old serpent, shall now be dragged up out of hell. He that first procured the Fall and misery of mankind, and has so set himself against their redemption, and has all along shown himself such an inveterate enemy to the Redeemer, now he shall never more have any thing to do with the church of God, or be suffered in the least to afflict or molest any member of it any more for ever. Instead of that, now he must be judged, and receive the due reward of his deeds. Now is come the time which he has always dreaded, and trembled at the thought of; the time wherein he must be judged, and receive his full punishment. He who by his temptation maliciously procured Christ's crucifixion, and triumphed upon it, as though he had obtained the victory, even he shall see the consequences of the death of Christ which he procured: for Christ's coming to judge him in his human nature is the consequence of it; for Christ obtained and purchased this glory to himself by that death. Now he must stand before that same Jesus whose death he procured, to be judged, condemned, and eternally destroyed by him. If Satan, the prince of hell, trembles at the thought of it thousands of years beforehand, how much more will he tremble, proud and stubborn as he is, when he comes to stand at Christ's bar!

Then shall he also stand at the bar of the saints whom he has so hated, and afflicted, and molested, for the saints shall judge him with Christ: 'Know ye not that we shall judge angels?' (*1 Cor.* 6:3). Now shall he be as it were subdued under the church's feet, agreeable to Romans 16:20. Satan, when he first tempted our first parents to fall, deceitfully and lyingly told them that they should be as gods; but little did he think that the consequence should be that they should indeed be so much as gods as to be assessors with God to judge him. Much less did he think, that that consequence would follow that one of that nature which he then tempted, one of the posterity of those persons whom he tempted, should actually be united to God, and that as God he should judge the world, and that he himself must stand trembling and astonished before his judgment seat. But thus all the devils in hell, who have so opposed Christ and his kingdom, shall now at last stand in utmost amazement and horror before Christ and his church, who shall appear to condemn them.

Now also shall all Christ's other enemies be brought to appear before him. Now shall the wicked proud scribes and Pharisees, who had such a malignant hatred of Christ while in his state of humiliation, and who persecuted Christ to death, those before whose judgment seat Christ was once called and stood, as a malefactor at their bar, and those who mocked him, and buffeted him, and spit in his face; now shall they see Christ in his glory, as Christ forewarned them in the time of it (*Matt.* 26:64-65). Then Christ was before their judgment seat; but now it is their turn. They shall stand before his judgment seat with inconceivable horror and amazement, with ghastly countenances, and quaking limbs, and chattering teeth, and knees smiting one against another.

Now also all the cruel enemies and persecutors of the church that have been in all ages, shall come in sight together. Pharaoh and the Egyptians, Antiochus Epiphanes, the persecuting scribes and Pharisees, the persecuting heathen Emperors, Julian the Apostate, the cruel persecuting Popes and Papists, Gog and Magog, shall all appear at once before the judgment seat of Christ. They and the saints who have in every age been persecuted by them, shall come in sight one of another, and must confront one another before the great Judge. And now shall the saints on their glorious thrones be made the judges of those unjust kings and rulers who have before judged and condemned them, and cruelly put them to death. Now shall those persecutors behold the glory to which they are arrived whom they before so cruelly despised and so cruelly used; and Christ will make those holy martyrs as it were to come and set their feet on the necks of their persecutors; they shall be made their footstool.

Thus wonderfully will the face of things be altered from what used to be in the former times of the world. Now will all things be coming to rights.

4. *The righteousness of the church shall be manifested, and all the wickedness of their enemies shall be brought to light.* Those saints who had been the objects of hatred, reproach, and contempt in the world, and were reviled and condemned by their persecutors without a cause, shall now be fully vindicated. They shall now appear clothed with the glorious robe of Christ's righteousness. It shall be most manifest before the world, that Christ's righteousness is theirs, and they shall as it were gloriously shine forth in it. And then also shall their inherent holiness be made manifest, and all their good works shall be brought to light. The good things which they did in secret shall now be manifested openly. Those holy ones of God, who had been treated as though they were the filth and offscouring of the earth, as though they were not fit to live upon earth, as worse than beasts or devils, shall now, when things shall appear as they are, appear to have been the excellent of the earth. Now God will bring forth their righteousness as the light, and their judgment as the noonday. And now it shall appear who were those wicked persons that were not fit to live, when all the wickedness of the enemies of

[413]

Christ and his church, their pride, their malice, their cruelty, their hatred of true religion, shall be set forth in all the horrid acts of it, and with all its aggravations in its proper colours.

And now the righteous may be heard before this great Judge, who could not be heard before those unjust judges. Now they shall declare their cause and shall rise up in judgment against their persecutors and shall declare how they have been treated by them. And now all the wickedness of the wicked of the whole world shall be brought to light. All their secret wickedness, and their very hearts, shall be opened to view and as it were turned inside out before the bright light of that great day: and things that have been spoken in the ear in the closet, and done in the dark, shall be manifested in the light and proclaimed before all angels and men that are, ever were, or shall be.

5. *The sentence shall be pronounced on the righteous and the wicked.* Christ, the glorious judge, shall pass that blessed sentence on the church at his right hand, 'Come, ye blessed of my Father, inherit the kingdom prepared for you from the foundation of the world.' This sentence shall be pronounced with infinite love, and the voice will be most sweet, causing every heart to flow with joy. Thus Christ shall pronounce a sentence of justification on thousands and millions who have before had a sentence of condemnation passed upon them by their persecuting rulers. He will thus put honour upon those who have been before despised. He will own them for his, and will as it were put a crown of glory upon their heads before the world; and then shall they shine forth as the sun with Jesus Christ in glory and joy, in the sight of all their enemies.

And then shall the sentence of condemnation be passed on the wicked, 'Depart, ye cursed, into everlasting fire, prepared for the devil and his angels.' Thus shall the church's enemies be condemned; in which sentence of condemnation the holy martyrs, who have suffered from them, shall concur. When the words of this sentence are pronounced, they will strike every heart of those at the left hand with inconceivable horror and amazement. Every syllable of it will be more terrible than a stream of lightning through their hearts. We can conceive but very little of those signs and expressions of horror which there will be upon it, of shrieking, quaking, gnashing of teeth, distortions of countenance, hideous looks, hideous actions, and hideous voices, through all that vast throng.

6. *Christ and all his church of saints, and all the holy angels ministering to them, shall leave this lower world, and ascend up towards the highest heavens.* Christ shall ascend in as great glory as he descended, and in some respects greater; for now he shall ascend with his elect church with him, glorified in both body and soul. Christ's first ascension to heaven soon after his own resurrection was very glorious. But this, his second ascension, the ascension of his mystical body, his whole church, shall be far more glorious. The redeemed church shall all ascend with him in a most joyful and triumphant manner; and all their enemies and persecutors, who shall be left behind on the accursed ground to be consumed, shall see the sight and hear their songs.

And thus Christ's church shall forever leave this accursed world, to go into that more glorious world, the highest heavens, into the paradise of God, the kingdom that was prepared for them from the foundation of the world.

7. *When they are gone, this world shall be set on fire and turned into a great furnace*, wherein all the enemies of Christ and his church shall be tormented forever and ever. This is manifest by 2 Peter 3:7, 'But the heavens and the earth, which are now, by the same word are kept in store, reserved unto fire against the day of judgment, and perdition of ungodly men.'

When Christ and his church are ascended to a distance from this world, that miserable company of wicked being left behind to have their sentence executed upon them here, then, some way or other, this whole lower world shall be set on fire, either by fire from heaven or by fire breaking out of the bowels of the earth, or both, as it was with the water in the time of the deluge. However, this lower world shall be set all on fire. How will it strike the wicked with horror when the fire begins to lay hold upon them, and they find no way to escape it, or flee or hide from it! What shrieking and crying will there be among those many thousands and millions, when they begin to enter into this great furnace, when the whole world shall be a furnace of the fiercest and most raging heat, insomuch that the Apostle Peter says that 'the heavens shall pass away with a great noise, and the elements shall melt with fervent heat, the earth also and the works that are therein shall be burnt up'; and that 'the heavens being on fire shall be dissolved, and the elements shall melt with fervent heat' (2 *Pet.* 3:10,12). And so fierce shall be its heat that it shall burn the earth into its very centre, which seems to be what is meant, 'For a fire is kindled in my anger, and shall burn unto the lowest hell, and shall consume the earth with her increase, and set on fire the foundations of the mountains' (*Deut.* 32:22).

And here shall all the persecutors of the church of God burn in everlasting fire, who have before burnt the saints at the stake, and shall suffer torments far beyond all that their utmost wit and malice could inflict on the saints. And here the bodies of all the wicked shall burn, and be tormented to all eternity, and never be consumed; and the wrath of God shall be poured out on their souls. Though the souls of the wicked in hell do now suffer dreadful punishment, yet their punishment will be so increased at the day of judgment that what they suffered before is, in comparison with it, as an imprisonment to the execution which follows it. And now the devil, that old serpent, shall receive his full punishment; now shall that which he before trembled for fear of fully come upon him. This world, which formerly used to be the place of his kingdom, where he set up himself as God, shall now be the place of his complete punishment, and full and everlasting torment.

And in this one design of the work of redemption which has been mentioned, namely, putting Christ's enemies under his feet, shall be perfectly accomplished. His enemies shall now be made his footstool, in the fullest degree. Now shall be the most perfect fulfilment of that in Genesis 3:15, 'It shall bruise thy head.'

8. *At the same time, all the church shall enter with Christ, their glorious Lord, into the highest heaven,* and there shall enter on the state of their highest and eternal blessedness and glory. While the lower world, which they have left under their feet, is seized with the fire of God's vengeance, and flames are kindling upon it, and the wicked are entering into everlasting fire, the whole church shall enter, with their glorious head, and all the holy angels attending, in a joyful manner into the eternal paradise of God, the palace of the great Jehovah, their heavenly Father. The gates shall open wide for them to enter, and there Christ will bring them into his chambers in the highest sense.

He will bring them into his Father's house, into a world not like that which they have left. Here Christ will bring them, and present them in glory to his Father, saying, 'Here am I, and the children which thou hast given me'; as much as to say, Here am I, with every one of those whom thou gavest me from eternity to take care of, that they might be redeemed and glorified, and to redeem whom I have done and suffered so much, and to make way for the redemption of whom I have for so many ages been accomplishing such great changes. Here they are now perfectly redeemed in body and soul. I have perfectly delivered them from all the ill fruits of the fall, and perfectly freed them from all their enemies. I have brought them all together into one glorious society, and united them all in myself. I have openly justified them before all angels and men, and here I have brought them all away from that accursed world where they have suffered so much, and have brought them before thy throne. I have done all that for them which thou hast appointed me. I have perfectly cleansed them from all filthiness in my blood, and here they are in perfect holiness, shining with thy perfect image.

And then the Father will accept of them, and own them all for his children, and will welcome them to the eternal and perfect inheritance and glory of his house, and will on this occasion give more glorious manifestations of his love than ever before, and will admit them to a more full and perfect enjoyment of himself.

And now shall be the marriage of the Lamb in the most perfect sense. The commencement of the glorious times of the church on earth, after the fall of Antichrist, is represented as the marriage of the Lamb; and this shall be the marriage of the Lamb in the highest sense that ever shall be on earth; but after this we read of another marriage of the Lamb, at the close of the day of judgment. After the beloved disciple had given an account of the day of judgment, in the close of the Revelation chapter 20, then he proceeds to give an account of what follows, in chapters 21 and 22; and in the second verse of chapter 21, he gives an account of his seeing the holy city, the new Jerusalem, prepared as a bride adorned for her husband. And when Christ shall bring his church into his Father's house in heaven, after the judgment, he shall bring her thither as his bride, having there presented her, whom he loved, and gave himself for, to himself without spot or wrinkle, or any such thing.

The bridegroom and the bride shall then enter into heaven, both having on their wedding robes, attended with all the glorious angels. And there they enter on the feast and joys of their marriage before the Father. They shall then begin an everlasting wedding day. This shall be the day of the gladness of Christ's heart, wherein he will greatly rejoice, and all the saints shall rejoice with him. Christ shall rejoice over his bride, and the bride shall rejoice in her husband, in the state of her consummate and everlasting blessedness, of which we have a particular description in Revelation 21 and 22.

And now the whole work of redemption is finished. We have seen how it has been carrying on from theFall of man to this time. But now it is complete with respect to all that belongs to it. Now the top stone of the building is laid. In the progress of the discourse on this subject, we have followed the church of God in all the great changes, all her tossings to and fro that she has been subject to, in all the storms and tempests through the many ages of the world, until at length we have seen an end to all these storms. We have seen her enter the harbour, and landed in the highest heavens, in complete and eternal glory, in all her members, soul and body. We have gone through time, and the several ages of it, as the providence of God, and the Word of God, have led us; and now we have issued into eternity after time shall be no more. We have seen all the church's enemies fixed in endless misery, and have seen the church presented in her perfect redemption before the Father in heaven, there to enjoy this most unspeakable and inconceivable glory and blessedness; and there we leave her to enjoy this glory throughout the never-ending ages of eternity.

Now all Christ's enemies will be perfectly put under his feet, and he shall have his most perfect triumph over sin and Satan, and all his instruments, and death, and hell. Now shall all the promises made to Christ by God the Father before the foundation of the world, the promises of the covenant of redemption, be fully accomplished. And Christ shall now perfectly have obtained the joy that was set before him, for which he undertook those great sufferings which he underwent in his state of humiliation. Now shall all the hopes and expectations of the saints be fulfilled. The state of things that the church was in before was a progressive and preparatory state, but now she is arrived at her most perfect state of glory. All the glory of the glorious times of the church on earth is but a faint shadow of this her consummate glory in heaven.

And now Christ the great Redeemer shall be most perfectly glorified, and God the Father shall be glorified in him, and the Holy Ghost shall be most fully glorified in the perfection of his work on the hearts of all the church. And now shall that new heaven and new earth, or that renewed state of things, which had been building up ever since Christ's resurrection, be completely finished, after the very material frame of the old heavens and old earth are destroyed: 'And I saw a new heaven and a new earth: for the first heaven and the first earth were passed away' (*Rev.* 21:1).

And now will the great Redeemer have perfected every thing that appertains to the work of redemption, which he began so soon after the Fall of man. And who can conceive of the triumph of those praises which shall be sung in heaven on this great occasion, so much greater than that of the fall of Antichrist, which occasions such praises as we have described in Revelation chapter 19! The beloved disciple John seems to want expressions to describe those praises, and says, 'It was as the voice of many waters, and as the voice of mighty thunderings, saying, Alleluia: for the Lord God omnipotent reigneth.' But much more inexpressible will those praises be which will be sung in heaven after the final consummation of all things. Now shall the praises of that vast and glorious multitude be as mighty thunderings indeed!

And now, how are all the former things passed away, and what a glorious state are things fixed in, to remain to all eternity! And as Christ, when he first entered upon the work of redemption after the Fall of man, had the kingdom committed to him of the Father, and took on himself the administration of the affairs of the universe, to manage all so as to subserve the purposes of this affair, so now, the work being finished, he will deliver up the kingdom to God, even the Father, 'Then cometh the end, when he shall have delivered up the kingdom to God, even the Father; when he shall have put down all rule, and all authority and power' (*1 Cor.* 15:24). Not that Christ shall cease to reign or have a kingdom after this, for it is said, 'He shall reign over the house of Jacob for ever, and of his kingdom there shall be no end' (*Luke* 1:33). So in Daniel 7:14 it is said, 'His dominion is an everlasting dominion, which shall not pass away, and his kingdom that which shall not be destroyed.' But the meaning is that Christ shall deliver up that kingdom or dominion which he has over the world, as the Father's delegate or vicegerent, which the Father committed to him, to be managed in subserviency to this great design of redemption. The end of this commission, or delegation, which he had from the Father, seems to be to subserve this particular design of redemption; and therefore, when that design is fully accomplished, the commission will cease, and Christ will deliver it up to the Father, from whom he received it.

IMPROVEMENT OF THE WHOLE

I proceed now to enter upon some improvement of all that has been said from this doctrine.

1. Hence we may learn *how great a work this work of redemption is.* We have now had it in a very imperfect manner set forth before us, in the whole progress of it, from its first beginning after the Fall to the end of the world, when it is finished. We have seen how God has carried on this building from the first foundation of it, by a long succession of wonderful works, advancing it higher and higher from one age to another, until the top stone is laid at the end of the world. And now let us consider how great a work this is. Do men, when they behold some great palaces or churches, sometimes admire their magnificence, and are almost astonished to consider how great a piece of work it was to build such an house? Then how well may we admire the greatness of this building of God, which he builds up age after age, by a series of such great things which he brings to pass? There are three things that have been exhibited to us in what has been said, which do especially show the greatness of the work of redemption.

i. The greatness of those *particular events, and dispens-ations of providence,* by which it is accomplished. How great are those things which God has done, which are but so many parts of this great work! What great things were done in the world to prepare the way for Christ's coming to purchase, and what great things were done in the purchase of redemption! What a wonderful thing was that which was accomplished to put Christ in an immediate capacity for this purchase, that is, his incarnation, that God should become man! And what great things were done in that purchase, that a person who is the eternal Jehovah, should live upon earth for four or five and thirty years together, in a mean despised condition, and that he should spend his life in such labours and sufferings, and that at last he should die upon the cross! And what great things have been done to accomplish the success of Christ's redemption! What great things to put him into a capacity to accomplish this success! For this purpose he rose from the dead, and ascended up into heaven, and all things were made subject to him. How many miracles have been wrought, what mighty revolutions have been brought to pass in the world already, and how much greater shall be brought to pass, in order to it!

ii. The *number of those great events* by which God carries on this work, shows the greatness of the work. Those mighty revolutions are so many as to fill up many ages. The particular wonderful events by which the work of *creation* was carried on filled up six days: but the great dispensations by which the work of *redemption* is carried on are so many, that they fill up six or seven thousand years at least, as we have reason to conclude from the Word of God. There were great things wrought in this affair before the Flood, and in the Flood the world was once destroyed by water, and God's church was so wonderfully preserved from the Flood in order to carry on this work. And after the Flood, what great things did God work relating to the resettling of the world, to the building of Babel, the dispersing of the nations, the shortening of the days of man's life, the calling of Abraham, the destruction of Sodom and Gomorrah, and that long series of wonderful providences relating to Abraham, Isaac, Jacob, and Joseph, and those wonders in Egypt, and at the Red Sea, and in the wilderness, and in Canaan in Joshua's time, and by a long succession of wonderful providences from age to age, towards the nation of the Jews!

[423]

What great things were wrought by God, in so often over-turning the world before Christ came, to make way for his coming! What great things were done also in Christ's time, and then after that in overturning Satan's kingdom in the heathen empire, and in so preserving his church in the dark times of Popery, and in bringing about a Reformation! How many great and wonderful things will be effected in accomplishing the glorious times of the church, and at Christ's last coming on the day of judgment, in the destruction of the world, and in carrying the whole church into heaven.

iii. The *glorious issue* of this whole affair, in the perfect and external destruction of the wicked, and in the consummate glory of the righteous. And now let us once more take a view of this building, now all is finished and the top stone laid. It appeared in a glorious height in the apostles' time, and much more glorious in the time of Constantine and will appear much more glorious still after the fall of Antichrist; but at the consummation of all things, it appears in an immensely more glorious height than ever before. Now it appears in its greatest magnificence, as a complete lofty structure, whose top reaches to the heaven of heavens; a building worthy of the great God, the King of kings. And from what has been said, one may argue that the work of redemption is the greatest of all God's works of which we have any notice, and is the end of all his other works. It appears plainly from what has been said that this work is the principal of all God's works of providence, and that all other works of providence are reducible hither. They are all subordinate to the great affair of redemption. We see that all the revolutions in the world are to subserve this grand design; so that the work of redemption is, as it were, the sum of God's works of providence.

This shows us how much greater the work of redemption is, than the work of creation; for I have several times observed that the work of providence is greater than the work of creation, because it is the end of it, as the use of a house is the end of the building of the house. But the work of redemption is the sum of all God's works of providence; all are subordinate to it; so the work of the new creation is more excellent than the old. So it ever is that, when one thing is removed by God to make way for another, the new one excels the old. Thus the temple excelled the tabernacle; the new covenant the old; the new dispensation of the gospel the dispensation of Moses; the throne of David the throne of Saul; the priesthood of Christ the priesthood of Aaron; the new Jerusalem the old; and so the new creation far excels the old.

God has used the creation which he has made for no other purpose but to subserve the designs of this affair. To answer this end, he hath created and disposed of mankind, to this the angels, to this the earth, to this the highest heavens. God created the world to provide a spouse and a kingdom for his Son; and the setting up of the kingdom of Christ, and the spiritual marriage of the spouse to him, is what the whole creation labours and travails in pain to bring to pass. This work of redemption is so much the greatest of all the works of God that all other works are to be looked upon either as parts of it, or appendages to it, or are some way reducible to it; and so all the decrees of God do some way or other belong to that eternal covenant of redemption which was between the Father and the Son before the foundation of the world. Every decree of God is in some way or other reducible to that covenant.

And seeing this work of redemption is so great a work, hence we need not wonder that the angels desire to look into it. And we need not wonder that so much is made of it in Scripture, and that it is so much insisted on in the histories, prophecies, and songs of the Bible; for the work of redemption is the great subject of the whole of its doctrines, its promises, its types, its songs, its histories, and its prophecies.

2. Hence we may learn how *God is the Alpha and Omega, the beginning and ending of all things.* Such are the characters and titles we find often ascribed to God in Scripture, in those places where the Scripture speaks of the course of things, and the series of events in providence: 'Who hath wrought and done it, calling the generations from the beginning? I the LORD, the first, and with the last, I am he' (*Isa.* 41:4). And particularly does the Scripture ascribe such titles to God where it speaks of the providence of God as it relates to, and is summed up in, the great work of redemption; as in Isaiah. 44:6-7 and Isaiah 48:12, with the context, beginning with the ninth verse. So God eminently appears as the first and the last by considering the whole scheme of divine providence as we have considered it, that is, as all reducible to that one great work of redemption.

And therefore, when Christ reveals the future great events of providence relating to his church and people, and this affair of redemption, to the end of the world, to his disciple John, he often reveals himself under this character. So Revelation 1:8, 'I am Alpha and Omega, the beginning and the ending, saith the Lord, which is, and which was, and which is to come, the Almighty.' So again in verses 10 and 11, 'I heard behind me a great voice as of a trumpet, saying, I am Alpha and Omega, the first and the last.' Alpha and Omega are the names of the first and last letters of the Greek alphabet, as A and Z are of ours; and therefore it signifies the same as his being the first and the last, the beginning and the ending.

Thus God is called in the beginning of this book of Revelation, before the course of the prophecy begins; and so again he is called at the end of it, after the course of events is gone through, and the final issue of things is seen, as in Revelation 21:6, 'And he said unto me, It is done. I am Alpha and Omega, the beginning and the end.' And so in Revelation 22:12-13, 'And, behold, I come quickly; and my reward is with me, to give every man according as his work shall be. I am Alpha and Omega, the beginning and the end, the first and the last.'

We have seen how this is true in the course of what I have laid before you upon this subject. We have seen how things were from God in the beginning; on what design God began the course of his providence in the beginning of the generations of men upon the earth; and we have seen how it is God that has all along carried things on agreeable to the same designs without ever failing; and how at last the conclusion and final issue of things are to God; and so we have seen how all things are of him, and through him, and to him; and therefore we may well now cry out with the apostle, 'O the depth of the riches both of the wisdom and knowledge of God! How unsearchable are his judgments, and his ways past finding out! . . . For of him, and through him, and to him, are all things: to whom be glory for ever. Amen' (*Rom.* 11:33,36).

We have seen how other things came to an end, one after another; how states, and kingdoms, and empires, one after another, fell and came to nothing, even the greatest and strongest of them. We have seen how the world has been often overturned, and will be more remarkably overturned than ever it has been yet; we have seen how the world comes to an end, how it was first destroyed by water, and how at last it shall be utterly destroyed by fire: but yet God remains the same through all ages. He was before the beginning of this course of things, and he will be after the end of them; agreeable to Psalm 102:25-26. Thus God is he that is, and that was, and that is to come.

We have seen in a variety of instances how all other gods perish; we have seen how the ancient gods of the heathen in the nations about Canaan, and throughout the Roman Empire, are all destroyed, and their worship long since overthrown; we have heard how Antichrist, who has called himself a god on earth, and how Mahomet, who claims religious honours, and how all the gods of the heathen through the world, will come to an end; and how Satan, the great dragon, that old serpent, who has set up himself as god of this world, will be cast into the lake of fire, there to suffer his complete punishments: but Jehovah remains, and his kingdom is an everlasting kingdom, and of his dominions there is no end. We have seen what mighty changes there have been in the world but God is unchangeable, 'the same yesterday, and today, and for ever'.

We began at the head of the stream of divine providence, and have followed and traced it through its various windings and turnings until we are come to the end of it, and we see where it issues. As it began in God, so it ends in God. God is the infinite ocean into which it empties itself. Providence is like a mighty wheel whose circumference is so high that it is dreadful, with the glory of the God of Israel above upon it, as it is represented in Ezekiel's vision. We have seen the revolution of this wheel and how, as it was from God, so its return has been to God again. All the events of divine providence are like the links of a chain; the first link is *from* God, and the last is *to* him.

3. We may see by what has been said *how Christ in all things has the pre-eminence*. For this great work of redemption is all his work. He is the great Redeemer, and therefore the work of redemption, as the sum of God's works of providence, shows the glory of our Lord Jesus Christ as being above all, and through all, and in all. That God intended the world for his Son's use in the affair of redemption is one reason that is to be given why he created the world by him, which seems to be intimated by the apostle in Ephesians 3:9–12. What has been said shows how all the purposes of God are purposed in Christ, and how he is before all and above all, and all things

consist by him, and are governed by him, and are for him (*Col.* 1:15–18).

We see by what has been said how God makes him, his first-born, higher than the kings of the earth, and sets his throne above their thrones; how God has always upheld his kingdom, when the kingdoms of others have come to an end; how that appears at last above all, however greatly opposed for so many ages; how finally all other kingdoms fall, and his kingdom is the last kingdom, and never gives place to any other.

We see that, whatever changes there are, and however highly Christ's enemies exalt themselves, that yet finally all his enemies become his footstool, and he reigns in uncontrolled power and immense glory. In the end his people are all perfectly saved and made happy, and his enemies all become his footstool. And thus God gives the world to his Son for his inheritance.

4. Hence we may see *what a consistent thing divine providence is.* The consideration of what has been said, may greatly serve to show us the consistency, order and beauty, of God's works of providence. If we behold the events of providence in any other view than that in which it has been set before us, it will all look like confusion, like a number of jumbled events coming to pass without any order or method, like the tossing of the waves of the sea. Things will look as though one confused revolution came to pass after another, merely by blind chance, without any regular or certain end.

But if we consider the events of providence in the light in which they have been set before us under this doctrine, in which the Scriptures set them before us, they appear, far from being jumbled and confused, an orderly series of events, all wisely ordered and directed in excellent harmony and consistency, tending all to one end. The wheels of providence are not turned round by blind chance, but they are full of eyes round about, as Ezekiel represents, and they are guided by the Spirit of God. Where the Spirit goes, they go; and all God's works of providence through all ages meet in one at last, as so many lines meeting in one centre.

It is with God's work of providence as it is with his work of creation: it is but one work. The events of providence are not so many distinct, independent works of providence, but they are rather so many different parts of one work of providence. It is all one work, one regular scheme. God's works of providence are not disunited and jumbled without connection or dependence, but are all united, just as the several parts of one building. There are many stones, many pieces of timber, but all are so joined, and fitly formed together, that they make but one building. They have all but one foundation, and are united at last in one top stone.

God's providence may not unfitly be compared to a large and long river, having innumerable branches, beginning in different regions, and at a great distance one from another, and all conspiring to one common issue. After their very diverse and contrary courses which they hold for a while, yet they all gather more and more together, the nearer they come to their common end, and all at length discharge themselves at one mouth into the same ocean. The different streams of this river are apt to appear like mere jumble and confusion to us, because of the limitedness of our sight, whereby we cannot see from one branch to another, and cannot see the whole at once, so as to see how all are united in one.

A man who sees but one or two streams at a time cannot tell what their course tends to. Their course seems very crooked, and different streams seem to run for a while different and contrary ways: and if we view things at a distance, there seem to be innumerable obstacles and impediments in the way to hinder their ever uniting and coming to the ocean, as rocks and mountains, and the like; but yet if we trace them, they all unite at last, and all come to the same issue, disgorg-ing themselves in one into the same great ocean. Not one of all the streams fails of coming hither at last.

5. From the whole that has been said, we may strongly argue that *the Scriptures are the Word of God*, because they alone inform us what God is about, or what he aims at, in these works which he is doing in the world. God doubtless is pursuing some design, and carrying on some scheme, in the various changes and revolutions which from age to age come to pass in the world.

It is most reasonable to suppose that there is some certain great design to which providence subordinates all the great successive changes in the affairs of the world which God has made. It is reasonable to suppose that all revolutions, from the beginning of the world to the end of it, are but the various parts of the same scheme, all conspiring to bring to pass that great event which the great Creator and Governor of the world has ultimately in view; and that the scheme will not be finished, nor the design fully accomplished, and the great and ultimate event fully brought to pass, until the end of the world and the last revolution is brought about.

Now there is nothing else that informs us what this scheme and design of God in his works is, but only the holy Scrip-tures. Nothing else pretends to set in view the whole series of God's works of providence from beginning to end, and to inform us how all things were from God at first, and for what end they are, and how they were ordered from the beginning, and how they will proceed to the end of the world, and what they will come to at last, and how then all things shall be to God.

Nothing else but the Scriptures has any pretence for show-ing any manner of regular scheme or drift in those revolutions which God orders from age to age. Nothing else pretends to show what God would by the things which he has done, and is doing, and will do; what he seeks and intends by them. Nothing else pretends to show, with any distinctness or certainty, how the world began at first, or to tell us the original of things. Nothing but the Scriptures sets forth how God governed the world from the beginning of the generations of men upon the earth, in an orderly history; and nothing else sets before us how he will govern it to the end, by an orderly prophecy of future events; agreeable to the challenge which God makes to the gods, prophets, and teachers of the heathen in Isaiah 41:22-23, 'Let them bring them forth, and shew us what shall happen: let them shew the former things, what they be, that we may consider them, and know the latter end of them; or declare us things for to come. Shew the things that are to come hereafter, that we may know that ye are gods.'

Reason shows that it is fit and requisite, that the intelligent and rational beings of the world should know something of God's scheme and design in his works; for they doubtless are the beings that are principally concerned. God's great design in his works is doubtless something concerning his reasonable creatures, rather than brute beasts and lifeless things. The revolutions by which God's great design is brought to pass, are doubtless revolutions chiefly among them, and which concern their state, and not the state of things without life or reason. And therefore surely it is requisite that they should know something of it; especially seeing that reason teaches that God has given his rational creatures reason, and a capacity of seeing God in his works; for this end, that they may see God's glory in them, and give him the glory of them. But, how can they see God's glory in his works, if they do not know what God's design in them is, and what he aims at by what he is doing in the world?

And further, it is fit that mankind should be informed something of God's design in the government of the world, because they are made capable of actively falling in with that design, and promoting it, and acting herein as his friends and subjects; it is therefore reasonable to suppose that God has given mankind some revelation to inform them of this. But there is nothing else that does it but the Bible.

In the Bible this is done. Hence we may learn an account of the first original of things, and an orderly account of the scheme of God's works from the first beginning, through those ages that are beyond the reach of all other histories. Here we are told what God aims at in the whole, what is the great end, how he has contrived the grand design he drives at, and the great things he would accomplish by all. Here we have a most rational excellent account of this matter, worthy of God, and exceedingly shewing forth the glory of his perfections, his majesty, his wisdom, his glorious holiness, and grace, and love, and his exaltation above all, showing how he is the first and the last.

Here we are shown the connection of the various parts of the work of providence, and how all harmonizes and is connected together in a regular, beautiful, and glorious frame. In the Bible we have an account of the whole scheme of providence, from the beginning of the world to the end of it, either in history or prophecy, and are told what will become of things at last; how they will be finished off by a great day of judgment, and will issue in the subduing of God's enemies, and in the salvation and glory of his church, and setting up of the everlasting kingdom of his Son.

How rational, worthy, and excellent a revelation is this! And how excellent a book is the Bible, which contains so much beyond all other books in the world! And what characters are here of its being indeed a divine book! – a book that the great Jehovah has given to mankind for their instruction, without which we should be left in miserable darkness and confusion.

[433]

6. From what has been said, we may see *the glorious majesty and power of God in this affair of redemption*. Especially is God glorious in power. His glorious power appears in upholding his church for so long a time and carrying on this work; upholding it oftentimes when it was but as a little spark of fire, or as smoking flax, in which the fire was almost gone out, and the power of earth and hell were combined to destroy it. Yet God has never suffered them to quench it, and finally will bring forth judgment unto victory. God glorifies his strength in his church's weakness; in causing his people, who are like a number of little infants, finally to triumph over all earth and hell; so that they shall tread on the lion and adder; the young lion and dragon shall they trample under foot. The glorious power of God appears in conquering his many and mighty enemies by that Person who was once an infant in a manger, and appeared as a poor, weak, despised man. He conquers them and triumphs over them in their own weapon, the cross.

The glorious majesty of God appears in conquering all those mighty enemies of the church one age after another; in conquering Satan, that proud and strong spirit, and all his hellish host; in bringing him down under foot, long after he had vaunted himself as god of this world, and when he did his utmost to support himself in his kingdom.

God's power gloriously appears in conquering Satan when exalted in that strongest and most potent heathen kingdom that ever he had, the Roman Empire. Christ, our Michael, has overcome him, and the devil was cast out, and there was found no more place for him in heaven; but 'he was cast out unto the earth, and his angels were cast out with him'. Again, his power gloriously appears in conquering him in that kingdom wherein his pride, subtlety, and cruelty above all appear, that is, the kingdom of Antichrist. It gloriously appears in conquering him in that greatest and strongest combination and opposition of the devil and his adherents against Christ and his church, just before the fall of Antichrist, wherein his visible kingdom has a fatal blow given it, on which a universal downfall of it follows all over the world.

The glorious power of God appears in thus conquering the devil, and bringing him under foot, time after time, after long time given him to strengthen himself to his utmost, as he was once overthrown in his heathen Roman Empire, after he had been making himself strong in those parts of the world ever since the building of Babel. It appears also in overthrowing his kingdom more fatally and universally all over the world, after he had again another opportunity given him to strengthen himself to his utmost for many ages, by setting up those two great kingdoms of Antichrist and Mahomet, and to establish his interest in the heathen world. We have seen how these kingdoms of God's enemies, that, before God appears, look strong, as though it was impossible to overthrow them; yet, time after time, when God appears, they seem to melt away as the fat of lambs before the fire, and are driven away as the chaff before the whirlwind, or the smoke out of the chimney.

Those mighty kingdoms of Antichrist and Mahomet which have made such a figure for so many ages together and have trampled the world under foot, when God comes to appear, will vanish away like a shadow, and will as it were disappear of themselves, and come to nothing, as the darkness in a room does when the light is brought in. What are God's enemies in his hands? How is their greatest strength weakness when he rises up! And how weak will they all appear together at the day of judgment! Thus we may apply those words in the song of Moses, 'Thy right hand, O LORD, is become glorious in power: thy right hand, O LORD, hath dashed in pieces the enemy' (*Exod.* 15:6). And how great doth the majesty of God appear in overturning the world from time to time, to accomplish his designs, and at last in causing the earth and heavens to flee away, for the advancement of the glory of his kingdom!

7. From what has been said, we may see *the glorious wisdom of God*. It shows the wisdom of God in creating the world that he has created it for such an excellent use, to accomplish in it so glorious a work. And it shows the wisdom of divine providence, that he brings such great good out of such great evil, in making the Fall and ruin of mankind, which in itself is so sorrowful and deplorable, an occasion of accomplishing such a glorious work as this work of redemption, and of erecting such a glorious building, whose top should reach unto heaven, and of bringing his elect to a state of such unspeakable happiness. And how glorious doth the wisdom of God appear in that long course and series of great changes in the world, in bringing such order out of confusion, in so frustrating the devil, and so wonderfully turning all his most subtle machinations to his own glory, and the glory of his Son Jesus Christ; and in causing the greatest works of Satan, those in which he has most glorified himself, to be wholly turned into occasions of so much the more glorious triumph of his Son Jesus Christ! And how wonderful is the wisdom of God in bringing all such manifold and various changes and overturnings in the world to such a glorious period at last, and in so directing all the wheels of providence by his skilful hand that every one of them conspires, as the manifold wheels of a most curious machine, at last to strike out such an excellent issue, such a manifestation of the divine glory, such happiness to his people, and such a glorious and everlasting kingdom to his Son!

8. From what has been said, we may see *the stability of God's mercy and faithfulness to his people*; how he never forsakes his inheritance, and remembers his covenant to them through all generations. Now we may see what reason there was for the words of the text, 'The moth shall eat them up like a garment, and the worm shall eat them like wool; but my

righteousness shall endure for ever and ever, and my salvation from generation to generation.' And now we may see abundant reason for that name of God which he reveals to Moses, 'And God said unto Moses, I AM THAT I AM' (*Exod.* 3:14), that is, I am the same that I was when I entered into covenant with Abraham, Isaac, and Jacob, and ever shall be the same; I shall keep covenant forever: I am self-sufficient, all-sufficient, and immutable.

And now we may see the truth of that in Psalm 36:5-6, 'Thy mercy, O LORD, is in the heavens; and thy faithfulness reacheth unto the clouds. Thy righteousness is like the great mountains; thy judgments are a great deep.' And if we consider what has been said, we need not wonder that the Psalmist, in the 136th Psalm, so often repeats this, 'For his mercy endureth for ever'; as if he were in an ecstasy at the consideration of the perpetuity of God's mercy to his church, and delighted to think of it, and knew not how but continually to express it. Let us with like pleasure and joy celebrate the everlasting duration of God's mercy and faithfulness to his church and people, and let us be comforted by it under the present dark circumstances of the church of God, and all the uproar and confusions that are in the world, and all the threatenings of the church's enemies. And let us take encouragement earnestly to pray for those glorious things which God has promised to accomplish for his church.

9. Hence we may learn *how happy a society the church of Christ is*, for all this great work is for them. Christ undertook it for their sakes, and for their sakes he carries it on, from the Fall of man to the end of the world. It is because he has loved them with an everlasting love. For their sakes he overturns states and kingdoms. For their sakes he shakes heaven and earth. He gives men for them, and people for their life. Since they have been precious in God's sight, they have been

honourable; and therefore he first gives the blood of his own Son to them, and then, for their sakes, gives the blood of all their enemies, many thousands and millions, all nations that stand in their way, as a sacrifice to their good.

For their sakes he made the world, and for their sakes he will destroy it; for their sakes he built heaven, and for their sakes he makes his angels ministering spirits. Therefore the Apostle says, 'All things are yours: whether Paul, or Apollos, or Cephas, or the world, or life, or death, or things present, or things to come; all are yours' (*1 Cor.* 3:21-22). How blessed is this people who are redeemed from among men, and are the first-fruits unto God, and to the Lamb; who have God in all ages for their protection and help! 'Happy art thou, O Israel: who is like unto thee, O people saved by the LORD, the shield of thy help, and who is the sword of thy excellency! and thine enemies shall be found liars unto thee; and thou shalt tread upon their high places' (*Deut.* 33:29).

Let who will prevail now, let the enemies of the church exalt themselves as much as they will, these are the people that shall finally prevail. The last kingdom shall finally be theirs; the kingdom shall finally be given into their hands, and shall not be left to other people. We have seen what a blessed issue things shall finally be brought to as to them, and what glory they shall arrive at, and remain in possession of, for ever and ever, after all the kingdoms of the world are come to an end, and the earth is removed, and mountains are carried into the depth of the sea, or where the sea was, and this lower earth shall all be dissolved. O happy people, and blessed society! Well may they spend an eternity in praises and hallelujahs to him who hath loved them *from* eternity, and will love them *to* eternity.

10. And, lastly, hence *all wicked men, all that are in a Christless condition, may see their exceeding misery.* You that

are such, whoever you are, you are those who shall have no part or lot in this matter. You are never the better for any of those things of which you have heard: yea, your guilt is but so much the greater, and the misery you are exposed to so much the more dreadful. You are some of that sort against whom God, in the progress of the work, exercises so much manifest wrath; some of those enemies who are liable to be made Christ's footstool, and to be ruled with a rod of iron, and to be dashed in pieces. You are some of the seed of the serpent, to bruise the head of which is one great design of all this work.

Whatever glorious things God accomplishes for his church, if you continue in the state you are now in, they will not be glorious to you. The most glorious times of the church are always the most dismal times to the wicked and impenitent. This we are taught in Isaiah 66:14. And so we find: wherever glorious things are foretold concerning the church, there terrible things are foretold concerning the wicked, its enemies. And so it ever has been in fact. In all remarkable deliverances wrought for the church, there has been also a remarkable execution of wrath on its enemies.

So it was when God delivered the children of Israel out of Egypt. At the same time he remarkably poured out his wrath on Pharaoh and the Egyptians. So when he brought them into Canaan by Joshua, and gave them that good land, he remarkably executed wrath upon the Canaanites. So when they were delivered out of their Babylonish captivity, signal vengeance was inflicted on the Babylonians. So when the Gentiles were called, and the elect of God were saved by the preaching of the apostles, Jerusalem and the persecuting Jews were destroyed in a most awful manner. I might observe the same concerning the glory accomplished to the church in the days of Constantine, at the overthrow of Satan's visible kingdom in the downfall of Antichrist, and at the day of judgment. In all these instances, and especially in the last, there have been, or will be, exhibited most awful tokens of the divine wrath against the wicked. And to this class you belong.

You are indeed some of that sort that God will make use of in this affair, but it will be for the glory of his justice, and not of his mercy. You are some of those enemies of God who are reserved for the triumph of Christ's glorious power in overcoming and punishing them. You are some of that sort that shall be consumed with this accursed world after the day of judgment, when Christ and his church shall triumphantly and gloriously ascend to heaven.

Therefore let all that are in a Christless condition amongst us seriously consider these things, and not be like the foolish people of the old world, who would not take warning when Noah told them that the Lord was about to bring a flood of waters upon the earth; or like the people of Sodom, who would not regard when Lot told them that God would destroy that city, and would not flee from the wrath to come, and so were consumed in that terrible destruction.

And now I would conclude my whole discourse on this subject in words like those in the last chapter of Revelation: These sayings are faithful and true, and blessed is he that keepeth these sayings. Behold, Christ cometh quickly, and his reward is with him, to render to every man according as his work shall be. And he that is unjust shall be unjust still; and he that is filthy shall be filthy still; and he that is holy shall be holy still.

'Blessed are they that do his commandments, that they may have right to the tree of life, and may enter in through the gates into the city. For without are dogs, and sorcerers, and whoremongers, and murderers, and idolaters, and whosoever loveth and maketh a lie . . . He which testifieth these things, saith, Surely I come quickly.

'Amen. Even so, come, Lord Jesus.'